Brainchildren

Representation and Mind
Hilary Putnam and Ned Block, editors

Hilary Putnam, *Representation and Reality*

Fred Dretske, *Explaining Behavior: Reasons in a World of Causes*

Jerrold J. Katz, *The Metaphysics of Meaning*

Jerry A. Fodor, *A Theory of Content and Other Essays*

Cora Diamond, *The Realistic Spirit: Wittgenstein, Philosophy, and the Mind*

Stephen L. White, *The Unity of the Self*

Michael Tye, *The Imagery Debate*

Christopher Peacocke, *A Study of Concepts*

John R. Searle, *The Rediscovery of the Mind*

John Campbell, *Past, Space, and Self*

Galen Strawson, *Mental Reality*

Michael Tye, *Ten Problems of Consciousness: A Representational Theory of the Phenomenal Mind*

Robert Cummins, *Representations, Targets, and Attitudes*

Edited by Peter J. McCormick, *Starmaking: Realism, Anti-Realism, and Irrealism*

Hao Wang, *A Logical Journey: From Gödel to Philosophy*

Jerrold J. Katz, *Realistic Rationalism*

Daniel C. Dennett, *Brainchildren: Essays on Designing Minds*

Brainchildren

Essays on Designing Minds

Daniel C. Dennett

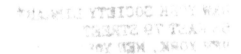

A Bradford Book
The MIT Press
Cambridge, Massachusetts

This book was set in Palatino by Achorn Graphic Services and was printed and bound in the United States of America.

Library of Congress Cataloging-in-Publication Data

Dennett, Daniel Clement.
 Brainchildren: essays on designing minds / Daniel C. Dennett.
 p. cm.—(Representation and mind. A Bradford Book)
 Includes bibliographical references and index.
 ISBN 0-262-04166-9 (hardcover: alk. paper).—ISBN 0-262-54090-8 (pbk.: alk. paper)
 1. Philosophy of mind. 2. Artificial intelligence. 3. Animal intelligence.
I. Title. II. Series.
BD418.3.D46 1998
128′.2–dc21   97–9440
                                                                          CIP

For Harry and Betty Stanton

Contents

Preface   xi

I Philosophy of Mind

1 Can Machines Think?   3

   Postscript [1985]: Eyes, Ears, Hands, and History
   Postscript [1997]

2 Speaking for Our Selves   31
   Nicholas Humphrey and Daniel C. Dennett

   Postscript

3 Do-It-Yourself Understanding   59

4 Two Contrasts: Folk Craft versus Folk Science, and Belief versus
   Opinion   81

5 Real Patterns   95

6 Julian Jaynes's Software Archeology   121

7 Real Consciousness   131

8 Instead of Qualia   141

9 The Practical Requirements for Making a Conscious Robot   153

10 The Unimagined Preposterousness of Zombies: Commentary on
    Moody, Flanagan, and Polger   171

II Artificial Intelligence and Artificial Life

11 Cognitive Wheels: The Frame Problem of AI   181

12 Producing Future by Telling Stories   207

13 The Logical Geography of Computational Approaches: A View
    from the East Pole   215

14 Hofstadter's Quest: A Tale of Cognitive Pursuit   235

15 Foreword to Robert French, *The Subtlety of Sameness*   243

16 Cognitive Science as Reverse Engineering: Several Meanings of
    "Top-Down" and "Bottom-Up"   249

17 Artificial Life as Philosophy   261

18 When Philosophers Encounter Artificial Intelligence   265

19 Review of Allen Newell, *Unified Theories of Cognition*   277

III Ethology, Animal Mind

20 Out of the Armchair and into the Field   289

21 Cognitive Ethology: Hunting for Bargains or a Wild Goose
    Chase   307

22 Do Animals Have Beliefs?   323

23 Why Creative Intelligence Is Hard to Find: Commentary on
    Whiten and Byrne   333

24 Animal Consciousness: What Matters and Why   337

    Postscript: Pain, Suffering, and Morality

IV Standing Back

25 Self-Portrait   355

26 Information, Technology, and the Virtues of Ignorance   367

Bibliography   385
Index   401

Preface

The point of this collection is to bring together, for the convenience of students and other readers who do not have ready access to a major university library, essays on the mind that I have published over the last dozen years in a wide variety of relatively inaccessible publications. With one exception, these essays all appeared in conference volumes or in specialized journals that are often not found in undergraduate college libraries. Juxtaposing them has shown me patterns in the development of my own thinking that I myself had not recognized, uncovering both strengths and weaknesses in my positions, so I expect others will benefit from a clearer view as well.

I have grouped the essays into four categories, but the boundaries between them are porous. All the essays belong to the philosophy of mind broadly conceived—as it ought to be these days—but I have bundled two groups that are directed more narrowly to topics in Artificial Intelligence and Artificial Life on the one hand, and ethology and animal psychology on the other, and added a final pair, one providing an overview and the other looking toward future work.

I am indebted to Alicia Smith for the fine job she did obtaining all the necessary permissions, and gathering, proofreading, and formatting all the pieces for the press. I am grateful to Betty Stanton at the MIT Press and Stefan McGrath at Penguin for working with us to bring out the book in timely and affordable fashion.

I   Philosophy of Mind

1 Can Machines Think?

Much has been written about the Turing test in the last few years, some of it preposterously off the mark. People typically mis-imagine the test by orders of magnitude. This essay is an antidote, a prosthesis for the imagination, showing how huge the task posed by the Turing test is, and hence how unlikely it is that any computer will ever pass it. It does not go far enough in the imagination-enhancement department, however, and I have updated the essay with a new postscript.

Can machines think? This has been a conundrum for philosophers for years, but in their fascination with the pure conceptual issues they have for the most part overlooked the real social importance of the answer. It is of more than academic importance that we learn to think clearly about the actual cognitive powers of computers, for they are now being introduced into a variety of sensitive social roles, where their powers will be put to the ultimate test: In a wide variety of areas, we are on the verge of making ourselves dependent upon their cognitive powers. The cost of overestimating them could be enormous.

One of the principal inventors of the computer was the great British mathematician Alan Turing. It was he who first figured out, in highly abstract terms, how to design a programmable computing device—what we now call a universal Turing machine. All programmable computers in use today are in essence Turing machines. Over thirty years ago, at the dawn of the computer age, Turing began a classic article, "Computing Machinery and Intelligence" with the words: "I propose to consider the question, 'Can machines think?' "—but then went on to say this was a bad question, a question that leads only to sterile debate and haggling over definitions, a question, as he put it, "too mean-

Originally appeared in Shafto, M., ed., *How We Know* (San Francisco: Harper & Row, 1985).

ingless to deserve discussion" (Turing, 1950). In its place he substituted what he took to be a much better question, a question that would be crisply answerable and intuitively satisfying—in every way an acceptable substitute for the philosophic puzzler with which he began.

First he described a parlor game of sorts, the "imitation game," to be played by a man, a woman, and a judge (of either gender). The man and woman are hidden from the judge's view but able to communicate with the judge by teletype; the judge's task is to guess, after a period of questioning each contestant, which interlocutor is the man and which the woman. The man tries to convince the judge he is the woman (and the woman tries to convince the judge of the truth), and the man wins if the judge makes the wrong identification. A little reflection will convince you, I am sure, that, aside from lucky breaks, it would take a clever man to convince the judge that he was a woman—assuming the judge is clever too, of course.

Now suppose, Turing said, we replace the man or woman with a computer, and give the judge the task of determining which is the human being and which is the computer. Turing proposed that any computer that can regularly or often fool a discerning judge in this game would be intelligent—would be a computer that thinks—*beyond any reasonable doubt*. Now, it is important to realize that failing this test is not supposed to be a sign of lack of intelligence. Many intelligent people, after all, might not be willing or able to play the imitation game, and we should allow computers the same opportunity to decline to prove themselves. This is, then, a one-way test; failing it proves nothing.

Furthermore, Turing was not committing himself to the view (although it is easy to see how one might think he was) that to think is to think just like a human being—any more than he was committing himself to the view that for a man to think, he must think exactly like a woman. Men and women, and computers, may all have different ways of thinking. But surely, he thought, if one can think in one's own peculiar style well enough to imitate a thinking man or woman, one can think well, indeed. This imagined exercise has come to be known as the Turing test.

It is a sad irony that Turing's proposal has had exactly the opposite effect on the discussion of that which he intended. Turing didn't design the test as a useful tool in scientific psychology, a method of confirming or disconfirming scientific theories or evaluating particular models of mental function; he designed it to be nothing more than a philosophical conversation-stopper. He proposed—in the spirit of "Put up or shut up!"—a simple test for thinking that was *surely* strong enough to satisfy the sternest skeptic (or so he thought). He was saying, in effect, "Instead of arguing interminably about the ultimate nature and essence of thinking, why don't we all agree that whatever that nature is, anything that could pass this test would surely have it; then we could turn to asking how or whether some machine could be designed and built that might pass the test fair and square." Alas, philosophers—amateur and professional—have instead taken Turing's proposal as the pretext for just the sort of definitional haggling and interminable arguing about imaginary counterexamples he was hoping to squelch.

This thirty-year preoccupation with the Turing test has been all the more regrettable because it has focused attention on the wrong issues. There are *real world* problems that are revealed by considering the strengths and weaknesses of the Turing test, but these have been concealed behind a smokescreen of misguided criticisms. A failure to think imaginatively about the test actually proposed by Turing has led many to underestimate its severity and to confuse it with much less interesting proposals.

So first I want to show that the Turing test, conceived as he conceived it, is (as he thought) plenty strong enough as a test of thinking. I defy anyone to improve upon it. But here is the point almost universally overlooked by the literature: There is a common *misapplication* of the sort of testing exhibited by the Turing test that often leads to drastic overestimation of the powers of actually existing computer systems. The follies of this familiar sort of thinking about computers can best be brought out by a reconsideration of the Turing test itself.

The insight underlying the Turing test is the same insight that inspires the new practice among symphony orchestras of conducting auditions with an opaque screen between the jury and the musician. What matters in a musician, obviously, is musical ability and only musical ability; such features as sex, hair length, skin color, and weight are strictly irrelevant. Since juries might be biased—even innocently and unawares—by these irrelevant features, they are carefully screened off so only the essential feature, musicianship, can be examined. Turing recognized that people similarly might be biased in their judgments of intelligence by whether the contestant had soft skin, warm blood, facial features, hands and eyes—which are obviously not themselves essential components of intelligence—so he devised a screen that would let through only a sample of what really mattered: the capacity to understand, and think cleverly about, challenging problems. Perhaps he was inspired by Descartes, who in his *Discourse on Method* (1637) plausibly argued that there was no more demanding test of human mentality than the capacity to hold an intelligent conversation:

It is indeed conceivable that a machine could be so made that it would utter words, and even words appropriate to the presence of physical acts or objects which cause some change in its organs; as, for example, if it was touched in some spot that it would ask what you wanted to say to it; if in another, that it would cry that it was hurt, and so on for similar things. But it could never modify its phrases to reply to the sense of whatever was said in its presence, as even the most stupid men can do.

This seemed obvious to Descartes in the seventeenth century, but of course the fanciest machines he knew were elaborate clockwork figures, not electronic computers. Today it is far from obvious that such machines are impossible, but Descartes's hunch that ordinary conversation would put as severe a strain on artificial intelligence as any other test was shared by Turing. Of course there is nothing sacred about the particular conversational game chosen by Turing for his test; it is just a cannily chosen test of more general intelligence. The assumption Turing was prepared to make was this: Nothing could possibly pass the Turing test by winning the imitation game without being able to perform indefinitely many other clearly intelligent actions. Let us call that assumption the quick-probe assumption. Turing realized, as anyone would, that there are hundreds and thousands of telling signs of intelligent thinking to be observed in our fellow creatures, and one could, if one wanted, compile a vast battery of different tests to assay the capacity for intelligent thought. But success on his chosen test, he thought, would be highly predictive of success on many other intuitively acceptable tests of intelligence. Remember, failure on the Turing test does not predict failure on those others, but success would surely predict success. His test was so severe, he thought, that nothing that could pass it fair and square would disappoint us in other quarters. Maybe it wouldn't do everything we hoped—maybe it wouldn't appreciate ballet, or understand quantum physics, or have a good plan for world peace, but we'd all see that it was surely one of the intelligent, thinking entities in the neighborhood.

Is this high opinion of the Turing test's severity misguided? Certainly many have thought so—but usually because they have not imagined the test in sufficient detail, and hence have underestimated it. Trying to forestall this skepticism, Turing imagined several lines of questioning that a judge might employ in this game—about writing poetry, or playing chess—that would be taxing indeed, but with thirty years' experience with the actual talents and foibles of computers behind us, perhaps we can add a few more tough lines of questioning.

Terry Winograd, a leader in artificial intelligence efforts to produce conversational ability in a computer, draws our attention to a pair of sentences (Winograd, 1972). They differ in only one word. The first sentence is this:

The committee denied the group a parade permit because they advocated violence.

Here's the second sentence:

The committee denied the group a parade permit because they feared violence.

The difference is just in the verb—*advocated* or *feared*. As Winograd points out, the pronoun *they* in each sentence is officially ambiguous. Both readings of the pronoun are always legal. Thus we can imagine a world in which governmental committees in charge of parade permits advocate violence in the streets and, for some strange reason, use this as their pretext for denying a parade permit. But the natural, reasonable, intelligent reading of the first sentence is that it's the group that advocated violence, and of the second, that it's the committee that feared violence.

Now if sentences like this are embedded in a conversation, the computer must figure out which reading of the pronoun is meant, if it is to respond intelligently. But mere rules of grammar or vocabulary will not fix the right reading. What fixes the right reading for us is knowledge about the world, about politics, social circumstances, committees and their attitudes, groups that want to parade, how they tend to behave, and the like. One must know about the world, in short, to make sense of such a sentence.

In the jargon of Artificial Intelligence (AI), a conversational computer needs a lot of *world knowledge* to do its job. But, it seems, if somehow it is endowed with that world knowledge on many topics, it should be able to do much more with that world knowledge than merely make sense of a conversation containing just that sentence. The only way, it appears, for a computer to disambiguate that sentence and keep up its end of a conversation that uses that sentence would be for it to have a much more general ability to respond intelligently to information about social and political circumstances, and many other topics. Thus, such sentences, by putting a demand on such abilities, are good quick-probes. That is, they test for a wider competence.

People typically ignore the prospect of having the judge ask off-the-wall questions in the Turing test, and hence they underestimate the competence a computer would have to have to pass the test. But remember, the rules of the imitation game as Turing presented it permit the judge to ask any question that could be asked of a human being—no holds barred. Suppose then we give a contestant in the game this question:

An Irishman found a genie in a bottle who offered him two wishes. "First I'll have a pint of Guinness," said the Irishman, and when it appeared he took several long drinks from it and was delighted to see that the glass filled itself magically as he drank. "What about your second wish?" asked the genie. "Oh well," said the Irishman, "that's easy. I'll have another one of these!"

—Please explain this story to me, and tell me if there is anything funny or sad about it.

Now even a child could express, if not eloquently, the understanding that is required to get this joke. But think of how much one has to know and understand about human culture, to put it pompously, to be able to give any account of the point of this joke. I am not supposing that the computer would have to laugh at, or be amused by, the joke. But if it wants to win the imitation game—and that's the test, after all—it had better know enough in its own alien, humorless way about human psychology and culture to be able to pretend effectively that it was amused and explain why.

It may seem to you that we could devise a better test. Let's compare the Turing test with some other candidates.

Candidate 1: A computer is intelligent if it wins the World Chess Championship.

That's not a good test, as it turns out. Chess prowess has proven to be an isolatable talent. There are programs today that can play fine chess but can do nothing else. So the quick-probe assumption is false for the test of playing winning chess.

Candidate 2: The computer is intelligent if it solves the Arab-Israeli conflict.

This is surely a more severe test than Turing's. But it has some defects: it is unrepeatable, if passed once; slow, no doubt; and it is not crisply clear what would count as passing it. Here's another prospect, then:

Candidate 3: A computer is intelligent if it succeeds in stealing the British crown jewels without the use of force or violence.

Now this is better. First, it could be repeated again and again, though of course each repeat test would presumably be harder—but this is a feature it shares with the Turing test. Second, the mark of success is clear—either you've got the jewels to show for your efforts or you don't. But it is expensive and slow, a socially dubious caper at best, and no doubt luck would play too great a role.

With ingenuity and effort one might be able to come up with other candidates that would equal the Turing test in severity, fairness, and efficiency, but I think these few examples should suffice to convince us that it would be hard to improve on Turing's original proposal.

But still, you may protest, something might pass the Turing test and still not be intelligent, not be a thinker. What does *might* mean here? If what you have in mind is that by cosmic accident, by a supernatural coincidence, a stupid person or a stupid computer *might* fool a clever judge repeatedly, well, yes, but so what? The same frivolous possibility "in principle" holds for any test whatever. A playful god, or evil demon, let us agree, could fool the world's scientific community about the presence of H_2O in the Pacific Ocean. But still, the tests they rely on to establish that there is H_2O in the Pacific Ocean are quite beyond reasonable criticism. If the Turing test for thinking is no worse than any well-established scientific test, we can set skepticism aside and go back to serious matters. Is there any more likelihood of a "false positive" result on the Turing test than on, say, the test currently used for the presence of iron in an ore sample?

This question is often obscured by a "move" that philosophers have sometimes made called operationalism. Turing and those who think well of his test are often accused of being operationalists. Operationalism is the tactic of *defining* the presence of some property, for instance, intelligence, as being established once and for all by the passing of some test. Let's illustrate this with a different example.

Suppose I offer the following test—we'll call it the Dennett test—for being a great city:

A great city is one in which, on a randomly chosen day, one can do all three of the following:

Hear a symphony orchestra
See a Rembrandt *and* a professional athletic contest
Eat *quenelles de brochet à la Nantua* for lunch

To make the operationalist move would be to declare that any city that passes the Dennett test is *by definition* a great city. What being a great city *amounts to* is just passing the Dennett test. Well then, if the Chamber of Commerce of Great Falls, Montana, wanted—and I can't imagine why—to get their hometown on my list of great cities, they could accomplish this by the relatively inexpensive route of hiring full time about ten basketball players, forty musicians, and a quick-order quenelle chef and renting a cheap Rembrandt from some museum. An idiotic operationalist would then be stuck admitting that Great Falls, Montana, was in fact a great city, since all he or she cares about in great cities is that they pass the Dennett test.

Sane operationalists (who for that very reason are perhaps not operationalists at all, since *operationalist* seems to be a dirty word) would cling confidently to their test, but only because they have what they consider to be very good reasons for thinking the odds against a false positive result, like the imagined Chamber of Commerce caper, are astronomical. I devised the Dennett test, of course, with the realization that no one would be both stupid and rich enough to go to such preposterous lengths to foil the test. In the actual world, wherever you find symphony orchestras, *quenelles,* Rembrandts, and professional sports, you also find daily newspapers, parks, repertory theaters, libraries, fine architecture, and all the other things that go to make a city great. My test was simply devised to locate a telling sample that could not help but be representative of the rest of the city's treasures. I would cheerfully run the minuscule risk of having my bluff called. Obviously, the test items are not all that I care about in a city. In fact, some of them I don't care about at all. I just think they would be cheap and easy ways of assuring myself that the subtle things I do care about in cities are present. Similarly, I think it would be entirely unreasonable to suppose that Alan Turing had an inordinate fondness for party games, or put too high a value on party game prowess in his test. In both the Turing and the Dennett test, a very unrisky gamble is being taken: the gamble that the quick-probe assumption is, in general, safe.

But two can play this game of playing the odds. Suppose some computer programmer happens to be, for whatever strange reason, dead set on tricking me into judging an entity to be a thinking, intelligent thing when it is not. Such a trickster could rely as well as I can on unlikelihood and take a few gambles. Thus, if the programmer can expect that it is not remotely likely that I, as the judge, will bring up the topic of children's birthday parties, or baseball, or moon rocks, then he or she can avoid the trouble of building world knowledge on those topics into the data base. Whereas if I do improbably raise these issues, the system will draw a blank and I will unmask the pretender easily. But given all the topics and words that I *might* raise, such a savings would no doubt be negligible. Turn the idea inside out, however, and the trickster would have a fighting chance. Suppose the programmer has reason to believe that I will ask *only* about children's birthday parties, or baseball, or moon rocks—all other topics being, for one reason or another, out of bounds. Not only does the task shrink dramatically, but there already exist systems or preliminary sketches of systems in artificial intelligence that can do a whiz-bang job of responding with apparent intelligence on just those specialized topics.

William Wood's LUNAR program, to take what is perhaps the best example, answers scientists' questions—posed in ordinary English—about moon rocks. In one test it answered correctly and appropriately something like 90 percent of the questions that geologists and other experts thought of asking it about moon rocks. (In 12 percent of those correct responses there were trivial, correctable defects.) Of course, Wood's motive in creating LUNAR was not to trick unwary geologists into thinking they were conversing with an intelligent being. And if that had been his motive, his project would still be a long way from success.

For it is easy enough to unmask LUNAR without ever straying from the prescribed topic of moon rocks. Put LUNAR in one room and a moon rock specialist in another, and then ask them both their opinion of the social value of the moon-rocks-gathering expeditions, for instance. Or ask the contestants their opinion of the suitability of moon rocks as ashtrays, or whether people who have touched moon rocks are ineligible for the draft. Any intelligent person knows a lot more about moon rocks than their geology. Although it might be *unfair* to demand this extra knowledge of a computer moon rock specialist, it would be an easy way to get it to fail the Turing test.

But just suppose that someone could extend LUNAR to cover itself plausibly on such probes, so long as the topic was still, however indirectly, moon rocks. We might come to think it was a lot more like the human moon rocks specialist than it really was. The moral we should draw is that as Turing test judges we should resist all limitations and waterings-down of the Turing test. They make the game too easy— vastly easier than the original test. Hence they lead us into the risk of overestimating the actual comprehension of the system being tested.

Consider a different limitation of the Turing test that should strike a suspicious chord in us as soon as we hear it. This is a variation on a theme developed in an article by Ned Block (1982). Suppose someone were to propose to restrict the judge to a vocabulary of, say, the 850 words of "Basic English," and to single-sentence probes—that is "moves"—of no more than four words. Moreover, contestants must respond to these probes with no more than four words per move, and a test may involve no more than forty questions.

Is this an innocent variation on Turing's original test? These restrictions would make the imitation game clearly finite. That is, the total number of all possible permissible games is a large, but finite, number. One might suspect that such a limitation would permit the trickster simply to store, in alphabetical order, all the possible good conversations within the limits and beat the judge with nothing more sophisticated than a system of table lookup. In fact, that isn't in the cards. Even with these severe and improbable and suspicious restrictions imposed upon the imitation game, the number of legal games, though finite, is mind-bogglingly large. I haven't bothered trying to calculate it, but it surely exceeds astronomically the number of possible chess games with no more than forty moves, and that number has been calculated. John Haugeland says it's in the neighborhood of ten to the one hundred twentieth power. For comparison, Haugeland (1981, p. 16) suggests that there have only been ten to the eighteenth seconds since the beginning of the universe.

Of course, the number of good, sensible conversations under these limits is a tiny fraction, maybe one quadrillionth, of the number of merely grammatically well formed conversations. So let's say, to be very conservative, that there are only ten to the fiftieth different smart conversations such a computer would have to store. Well, the task shouldn't take more than a few trillion years—given generous government support. Finite numbers can be very large.

So though we needn't worry that this particular trick of storing all the smart conversations would work, we can appreciate that there are lots of ways of making the task easier that may appear innocent at first. We also get a reassuring measure of just how severe the unrestricted Turing test is by reflecting on the more than astronomical size of even that severely restricted version of it.

Block's imagined—and utterly impossible—program exhibits the dreaded feature know in computer science circles as *combinatorial explosion*. No conceivable computer could overpower a combinatorial explosion with sheer speed and size. Since the problem areas addressed by artificial intelligence are veritable minefields of combinatorial explosion, and since it has often proven difficult to find *any* solution to a problem that avoids them, there is considerable plausibility in Newell and Simon's proposal that avoiding combinatorial explosion (by any means at all) be viewed as one of the hallmarks of intelligence.

Our brains are millions of times bigger than the brains of gnats, but they are still, for all their vast complexity, compact, efficient, timely organs that somehow or other manage to perform all their tasks while avoiding combinatorial explosion. A computer a million times bigger or faster than a human brain might not look like the brain of a human being, or even be internally organized like the brain of a human being, but if, for all its differences, it somehow managed to control a wise and timely set of activities, it would have to be the beneficiary of a very special design that avoided combinatorial explosion, and whatever that design was, would we not be right to consider the entity intelligent?

Turing's test was designed to allow for this possibility. His point was that we should not be species-chauvinistic, or anthropocentric, about the insides of an intelligent being, for there might be inhuman ways of being intelligent.

To my knowledge, the only serious and interesting attempt by any program designer to win even a severely modified Turing test has been Kenneth Colby's. Colby is a psychiatrist and intelligence artificer at UCLA. He has a program called PARRY, which is a computer simulation of a paranoid patient who has delusions about the Mafia being out to get him. As you do with other conversational programs, you interact with it by sitting at a terminal and typing questions and answers back and forth. A number of years ago, Colby put PARRY to a very restricted test. He had genuine psychiatrists interview PARRY. He did not suggest to them that they might be talking or typing to a computer; rather, he made up some plausible story about why they were communicating with a real live patient by teletype. He also had the psychiatrists interview real, human paranoids via teletype. Then he took a PARRY transcript, inserted it in a group of teletype transcripts from real patients, gave them to *another* group of experts—more psychiatrists—and said, "One of these was a conversation with a computer. Can you figure out which one it was?" They couldn't. They didn't do better than chance.

Colby presented this with some huzzah, but critics scoffed at the suggestions that this was a legitimate Turing test. My favorite commentary on it was Joseph Weizenbaum's; in a letter to the *Communications of the Association of Computing Machinery* (Weizenbaum, 1974, p. 543), he said that, inspired by Colby, he had designed an even better program, which passed the same test. His also had the virtue of being a very inexpensive program, in these times of tight money. In fact you didn't even need a computer for it. All you needed was an electric typewriter. His program modeled infant autism. And the transcripts— you type in your questions, and the thing just sits there and hums— cannot be distinguished by experts from transcripts of real conversations with infantile autistic patients. What was wrong, of course, with Colby's test was that the unsuspecting interviewers had no motivation at all to try out any of the sorts of questions that easily would have unmasked PARRY.

Colby was undaunted, and after his team had improved PARRY he put it to a much more severe test—a surprisingly severe test. This time, the interviewers—again, psychiatrists—*were* given the task at the outset of telling the computer from the real patient. They were set up in a classic Turing test: the patient in one room, the computer PARRY in the other room, with the judges conducting interviews with both of them (on successive days). The judges' task was to find out which one was the computer and which one was the real patient. Amazingly, they didn't do much better, which leads some people to say, "Well, that just confirms my impression of the intelligence of psychiatrists!"

But now, more seriously, was this an honest-to-goodness Turing test? Were there tacit restrictions on the lines of questioning of the judges? Like the geologists interacting with LUNAR, the psychiatrists' professional preoccupations and habits kept them from asking the sorts of unlikely questions that would have easily unmasked PARRY. After all, they realized that since one of the contestants was a real, live paranoid person, medical ethics virtually forbade them from toying with, upsetting, or attempting to confuse their interlocutors. Moreover, they also knew that this was a test of a model of paranoia, so there were certain questions that wouldn't be deemed to be relevant to testing the model *as a model of paranoia*. So, they asked just the sort of questions that therapists *typically* ask of such patients, and of course PARRY had been ingeniously and laboriously prepared to deal with just that sort of question.

One of the psychiatrist judges did, in fact, make a rather half-hearted attempt to break out of the mold and ask some telling questions: "Maybe you've heard of the saying 'Don't cry over spilled milk.' What does that mean to you?" PARRY answered: "Maybe it means you have to watch out for the Mafia." When then asked "Okay, now if you were in a movie theater watching a movie and smelled something like burning wood or rubber, what would you do?" PARRY replied: "You know, they know me." And the next question was, "If you found a stamped, addressed letter in your path as you were walking down the street, what would you do?" PARRY replied: "What else do you want to know?"[1]

Clearly PARRY was, you might say, *parrying* these questions, which were incomprehensible to it, with more or less stock paranoid formulas. We see a bit of a dodge, which is apt to work, apt to seem plausible to the judge, only because the "contestant" is *supposed* to be paranoid, and such people are expected to respond uncooperatively on such occasions. These unimpressive responses didn't particularly arouse the suspicions of the judge, as a matter of fact, though probably they should have.

PARRY, like all other large computer programs, is dramatically bound by limitations of cost-effectiveness. What was important to Colby and his crew was simulating his model of paranoia. This was a massive effort. PARRY has a thesaurus or dictionary of about 4500 words and 700 idioms and the grammatical competence to use it—a *parser*, in the jargon of computational linguistics. The entire PARRY program takes up about 200, 000 words of computer memory, all laboriously installed by the programming team. Now once all the effort had gone into devising the model of paranoid thought processes and linguistic ability, there was little if any time, energy, money, or interest left over to build in huge amounts of world knowledge of the sort that any actual paranoid, of course, would have. (Not that anyone yet knows how to build in world knowledge in the first place.) Building in the world knowledge, if one could even do it, would no doubt have made PARRY orders of magnitude larger and slower. And what would have been the point, given Colby's theoretical aims?

PARRY is a theoretician's model of a psychological phenomenon: paranoia. It is not intended to have practical applications. But in recent years a branch of AI (knowledge engineering) has appeared that develops what are now called expert systems. Expert systems *are* designed to be practical. They are software superspecialist consultants, typically, that can be asked to diagnose medical problems, to analyze geological data, to analyze the results of scientific experiments, and the like. Some

---

1. I thank Kenneth Colby for providing me with the complete transcripts (including the Judges' commentaries and reactions), from which these exchanges are quoted. The first published account of the experiment is Heiser, et al. (1980, pp. 149–162). Colby (1981, pp. 515–560) discusses PARRY and its implications.

of them are very impressive. SRI in California announced in the mid-eighties that PROSPECTOR, an SRI-developed expert system in geology, had correctly predicted the existence of a large, important mineral deposit that had been entirely unanticipated by the human geologists who had fed it its data. MYCIN, perhaps the most famous of these expert systems, diagnoses infections of the blood, and it does probably as well as, maybe better than, any human consultants. And many other expert systems are on the way.

All expert systems, like all other large AI programs, are what you might call Potemkin villages. That is, they are cleverly constructed facades, like cinema sets. The actual filling-in of details of AI programs is time-consuming, costly work, so economy dictates that only those surfaces of the phenomenon that are like to be probed or observed are represented.

Consider, for example, the CYRUS program developed by Janet Kolodner in Roger Schank's AI group at Yale a few years ago (see Kolodner, 1983a; 1983b, pp. 243–280; 1983c, pp. 281–328). CYRUS stands (we are told) for Computerized Yale Retrieval Updating System, but surely it is no accident that CYRUS modeled the memory of Cyrus Vance, who was then secretary of state in the Carter administration. The point of the CYRUS project was to devise and test some plausible ideas about how people organize their memories of the events they participate in; hence it was meant to be a "pure" AI system, a scientific model, not an expert system intended for any practical purpose. CYRUS was updated daily by being fed all UPI wire service news stories that mentioned Vance, and it was fed them directly, with no doctoring and no human intervention. Thanks to an ingenious news-reading program called FRUMP, it could take any story just as it came in on the wire and could digest it and use it to update its data base so that it could answer more questions. You could address questions to CYRUS in English by typing at a terminal. You addressed them in the second person, as if you were talking with Cyrus Vance himself. The results looked like this:

Q: *Last time you went to Saudi Arabia, where did you stay?*
A: In a palace in Saudi Arabia on September 23, 1978.

Q: *Did you go sightseeing there?*
A: Yes, at an oilfield in Dhahran on September 23, 1978.

Q: *Has your wife even met Mrs. Begin?*
A: Yes, most recently at a state dinner in Israel in January 1980.

CYRUS could correctly answer thousands of questions—almost any fair question one could think of asking it. But if one actually set out to explore the boundaries of its facade and find the questions that overshot the mark, one could soon find them. "Have you ever met a female head of state?" was a question I asked it, wondering if CYRUS knew that Indira Ghandi and Margaret Thatcher were women. But for some reason the connection could not be drawn, and CYRUS failed to answer either yes or no. I had stumped it, in spite of the fact that CYRUS could handle a host of what you might call neighboring questions flawlessly. One soon learns from this sort of probing exercise that it is very hard to extrapolate accurately from a sample performance that one has observed to such a system's total competence. It's also very hard to keep from extrapolating much too generously.

While I was visiting Schank's laboratory in the spring of 1980, something revealing happened. The real Cyrus Vance resigned suddenly. The effect on the program CYRUS was chaotic. It was utterly unable to cope with the flood of "unusual" news about Cyrus Vance. The only sorts of episodes CYRUS could understand at all were diplomatic meetings, flights, press conferences, state dinners, and the like—less than two dozen general sorts of activities (the kinds that are newsworthy and typical of secretaries of state). It had no provision for sudden resignation. It was as if the UPI had reported that a wicked witch had turned Vance into a frog. It is distinctly possible that CYRUS would have taken that report more in stride that the actual news. One can imagine the conversation:

Q: *Hello, Mr. Vance, what's new?*
A: I was turned into a frog yesterday.

But of course it wouldn't know enough about what it had just written to be puzzled, or startled, or embarrassed. The reason is obvious. When you look inside CYRUS, you find that it has skeletal definitions of thousands of words, but these definitions are minimal. They contain as little as the system designers think that they can get away with. Thus, perhaps, *lawyer* would be defined as synonymous with *attorney* and *legal counsel*, but aside from that, all one would discover about lawyers is that they are adult human beings and that they perform various functions in legal areas. If you then traced out the path to *human being,* you'd find out various obvious things CYRUS "knew" about human beings (hence about lawyers), but that is not a lot. That lawyers are university graduates, that they are better paid than chambermaids, that they know how to tie their shoes, that they are unlikely to be found in the company of lumberjacks—these trivial, if weird, facts about lawyers would not be explicit or implicit anywhere in this system. In other words, a very thin stereotype of a lawyer would be incorporated into the system, so that almost nothing you could tell it about a lawyer would surprise it.

So long as surprising things don't happen, so long as Mr. Vance, for instance, leads a typical diplomat's life, attending state dinners, giving speeches, flying from Cairo to Rome, and so forth, this system works very well. But as soon as his path is crossed by an important anomaly, the system is unable to cope, and unable to recover without fairly massive human intervention. In the case of the sudden resignation, Kolodner and her associates soon had CYRUS up and running again, with a new talent—answering questions about Edmund Muskie, Vance's successor—but it was no less vulnerable to unexpected events. Not that it mattered particularly since CYRUS was a theoretical model, not a practical system.

There are a host of ways of improving the performance of such systems, and of course, some systems are much better than others. But all AI programs in one way or another have this facade-like quality, simply for reasons of economy. For instance, most expert systems in medical diagnosis so far developed operate with statistical information. They have no deep or even shallow knowledge of the underlying causal mechanisms of the phenomena that they are diagnosing. To take an imaginary example, an expert system asked to diagnose an abdominal pain would be oblivious to the potential import of the fact that the patient had recently been employed as a sparring partner by Muhammad Ali—there being no statistical data available to it on the rate of kidney stones among athlete's assistants. That's a fanciful case no doubt—too obvious, perhaps, to lead to an actual failure of diagnosis and practice. But more subtle and hard-to-detect limits to comprehension are always present, and even experts, even the system's designers, can be uncertain of where and how these limits will interfere with the desired operation of the system. Again, steps can be taken and are being taken to correct these flaws. For instance, my former colleague at Tufts, Benjamin Kuipers, is currently working on an expert system in nephrology—for diagnosing kidney ailments—that will be based on an elaborate system of causal reasoning about the phenomena being diagnosed. But this is a very ambitious, long-range project of considerable theoretical difficulty. And even if all the reasonable, cost-effective steps are taken to minimize the superficiality of expert systems, they will still be facades, just somewhat thicker or wider facades.

When we were considering the fantastic case of the crazy Chamber of Commerce of Great Falls, Montana, we couldn't imagine a plausible motive for anyone going to any sort of trouble to trick the Dennett test. The quick-probe assumption for the Dennett test looked quite secure. But when we look at expert systems, we see that, however innocently, their designers do have motivation for doing exactly the sort of trick that would fool an unsuspicious Turing tester. First, since expert systems are all superspecialists who are only supposed to know about some narrow subject, users of such systems, not having much time to kill, do not bother probing them at the boundaries at all. They don't bother asking "silly" or irrelevant questions. Instead, they concentrate—not unreasonably—on exploiting the system's strengths. But shouldn't they try to obtain a clear vision of such a system's weaknesses as well? The normal habit of human thought when conversing with one another is to assume general comprehension, to assume rationality, to assume, moreover, that the quick-probe assumption is, in general, sound. This amiable habit of thought almost irresistibly leads to putting too much faith in computer systems, especially user-friendly systems that present themselves in a very anthropomorphic manner.

Part of the solution to this problem is to teach all users of computers, especially users of expert systems, how to probe their systems before they rely on them, how to search out and explore the boundaries of the facade. This is an exercise that calls not only for intelligence and imagination, but also a bit of special understanding about the limitations and actual structure of computer programs. It would help, of course, if we had standards of truth in advertising, in effect, for expert systems. For instance, each such system should come with a special demonstration routine that exhibits the sorts of shortcomings and failures that the designer knows the system to have. This would not be a substitute, however, for an attitude of cautious, almost obsessive, skepticism on the part of the users, for designers are often, if not always, unaware of the subtler flaws in the products they produce. That is inevitable and natural, given the way system designers must think. They are trained to think positively—constructively, one might say—about the designs that they are constructing.

I come, then, to my conclusions. First, a philosophical or theoretical conclusion: The Turing test in unadulterated, unrestricted from, as

Turing presented it, is plenty strong if well used. I am confident that no computer in the next twenty years is going to pass an unrestricted Turing test. They may well win the World Chess Championship or even a Nobel Prize in physics, but they won't pass the unrestricted Turing test. Nevertheless, it is not, I think, impossible in principle for a computer to pass the test, fair and square. I'm not running one of those a priori "computers can't think" arguments. I stand unabashedly ready, moreover, to declare that any computer that actually passes the unrestricted Turing test will be, in every theoretically interesting sense, a thinking thing.

But remembering how very strong the Turing test is, we must also recognize that there may also be interesting varieties of thinking or intelligence that are not well poised to play and win the imitation game. That no nonhuman Turing test winners are yet visible on the horizon does not mean that there aren't machines that already exhibit *some* of the important features of thought. About them, it is probably futile to ask my title question, Do they think? Do they *really* think? In some regards they do, and in some regards they don't. Only a detailed look at what they do, and how they are structured, will reveal what is interesting about them. The Turing test, not being a scientific test, is of scant help on that task, but there are plenty of other ways of examining such systems. Verdicts on their intelligence or capacity for thought or consciousness would be only as informative and persuasive as the theories of intelligence or thought or consciousness the verdicts are based on and since our task is to create such theories, we should get on with it and leave the Big Verdict for another occasion. In the meantime, should anyone want a surefire, almost-guaranteed-to-be-fail-safe test of thinking by a computer, the Turing test will do very nicely.

My second conclusion is more practical, and hence in one clear sense more important. Cheapened versions of the Turing test are everywhere in the air. Turing's test in not just effective, it is entirely natural—this is, after all, the way we assay the intelligence of each other every day. And since incautious use of such judgments and such tests is the norm, we are in some considerable danger of extrapolating too easily, and judging too generously, about the understanding of the systems we are using. The problem of overestimation of cognitive prowess, of comprehension, of intelligence, is not, then, just a philosophical problem, but a real social problem, and we should alert ourselves to it, and take steps to avert it.

*Postscript [1985]: Eyes,
Ears, Hands, and History*

My philosophical conclusion in this paper is that any computer that
actually passes the Turing test would be a thinking thing in every theoretically interesting sense. This conclusion seems to some people to fly
in the face of what I have myself argued on other occasions. Peter Bieri,
commenting on this paper at Boston University, noted that I have often
claimed to show the importance to genuine understanding of a rich
and intimate perceptual interconnection between an entity and its surrounding world—the need for something like eyes and ears—and a
similarly complex active engagement with elements in that world—the
need for something like hands with which to do things in that world.
Moreover, I have often held that only a biography of sorts, a history
of actual projects, learning experiences, and other bouts with reality,
could produce the sorts of complexities (both external, or behavioral,
and internal) that are needed to ground a principled interpretation of
an entity as a thinking thing, an entity with beliefs, desires, intentions,
and other mental attitudes.

But the opaque screen in the Turing test discounts or dismisses these
factors altogether, it seems, by focusing attention on only the contem-
poraneous capacity to engage in one very limited sort of activity:
verbal communication. (I have coined a pejorative label for such purely
language-using systems: bedridden.) Am I going back on my earlier
claims? Not at all. I am merely pointing out that the Turing test is so
powerful that it will ensure indirectly that these conditions, if they are
truly necessary, are met by any successful contestant.

"You may well be right," Turing could say, "that eyes, ears, hands,
and a history are necessary conditions for thinking. If so, then I submit
that nothing could pass the Turing test that didn't have eyes, ears,
hands, and a history. That is an empirical claim, which we can someday

hope to test. If you suggest that these are conceptually necessary, not just practically or physically necessary, conditions for thinking, you make a philosophical claim that I for one would not know how, or care, to assess. Isn't it more interesting and important in the end to discover whether or not it is true that no bedridden system could pass a demanding Turing test?"

Suppose we put to Turing the suggestion that he add another component to his test: Not only must an entity win the imitation game, but also must be able to identify—using whatever sensory apparatus it has available to it—a variety of familiar objects placed in its room: a tennis racket, a potted palm, a bucket of yellow paint, a live dog. This would ensure that somehow the other entity was capable of moving around and distinguishing things in the world. Turing could reply, I am asserting, that this is an utterly unnecessary addition to his test, making it no more demanding than it already was. A suitable probing conversation would surely establish, beyond a shadow of a doubt, that the contestant knew its way around the world. The imagined alternative of somehow "prestocking" a bedridden, blind computer with enough information, and a clever enough program, to trick the Turing test is science fiction of the worst kind—possible "in principle" but not remotely possible in fact, given the combinatorial explosion of possible variation such a system would have to cope with.

"But suppose you're wrong. What would you say of an entity that was created all at once (by some programmers, perhaps), an instant individual with all the conversational talents of an embodied, experienced human being?" This is like the question: "Would you call a hunk of H_2O that was as hard as steel at room temperature ice?" I do not know what Turing would say, of course, so I will speak for myself. Faced with such an improbable violation of what I take to be the laws of nature, I would probably be speechless. The least of my worries would be about which lexicographical leap to take:

A: "It turns out, to my amazement, that something can think without having had the benefit of eyes, ears, hands, and a history."
B: "It turns out, to my amazement, that something can pass the Turing test without thinking."

Choosing between these ways of expressing my astonishment would be asking myself a question "too meaningless to deserve discussion."

Discussion

Q: *Why was Turing interested in differentiating a man from a woman in his famous test?*

A: That was just an example. He described a parlor game in which a man would try to fool the judge by answering questions as a woman would answer. I suppose that Turing was playing on the idea that maybe, just maybe, there is a big difference between the way men think and the way women think. But of course they're both thinkers. He wanted to use that fact to make us realize that, even if there were clear differences between the way a computer and a person thought, they'd both still be thinking.

Q: *Why does it seem that some people are upset by AI research? Does AI research threaten our self-esteem?*

A: I think Herb Simon has already given the canniest diagnosis of that. For many people the mind is the last refuge of mystery against the encroaching spread of science, and they don't like the idea of science engulfing the last bit of *terra incognita*. This means that they are threatened, I think irrationally, by the prospect that researchers in Artificial Intelligence may come to understand the human mind as well as biologists understand the genetic code, or as well as physicists understand electricity and magnetism. This could lead to the "evil scientist" (to take a stock character from science fiction) who can control you because he or she has a deep understanding of what's going on in your mind. This seems to me to be a totally valueless fear, one that you can set aside, for the simple reason that the human mind is full of an extraordinary amount of detailed knowledge, as, for example, Roger Schank has been pointing out.

As long as the scientist who is attempting to manipulate you does not share all your knowledge, his or her chances of manipulating you are minimal. People can always hit you over the head. They can do that now. We don't need Artificial Intelligence to manipulate people by putting them in chains or torturing them. But if someone tries to manipulate you by controlling your thoughts and ideas, that person will have to know what you know and more. The best way to keep yourself safe from that kind of manipulation is to be well informed.

Q: *Do you think we will be able to program self-consciousness into a computer?*

A: Yes, I do think that it's possible to program self-consciousness into a computer. *Self-consciousness* can mean many things. If you take the simplest, crudest notion of self-consciousness, I suppose that would be the sort of self-consciousness that a lobster has: When it's hungry, it eats something, but it never eats itself. It has some way of distinguishing between itself and the rest of the world, and it has a rather special regard for itself.

The lowly lobster is, in one regard, self-conscious. If you want to know whether or not you can create that on the computer, the answer is yes. It's no trouble at all. The computer is already a self-watching, self-monitoring sort of thing. That is an established part of the technology.

But, of course, most people have something more in mind when they speak of self-consciousness. It is that special inner light, that private way that it is with you that nobody else can share, something that is forever outside the bounds of computer science. How could a computer ever be conscious in this sense?

That belief, that very gripping, powerful intuition is, I think, in the end simply an illusion of common sense. It is as gripping as the common-sense illusion that the earth stands still and the sun goes around the earth. But the only way that those of us who do not believe in the illusion will ever convince the general public that it *is* an illusion is by gradually unfolding a very difficult and fascinating story about just what is going on in our minds.

In the interim, people like me—philosophers who have to live by our wits and tell a lot of stories—use what I call intuition pumps, little examples that help free up the imagination. I simply want to draw your attention to one fact. If you look at a computer—I don't care whether it's a giant Cray or a personal computer—if you open up the box and look inside and see those chips, you say, "No way could that be conscious. No way could that be self-conscious." But the same thing is true if you take the top off somebody's skull and look at the gray matter pulsing away in there. You think, "That is conscious? No way could that lump of stuff be conscious."

Of course, it makes no difference whether you look at it with a microscope or with a macroscope: At no level of inspection does a brain look like the seat of consciousness. Therefore, don't expect a computer to look like the seat of consciousness. If you want to get a grasp of how a computer could be conscious, it's no more difficult in the end than getting a grasp of how a brain could be conscious.

As we develop good accounts of consciousness, it will no longer seem so obvious to everyone that the idea of a self-conscious computer is a contradiction in terms. At the same time, I doubt that there will ever be self-conscious robots. But for boring reasons. There won't be any point in making them. Theoretically, could we make a gall bladder out of atoms? In principle we could. A gall bladder is just a collection of atoms, but manufacturing one would cost the moon. It would be more expensive than every project NASA has ever dreamed of, and there would be no scientific payoff. We wouldn't learn anything new about how gall bladders work. For the same reason, I don't think we're going to see really humanoid robots, because practical, cost-effective robots don't need to be very humanoid at all. They need to be like the robots you can already see at General Motors, or like boxy little computers that do special-purpose things.

The theoretical issues will be studied by artificial intelligence researchers by looking at models that, to the layman, will show very little sign of humanity at all, and it will be only by rather indirect arguments that anyone will be able to appreciate that these models cast light on the deep theoretical question of how the mind is organized.

Postscript [1997]

In 1991, the First Annual Loebner Prize Competition was held in Boston at the Computer Museum. Hugh Loebner, a New York manufacturer, had put up the money for a prize—a bronze medal and $100,000—for the first computer program to pass the Turing test fair and square. The Prize Committee, of which I was Chairman until my resignation after the third competition, recognized that no program on the horizon could come close to passing the unrestricted test—the only test that is of any theoretical interest at all, as this essay has explained. So to make the competition interesting during the early years, some restrictions were adopted (and the award for winning the restricted test was dropped to $2000). The first year there were ten terminals, with ten judges shuffling from terminal to terminal, each spending fifteen minutes in conversation with each terminal. Six of the ten contestants were programs, four were human "confederates" behind the scenes.

Each judge had to rank order all ten terminals from most human to least human. The winner of the restricted test would be the computer with the highest mean rating. The winning program would not have to fool any of the judges, nor would fooling a judge be in itself grounds for winning; highest mean ranking was all. But just in case some program *did* fool a judge, we thought this fact should be revealed, so judges were required to draw a line somewhere across their rank ordering, separating the humans from the machines.

We on the Prize Committee knew the low quality of the contesting programs that first year, and it seemed obvious to us that no program would be so lucky as to fool a single judge, but on the day of the competition, I got nervous. Just to be safe, I thought, we should have some certificate prepared to award to any programmer who happened to pull off this unlikely feat. While the press and the audience were assembling for the beginning of the competition, I rushed into a back room at the Computer Museum with a member of the staff and we cobbled up a handsome certificate with the aid of a handy desktop publisher. In the event, we had to hand out three of these certificates, for a total of seven positive misjudgments out of a possible sixty! The gullibility of the judges was simply astonishing to me. How *could* they have mis-judged so badly? Here I had committed the sin I'd so often found in others: treating a failure of imagination as an insight into necessity. But remember that in order to make the competition much easier, we had tied the judges' hands in various ways—too many ways. The judges had been forbidden to *probe* the contestants aggressively, to con-duct conversational experiments. (I may have chaired the committee, but I didn't always succeed in persuading a majority to adopt the rules I favored.) When the judges sat back passively, as instructed, and let the contestants lead them, they were readily taken in by the Potemkin village effect described in the essay.

None of the misjudgments counted as a real case of a computer pass-ing the unrestricted Turing test, but they were still surprising to me. In the second year of the competition, we uncovered another unantici-pated loophole: due to faulty briefing of the confederates, several of them gave deliberately clunky, automaton-like answers. It turned out that they had decided to give the silicon contestants a sporting chance by acting as if they were programs! But once we'd straightened out these glitches in the rules and procedures, the competition worked out just as I had originally predicted: the computers stood out like sore thumbs even though there were still huge restrictions on topic. In the third year, two of the judges—journalists—each made a false *negative* judgment, declaring one of the less eloquent human confederates to be a computer. On debriefing, their explanation showed just how vast the gulf was between the computer programs and the people: they rea-soned that the competition would not have been held if there weren't at least one halfway decent computer contestant, so they simply picked the least impressive human being and declared it to be a computer. But they could see the gap between the computers and the people as well as everybody else could.

The Loebner Prize Competition was a fascinating social experiment, and some day I hope to write up the inside story—a tale of sometimes hilarious misadventure, bizarre characters, interesting technical chal-lenges, and more. But it never succeeded in attracting serious contes-tants from the world's best AI labs. Why not? In part because, as the essay argues, passing the Turing test is not a sensible research and development goal for serious AI. It requires too much Disney and not enough science. We might have corrected that flaw by introducing into the Loebner Competition something analogous to the "school figures" in ice-skating competition: theoretically interesting (but not crowd-pleasing) technical challenges such as parsing pronouns, or dealing creatively with enthymemes (arguments with unstated premises). Only those programs that performed well in the school figures—the serious competition—would be permitted into the final show-off round, where they could dazzle and amuse the onlookers with some cute Disney touches. Some such change in the rules would have wiped out all but the most serious and dedicated of the home hobbyists, and made the Loebner Competition worth winning (and not too embarrassing to lose). When my proposals along these lines were rejected, however, I resigned from the committee. The annual competitions continue, apparently, under the direction of Hugh Loebner. On the World Wide Web I just found the transcript of the conversation of the winning program in the 1996 completion. It was a scant improvement over 1991, still a bag of cheap tricks with no serious analysis of the meaning of the sentences. The Turing test is too difficult for the real world.

2

Speaking for Our Selves

Nicholas Humphrey and
Daniel C. Dennett

In 1988, the British psychologist Nicholas Humphrey came to work with me at the Center for Cognitive Studies at Tufts. Among our projects was investigating the curious phenomenon of Multiple Personality Disorder. Our jointly authored essay was originally commissioned by the New York Review of Books, *but when we submitted the draft (in roughly the form presented here), we encountered an esculating series of ever more impenetrable editorial "objections"; it finally became clear to us that these objections had more to do with feelings of intellectual queasiness than with scientific disagreement, and that nothing we could do would make the article acceptable. Since we were eager to publish it swiftly, in a journal of general intellectual interest, we submitted it to* Raritan. *That journal does not permit footnotes, so the footnotes as printed here are from the version reprinted as* Occasional Paper #8, Center on Violence and Human Survival, John Jay College of Criminal Justice, The City University of New York, 1991. *The topic of MPD has something for everyone: self, science, sex, violence, literary theory, and much, much more. We think we did justice to the phenomena, and we have often wondered about the emotional politics that lay behind the* New York Review of Books' *decision to keep our observations from their readers.*

"Thus play I in one person many people, and none contented."

—Richard II

In the early 1960s when the laws of England allowed nudity on stage only if the actor did not move, a tent at the Midsummer Fair in Cambridge offered an interesting display. "The one and only Chameleon Lady," the poster read, "becomes Great Women in History." The inside

Originally appeared in *Raritan: A Quarterly Review*, IX (1), Summer 1989, pp. 68–98.

of the tent was dark. "Florence Nightingale!" the showman bellowed, and the lights came up on a naked woman, motionless as marble, holding up a lamp. The audience cheered. The lights went down. There was a moment's shuffling on the stage. "Joan of Arc!" and here she was, lit from a different angle, leaning on a sword. "Good Queen Bess!" and now she had on a red wig and was carrying an orb and scepter.

"But it's the same *person*," said a know-all schoolboy.

Imagine now, thirty years later, a commercial for an IBM computer. A poster on a tent announces, "The one and only IBM PC becomes Great Information Processors of History." The tent is dark. "Word-Star!" shouts the showman, and the lights come up on a desktop computer, displaying a characteristic menu of commands. The lights go down. There is the sound of changing disks. "Paintbrush!" and here is the computer displaying a different menu. "Now, what you've all been waiting for, Lotus 123!"

"But it's just a different *program*," says the schoolboy.

Somewhere between these two scenarios lies the phenomenon of *multiple personality* in human beings. And somewhere between these two over-easy assessments of it are we. One of us is a theoretical psychologist, the other is a philosopher, both with a long-standing interest in the nature of personhood and of the self. We have had the opportunity during the past year to meet several "multiples," to talk with their therapists, and to savor the world from which they come. We give here an outsider's inside view.

We had been at the conference on Multiple Personality Disorder for two full days before someone made the inevitable joke: "The problem with those who don't believe in MPD is they've got Single Personality Disorder." In the mirror-world that we had entered, almost no one laughed.

The occasion was the Fifth International Conference on Multiple Personality/Dissociative States in Chicago,[1] attended by upwards of five hundred psychotherapists and a large but unquantifiable number of former patients.

The Movement or the Cause (as it was called) of MPD has been undergoing an exponential growth. Two hundred cases of multiplicity reported up till 1980, 1,000 known to be in treatment by 1984, 4,000

---

1. The International Society for the study of Multiple Personality and Dissociation (2506 Gross Point Road, Evanston, IL 60201) in 1989 had over a thousand members. The proceedings of the 1988 Chicago meeting are published in Braun (1988).

now. Women outnumber men by at least four to one, and there is reason to believe that the vast majority—perhaps 95%—have been sexually or physically abused as children. We heard it said there are currently more than 25,000 multiples in North America.[2]

The accolade of "official diagnosis" was granted in 1980, with an entry in the clinician's handbook, *DSM-III:*[3]

Multiple Personality. 1. The existence within an individual of two or more distinct personalities, each of which is dominant at a particular time. 2. The personality that is dominant at any particular time determines the individual's behavior. 3. Each individual personality is complex and integrated with its own unique behavior patterns and social relationships. [The official name of the disorder was changed in (1994) to Dissociative Identity Disorder. See the revised definition in *DSM-IV.*—DCD, 1997]

Typically there is said to exist a "host" personality, and several alternative personalities or "alters." Usually, though not always, these personalities call themselves by different names. They may talk with different accents, dress by choice in different clothes, frequent different locales.

None of the personalities is emotionally well-rounded. The host is often emotionally flat, and different alters express exaggerated moods: Anger, Nurturance, Childishness, Sexiness. Because of their different affective competence, it falls to different alters to handle different social situations. Thus one may come out for lovemaking, another for playing with the kids, another for picking a fight, and so on.

The host personality is on stage most of the time, but the alters cut in and displace the host when for one reason or another the host cannot cope. The host is usually amnesic for those episodes when an alter is in charge; hence the host is likely to have blank spots or missing time. Although general knowledge is shared between them, particular memories are not.

The life experience of each alter is formed primarily by the episodes when she or he is in control. Over time, and many episodes, this experience is aggregated into a discordant view of who he or she is—and hence a separate sense of self.

The number of alters varies greatly between patients, from just one (dual personality), to several dozen. In the early literature most pa-

---

2. For the statistics cited on MPD, see Putnam, F. W., et 2 al. (1986, p. 285–293).
3. *DMS-III* is *Diagnostic and Statistical Manual III,* Washington, DC: American Psychiatric Association, 1980.

tients were reported to have two or three, but there has been a steady increase, with a recent survey suggesting the median number is eleven. When the family has grown this large, one or more of the alters is likely to claim to be of different gender from the host.

This at least is how we first heard multiplicity described to us. It was not however until we were exposed to particular case histories, that we ourselves began to have any feeling for the human texture of the syndrome or for the analysis being put on it by MPD professionals. Each case must be, of course, unique. But it is clear that common themes are beginning to emerge, and that, based on their pooled experience, therapists are beginning to think in terms of a "typical case history." The case that follows, although in part a reconstruction, is true to type (and life).[4]

Mary, in her early thirties, has been suffering from depression, confusional states and lapses of memory. During the last few years she has been in and out of the hospital, where she has been diagnosed variously as schizophrenic, borderline, and manic depressive. Failing to respond to any kind of drug treatment, she has also been suspected of malingering. She ends up eventually in the hands of Doctor R, who specializes in treating dissociative disorders. More trusting of him than of previous doctors, Mary comes out with the following telltale information.

Mary's father died when she was two years old, and her mother almost immediately remarried. Her stepfather, she says, was kind to her, although "he sometimes went too far." Through childhood she suffered from sick-headaches. Her teenage years were stormy, with dramatic swings in mood. She vaguely recalls being suspended from her high school for a misdemeanor, but her memory for her school years is patchy. In describing them she occasionally resorts—without notice—to the third person ("She did this . . . That happened to her"), or sometimes the first person plural ("We [meaning herself] went to Grandma's"). She is artistically creative and can play the guitar, but when asked where she learned it, she says she does not know and

---

4. Among the recent autobiographical accounts of cases, by far the best written is Sylvia Fraser (1988). Many short case histories have been published in the clinical literature. Damgaard, J., et al, (1985, pp. 131–137) is a comprehensive recent bibliography. See also the special issue on MPD of *Psychiatric Clinics of North America* (Braun, 1984). Other useful entry points into the vast literature: Philip Coons (1986, pp. 715–721); Richard Kluft (1988, pp. 557–585); and, for a more skeptical treatment, Thomas A. Fahy, (1988, pp. 509–606).

deflects attention to something else. She agrees that she is "absent-minded"—"but aren't we all?" She might find there are clothes in her closet that she can't remember buying, or discover she has sent her niece two birthday cards. She claims to have strong moral values; but other people, she admits, call her a hypocrite and liar. She keeps a diary—"to keep up," she says, "with where we're at."

Dr. R (who already has four multiples in treatment), is beginning to recognize a pattern. When, some months into treatment, he sees Mary's diary and observes that the handwriting varies from one entry to the next, as if written by several different people, he decides (in his own words) "to go for gold." With Mary's agreement, he suggests they undertake an exploratory session of hypnosis. He puts her into a light trance and requests that the "part of Mary that hasn't yet come forward" should make herself known. A sea change occurs in the woman in front of him. Mary, until then a model of decorum, throws him a flirtatious smile. "Hi, Doctor," she says, "I'm Sally . . . Mary's a wimp. She thinks she knows it all, but I can tell you . . ."

But Sally does not tell him much, at least not yet. In subsequent sessions (conducted now without hypnosis) Sally comes and goes, almost as if she were playing games with Dr. R. She allows him glimpses of what she calls the "happy hours," and hints at having a separate and exotic history unknown to Mary. But then with a toss of the head she slips away—leaving Mary, apparently no party to the foregoing conversation, to explain where *she* has been.

Now Dr. R starts seeing his patient twice a week, for sessions that are several hours in length. In the course of the next year he uncovers the existence not just of Sally but of a whole family of alter personalities, each with its own characteristic style. "Sally" is coquettish, "Hatey" is angry, "Peggy" is young and malleable. Each has a story to tell about the times when she is "out in front"; and each has her own set of special memories. While each of the alters claims to know most of what goes on in Mary's life, Mary herself denies anything but hearsay knowledge of *their* roles.

To begin with, the changeover from one personality to another is unpredictable and apparently spontaneous. The only clue that a switch is imminent is a sudden look of vacancy, marked perhaps by Mary's rubbing her brow, or covering her eyes with her hand (as if in momentary pain). But as their confidence grows, it becomes easier for Dr. R to summon different alters "on demand."

Dr. R's goal for Mary now becomes that of "integration"—a fusing of the different personalities into one self. To achieve this he has not only to acquaint the different alters with each other, but also to probe the origins of the disorder. Thus he presses slowly for more information about the circumstances that led to Mary's "splitting." Piecing together the evidence from every side, he arrives at a version of events that he has already partly guessed. This is the story that Mary and the others eventually agree upon:

When Mary was four years old, her stepfather started to take her into his bed. He gave her the pet name Sandra, and told her that "Daddy-love" was to be Sandra's and his little secret. He caressed her and asked for her caresses. He ejaculated against her tummy. He did it in her bottom and her mouth. Sometimes Mary tried to please him, sometimes she lay still like a doll. Sometimes she was sick and cried that she could take no more. One time she said that she would tell— but the stepfather hit her and said that both of them would go to prison. Eventually, when the pain, dirt, and disgrace became too much to bear, Mary simply "left it all behind": while the man abused her, she *dissociated* and took off to another world. She left—and left Sandra in her place.

What happened next is, Dr. R insists, no more than speculation. But he pictures the development as follows. During the next few crucial years—those years when a child typically puts down roots into the fabric of human society, and develops a unitary sense of "I" and "Me"—Mary was able to function quite effectively. Protected from all knowledge of the horror, she had a comprehensible history, comprehensible feelings, and comprehensible relationships with members of her family. The "Mary-person" that she was becoming was one person with one story.

Mary's gain was however Sandra's loss. For Sandra *knew*. And this knowledge, in the early years, was crippling. Try as she might, there was no single story that she could tell that would embrace her contradictory experiences; no one "Sandra-person" for her to become. So Sandra, in a state of inchoateness, retreated to the shadows, while Mary— except for "Daddy-love"—stayed out front.

Yet if Mary could split, then so could Sandra. And this, it seems, is what occurred. Unable to make it *all* make sense, Sandra made sense from the pieces—not consciously and deliberately, of course, but with the cunning of unconscious design: She parceled out the different aspects of her abuse-experience, and assigned each aspect to a different self (grafting, as it were, each set of memories as a side-branch to the existing stock she shared with Mary). Thus her experience of *liking to please Daddy* gave rise to what became the Sally-self. Her experience of *the pain and anger* gave rise to Hatey. And her experience of *playing at being a doll* gave rise to Peggy.

Now these descendants of the original Sandra could, with relative safety, come out into the open. And before long, opportunities arose for them to try their newfound strength in settings other than that of the original abuse. When Mary lost her temper with her mother, Hatey could chip in to do the screaming. When Mary was kissed by a boy in the playground, Sally could kiss him back. Everyone could do what they were "good at"—and Mary's own life was made that much simpler. This pattern of what might be termed "the division of emotional labor" or "self-replacement therapy" proved not only to be viable, but to be rewarding all around.

Subsequently this became the habitual way of life. Over time each member of the family progressively built up her own separate store of memories, competencies, idiosyncrasies, and social styles. But they were living in a branching house of cards. During her teenage years, Mary's varying moods and waywardness could be passed off as "adolescent rebelliousness." But in her late twenties, her true fragility began to show—and she lapsed into confusion and depression.

Although we have told this story in what amounts to cartoon form, we have no doubts that cases like Mary's are authentic. Or, rather, we should say we have no doubts that there are real people and real doctors to whom this case history could very well apply. Yet—like many others who have taken a skeptical position about MPD—we ourselves have reservations about what such a case history in fact amounts to.

How could anyone know for sure the events were as described? Is there independent confirmation that Mary was abused? Does her story match with what other people say about her? How do we know the whole thing is not just an hysterical invention? To what extent did the doctor lead her on? What transpired during the sessions of hypnosis? And, anyway, what does it all really mean? What should we make of Dr. R's interpretation? Is it really possible for a single human being to have several different "selves"?

The last problem—that of providing a philosophically and scientifically acceptable theory of MPD—is the one we have a special interest in addressing. You might think, however, we ought to start with a discussion of the "factual evidence": for why discuss the theoretical basis of something that has not yet been proven to exist? Our answer is that unless and until MPD can be shown to be theoretically possible—that is, to be neither a logical nor a scientific contradiction—any discussion of the evidence is likely to be compromised by a priori disbelief.

As Hume remarked in his essay "Of Miracles": "it is a general maxim worthy of our attention . . . that no testimony is sufficient to establish a miracle unless the testimony be of such a kind that its falsehood would be more miraculous than the fact which it endeavors to establish" (1748, section 10 [p. 123 in Bobbs Merrill, 1973]). In the history of science there have been many occasions in which seemingly miraculous phenomena were not and perhaps could not be taken seriously until some form of theoretical permission for them had been devised (the claims of acupuncture, for example, were assumed by Western scientists to make no sense—and hence be false—until the discovery of endogenous opiates paved the way for a scientific explanation). We shall, we hope, be in a better position to assess the testimony concerning MPD—that is, to be both critical and generous—if we can first make a case that the phenomenon is not only possible but even (in certain circumstances) plausible.

Many people who find it convenient or compelling to talk about the "self" would prefer not to be asked the emperor's-new-clothes question: Just what, exactly, is a "self"? When confronted by an issue that seems embarrassingly metaphysical, it is tempting to temporize and wave one's hands: "It's not a thing, exactly, but more a sort of, well, a *concept* or an *organizing principle* or . . ." This will not do. And yet what will?

Two extreme views can be and have been taken. Ask a layman what he thinks a self is, and his unreflecting answer will probably be that a person's self is indeed some kind of real *thing*: a ghostly supervisor who lives inside his head, the thinker of his thoughts, the repository of his memories, the holder of his values, his conscious inner "I." Although he might be unlikely these days to use the term "soul," it would be very much the age-old conception of the soul that he would have in mind. A self (or soul) is an existent entity with executive powers over the body and its own enduring qualities. Let's call this realist picture of the self, the idea of a "proper-self."

Contrast it, however, with the revisionist picture of the self which has become popular among certain psychoanalysts and philosophers of mind. In this view, selves are not things at all, but *explanatory fictions*.

Nobody really has a soul-like agency inside them: we just find it useful to imagine the existence of this conscious inner "I" when we try to account for their behavior (and, in our own case, our private stream of consciousness). We might say indeed that the self is rather like the "center of narrative gravity" of a set of biographical events and tendencies; but, as with a center of physical gravity, there's really no such *thing* (with mass or shape). Let's call this nonrealist picture of the self, the idea of a "fictive-self."

Now maybe (one might think) it is just a matter of the level of description: The plain man's proper-self corresponds to the intrinsic reality, while the philosopher's fictive-selves correspond to people's (necessarily inadequate) attempts to grasp that intrinsic reality. So there is indeed a "proper-self" that actually resides inside everyone, and alongside it there are the various "fictive-selves" that each person (and his or her acquaintances) have reconstructed.

This suggestion, however, would miss that point of the revisionist critique. The revisionist case is that there really is no proper-self: none of the fictive-selves—including one's own firsthand version—corresponds to anything that actually exists in one's head.

At first sight this may not seem reasonable. Granted that whatever *is* inside the head might be difficult to observe, and granted also that it might be a mistake to talk about a "ghostly supervisor," nonetheless there surely has to be some kind of a supervisor in there: a supervisory brain program, a central controller, or whatever. How else could anybody function—as most people clearly do function—as a purposeful and relatively well-integrated agent?

The answer that is emerging from both biology and Artificial Intelligence is that complex systems can in fact function in what seems to be a thoroughly "purposeful and integrated" way simply by having *lots of subsystems doing their own thing* without any central supervision. Indeed most systems on earth that appear to have central controllers (and are usefully described as having them) do not. The behavior of a termite colony provides a wonderful example of it. The colony as a whole builds elaborate mounds, gets to know its territory, organizes foraging expeditions, sends out raiding parties against other colonies, and so on. The group cohesion and coordination is so remarkable that hardheaded observers have been led to postulate the existence of a colony's "group soul" (*vide* Marais's *The Soul of the White Ant*). Yet, in fact, all this group wisdom results from nothing other than myriads of individual termites, specialized as several different castes, going about their individual business—influenced by each other, but quite uninfluenced by any master-plan (Marais, 1937)[5]

Then is the argument between the realists and the revisionists being won hands down by the revisionists? No, not completely. Something (some thing?) is missing here. But the question of what the "missing something" is, is being hotly debated by cognitive scientists in terms that have become increasingly abstruse. Fortunately we can avoid— maybe even leapfrog—much of the technical discussion by the use of an illustrative metaphor (reminiscent of Plato's *Republic*, but put to quite a different use).

Consider the United States of America. At the fictive level there is surely nothing wrong with personifying the USA and talking about it (rather like the termite colony) as if it had an inner self. The USA has memories, feelings, likes and dislikes, hopes, talents, and so on. It hates Communism, is haunted by the memory of Vietnam, is scientifically creative, socially clumsy, somewhat given to self-righteousness, rather sentimental. But does that mean (here is the revisionist speaking) there is one central agency inside the USA which embodies all those qualities? Of course not. There is, as it happens, a specific area of the country where much of it comes together. But go to Washington and ask to speak to Mr. American Self, and you'd find there was nobody home: instead you'd find a lot of different agencies (the Defense Department, the Treasury, the courts, the Library of Congress, the National Science Foundation, etc.) operating in relative independence of each other.

There is no such thing as Mr. American Self, but as a matter of fact there is in every country a Head of State. The Head of State may actually be non-executive, and certainly does not enact all the subsidiary roles (the US President does not bear arms, sit in the courts, play baseball, or travel to the Moon).

But nevertheless the Head of State is expected to take an active interest in all these national pursuits. The President is meant to appreciate better than anyone the "State of the Union." He is meant to *represent* different parts of the nation *to* each other, and to inculcate a common value system. Moreover—and this is most important—he is the "spokesman" when it comes to dealing with other nation states.

---

5. Douglas Hofstadter (1979, pp. 275–336) has developed the analogy between mind and ant colony in the chapter "Prelude . . . Ant Fugue." The "distributed control" approach to designing intelligent machines has in fact had a long history in Artificial Intelligence, going back as far as Selfridge's early "Pandemonium" model of 1959, and finding recent expression in Marvin Minsky (1985).

That is not to say that a nation, lacking such a figurehead, would cease to function day-to-day. But it is to say that in the longer term it may function much better if it does have one. Indeed a good case can be made that nations, unlike termite colonies, require this kind of figurehead as a condition of their political survival—especially given the complexity of international affairs.

The drift of this analogy is obvious. In short, a human being too may need an inner figurehead—especially given the complexities of human social life.[6] Thus we come back full circle, though a little lower down, to the idea of a proper-self: not a ghostly supervisor, but something more like a "Head of Mind" with a real, if limited, causal role to play in representing the person to himself and to the world.

If this is accepted (as we think it should be), we can turn to the vexed question of self-development or self-establishment. Here the Head of State analogy may seem at first less helpful. For one thing, in the USA at least, the President is democratically *elected* by the population. For another, the *candidates* for the presidency are pre-formed entities, already waiting in the wings.

Yet is this really so? It could equally be argued that the presidential candidates, rather than being pre-formed, are actually brought into being—through a narrative dialectical process—by the very population to which they offer their services as president. Thus the population (or the news media) first try out various *fictive versions* of what they think their "ideal president" should be, and *then* the candidates adapt themselves as best they can to fill the bill. To the extent that there is more than one dominant fiction about "what it means to be American," different candidates mold themselves in different ways. But in the end only one can be elected—and will, of course, claim to speak for the whole nation.

In very much a parallel way, we suggest, a human being first creates—unconsciously—one or more ideal fictive-selves and then elects the best supported of these into office as her Head of Mind. A significant difference in the human case, however, is that there is likely to be considerably more *outside influence.* Parents, friends, and even enemies may all contribute to the image of "what it means to be me," as well as—and maybe over and above—the internal news media. Daddy, for

6. The social function of self-knowledge has been stressed particularly by Humphrey (1983; 1986). For a suggestive discussion of "active symbols" as something not unlike our notion of a Figurehead of Mind, see Douglas Hofstadter (1979; 1985, esp. pp. 646–665).

example, might lean on the growing child to impose an *invasive* fictive-self.

Thus a human being does not start out as single *or* as multiple—but without any Head of Mind at all. In the normal course of development, the individual slowly gets acquainted with the various possibilities of selfhood that "make sense"—partly through observation, partly through outside influence. In most cases a majority view emerges, strongly favoring one version of "the real me," and it is that version which is installed as her elected Head of Mind. But in some cases the competing fictive-selves are so equally balanced, or different constituencies within are so unwilling to accept the result of the election, that constitutional chaos reigns—and there are snap elections (or coups d'état) all the time.

Could a model inspired by (underlying) this analogy account for the memory black-spots, differences in style, and other symptomatology of MPD? Certainly the analogy provides a wealth of detail suggesting so. Once in office a new Head of State typically downplays certain "unfortunate" aspects of his nation's history (especially those associated with the rival, preceding Head of State). Moreover, by standing for particular national values, the Head of State affects the course of future history by encouraging the expression of those values by the population (and so, by a kind of feedback, confirming his or her own role).

Let's go back to the case of Mary. As a result of her experience of abuse, she (the whole, disorganized, conglomeration of parts) came to have several alternative pictures of the real Mary, each championed by different constituencies within her. So incompatible were these pictures, yet so strong were the electoral forces, that there could be no lasting agreement on who should represent her. For a time the Mary constituency got its way, overriding the Sandra constituency. But later the Sandra forces subdivided, to yield Sally, Hatey, Peggy; and when the opportunities arose, these reformed forces began to win electoral battles. She became thus constitutionally unstable, with no permanent solution to the question of "who I really am." Each new (temporarily elected) Head of Mind emphasized different aspects of her experience and blocked off others; and each brought out exaggerated character traits.

We have talked here in metaphors. But translations into the terms of current cognitive science would not be difficult to formulate. First, what sense can be given to the notion of a "Head of Mind"? The analogy with a *spokesman* may not be far off the literal truth. The language-producing systems of the brain have to get their instructions from somewhere, and the very demands of pragmatics and grammar would conspire to confer something like Head of Mind authority on whatever subsystem currently controls their input. E. M. Forster once remarked "How can I tell what I think until I see what I say?" The four "I" 's in this sentence are meant to refer to the same thing. But this grammatical tradition may depend—and may always have depended—on the fact that the thought expressed in Forster's question is quite literally self-confirming: what "I" (my self) thinks *is* what "I" (my language apparatus) says.

There can, however, be no guarantee that either the speaker or anyone else who hears him over an extended period will settle on there being just a single "I." Suppose, at different times, different subsystems within the brain produce "clusters" of speech that simply cannot easily be interpreted as the output of a single self. Then—as a Bible scholar may discover when working on the authorship of what is putatively a single-authored text—it may turn out that the clusters make *best sense* when attributed to different selves.

How about the selective amnesia shown by different Heads of Mind? To readers who have even a passing knowledge of computer information processing, the idea of mutually inaccessible "directories" of stored information will already be familiar. In cognitive psychology, new discoveries about state-dependent learning and other evidence of modularization in the brain have led people to recognize that *failure* of access between different subsystems is the norm rather than the exception. Indeed the old Cartesian picture of the mind "transparent to itself" now appears to be rarely if ever achievable (or even desirable) in practice. In this context the out-of-touchness of different selves no longer looks so startling.

What could be the basis for the different "value systems" associated with rival Heads of Mind? Psychopharmacological evidence suggests that the characteristic emotional style of different personalities could correspond to the brain-wide activation or inhibition of neural pathways that rely on different neurotransmitter chemicals. Thus the phlegmatic style of Mary's host personality could be associated with low norepinephrine levels, the shift to the carnal style of Sally with high norepinephrine, and the out-of-control Hatey with low dopamine.

Even the idea of an "election" of the current Head of Mind is not implausible. Events very like elections take place in the brain all the time—whenever coherent patterns of activity compete for control of the same network. Consider what happens, for example, when the visual system receives two conflicting images at the two eyes. First there is an attempt at fusion; but if this proves to be unstable, "binocular rivalry" results, with the input from one eye completely taking over while the other is suppressed. Thus we already have, at the level of visual neurophysiology, clear evidence of the mind's general preference for single-mindedness over completeness.

These ideas about the nature of selves are by no means altogether new. C. S. Peirce (1905), for instance, expressed a similar vision:

A person is not absolutely an individual. His thoughts are what he is "saying to himself," that is, is saying to that other self that is just coming into life in the flow of time.

From within the psychoanalytic tradition, Heinz Kohut wrote (in "On Courage," 1985, p. 33):

I feel that a formulation which puts *the* self into the center of the personality as the initiator of all actions and as the recipient of all impressions exacts too high a price. . . . If we instead put our trust in empirical observation . . . we will see different selves, each of them a lasting psychological configuration, . . . fighting for ascendancy, one blocking out the other, forming compromises with each other, and acting inconsistently with each other at the same time. In general, we will witness what appears to be an uneasy victory of one self over all others.

Robert Jay Lifton (1979, 1986) has defined the self as the "inclusive symbol of one's own organism"; and in his discussions of what he calls "proteanism" (an endemic form of multiplicity in modern human beings) and "doubling" (as in the double-life led by Nazi doctors) he has stressed the struggle that all human beings have to keep their rival self-symbols in symbiotic harmony.

These ideas have, however, been formulated without reference to the newly gathered evidence on MPD. Moreover the emphasis of almost all the earlier work has been on the *underlying continuity* of human psychic structure: a *single* stream of consciousness manifesting itself in now this, now that configuration. Nothing in the writings of Kohut or of Lifton would have prepared us for the radical *discontinuity* of consciousness that—if it really exists—is manifest in the case of a multiple like Mary.

Which brings us to the question that has been left hanging all along: *Does* "real MPD" exist? We hope that, in the light of the preceding discussion, we shall be able to come closer to an answer.

What would it mean for MPD to be "real"? We suggest that, if the model we have outlined is anything like right, it would mean at least the following:

1. The subject will have, at different times, different "spokesmen," corresponding to separate Heads of Mind. Both objectively and subjectively, this will be tantamount to having different "selves" because the access each such spokesman will have to the memories, attitudes, and thoughts of other spokesmen will be, in general, as indirect and intermittent as the access one human being can have to the mind of another.

2. Each self, when present, will claim to have conscious control over the subject's behavior. That is, this self will consider the subject's current actions to be *her* actions, experiences to be *her* experiences, memories to be *her* memories, and so on. (At times the self out front may be conscious *of* the existence of other selves—she may even hear them talking in the background—but she will not be conscious *with* them).

3. Each self will be convinced—as it were by "her own rhetoric"— about her own integrity and personal importance.

4. This self-rhetoric will be convincing not only to the subject but also (other things being equal) to other people with whom she interacts.

5. Different selves will be interestingly different. That is, each will adopt a distinctive style of presentation—which very likely will be associated with differences in physiology.

6. The "splitting" into separate selves will generally have occurred before the patient entered therapy.

Now, what are the facts about MPD? The first thing to say is that in *no* case do we *know* that all these criteria have been met. What we have to go on instead is a plethora of isolated stories, autobiographical accounts, clinical reports, police records, and just a few scientific studies. Out of those the following questions and answers form.

Does the Phenomenon Exist?

There can be no doubt that what might be called a "candidate phenomenon" exists. There are literally thousands of people living today who, in the course of clinical investigation, have presented themselves as having several independent selves (or "spokesmen" for their minds). Such cases have been described in reputable scientific journals, recorded on film, shown on television, cross-examined in law courts. We ourselves have met with several of them and have even argued with these separate selves about why we should believe the stories that they tell us. Skeptics may still choose to doubt what the phenomenon *amounts to*, but they should no longer doubt that it *occurs*.

Do Multiples Themselves Believe in What They Are Saying?

Certainly they seem to do so. In the clinic, at least, different selves stoutly insist on their own integrity, and resist any suggestion that they might be "play-acting" (a suggestion, which, admittedly, most therapists avoid). The impression they make is not of someone who is acting, but rather of a troubled individual who is doing her best—in what can only be described as difficult circumstances—to make sense of what she takes to be the facts of her experience.

As persuasive as anything is the apparently genuine puzzlement that patients show when confronted by facts they *can't* make sense of. Thus one woman told us of when—as frequently happened—she came home and found her neat living room all messed up, she suspected that other people must be playing tricks on her. A young man described how he found himself being laughed at by his friends for having been seen around gay bars: he tried over several months to grow a beard to prove his manhood, but as soon as the stubble began to sprout, someone—he did not know who—shaved it off. A woman discovered that money was being mysteriously drawn from her bank account, and told the police that she was being impersonated. We have heard of a case of a highly skeptical patient who refused to accept her therapist's diagnosis until they both learned that one of her alters was seeing *another* therapist.

That is not to say that such stories would always stand up to critical examination: examination, that is, by the standards of "normal human life." But this, it seems, is quite as much a problem for the patient as for anyone else. These people clearly know as well as anybody that there is *something* wrong with them and that their lives don't seem to run as smoothly as other people's. In fact it would be astonishing (and grounds for our suspicion) if they did not: for they are generally too intelligent not to recognize that in some respects their experience is bizarre. We met a woman, Gina, with a male alter, Bruce, and asked Bruce the obvious "normal" question: When he goes to the bathroom, does he choose the Ladies or the Gents? He confessed that he goes to the Ladies—because "something went wrong with my anatomy" and "I turned out to be a male living in a woman's body."

For several years a multiple newsletter—*S4OS* (Speaking for Our Selves)—circulated, in which patients shared with each other their experiences and strategies. In September 1987 *S4OS* claimed 691 subscribers.[7]

Do They Succeed in Persuading Other People to Believe in Them?

We have no doubt that the therapist who diagnoses MPD is fully convinced that he is dealing with several different selves. But, from our standpoint, a more crucial issue is whether other people who are not already *au fait* with the diagnosis accept this way of looking at things. According to our analysis (or indeed any other we can think of) selves have a public as well as a private role to play: indeed they exist *primarily* to handle social interactions. It would therefore be odd, to say the least, if some or all of a patient's selves were to be kept entirely secret from the world.

On this point the evidence is surprisingly patchy. True enough, in many cases the patient herself will—in the context of the therapeutic situation—tell stories of her encounters in the outside world. But what we need is evidence from a third source: a neutral source that is in no way linked to the context in which splitting is "expected" (as might still be the case with another doctor, or another patient, or even a television journalist). We need to know whether the picture of her multiple life that the therapist and patient have worked out together jibes with what other people have independently observed.

Prima facie, it sounds like the kind of evidence it would be easy to obtain—by asking family, friends, fellow workers. There is the problem of course that certain lines of enquiry are ruled out on ethical grounds, or because their pursuit would jeopardize the patient's ongoing therapy, or would simply involve an unjustifiable amount of time. Nonetheless it is disappointing to discover how few such enquiries have been made.

Many multiple patients are married and have families; many have regular employment. Yet, again and again it seems that no one on the outside has in fact noticed anything peculiar—at least not *so* peculiar.

---

7. *S4OS — Speaking For Our Selves: a Newsletter By, For, and About People With Multiple Personality*, P.O. Box 4830, Long Beach, California, 90804, published quarterly between October 1985 and December 1987, when publication was suspended (temporarily, it was hoped) due to a personal crisis in the life of the editor. In September 1987 *S4OS* claimed 691 subscribers. Its contents were unquestionably the sincere writings and drawings of MPD patients, often more convincing—and moving—than the many more professional autobiographical accounts that have been published.

Maybe, as several therapists explained to us, their patients are surprisingly good at "covering up" (secrecy, beginning in childhood, is part and parcel of the syndrome—and in any case the patient has probably learned to avoid putting herself or others on the spot). Maybe other people have detected something odd and dismissed it as nothing more than inconstancy or unreliability (after all, everyone has changing moods, most people are forgetful, and many people lie). Gina told us of how she started to make love to a man she met at an office party but grew bored with him and left—leaving "one of the kids" (another alter) cringing in her place. The man, she said, was quite upset. But no one has heard his side of the story.

To be sure, in many cases, perhaps even most, there is some form of *postdiagnostic* confirmation from outside: the husband who, when the diagnosis is explained to him, exclaims "Now it all makes sense!" or the boyfriend who volunteers to the therapist tales of what it is like to be "jerked around" by the tag-team alters of his partner. One patient's husband admitted to mixed emotions about the impending cure or integration of his wife: "I'll miss the little ones!"

The problem with such retrospective evidence is, however, that the informant may simply be acceding to what might be termed a "diagnosis of convenience." It is probably the general rule that once multiplicity has been recognized *in therapy*, and the alters have been "given permission" to come out, there are gains to be had all round from adopting the patient's preferred style of presentation. When we ourselves were introduced to a patient who switched three times in the course of half an hour, we were chastened to discover how easily we ourselves fell in with addressing her as if she were now a man, now a woman, now a child—a combination of good manners on our part and an anxiety not to drive the alter personality away (as Peter Pan said "Every time someone says 'I don't believe in fairies,' there is a fairy somewhere who falls down dead").

Any interaction with a patient involves cooperation and respect, which shade imperceptibly into collusion. The alternative might be surreptitious observation in extra-clinical situations, but this would be as hard to justify as to execute. The result is that one is limited to encounters that—in our limited experience-have an inevitable séance-like quality to them.

Therapists with whom we have talked are defensive on this issue. We have to say, however, that, so far as we can gather, evidence for the external social reality of MPD is weak.

Are There "Real" Differences between the Different Selves?

One therapist confided to us that, in his view, it was not uncommon for the different selves belonging to a single patient to be more or less identical—the *only* thing distinguishing them being their selective memories. More usually, however, the selves are described as being manifestly different in both mental and bodily character. The question is: do such differences go beyond the range of "normal" acting out?

At the anecdotal level, the evidence is tantalizing. For example a psychopharmacologist (whom we have reason to consider as hard-headed as they come) told us of how he discovered to his astonishment that a male patient, whose host personality could be sedated with 5mg of valium, had an alter personality who was apparently quite impervious to the drug: The alter remained as lively as ever when given a 50mg intravenous dose (sufficient in most people to produce anaesthesia).

Any would-be objective investigator of MPD is soon struck by the systematic elusiveness of the phenomena. Well-controlled scientific studies are few (and for obvious reasons difficult to do). Nonetheless, what data there are all go to show that multiple patients—in the context of the clinic—may indeed undergo profound psycho-physiological changes when they change personality state (Putnam, 1984, pp. 31–39; Miller, 1988; Nissen, et al., 1988; 1994). There is preliminary evidence, for example, of changes in handedness, voice-patterns, evoked-response brain-activity, and cerebral blood flow. When samples of the different handwritings of a multiple are mixed with samples by different hands, police handwriting experts have been unable to identify them. There are data to suggest differences in allergic reactions and thyroid functioning. Drug studies have shown differences in responsivity to alcohol and tranquilizers. Tests of memory have indicated genuine cross-personality amnesia for newly acquired information (while, interestingly enough, newly acquired motor-skills are carried over).

When and How Did the Multiplicity Come into Being?

The assumption made by most people in the MPD Movement—and which we so far have gone along with—is that the splitting into several selves *originates* in early childhood. The therapist therefore brings to light a pre-existing syndrome, and in no way is he or she responsible for *creating* MPD. But an alternative possibility of course exists, namely that the phenomenon—however genuine at the time that it is described—has been brought into being (and perhaps is being maintained) by the therapist himself.

We have hinted already at how little evidence there is that multiplicity has existed before the start of treatment. A lack of evidence that something exists is not evidence that it does not, and several papers at the Chicago meeting reported recently discovered cases of what seems to have been *incipient* multiplicity in children.[8] Nonetheless, the suspicion must surely arise that MPD is an "iatrogenic" condition (i.e., generated by the doctor).

Folie à deux between doctor and patient would be, in the annals of psychiatry, nothing new. It is now generally recognized that the outbreak of "hysterical symptoms" in female patients at the end of the last century (including paralysis, anesthesia, and so on) was brought about by the overenthusiastic attention of doctors (such as Charcot) who succeeded in creating the symptoms they were looking for. In this regard, hypnosis, in particular, has always been a dangerous tool. The fact that in the diagnosis of multiplicity hypnosis is frequently (although not always) employed, the closeness of the therapist-patient relationship, and the intense interest shown by therapists in the "drama" of MPD, are clearly grounds for legitimate concern.[9]

This concern is in fact one that senior members of the MPD Movement openly share. At the Chicago conference a full day was given to discussing the problem of iatrogenesis. Speaker after speaker weighed in to warn their fellow therapists against "fishing" for multiplicity, misuse of hypnosis, the "Pygmalion effect," uncontrolled "countertransference," and what was bravely called "major league malpractice" (i.e., sexual intimacy with patients).

A patient presents herself with a history of, let's call it, "general muddle." She is worried by odd juxtapositions and gaps in her life, by signs that she has sometimes behaved in ways that seem strange to her; she is worried she's going mad. Under hypnosis the therapist suggests that it is not her, but some other part of her that is the cause of trouble. And lo, some other part of her emerges. But since this *is* some other part, she requires—and hence acquires—another name. And since a person with a different name must be a different person, she requires—and hence acquires—another character. Easy; especially easy if the patient is the kind of person who is highly suggestible and

---

8. On incipient MPD in children, see David Mann and Jean Goodwin (1988); Carole Snowden (1988); and Theresa K. Albini (1988).

9. For a fascinating discussion of how individuals may mold themselves to fit "fashionable" categories, see Ian Hacking, (1986, pp. 222–236).

readily dissociates, as is typical of those who have been subjected to abuse.[10]

Could something like this possibly be the background to almost every case of MPD? We defer to the best and most experienced therapists in saying that it could not. In some cases there seems to be no question that the alternate personality makes its debut in therapy as if already formed. We have seen a videotape of one case where, in the first and only session of hypnosis, a pathetic young woman, Bonny, underwent a remarkable transformation into a character, calling herself "Death," who shouted murderous threats against both Bonny and the hypnotist. Bonny had previously made frequent suicide attempts, of which she denied any knowledge. Bonny subsequently tried to kill another patient on the hospital ward and was discovered by a nurse lapping her victim's blood. It would be difficult to write off Bonny / Death as the invention of an overeager therapist.

On the general run of cases, we can only withhold judgment, not just because we do not know the facts, but also because we are not sure a "judgmental" judgment is in order. Certainly we do not want to align ourselves with those who would jump to the conclusion that if MPD arises in the clinic rather than in a childhood situation it cannot be "real." The parallel with hysteria is worth pursuing. As Charcot himself demonstrated only too convincingly, a woman who feels no pain when a pin is stuck into her arm *feels no pain* — and calling her lack of reaction a "hysterical symptom" does not make it any the less remarkable. Likewise a woman who at the age of thirty is now living the life of several different selves *is now living the life of several different selves*—and any doubts we might have about how she came to be that way should not blind us to the fact that such is now the way she is.

According to the model we proposed, no one starts off as either multiple or single. In every case there has to be some sort of external influence that tips the balance this way or that (or back again). Childhood may indeed be the most vulnerable phase; but it may also very well be that in certain people a state of incipient multiplicity persists much longer, not coming to fruition until later life.

The following story is instructive. A patient, Frances, who is now completely integrated, was telling us about the family of selves she used to live with—among whom she counted Rachel, Esther, Daniel,

---

10. On suggestibility, see, for example, E. R. Hilgard's studies of the correlation between hypnotizability and early experience of physical punishment (1970).

Sarah, and Rebecca. We were curious as to why a White-Anglo-Saxon-Protestant should have taken on these Hebrew names, and asked her where the names had come from. "That's simple," she said, "Dad used to play Nazis and Jews with me; but he wanted me to be an innocent victim, so every time he raped me he gave me a new Jewish name."

Here, it seems, that (as with Mary) the abuser at the time of the abuse explicitly, even if unwittingly, suggested the personality structure of MPD. But suppose that Frances had not had the "help" of her father in reaching this "solution." Suppose she had remained in a state of self confusion, muddling through her first thirty years, *until* a sympathetic therapist provided her with a way out (and a way forward). Would Frances have been less of a multiple than she turned out to be? In our view, no.

There must be, of course, a world of difference between an abuser's and a therapist's intentions in suggesting that a person contains several separate selves. Nonetheless the consequences for the structure of the patient / victim's mind would not be so dissimilar. "Patrogenic" and "iatrogenic" multiplicity could be—and in our view would be—equally *real.*

Forty years ago two early commentators, W. S. Taylor and M. F. Martin, wrote:

Apparently most ready to accept multiple personality are (a) persons who are very naive and (b) persons who have worked with cases or near cases (1944, p. 284).

The same is still largely true today. Indeed the medical world remains in general hostile to—even contemptuous of—MPD. Why?

We have pointed to several of the reasons. The phenomenon is considered by many people to be scientifically or philosophically absurd. We think that is a mistake. It is considered to be unsupported by objective evidence. We think that is untrue. It is considered to be an iatrogenic folly. We think that, even where that's so, the syndrome is a real one nonetheless.

But there is another reason, which we cannot brush aside: and that is the cliquish—almost cultish—character of those who currently espouse the cause of MPD. In a world where those who are not for MPD are against it, it is perhaps not surprising that "believers" have tended to close ranks. Maybe it is not surprising either that at meetings like the one we attended in Chicago there is a certain amount of well-meaning exaggeration and one-upmanship. We were however not prepared for what—if it occurred in a church—would amount to "bearing witness."

"How many multiples have you got?" one therapist asks another over breakfast in Chicago, "I'm on my fifth." "Oh, I'm just a novice—two, so far." "You know Dr. Q—she's got fifteen in treatment; and I gather she's a multiple herself." At lunch: "I've got a patient whose eyes change color." "I've got one whose different personalities speak six different languages, none of which they could possibly have learned." "My patient Myra had her fallopian tubes tied, but when she switched to Katey she got pregnant." At supper: "Her parents got her to breed babies for human sacrifice; she was a surrogate mother three times before her eighteenth birthday." "At three years old, Peter was made to kill his baby brother and eat his flesh." "There's a lot of it about: They reckon that a quarter of our patients have been victims of satanic rituals."

To be fair, this kind of gossip belies the deeper seriousness of the majority of therapists who deal with MPD. But that it occurs at all, and is seemingly so little challenged, could well explain why people outside the Movement want to keep their distance. Not to put too fine a point on it, there is everywhere the sense that both therapists and patients are participators in a Mystery, to which ordinary standards of objectivity do not apply. Multiplicity is seen as a semi-inspired, semiheroic condition: and almost every claim relating either to the patients' abilities or to the extent of their childhood suffering is listened to in sympathetic awe. Some therapists clearly consider it a privilege to be close to such extraordinary human beings (and the more of them in treatment, the more status the therapist acquires).

We were struck by the fact that some of the very specialists who have conducted the scientific investigations we mentioned earlier are sympathetic also to wild claims. We frankly cannot accept the truth of many of the circulating stories, and in particular we were unimpressed by this year's favorite—the "satanic cult" origins of many cases of MPD.

However, an astronomer who believes in astrology would not for that reason be untrustworthy as an astronomical observer, and it would be wrong to find the phenomenon of multiplicity guilty by association. The climate in which the discussion is currently occurring is regrettable but probably unavoidable, not because all the true believers are gullible and all the opponents narrow-minded, but because those who have worked with cases *know* they have seen something so remarkable as to defy conventional description, and, in the absence of an accepted conceptual framework for description, they are driven by a sense of fidelity to their own experience to making hyperbolic claims.

We draw, for the time being, the following conclusions:

1. While the unitary solution to the problem of human selfhood is for most people socially and psychologically desirable, it may not always be attainable.

2. The possibility of developing multiple selves is inherent in every human being. Multiplicity is not only biologically and psychologically plausible, but in some cases it may be the best—even the only—available way of coping with a person's life experience.

3. Childhood trauma (usually, though not necessarily, sexual) is especially likely to push a person toward incipient multiplicity. It is possible that the child may progress from there to becoming a full-fledged multiple of his or her own accord; but in general it seems more likely that external pressure—or sanction—is required.

4. The diagnosis of MPD has become, within a particular psychiatric lobby, a diagnostic fad. Although the existence of the clinical syndrome is now beyond dispute, there is as yet no certainty as to how much of the multiplicity currently being reported has existed prior to therapeutic intervention.

5. Whatever the particular history, the end result would appear to be in many cases a person who is genuinely split. That is, the grounds for assigning several selves to such a human being *can be as good as — indeed the same as — those for assigning a single self to a normal human being.*

It remains the case that even in North America, the diagnosis of MPD has become common only recently, and elsewhere in the world it is still seldom made at all. We must surely assume that the predisposing factors have always been widely present in the human population. So where has all the multiplicity been hiding?

To end with further questions, and not answer them, may be the best way of conveying where we ourselves have arrived. Here are some (almost random) puzzles that occur to us about the wider cultural significance of the phenomenon.

In many parts of the world the initiation of children into adult society has, in the past, involved cruel rites, involving sexual and physical abuse (sodomy, mutilation, and other forms of battering). Is the effect (maybe even the intention) of such rites to create adults with a tendency to MPD? Are there contexts where an ability to split might be (or have been thought to be) a positive advantage—for example when it comes to coping with physical or social hardship? Do multiples make better warriors?

In contemporary America, many hundreds of people claim to have been abducted by aliens from UFOs. The abduction experience is not recognized as such at first, and is described instead as "missing time" for which the person has no memories. Under hypnosis, however, the subject typically recalls having been kidnapped by humanoid creatures who did harmful things to her or him—typically involving some kind of sex-related surgical operation (for example, sharp objects being thrust into the vagina). Are these people recounting a mythic version of an actual childhood experience? During the period described as missing time, was another personality in charge—a personality for whom the experience of abuse was all too real?

Plato banned actors from his Republic on the grounds that they were capable of "transforming themselves into all sorts of characters"—a bad example, he thought, for solid citizens. Actors commonly talk about "losing" themselves in their roles. How many of the best actors have been abused as children? For how many is acting a culturally sanctioned way of letting their multiplicity come out?

The therapists we talked to were struck by the "charisma" of their patients. Charisma is often associated with a lack of personal boundaries, as if the subject is inviting everyone to share some part of him. How often have beguiling demagogues been multiples? Do we have here another explanation for the myth of the "wound and the bow"?

Queen Elizabeth I, at the age of two, went through the experience of having her father, Henry VIII, cut off her mother's head. Elizabeth in later life was notoriously changeable, loving and vindictive. Was Elizabeth a multiple? Joan of Arc had trances, and cross-dressed as a boy. Was she?

Postscript

In the course of writing and rewriting this essay, we encountered two problems of exposition that we eventually recognized to be important factors contributing to the phenomenon of MPD itself. First, the lure of hyperbolic claims mentioned in the essay was a pressure we experienced ourselves, even in comparing notes on our own observations. It is not just that one wants to tell a good story, but that one wants to tell a consistent story, and the resources of English currently conspire to force one into one overstatement or another. Readers of early drafts of this essay, both initiates and laypeople, made widely varied criticisms and suggestions, but there was one point of near unison: they felt cheated or unfulfilled because we were "equivocal" about the existence of the phenomenon; we didn't make clear—or clear enough for them—whether MPD was *real.*

A particularly telling instance of this was the therapist who told us that one of her patients, with whom we had talked, would be deeply hurt by our claim that "that is all there is" to her various alters. It is interesting that the therapist didn't come up with the following crusher: *the alters* of this patient would be deeply offended by our claim that "that is all there is" to *them*; did we really want to call them "second-class citizens" or "subhuman" or "nonpersons"?

Yet alters must in general know perfectly well that they are not "people." But if they are not people, what are they? They are what they are—they are selves, for want of a better word. As selves, they are as real as any self could be; they are not just imaginary playmates or theatrical roles on the one hand, nor on the other hand are they ghostly people or eternal souls sharing a mortal body. It is possible for some therapists, apparently, to tiptoe between these extremes, *respecting* without quite *endorsing* the alters, sustaining enough trust and peace of mind in their patients to continue therapy effectively while eschewing the equally (or even more) effective therapeutic route of frank endorsement (with its attendant exaggerations) followed by "fusion" or "integration." Anyone who finds this middle road hard to imagine should *try harder to imagine it* before declaring it a conceptual impossibility.

A related but more subtle expository problem might be described as due to the lack of a middle voice between active and passive. When Mary, as a child, was confronted with that horrible cacophony of experience, *who* was confused, *who* "devised" the splitting stratagem, *who* was oblivious to *whose* pains? Prior to the consolidation of a proper person, there is no one home to play subject to the verbs, and yet—according to the model—there is all that clever *activity* of self-creation going on inside. The standard lame device for dealing with such issues—which are ubiquitous in cognitive science, not just in psychiatry—is to settle for the passive voice and declare the whole *process* to occur outside of consciousness: The psycholinguist informs us that the most likely interpretation of an ambiguous sentence *is chosen unconsciously,* not that the person "consciously notices" the ambiguity and then "deliberately chooses" the most likely interpretation. Initiates to this way of speaking tend to underestimate the amount of conceptual revision they have undergone.

Again, anyone who finds it hard to imagine how it can be right to talk of choices made without a chooser, disapproval without a disapprover, even thoughts occurring without a thinker (Descartes's *res cogitans*), should pause to consider the possibility that this barely conceivable step might be a breakthrough, not a mistake. Those who refuse to suspend their intuitive judgments about this insist on imposing categories on discussion that make MPD seem fraudulent if you're a skeptic, or paranormal if you're a believer. The principle aim of this essay has been to break down this polarity of thought.[11]

---

11. We are grateful to the many therapists and patients who have tried to explain things to us and put up with our questions.

3

Do-It-Yourself Understanding[1]

Fred Dretske's views on meaning have been deservedly influential, and I accept much of what he has urged, but there are still some points of stubborn disagreement. Roughly a third of this essay is a recapitulation of several earlier essays addressing the remaining points of contention, but this latest version is, I think, an improvement and not just an enlargement, and it has heretofore been published only in French.

One of the virtues of Fred Dretske's recent work has been the salutary openness with which he has described the motivations he discovers controlling his thought, and this candor has brought a submerged confusion close to the surface. Since this confusion is widely shared by philosophers and others working on the problem of content ascription, an analysis of its influence on Dretske will at the same time illuminate the difficulties it is creating for other writers.

I think the confusion is born of the misalliance of two background images we have, each of which is valuable in itself but liable to be subscribed to in exaggerated form.[2]

First, there is the image of *mining the past for the future.* The purpose of brains is to "produce future," as the poet Valéry said: to create anticipations and expectations that will guide an organism's actions along the paths that avoid harm and capture good.[3] The raw materials for

Originally appeared as "La Compréhension Artisinale" (French translation) in Fisette, D., ed., *Daniel C. Dennett et les Stratégies Intentionelles, Lekton,* 11, Winter 1992, pp. 27–52.
1. This paper incorporates portions of an earlier paper, "Ways of Establishing Harmony" (Dennett, 1990b).
2. This confusion was suggested to me by Kathleen Akins (1988), where she draws a similar distinction, but uses the distinction for quite different philosophical purposes.
3. See the discussion of the verbs of "making a difference," such as "avoid," "prevent," "foster," etc., in Dennett (1984d). See also my "Producing Future by Telling Stories" (chap. 12, this volume).

the production of reliable anticipations must come in via our sense organs, to be stored in our memories. The plasticity of our brains permits us to *learn*. As this image would have it, learning is a matter of *extracting meaning* from our interactions for use in the future. There is really no doubt that this is what our nervous systems are for, but how exactly this process of information-extraction and subsequent meaning-manufacture is accomplished remains a mystery. How, we ask, can we get the fruits of our transactions with the past to *inform* and guide our future acts? "Theories of meaning" or "theories of content ascription" or "psychosemantics" are all attempts either to answer this question or at least to erect and justify families of constraints on acceptable answers.

Second, there is the image of *what it feels like to come to understand something:* there you are, encountering something somewhat perplexing or indecipherable or at least as yet unknown—something that in one way or another creates the epistemic itch, when finally *Aha! I've got it!* Understanding dawns, and the item is transformed; it becomes useful, comprehended, within your control. Before time *t* the thing was not understood; after time *t*, it was understood—a clearly marked state transition that can often be accurately timed, even though it is, emphatically, a subjectively accessible, introspectively discovered transition.

Put these two good images together, and they tend to spawn the idea of *do-it-yourself understanding,* an alchemical process in which the individual, the agent (the inner I or inner eye or homunculus or self) transforms mere *information* into *understood content.*

Let me elaborate just a bit on these images, and the way they infuse our thinking. As we encounter things, our senses take in huge *amounts of information,* which, like ore, needs to be refined and converted into usable form; it is no use having the information that *p,* even if that is exactly the information you need, unless you have it in a *form you can understand.* So there must be a process (or perhaps a variety of processes) for turning raw or crude information into the useful materials from which "we" can construct our beliefs and plans. This refining / transforming process is largely if not entirely unconscious, and is often called *interpretation.* Its product is traditionally called *understanding.* According to this view, one moves from mere receipt of information via some sort of interpretive process to the desirable state of understanding that information. Once understanding has been achieved, the mind has something to work with, something in position to guide action, inform plans, persuade, warn, remind, illuminate.

There is something privileged—or perhaps *proprietary* would be a better term—about the state of understanding. The state of understanding doesn't do me any good unless it is *my* understanding. Just as you can't take my naps or eat my lunches, you can't understand my thoughts and perceptions. More precisely, you can, perhaps, eat my lunch or understand my thoughts, but this will do me no good. My goal is not just getting my lunch eaten, but getting my lunch eaten *by me*. Similarly, unless *I* am the one who understands the import of my sensory states, their information is unavailable to serve me. For instance, suppose you can tell, by observing a certain flush of my skin, that there is a dangerous amount of carbon monoxide in the vicinity; a state of mine contains information, and you extract that valuable information from my state and put it to use in guiding your own action; if only *I* could also extract that information, and get it into usable form, I could perhaps save my life!

Such is the way we are all apt to think. There is surely a lot that is right about this way of thinking, but it also engenders some extraordinarily persistent illusions and false hopes. In particular, it engenders the hopeless and ultimately ill-motivated quest for *do-it-yourself understanding,* an infatuation we can best unmask by examining some of its kin.

Consider the earnest homeowner and handyman who shuns plumbers and electricians and wants to do it all himself. Moreover, when it comes to doing it himself, no prefabricated units or kits (with "some assembly required") find favor with him. He insists on building everything from scratch; he cuts down the trees, saws out the boards, mines the ore from which to smelt the iron from which to make the steel from which to draw the wire from which to make the nails. This is a fanatic do-it-yourselfer. And also, of course, a fool. Why not take advantage of the huge efforts of partial design and partial construction whose products are so readily available, we might well ask. Do you really insist on fashioning your own light bulbs?

Consider now a rather opposite sort of fool, the person who claims to be an artist, but whose oeuvres are "paint by numbers" paintings, and sculptures made by pouring plaster of paris into purchased rubber molds. This man boasts of building his own bicycle; it turns out that when it arrived in its crate, the wheels had to be put on. He "designed and built his own house" he says; what he means is that when he ordered his tract house, he specified color combination D (from the available options A–G), and put in all the light bulbs himself.

Somewhere in between these extremes lie both sanity and the responsibility of authorship (if that really matters to you). That is, you
can quite properly claim—if you feel the need so to claim—that you
are the sole creator of the coffee table, even if you did purchase the
woodscrews ready-made, and the oak boards came already planed to
their proper thickness.

We can now anticipate the moral for our story about understanding: there can be no central workshop of the mind / brain in which the
agent "all by himself" achieves understanding by fashioning raw
materials (materials that are not already pre-understood to some
degree by some agency other than him*self*) into genuinely meaningful or contentful objects or structures. The processes responsible for
understanding must be distributed, in both time and space, so that we
make a mistake if we pose the following tempting questions: where
does the understanding happen? Has he understood it yet? (Has *he*
understood it yet? Has he *understood* it yet?) The introspectively familiar phenomenon of coming to understand something does happen—
and people do make things for themselves on occasion—but these
phenomena must be viewed as only relatively salient turning points
in processes in which responsibility or authorship or agency is also
diffused.[4]

Now we are ready to look at the quest for do-it-yourself understanding in Fred Dretske's recent work. In a recent paper (1985, p. 31), he
gives a particularly clear and telling example of the elusive difference
that he is trying to capture: the marijuana-detecting dog whose tail
wags because an event occurs in its brain "meaning" (carrying the information) that marijuana is present, but which doesn't wag *because*
the event means what it means. Unlike the dog's telltale tail-wag, Fred
insists, *our* bodily actions often happen *because of* what the states that
cause them mean: "it is the structure's having this meaning (its semantics, not just the structure that has this meaning (the syntax), which is
relevant to explaining behavior" (personal correspondence, quoted in
Dennett, 1987, p. 307).

In a more recent paper, "Does Meaning Matter?" (1990) he puts it
even better: he has been "increasingly preoccupied with the question,
not of what meaning (or content) *is*, but what meaning (or content)
does." He wants to give meaning "some explanatory bite" (p. 7), and

---

4. A related point about the fallacy of "Cartesian materialism," the view that the brain
has a privileged functional central point, is argued in Dennett, "Temporal Anomalies
of Consciousness" (1992b).

ideally, this would involve showing "the way meaning . . . *can* figure in the explanation of why" an event causes what it does.

What difficulty lies in the way of this goal? The arguments, from myself and others, to the effect that the meaning of a particular event always must be, in Dretske's terms, *epiphenomenal* with regard to that event's actual causal powers. In *Content and Consciousness* (1969), I argued that the intentional interpretation of neural events is always at best a "heuristic overlay," and in "Intentional Systems" (1971), I tried to show how physical-stance predictions of the effects of structures always had hegemony over predictions based on the powers attributable to those structures (in idealization) in virtue of their meaning— as discerned from the intentional stance. More recently (1981a; 1983a; 1990b), I have spoken, as Dretske notes, of the *impotence* of meaning; the brain is first and foremost a syntactic engine, which can be fruitfully viewed as reliably mimicking a semantic engine, but in which meanings themselves never overrule, overpower, or so much as influence the brute mechanistic or syntactic flow of local causation in the nervous system. (A semantic engine, I claim, is a mechanistic impossibility— like a perpetual motion machine, but a useful idealization in *setting the specs* for actual mechanisms.) Others have made similar claims: Fodor has long insisted on the inescapability of what he calls the Formality Constraint, and Dretske attributes to Schiffer (1987) the view that meaning is an "excrescence" which can do nothing and explain nothing.

Dretske's response to these claims is ambivalent. On the one hand he makes it clear that he would truly love to defend a doctrine of brains as real semantic engines, with real meanings locally throwing their weight around and making the most direct imaginable difference— but he knows better. He is convinced by the arguments that show, in LePore and Loewer's (1987) terms, that the historical facts on which the meaning of a structure supervenes are *screened off* from the explanation of the structure's causal powers and behavior. (In a similar vein, I have spoken of "inert historical facts.") Dretske's own presentation of the arguments for this conclusion are the clearest yet, and they draw, tellingly, on an analogy to the difference between value and perceived value, genuine currency versus counterfeit currency. In terms of our first image, Dretske acknowledges that there can be no guarantee that the precious ore of information actually mined from the past will be transformed into the appropriate future-guiding meaning-artifact (or "structure"). Conversely (and strangely, more importantly in the eyes of some), there is no guarantee that the "right" future-guiding structure was made out of the *right stuff*—that it was made from ore that was properly mined from the past.

Two kinds of all too familiar puzzle cases exhibit these dreaded dissociations. In one type, Tom *has the information* that the person standing before him is the murderer (let us say), but hasn't twigged. In some formulations, he *believes of* this individual that he is the murderer, but does not recognize or realize that he has this belief. That is, thanks to the proper sort of historical ancestry of his current state, the precious ore of information is in his possession, but for one reason or another it has not been transformed into a structure that he can put to the appropriate use on this occasion. The relevant understanding has not happened; or more pointedly, *he* doesn't understand the information he has. In the other, more science-fictional type, Tom (or Twin-Tom or Cosmic-Coincidence-simulacrum-of-Tom) is in just the right state so far as the future is concerned—given the structures present in his workshop he is well-poised to deal with the murderer or whatever— but these structures have bogus credentials. It is only *as if* he believed of the murderer that he was the murderer (and recognized this); it is only *as if* his counterfeit understanding were genuine. There may or may not have been understanding involved in the process that set up poor Tom in this way, but it was not *his* understanding. There are thus two ways such a structure can be disqualified according to this view: it isn't made of the right materials at all—cosmic coincidence cases in which the relevant information never was brought into the workshop—or it wasn't made *by the agent.* The policemen who trained Dretske's marijuana-sniffing dog to wag its tail when a certain aroma was present understood what they were designing, but since the dog it*self* is none the wiser, this doesn't count.

So Dretske wants to develop an account of content ascription that will ensure that only genuine, noncounterfeit contents get ascribed, and that moreover has the consequence that these contents "make a difference" in the only way that contents *as contents* could make a difference: by being understood. He wants meaning to have some explanatory bite, but since he endorses, and indeed strengthens, the arguments to the effect that the meaning of a particular event cannot directly and *ipso facto* account for the effects that flow from that event, he has a problem. The well-known responses to these arguments all involve finding some more indirect way in which there can be a regular, reliable correspondence between the meaning of a (neural) structure and its effects on behavior. For instance, Fodor's *language of thought* hypothesis is essentially an attempt to describe a system that satisfies what Haugeland has called the Formalists' Motto:

If you take care of the syntax, the semantics will take care of itself. (Haugeland, 1985, p. 106)

This motto lies at the heart of what Haugeland calls GOFAI (Good Old Fashioned AI) and I call "High Church Computationalism" (see chapter 13 of this volume). There are other, more noncommittal, ways in which materialists can postulate a reliable correspondence between semantics and mechanism, but Dretske calls all these theories "pre-established harmony" theories, and finds them all intolerable. He still yearns to establish a more direct and satisfying relation between meaning and mechanism than the rest of us have described.

I think it is wonderful that he chooses to illuminate this "corner materialists have painted themselves into" by some old-fashioned labels: "epiphenomenalism" and "pre-established harmony." These dreaded relics of prescientific philosophy of mind, these desperate and doomed escape routes from Cartesian dualism, are sure to strike terror in the heart of complacent materialists, and Dretske tells us exactly why he cannot abide them: any view of meaning according to which there is merely a pre-established harmony between the causal facts and the facts of meaning may permit us to *predict* an agent's behavior, and *control* an agent's behavior, but it will not permit us to *explain* an agent's behavior—"and that," he says quite reasonably, "is what it takes to vindicate belief-desire psychology or our ordinary view about the causal efficacy of thought—that we stopped, for example, *because* we thought the light was red."[5]

Our first image, of mining the past for the future, identifies two components or ingredients in meaning, reminiscent of Aristotle's matter and form: the informational ore is the matter or raw material, while the finished product has a behavior-directing competence or power which is directly a function of its structure or form. There is no meaning (in the relevant sense) without both contributions—something Dretske and I have both always insisted upon—but there is a temptation to think of meaning as somehow residing in the informational component, as *potential* meaning, perhaps, that just needs to be identified and

---

5. It is interesting that here Dretske announces his allegiance to the same goal that motivates Fodor—the vindication of folk psychology taken neat—while dismissing Fodor's own solution as insufficiently responding to the folk psychological intuition that (the Formality Condition be damned) *meanings make it happen.*

refined in the course of manufacture. But since Dretske has reluctantly accepted the conclusion that there can be no direct mechanical extraction of meaning, he realizes that a straightforward vindication of this intuition is not in the cards. What he offers us instead is an attempt to salvage, if not *locally potent meanings*, then the next best thing: "the fact that *A* means *M*, though it fails to explain why *B* occurred, may help explain a closely related fact, the fact that events of type *A*, when they occur, cause events of type *B* . . . And this fact, especially when we are trying to explain the behavior of a system, is a fact eminently worth explaining" (1990, pp. 9–10).

What we need, in short, is not just a brute pre-established harmony, but an *explanation* of why and how the harmony is pre-established. Moreover (if Dretske has his druthers) this explanation will make an ineliminable appeal to the meanings of the elements thus linked. Now apparently he thinks that we pre-established harmony theorists have failed to offer such an explanation, for he is forthright in his opposition: "I don't think this works. Or, if it does work, it does so at a cost that I'm not prepared (unless forced) to pay" (1990, p. 9). This is a mistake, for in the end, he does not offer us an alternative to pre-established harmony, but a version of it, a truncated version, in fact, of the version I have offered. I am pleased to see the convergence of our positions, which are now really very close. The main point of disagreement, as we shall see, stems from Dretske's quixotic quest for do-it-yourself-understanding.

There are exactly five ways in which such a correspondence—a "pre-established harmony" between the meanings of structures and their causal powers—could (in principle) come into existence. Dretske encounters them all, but fails to recognize them for what they are.

First, there are the Three Cousins:

1. the correspondence is designed by natural selection

2. the correspondence is designed by a learning process of some sort in the individual brain

3. the correspondence is designed by an engineer creating an artifact, such as a robot or computer

Then there is the Philosopher's Fantasy:

4. the correspondence is the result of a Cosmic Coincidence.

Finally, there is the Theologian's Hope:

5. the correspondence is created and maintained by God.

Eager though he is to wed meaning and causation together, Dretske rightly dismisses this fifth possibility with only a passing allusion, for the obvious reason that it would be, quite literally, a deus ex machina. It is interesting to me that philosophers who would be embarrassed to spend more than a passing moment dismissing this fifth alternative are nevertheless irresistibly drawn to extended discussions of the implications of the fourth, Cosmic Coincidence, which is actually a more fantastic and negligible "possibility in principle."

Notice that there really cannot be a sixth route to pre-established harmony. If such a harmony is not just a single, large ("Cosmic") coincidence (4), or a miracle (5), it must be the product, *somehow*, of lots of tiny, well-exploited coincidences. This is because, as we have already agreed, meanings cannot *directly* cause things to happen, so they cannot *directly* cause themselves to correspond to any causal regularities in the world. So it will have to be via an indirect process of fortuitous coincidences that are duly "appreciated" or "recognized" or "valued" or "selected" by something—either something blind and mechanical, such as natural selection or operant conditioning or "neural Darwinism" (Edelman, 1987) (1 and 2), or something foresightful and intelligent, such as an engineer (3). Any such process is a design process, and must consist, at bottom, of such generate-and-test cycles, where the generation of diversity to be tested is somewhat random or coincidental (see Dennett, 1973; 1974; 1978a).

Dretske ends up[6] endorsing only the second way—learning—as a way of giving meanings explanatory bite, but the argument by which he proceeds would seem to legitimate all Three Cousins for the same reasons. It is in his unwillingness to accept this implication of his own argument that we will find the traces of his misbegotten desire for do-it-yourself understanding. He begins his attempt to give meaning explanatory bite by distinguishing between explaining B's happening (A caused it) and explaining A's causing B. He then tells a story about how a neural assembly can come to have a meaning, via species evolution by natural selection. The upshot is that such a story can explain why it is that As, meaning what they do, cause Bs. So far as I can see, this account follows just the path I laid out in *Content and Consciousness*, in my discussion of "the evolution of appropriate structures" (1969, pp. 47–63). Dretske describes an organism with a need to develop an

---

6. Dretske's Tepoztlan paper ("The Causal Role of Content") appears to endorse natural selection as a legitimate way of establishing harmony—and I so interpreted his paper then—but in a note added later, he disavows that interpretation.

avoidance mechanism against the highly toxic condition F, while I described different strains of organism which were differently wired up to avoid, approach, or ignore a particular stimulus condition that happens to be "more often than not"—an important proviso—injurious (p. 49). The result of both thought experiments is the same: the lucky ones who happen to be wired up to avoid the toxic, ceteris paribus, are the ones who survive to reproduce, their coincidentally happy correspondence being selected for by natural selection.

Dretske goes on to suggest that the same result could also be achieved by redesign during an individual organism's lifetime via a conditioning process, or as I put it, via a process of "intracerebral evolution." (Dennett, 1969, pp. 56–63). In "Does Meaning Matter," he does not suggest that there is any important difference between the processes of species evolution and intracerebral evolution, but in his postscript, he insists that there is:

Natural selection gives us something quite different: reflex, instinct, tropisms, fixed-action-patterns, and other forms of involuntary behavior—behavior that is (typically) *not* explained in terms of the actors' beliefs and desires (if any). These genetically determined patterns of behavior often involve (as triggers for response) internal indicators (information-carrying elements), but, unlike belief, it isn't *their* content that explains the way they affect output. That is determined by the genes. (p. 15)

What exactly is the contrast?

In order to get meaning itself (and not just the structures that have meaning) to play an important role in the explanation of an *individual*'s behavior (as beliefs and desires do) one has to look at the meaning that was instrumental in shaping the behavior that is being explained. This occurs only during individual learning. Only then is the meaning of the structure type (the fact that it indicates so-and-so about the animal's surroundings) responsible for its recruitment as a control element in the production of appropriate action. (pp. 14–15)

The only difference I can discern, however, is that the "structure type" in the case of natural selection is a type that is identified in the genotype, while the structure type in the case of intracerebral evolution is a type that is identified only in the phenotype. In both cases "meaning was instrumental in shaping the behavior"—that is, in shaping the behavior-*type*, and in neither case was meaning instrumental in shaping any particular, individual token of a behavioral type.

Note, in any case, that while Dretske now endorses intracerebral evolution or conditioning as a process that yields meanings with explanatory bite, his doing so requires that he abandon, or at least soften, the hard line he has previously taken on these issues, in *Knowledge and the Flow of Information* (1981), and more recently in "Machines and the Mental" (1985) and "Misrepresentation" (1986). In his book, he attempted to erect meaning on a foundation of information. That is, he developed an account of semantic information (the sort of meaning needed for psychology—a *functional* notion that applies only to *designed* channels) from a base of nonfunctional, nonsemantic information channels, through which traveled items with "natural meaning"—items that informed (by definition) with *perfect reliability*; where natural meanings are concerned, no misrepresentation is possible. The task then was to turn the corner, somehow, from natural meaning to semantic or "natural functional meaning" (in which misrepresentation *is* possible), without, as he has more recently put it, "artificially *inflating*" the attributions of meaning to a structure one is so interpreting. Fred has tried to hold the line against inflation by insisting on what he now calls the "indicator relation." But the indicator relations he now endorses can only approximately carry information about the distal conditions one is tempted to say they are designed to inform the organism about.

The indicator relation, which he heralds as "a plausible, at least a *possible*, partial basis for meaning" need only be a rough-and-ready guide to the meaning of the chosen structure. At least Dretske *ought* to recognize this, for that is how evolution, at the species *or neural* level, works. Mother Nature is a stingy, opportunistic engineer who takes advantage of rough correspondences whenever they are good enough for the organism's purposes, given its budget. He correctly wants to boast that his account *does* find an explanatory role for meanings: it is *because of what a structure happens to indicate* that it is "selected for" or "reinforced in" a further causal role in the economy of control of the organism, but it will be selected for, or reinforced in, this role *whenever* it is "close enough for government work" as the engineers say.

Dretske shies away from embracing the First Cousin, then, in spite of his dalliance with it, but in any case the most he could get out of Cousins (1) and (2) would be an explanatory account that makes ineliminable appeal to *quasi-indicator relations* or *approximate meanings*. Mother Nature never holds out for high-priced indicator relations.

As my frequent allusions to engineering suggest, and as I have argued in Dennett (1987, chapter 8), the design processes one encounters in (1) and (2) are not only fundamentally the same, but fundamentally the same as the *artificial* design process encountered in (3). It is striking that Dretske resists this conclusion, most emphatically in "Machines and the Mental" but also, with somewhat difference emphasis, in "The Causal Role of Content." If it is an engineer or computer scientist— rather than a learning history—who does the selecting (who esteems a structure for its quasi-indicator relations and harnesses it in a particular functional role in a robot's control structure), this somehow gives the structure an illegitimate ancestry, in Dretske's eyes. But why?

Why should selection by an engineer disqualify a structure for one of Dretske's why-explanations? One might suppose that engineer-selection had an advantage over natural selection in this regard. One might say: whereas one must use scare-quotes when talking of natural selection's "appreciation" of the potential meaning of a structure, engineers sometimes really and truly respond to these potential meanings in the course of their conscious, deliberate, designing. But Dretske does not find this line of thought palatable, in spite of the fact that he often illustrates his point by the example of the wiring of a light switch, an example which explicitly appeals to just such different appreciations or intentions on the part of circuit designers. Is it just because he has a bad case of *organophilia* (otherwise known as *silicophobia*)? I think not. I suspect that he is distracted by an illusion: the illusion that somehow in ways (1) and (2)—but not in (3)—the organism itself (or even: its mind or soul) does the understanding—responds directly to the meaning.

After all, one might naturally but confusedly say, if some engineer is responsible for appreciating the meaning of a neural or computer structure, and is responsible for designing its further role in the light of that meaning, there is nothing left for the organism or robot to do— no *task of understanding* left over. The very same consideration would disqualify natural selection, for if it is the process of natural selection that has set up an innate correspondence between meaning and causation, there would likewise be no supervisory role for the organism (or its central, understanding homunculus) to play. (For more on this see Dennett, 1988a.) And this is, I suspect, exactly the natural confusion into which Dretske has fallen.

Both in his book, and more recently in his articles (and in personal correspondence, quoted in Dennett 1987, p. 306), he has held the line against innate, unlearned meanings. "Beliefs and desires, *reasons* in general (the sort of thing covered by the intentional stance), are (or so I would like to argue) invoked to explain patterns of behavior that are acquired during the life history of the organism exhibiting the behavior (i.e., learned)."

Why has he been tempted to favor individual learning histories exclusively? Because, apparently, they *seemed* to give the organism itself a proper role in the acquisition and appreciation of the meanings in question. But once again, of course, if "mere conditioning" is responsible for the redesign of the individual organism's brain, this too looks like taking responsibility away from the inner understander that Dretske is so loath to lose. Consider, in this connection, the marijuana-sniffing dog. It was carefully conditioned, presumably, to wag its tail (the conditioned response) when stimulated by the odor of marijuana. If we attend to the process by which the harmony was achieved, we can no longer see any role for "the dog itself" to play. The theoretical beauty, after all, of theories of learning that broke learning down, in one way or another, into "mere" conditioning was that they promised to explain learning without improper recourse to inner, mysterious processes or states of understanding.

"But where does the *understanding* happen?" one might ask, having been treated to an account of the way in which an organism was caused, thanks to its design, to respond appropriately (first internally, and eventually externally) to events impinging on it. The temptation here is to insist that in the case of the dog, the understanding is *all* in the trainers, and that *no amount* of "mere" conditioning or other design-by-outsiders could ever succeed in getting the dog to achieve *its own* understanding.

Here we see the unfortunate influence of our mis-united images, which tend to create the following barely submerged conviction: Understanding isn't *real* understanding, understanding for which the agent or organism is *responsible*, of which it is the proper *author*, unless it is entirely the product of the agent's own, do-it-yourself processes of interpretation. If the agent is "merely" the beneficiary of partially pre-understood, pre-interpreted, designed-by-other-agencies structures, then even if it appears *as if* the agent was understanding, there is really no agency there at all! Other, earlier creators are the proper authors of this design.

The appeal of the proprietary (it doesn't count unless it is *my* understanding!) turns Dretske's head against both natural selection and artificial intelligence. But its dire influence can also be seen, I believe, in Fodor's ever more mystical pronouncements about the psychosemantical relation, and the nonmodularity of "belief-fixation.") In *The Modu-*

larity of Mind (1983), Fodor argued heatedly for a vision of the mind in which the peripheral modules, both afferent and efferent, were blind, mechanical, encapsulated systems surrounding a central core, the arena of nonmodular, global "belief-fixation," a workshop in which the meanings of the products of the modules could be (somehow) *interpreted* by the mysterious central processes, of which Fodor emphatically insisted that neither he nor anyone else had any theories.

A lot is known about the transformations of representations which serve to get information into a form appropriate for central processing; practically nothing is known about what happens after the information gets there. The ghost has been chased further back into the machine, but it has not been exorcized. (1983, p. 127)

In effect Fodor is saying: "Here in the center is where understanding happens." Because of the Formality Constraint, Fodor is certain that the account to be given of the processes that achieve understanding will have to be, in the end, purely syntactically definable processes, and the only obvious candidate for such a Janus-faced process is *inference*, which can be viewed both semantically, as a meaning-extraction process, and syntactically, as a symbol-manipulation process. But aside from this dual-aspect appeal of inference as a potential gap-filler, there is little to recommend it. Such mechanistic accounts as there are of inference processes are hopelessly brittle and ineffective, as Fodor himself has insisted (in Fodor, 1983). He has not yet offered his own model of how inferences are supposed to work to turn mere information into meaning, but in any event, for meaning-extraction to occur, there has to be meaning present (if hidden) in the products' reaching the workshop via the senses—hence Fodor's attraction, in *Psychosemantics* (1987) and more recent work, to a purely denotational semantics that is somehow "information-based." Such a theory will ensure that the precious ore of information will make it into the home workshop, where the inner alchemist can turn it into useful products.

But this is an incoherent vision. No such account could work, in spite of its undeniable initial appeal. I have no formal proof of this, but an old thought experiment of mine shows why one might believe this:

Suppose you find yourself locked in a windowless room, with two walls covered with flashing lights, two walls covered with little buttons, and a note telling you that you are imprisoned in the control center of a giant robot on whose safety your own life now depends. Your task is simply to guide the robot through its somewhat perilous environment, learning to discriminate and cope with whatever comes along, finding "nourishment" and safe haven for the robot at night (so you can sleep), and avoiding dangers. All the *informa-tion* you need is conveyed by the flashing lights, and the robot's motor activity is controllable by pushing the buttons. To your dismay, however, you see that none of the lights or buttons are labeled. You can't tell whether the insistently flashing light in the upper left corner is warning danger, signaling a "full belly," informing you of the location of the sun, or requesting grease for a heel bearing. You don't know whether when you push a button and the light goes out, you've scratched an itch, occluded your view of something, or destroyed an attacker.

Clearly, if that is all you are given to go on, your task is impossible; if you succeeded in guiding your robot through the day it would be sheer luck. Yet in one sense (and a very familiar sense to cognitive psychologists) all the infor-mation you need is conveyed to you. For we needn't suppose the lights are mere repeaters of peripheral stimulation; their flashing can represent the prod-ucts of perceptual analysis machinery as sophisticated as you wish, and simi-larly the output can be supposed to initiate devious actions guided by hierarchical subroutine systems informed by multilayered feedback. In short, the entire array of systems devised by the cognitive psychologists could be built into this robot, so that it conveyed to its control center highly mediated and refined information, and yet, though in one sense the information would be there, in another more important sense, it would not. Yet the task just de-scribed is in a sense just the brain's task; it has no windows out which it can look in order to correlate features of the world with its input.

The problem of the control room could be solved for you, of course, if all the lights and buttons were correctly labeled (in a language you knew), but this can hardly be the brain's solution. The job of getting the input information *interpreted* correctly is thus *not* a matter of getting the information translated or transcribed into a particular internal code unless getting the information into that code is ipso facto getting it into functional position to govern the behavioral repertoire of the whole organism. (Dennett, 1978b, p. 258)

There is no way that pure do-it-yourself interpretation could get started; the only hope of creating a system—a brain or a computer system—that can bootstrap its way to understandings it was not born with is to create it with a goodly stock of pre-established harmony built in. It is not clear that Dretske would disagree with this conclusion, but then how are we to explain his earlier opposition to natural selection and his continuing opposition to engineering design as sources of har-mony? In recent correspondence with me, he has made it quite clear that he put so much stock in learning history that he was prepared to grant real meaning even to the structures in an artifact, *so long as they were produced, in part, by individual learning* by the artifact: "I think we could (logically) create an artifact that *acquired* original intentionality, but not one that (at the moment of creation as it were) *had* it" (personal correspondence, quoted in Dennett, 1987, p. 305).

Now here we must distinguish two claims, one plausible and important, and the other—Dretske's—obscurely motivated and, I think, strictly negligible. The plausible and important claim is that it is astronomically unfeasible to create, by the usual engineer's methods, the sorts of structures that are naturally and efficiently created by learning histories of the sort he champions. This suspicion strikes at the heart of a particular fantastic hope of some in AI, who would *handcraft* the myriads of beliefs that would constitute the "world knowledge" of an adroit robot. Not only have some thought this was possible in principle; there is a multimillion dollar project in AI with that as its explicit goal: Douglas Lenat's CYC project, an effort which Lenat himself supposes will take *person-centuries* of programming to accomplish. (See chap. 18 of this volume.) The majority opinion in AI, however, is that this is a hopeless approach, for reasons well canvassed by David Waltz (1988).

Dretske's point, in contrast, is philosophical, not practical. It is that even if the engineers could handcraft all those structures, they wouldn't have any meaning until they had been somehow annealed in the fire of experience. He puts the astronomically unfeasible product of engineering design in the same category with the even more astronomically unlikely case of Cosmic Coincidence, in spite of the fact that in the former case, there would be explanations of the provenance of structures that made appeal to meanings. He imagines that a physical duplicate of himself might "materialize—miraculously or randomly—out of some stray collection of molecules" (1990, p. 13), and goes to some length to insist that this biological twin's motions would not be *actions*, with *meanings* behind them.

I move my arm in this way *in order* to frighten away a pesky fly. With such a purpose I am, let us say, *shooing away a fly*. That is my *action*. My biological twin, though he moves his arm in the same way (with the same result) does not shoo away a fly. He doesn't have wants or beliefs, the kind of purposes I have in moving my arm. He isn't, therefore, performing the same action. (1990, pp. 13–14)

Your intuitions may agree with his, or recoil, but in either case, they concern something negligible, for as he goes on to acknowledge, there is a loophole: this metaphysically shocking state of affairs is apt to be short-lived, since it will persist only "until the twin accumulates enough experience—until, that is, his internal processes acquire the requisite extrinsic relations—to give his control processes, the processes governing the movement of his hand, the same kind of explanation as mine" (1990, p. 14).

How long, one wonders, should "acquiring the requisite extrinsic relations" take? I should think it would be instantaneous.[7] Signals from the bio-double's peripheral vision (or perhaps a faint blip from cutaneous sensors on the shoulder) happen to put the bio-double into what would be a bogus fly-out-there-sensing state—except that this time it is caused by a real fly. Moreover, the real fly's trajectory intimately determines the hand-eye coordination series that promptly leads to the (bogus or real?) "shooing" motions. How many flies must buzz around the head of a bio-double before he can start shooing them? If that isn't an angels-dancing-on-the-head-of-a-pin question, what would be?

This curious question, of how much traffic with the world is enough, somehow, to ensure that genuine meaning has been established, is simply the enlargement (via a *Cosmic* Coincidence) of the curious question that has bedeviled some evolutionary theorists: how much selection is required to endorse a tiny coincidence (a random mutation) as a genuine *adaptation*? See my discussion (Dennett, 1987, pp. 320–321) and footnotes on those pages, and in my response to commentary (1988d). But if nothing but arbitrary answers (e.g., forty-two generations of selection) could "settle" the question for natural selection, only arbitrary answers (e.g., forty-two flies must buzz) could settle the question for a learning history, for the processes have the same structure—they must begin with a fortuitous or coincidental coupling, thereupon favored—and they have the same power to design structures in indirect response to meaning.

Notice that these frivolous questions are analogous to the question of just how much *do-it-yourself* an agent must contribute before he is the *real* creator of something. The beneficiary of Cosmic Coincidence (or of interfering engineers) is like the sculptor who opportunistically avails himself of *objets trouvés*, taking advantage of unearned (unlearned) gifts. (As several punsters have noted, Dretske's view of content is that it must be acquired the old-fashioned way: you have to *learn* it.)

But where does this beneficiary keep the understanding required to appreciate these unearned gifts of meaning in the first place? The answer must be: there is no such original, central, untainted under-

---

7. See, for instance, my discussion (originally Dennett, 1973) of the parallel case of the bogus belief (that he has an older brother living in Cleveland) surgically inserted to Tom (in Dennett, 1978a, pp. 251–253); the discussion of the Panamanian debut of the two-bitser (how long does it take for the new functions to be "real"?); and my reply to Goldman (Dennett, 1988d).

standing; there are only the varieties of reliably meaning-tracking mechanical processes that, when reflected on themselves and their kin, tend to enhance the power of the indirect processes of meaning-extraction.

In *The Intentional Stance,* I looked at this issue from a slightly different perspective, using an example that might repay a second look in the present context.

The first thing a baby cuckoo does when it hatches is to look around the next for other eggs, its potential competitors for its adoptive parents' attention, and attempt to roll them over the edge. It surely has no inkling of the functional meaning of its activity, but that meaning is nevertheless there—*for* the organism and *to* the organism—unless we suppose by the latter phrase that the organism has to "have access" to that meaning, has to be in a position to reflect on it, or avow it, for instance. The rationale of the cuckoo's chillingly purposive activity is not in question; what remains to be investigated is to what extent the rationale is the fledgling's rationale and to what extend it is free-floating— merely what Mother Nature had in mind. . . . For Dretske, however, this is an all-or-nothing question, and it is tied to his intuition that there must be unique and unequivocal (natural functional) meanings for mental states.

Dretske seems to be trying to do two things at one stroke: first, he wants to draw a principled (and all-or-nothing) distinction between free-floating and— shall we say?—"fully appreciated" rationales; and second, he wants to remove all interpretive slack in the specification of the "actual" or "real" meaning of any such appreciated meaning-states. After all, if we appeal to our introspective intuitions, that is just how it seems: not only is there something we mean by our thoughts—something utterly determinate even if sometimes publicly ineffable—but it is our recognition or appreciation of *that meaning* that explains what we thereupon do. There certainly is a vast difference between the extremes represented by the fledgling cuckoo and, say, the cool-headed and cold-blooded human murderer who "knows just what he is doing, and why," but Dretske wants to turn it into the wrong sort of difference. (pp. 306–307)

The fledgling cuckoo, like Dretske's marijuana-sniffing dog and Ewert's prey-catching toads, doesn't seem to be "doing any of the understanding," doesn't seem, as I noted above, to "have access" to the meaning of its own states. The tempting idea is that there is not just a vast difference, but one big difference, a difference in kind, not degree, between such cases and the cases in which (as we notice "from the inside") we understand the meanings of our perceptual states and act upon them *because of* that understanding. But if we look closely, we will see that between the humble cuckoos and toads, and us, is a continuum of cases. The injury-feigning plover understands more about its broken-wing dance than one might skeptically have supposed at first, as revealed by its sensitivity to relevant variations. The deceptive acts of some primates (Whiten and Byrne, 1988a) apparently reveals a still more acute responsivity to the (approximate) meanings of the circumstances in which they act. And our own imperfect "grasp" of the implications of our perceptual states, beliefs, and intentions is the grist for hundreds of philosophical examples.

The human capacity to treat one's own states, reflexively, as the objects of further consideration—perception and thought—greatly enhances our powers of understanding.[8] Arguably, the sort of swift, sensitive self-redesign it permits is the basis for our undeniable cognitive superiority over all other organisms. But *being the product of such a process of auto-engineering* is neither a necessary nor a sufficient condition for being a type of structure whose meaning "has explanatory bite." As in other forms of design and manufacture, whether something works well or ill depends only indirectly and imperfectly on whether you made it yourself.

Dretske goes searching for a closer tie between meaning and structure because he is worried by the following argument:

If meaning supervenes, at least in part, on the *extrinsic* properties of an event—historical and relational facts that *need not* be mirrored in the event's current (= the time at which it has its effects) physical constitution or structure—then if A causes B, then the fact, if it is a fact, that A means M will not—indeed, cannot—figure in a causal explanation of B. It cannot because, in *similar circumstances* [my italics], an event lacking this meaning, but otherwise the same, will have exactly the same effects. So it isn't A's having meaning M that explains why B occurred. (1990, p. 9)

This would be a significant worry if "similar circumstances" were apt to be forthcoming with nonzero probability in cases where A did not mean M, but we can rest assured that we will virtually never encounter such an anomaly. That is to say, it is no accident that events with the meanings they have get to play the causal roles they play (and Dretske in fact gives a good account of this), but the other side of that coin is

8. In a valuable article that treats many of these issues, Robert van Gulick (1988) puts it this way: "The personal-level experience of understanding is nonetheless not an illusion. I, the personal subject of experience, do understand. I can make all the necessary connections with experience, calling up representations to immediately connect one with another. The fact that my ability is the result of my being composed of an organized system of subpersonal components which produce my orderly flow of thoughts does not impugn my ability. What is illusory or mistaken is only the view that I am some distinct substantial self who produces these connections in virtue of a totally non-behavioral form of understanding" (p. 96).

that the odds are astronomical against the occurrence of an event or structure that *lacked* the relevant meaning somehow arising to cause a bogus *B*-type event—at least more than once or twice. It is not just that *A*s cause *B*s, but that if *A*s cease to mean what they do, they will (shortly) cease to cause *B*s, thanks to the power of an adaptive (or learning) system to select against those of its structures that prove inappropriate. That is as tight a relationship as one can hope for, and it is tight enough to explain the admirable if imperfect human capacity for being responsive to content.

What Dretske misses is that it isn't only that *given the past,* the existence of these event types (meaning what they do) cause *those* event types (meaning what *they* do), but *in the future* should the sort of dissociation occur that leads Dretske to worry about "epiphenomenalism," it will (soon, not immediately or perfectly "locally") cause the causal link between *A*s and *B*s to lapse or be revised *because* it no longer serves the right behavior-guiding role. This is true, however, in all three cousins: the only difference is time scale. Engineers, as soon as they notice a glitch, will repair or debug or discard the system; natural selection takes longer, but works inexorably. Learning in the individual has the same effect. It is the fastest portable system of self-repair, but of course what gets repaired is not the self, and not the individual causes and effects, but only the event-type pairings.

If an artifact-Dretske (or robot) is well designed, then *even before* it has begun to interact with the world in a genuine causal way, it will be true that the desired counterfactual is true: *A*s (meaning that *p*) cause *B*s (meaning that *q*), but if *A*s stopped meaning that *p*, or *B*s stopped meaning that *q*, the causal link would soon be broken. *Almost* as soon as a change (or more realistically, a lapse) in meaning arises, a revision of causation will arise in response, thanks to the self-correcting capacities built in. I suppose the philosophers' limiting case is the robot that is so well designed to meet the future that it goes through its whole life without ever having to learn (repair) anything. The fact that it *would* have learned if it had had to learn is all that matters.

We don't need any special history of experience to ensure that any harmonies we encounter are robust, and Dretske's own arguments show that a learning history, the "acquisition of *extrinsic* relations," *could not* impart any *intrinsic* power to those harmonies. All there can be are better or worse harmonies, designed into the system thanks to various processes of trial-and-error research and development, some of them in the distant past of our species, some in our early learning histories, and some, no doubt, recent spur-of-the-moment revisions in the design of current structures—the sorts of sudden and introspectively memorable moments we take as our paradigms of *coming to understand*. We do get to do it ourselves, sometimes, but when we do, we are doing what we are designed to do, using parts and procedures that we have not ourselves designed, and taking full advantage of all the understanding that has gone into our design up to now.

4

Two Contrasts: Folk Craft versus Folk Science, and Belief versus Opinion

What is the status of folk psychology? Of the conferences I have attended on this topic, the best took place in Greensboro, North Carolina in 1988, and the papers presented were collected into the volume from which this essay is reprinted. The rise of connectionism seemed to many philosophers at first to be a harbinger of doom for folk psychology, when in fact it can be seen in retrospect to have cleared the decks for a much more realistic model of how the phenomena described in folk psychology might sit in the brain. Thanks to recent work, especially the books and articles by Andy Clark (1993, 1997, forthcoming, Clark and Karmiloff-Smith, 1993), we can begin to see the outlines of a hybrid architecture, composed of connectionist fabrics throughout, but shaped into a virtual machine capable of rather more introspectively familiar goings-on. This essay takes some groping steps toward that picture. The crucial idea is that the role of noise in the implementation of this virtual machine makes the implementation-relation nontrivial: unlike the situation in GOFAI or in the "classical" symbolic models of cognitive science, there can be effects at the higher level whose explanation requires delving deep into the underlying machinery.

Let us begin with what all of us here agree on: Folk psychology is not immune to revision. It has a certain vulnerability in principle. Any particular part of it might be overthrown and replaced by some other doctrine. Yet we disagree about how likely it is that that vulnerability in principle will turn into the actual demise of large portions—or all— of folk psychology. I believe that folk psychology will endure, and for some very good reasons, but I am not going to concentrate on that here. What I want to stress is that for all of its blemishes, warts, and

Originally appeared in Greenwood, J., ed., *The Future of Folk Psychology: Intentionality and Cognitive Science* (Cambridge: Cambridge University Press, 1991), pp. 135–148.

perplexities, folk psychology is an extraordinarily powerful source of prediction. It is not just prodigiously powerful but remarkably easy for human beings to use. We are virtuoso exploiters of not so much a theory as a craft. That is, we might better call it a folk craft rather than a folk theory. The *theory* of folk psychology is the ideology about the craft, and there is lots of room, as anthropologists will remind us, for false ideology.

What we learn at mother's knee as we are growing up, and what might be to some degree innate, is a multifarious talent for having expectations about the world. Much of that never gets articulated into anything remotely like propositions. (Here I am in partial agreement with the new Paul Churchland. He now wants to say that folk psychology is a theory; but theories don't have to be formulated the way they are formulated in books. I think that's a pretty good reason for not calling it a theory, since it doesn't consist of any explicit theorems or laws.) But now what is this thing that is folk psychology, if it is not a theory? What kind of a craft is it? I've certainly had my say about that, in *Brainstorms* (Dennett, 1978a) and *The Intentional Stance* (Dennett, 1987), and I'm not going to try to telescope all that I say there into a summary here. Instead, I am going to expand on the similarities between folk psychology and folk physics—two crafts that repay attention, and that *should* be studied with the methods of anthropology, not just the informal methods of philosophers.

If we look at folk physics, we discover some interesting anomalies. Folk physics is as effortless, as second-nature as folk psychology, and it keeps us one step ahead of harsh reality most of the time. A pioneering analysis of a portion of folk physics is found in Patrick Hayes's (1978, 1980) work on what he calls the "naive physics of liquids." Consider how robust and swift our anticipations are of the behavior of liquids under normal circumstances.

For instance, if you and I were seated at a table, and I happened to overturn a full glass of water, almost certainly you would push your chair back rather quickly, because you would expect that if you didn't, the water would run off the edge of the table onto your clothes. We do these things *almost* without thinking, but in fact, if the circumstances were slightly different—if there were a lip on the table, or a towel where the liquid was pouring—we would effortlessly have very different expectations, and behave differently. We know about how towels absorb liquids, and about how liquids don't roll up over the edge of lips under normal conditions. These are part of a huge family of expectations we have about liquids, which we would find very difficult to enunciate in a string of propositions—though that is just what Hayes very ingeniously attempted. He tried to do a formal, axiomatic folk physics of liquids. In the folk physics of liquids, he notes, siphons are impossible. So are pipettes—putting your finger over the top of the straw and drawing up the Pepsi. Hayes views this as a virtue of his theory, because that is what folk physics declares; it is different from academic physics. There is something counterintuitive about both pipettes and siphons. Therefore, if you want to codify à la anthropology what people actually think and do, you want to make folk physics *predict against* such things as siphons and pipettes.

Now when we turn to folk psychology, we should expect the same thing. We should expect that some deeply intuitive ideas of folk psychology will just turn out to be false. Folk physics would say that gyroscopes are impossible, and that sailing upwind is impossible, but we come to learn that they are not, strange as this seems. We were just wrong about these matters, but even after we learn this, the intuitions don't go away; the phenomena still seem counterintuitive. So we might expect that folk psychology, under the pressure of advanced academic psychology and brain science, will similarly come a cropper. Certain deeply intuitive principles of folk psychology, perhaps never before articulated, may have to be given up. (I presume that folk physics never *articulated* the principle that siphons were impossible until siphons were well known to be possible; when siphons were observed, people perhaps said, "Hey wait a minute! Things shouldn't happen that way!") So it would be surprising if we had already articulated the principles of folk psychology that academic psychology is going to undermine—if it undermines any. Rather, we will find ourselves beset with extremely counterintuitive clashes, and something will have to give. And what very likely will give is parts of folk psychology. That is to say, the craft itself will come to be adjusted to acknowledge the existence of perplexities and peculiarities and contrary predictions that the craft had never before made.

I want to distinguish between craft and ideology, between what we learn to do, and what our mothers and others have actually *told* us the craft was all about when they enunciated the lore, for what the anthropologists tell us is that craft and ideology are often quite distinct. If you ask the native potters how they make their pots they may tell you one thing and do another. It is not a question of lack of sophistication. Jet airplane pilots tell their students, "This is how you fly a jet plane." They even write books about how they fly jet planes, but often that is not how they fly. They often don't know what they're doing. Now, if you want to study that sort of thing, you should bring the particular talents of the anthropologist to the study, but pending that research I will hazard some informal observations. I suppose if we look carefully at the ideology of folk psychology, we find it is pretty much Cartesian—dualist through and through. Perhaps there are also other problems and perplexities within the ideology as it has come down to us through the tradition. But notice that nobody in philosophy working on folk psychology wants to take that part of the ideology seriously. We are all materialists today, so the issue about the future of folk psychology is not whether or not some Cartesian view will triumph. We have apparently just decided that dualism (if it really is, as some have argued, presupposed by "common sense") is an expendable feature of the ideology. The question that concerns us now is whether there are other, less expendable features of the ideology.

Consider what can happen: Fodor, for instance, looks at the craft of folk psychology and tries to come up with a theory about why it works. His theory is that it works because it's good natural history. It is actually an account of what is going on in the head, he thinks. All the things that seem to be salient in the practice of the craft actually have their isomorphs or homomorphs the head. So he comes up with what he calls "intentional realism." He notices that people say things like

Tom believes that p

and

Sam desires that q [actually, nobody ever uses this form, but bend a little!]

From this we note that there is an attitude slot and a p-or-q slot, a propositional slot. We have two different sources of variation, two different knobs that turn in the folk craft. The reason it works, Fodor thinks, is that in the head there are things which line up with those knobs in a nice way. If the attitude knob has fourteen settings on it, there have to be fourteen different state types in the brain. If the p-or-q knob has an infinity of settings, there has to be an infinity of possible different internal states, each of them distinct and discrete. But that is just one theory about why folk psychology works, and several other chapters in *The Future of Folk Psychology* demonstrate that there are some pretty good reasons for thinking it's a bad theory.

It's really rather curious to say "I'm going to show you that folk psychology is false by showing you that Jerry Fodor is mistaken." Yet that is pretty much the strategy of Ramsey, Stich, and Garon's chapter in Creenwood, 1991, "Connectionism, Eliminativism and the Future of Folk Psychology." It won't achieve its aim if Fodor is wrong about what is the most perspicuous ideology or explanation of the power of the folk craft. If he is wrong about that, then indeed you would expect that the vision he has of what is going on in the brain would not match what the brain people would discover; but that disparity wouldn't mean that folk psychology as a craft was on the way out, or even that no perspicuous account of the ontology or metaphysics of folk psychology as a craft would survive just fine on a connectionist day of glory. I think John Heil nicely explains in his commentary how one might imagine that happening. One can also see in Ramsey, Stich, and Garon's own account how they are using folk psychological terms simply in order to motivate their connectionist models, and explain how they are supposed to work. Why do they find they must do that, if there is no useful relationship between folk psychology and computational neuroscience? Is it just a temporary ladder that we will learn to throw away? If the ladder works so well, why contemplate discarding it?

We should acknowledge, then, that it doesn't matter if the folk ideology about the craft is wrong—unless you take the ideology too seriously! In *The Intentional Stance* (1987; p. 114), I comment at one point that Fodor's theory is a little like a curious folk theory of the common cold: a cold is a large collection of sneezes, some of which escape. Someone might actually think that that is what a cold was, and might wonder how many more sneezes had to escape before it was over. Fodor's theory is similar: it is that there are all these sentences in the head; some of them come out, and some of them go in, but aside from a bit of translation (between Mentalese and, say, English) basically they never get changed around all that much.

Some others, such as myself, have tried to give a rather different analysis of what folk psychology as a craft is, in terms of the intentional stance. I have insisted that far from being most perspicuously treated as (1) discrete, (2) semantically interpretable states, (3) playing a causal role, the beliefs and desires of the folk psychological craft are best viewed as *abstracta* — more like centers of gravity or vectors than as individualizable concrete states of a mechanism.

In chapter 4 of *The Future of Folk Psychology*, Ramsey, Stich, and Garon give some bottom-up reasons for being dubious about this

Fodorian triad of views about the nature of psychological states, and I'm going to try to give a few slightly different ones—you might call them top-down reasons—by performing a few quasi-experiments drawn from *The Intentional Stance*. (If you've read the book, you're not a naive subject.)

Here is a joke. See if you get it. ("Newfies" are people from Newfoundland; they are the Poles of Canada—or the Irish of Canada if you're British.)

A man went to visit his friend the Newfie and found him with both ears bandaged. "What happened?" he asked, and the Newfie replied, "I was ironing my shirt, you know, and the telephone rang." "That explains one ear, but what about the other?" "Well, you know, I had to call the doctor!"

The experiment works—with you as a subject—if you get the joke. Most, but not all, people do. If we were to pause, in the fashion of Eugene Charniak, whose story-understanding artificial intelligence (AI) program (Charniak, 1974) first explored this phenomenon, and ask what one has to believe in order to get the joke (and here we have a list of propositions or sentences-believed-true, individuated in the standard way), what we get is a long list of different propositions. You have to have beliefs about the shape of an iron, the shape of a telephone; the fact that when people are stupid they often can't coordinate left hand with the right hand doing different things; the fact that the heft of a telephone receiver and an iron are approximately the same; the fact that when telephones ring, people generally answer them, and many more.

What makes my narrative a joke and not just a boring story is that it is radically enthymematic; it leaves out a lot of facts and counts on the listener filling them in, but you could fill them in only if you had all those beliefs. Now an absolutely daft theory about how you got the joke—and this is probably not fair to Fodor but a caricature of sorts—is this: In come some sentences (in the ear—exactly the sentences I spoke), and their arrival provokes a mechanism that goes hunting for all the relevant sentences—all those on our list—and soon brings them into a common workspace, where a resolution theorem-prover takes over, filling in all the gaps by logical inference. That is the sort of sententialist theory of cognitive processing that Fodor has gestured in the direction of, but nobody has produced a plausible or even workable version, so far as I know. The sketch I have just given is an absolutely harebrained theory, which nobody could assert with a straight face.

Nobody believes that theory, I trust, but note that even if it and all its near kin (the other sententialist / inference engine theories) are rejected as theories about how you got the joke, our list of beliefs is not for that reason otiose, foolish, or spurious. It actually does describe cognitive conditions (very abstractly considered) that have to be met by anybody who gets the joke. We can imagine running the experiments that would prove this. Strike off one belief on that list and see what happens. That is, find some people who don't have that belief (but have all the others), and tell them the joke. They won't get it. They can't get it, because each of the beliefs is necessary for comprehension of the story.

Ramsey, Stich, and Garon discuss the phenomenon of forgetting one belief out of a list of beliefs. In the connectionist net they display, the way that you forget a belief is different from the way you might forget a belief in a Collins and Quillian network, but the point I would make here is that on either account, we have counterfactual-supporting generalizations of the following form: If you don't believe (have forgotten) that p, then you won't get the joke.

I am prepared in fact to make an empirical prediction, which relies on the scientific probity of talking about this list of beliefs, even though they don't represent anything salient in the head, but are mere abstracta. The joke that I just told and you just got is on its way out. It's going to be obsolete in a generation or two. Why? Because in this age of wash-and-wear clothing, the kids that are growing up have never seen anybody ironing. Some of them don't know what an iron looks and feels like, and their numbers are growing. For that matter, telephones are changing all the time, too, so the essential belief in the similarity of shape and heft of telephone receiver and iron is going to vanish; it is not going to be reliably in the belief pool of normal audiences. So they are not going to get the joke. You would have to explain it to them—"Well, back in the olden days, irons looked and felt like . . ."—and then, of course, it wouldn't be a joke anymore. This is an example which could be multiplied many times over, showing that the power of folk psychology or the intentional stance as a calculus of abstracta is not in the least threatened by the prospect that no version of Fodor's Intentional Realism is sustained by cognitive neuroscience.

Ramsey, Stich, and Garon also give some examples to show the presumed discreteness of beliefs on the folk-psychological model. They point out that an explanation can cite a single belief, and beliefs can come and go more or less atomistically—according to folk psychology. Heil comments usefully on what is misleading about this interpretation of such phenomena, so I'm going to extend his criticism via a different example. Suppose we explain Mary's suddenly running upstairs by citing her belief that she's left her purse behind on the bed, and her desire to take her purse with her when she goes out. According to the Realist interpretation of folk psychology, this would be a case in which we were not speaking metaphorically, and if we happen to speak imprecisely (did she really actually believe just that she had left her purse on some horizontal surface in the bedroom?), this is always correctable in principle because there is a definite fact of the matter, say the Realists, of just which beliefs and desires a person has. Now I take it that in a case like this, what creates the illusion of discrete, separate, individuatable beliefs is the fact that we talk about them: the fact that when we go to explain our anticipations, when we move from generating our own private expectations of what people are going to do, to telling others about these expectations we have, and explaining to them why we have them, we do it with language. What comes out, of course, are propositions. Given the demands for efficiency in communication, we have to highlight the presumably central content features of the explanation or prediction that we have in mind. A distilled essence—in fact, as we have seen, typically an enthymematic portion of the distilled essence—gets expressed in words.

In order to make any sense of what we are doing in the classical way that Fodor suggests, we have to carry a lot of further baggage along. Let me quote Davidson:

Without speech we cannot make the fine distinctions between thoughts that are essential to the explanations we can sometimes confidently supply. Our manner of attributing attitudes ensures that all the expressive power of language can be used to make such distinctions. (Davidson 1975, pp. 15–16)

I agree with that. It remains true, however, that in the ordinary run of affairs, large families of beliefs travel together in our mental lives. At one instant, Mary believes that her purse is on the bed, *and* believes her handbag is on some horizontal surface, *and* believes that the item containing her comb is supported by the article of furniture one sleeps in, and so forth. Now do all (or many) of these distinct states have to light up and team up to cause Mary to run upstairs? Or is there just one each from the belief family and desire family that are chosen to do the work? If we cling to Fodor's "classical" view of propositional attitudes, these are the only alternatives, and they are exclusive. That is not to say that there couldn't be overdetermination (e.g., fourteen

beliefs and seven desires were ON at that time, but any pair were sufficient to cause the decision), but that there has to be a fact of the matter
about exactly which of these discrete beliefs and desires existed at the
time, and whether or not it did, or could, contribute to the causation
of the decision.

This is related to a point that Heil makes. Folk psychology recognizes, if you like, the holism of belief attribution in everyday life, and
in fact boggles at the suggestion that somebody could believe that her
handbag was on the bed and not believe any of these other propositions. The idea that you could believe one of these without believing
the others—and not just the obvious logical consequences of it, but all
of the pragmatic neighbors of it—is something that folk psychology
does not anticipate, because it is not as staunchly Realist about beliefs
and desires as Fodor is.

So it seems to me that the illusion of realism arises from the fact that
we don't just use folk psychology privately to anticipate—each one of
us—the behavior of each other. In contrast, if chimpanzees, for instance, use folk psychology (Premack, 1986) they don't talk about it.
They are *individual* folk psychologists, but we're not. We're *communal*
folk psychologists who are constantly explaining to other people why
we think that so and so is going to do such and such. We have to talk,
and when we talk, since life is short, we have to give an edited version
of what we're actually thinking, so what comes out is a few sentences.
Then of course it's only too easy to suppose that those sentences are
not mere edited abstractions or distillations from, but are rather something like copies of or translations of the very states in the minds of
the beings we're talking about.

The fact that we talk has, I claim, an obvious but interesting further
effect: since we talk, and write, we have all these sentences lying
around—our own and other people's. We hear them, we remember
them, we write them down, we speak them ourselves, and with regard
to any such sentence in our language that we encounter or create, we
have a problem: what to do with it. We can discard it, forget it, or we
can decide to put it in the pile labeled TRUE or the pile labeled FALSE.
And this, I claim, creates a rather different sort of specialized state,
what in *Brainstorms* I called opinions. These are not just beliefs; these
are linguistically infected states—only language users have them.
Opinions are essentially bets on the truth of sentences in a language
that we understand. My empirical hunch is that a proper cognitive
psychology is going to have to make a very sharp distinction between

beliefs and opinions, that the psychology of opinions is really going to be rather different from the psychology of beliefs, and that the sorts of architecture that will do very well by, say, nonlinguistic perceptual beliefs (you might say "animal" beliefs) is going to have to be supplemented rather substantially in order to handle opinions. And I think it is confusion on this score—more specifically the failure to distinguish between believing a certain sentence of your natural language is true, and having the sort of belief that that sentence might be used to express—that has given Fodor's Intentional Realism the run that it's had.

It occurs to me that a further feature of this line of thought that Churchland and Stich might like is that if I'm right about the distinction between beliefs and opinions, then the following dizzy prospect opens up: Scientists (connectionist heroes of the near future) might "come to the *opinion*" that there are no such things as beliefs, without thereby having to *believe* there were no such things! If connectionists are right, after all, they just are connectionist systems that on occasion make bets on the truth of various sentences of their natural language. All of their science goes on—at least the public communication and confirmation part of it—at the level of opinions. Although they do not have beliefs, they do have opinions, since they are still using sentences and hence committing themselves to the truth of some of them. But they wouldn't have to say they *believe* that a particular sentence is true; they would just . . . *connect* that it was! Because of the settings of their connectionist networks, they would put that sentence in the TRUE pile, but putting that sentence in the TRUE pile (even in the TRUE pile of sentences you keep stored in your head) is distinct from believing—on the folk psychological model. (Those of us who are not Fodorians about belief can go on talking about what these connectionists *believe*, but the Fodorians and Stichians among them can consistently be of the *opinion* that they never in fact believe anything!)

I want to say a bit more about connectionism, for I want to throw a few more pails of cold water on the euphoria expressed if not induced by the San Diego papers (Churchland, chap. 2; and Ramsey, Stich, and Garon, chap. 4 of *The Future of Folk Psychology*). First, however, I want to make some remarks in favor of connectionism that they do not quite make. Ramsey, Stich, and Garon claim that connectionism isn't just implementation at a lower level of a traditional, hierarchical model, and I want to say something more in favor of that. Here is why I think connectionism is exciting.

Suppose you have what Haugeland (1985) would call a GOFAI (Good Old-Fashioned Artificial Intelligence) nonconnectionist AI theory: It postulates a certain level at which there are symbolic structures in something like a language of thought, and it has some mechanism for computing over these. Then, indeed, it makes little difference how you implement that. It makes no difference whether you use a VAX or a Cray, a compiled or interpreted language. It makes no difference how you determine the implementation, because all of the transitions are already explicitly stated at the higher level. That is to say, in technical terms, you have a flow graph and not merely a flow chart, which means that *all* the transition regularities are stipulated at that level, leaving nothing further to design, and it is simply a matter of engineering to make sure that the transition regularities are maintained. It makes no sense to look at different implementations, for the same reason it makes no sense to look at two different copies of the same newspaper. You might get some minor differences of implementation speed or something like that, but that is not apt to be interesting, whereas the relationship between the symbolic or cognitive level and the implementation level in connectionist networks is not that way. It really makes sense to look at different implementations of the cognitive-level sketch because you are counting on features of those implementations to fix details of the transitions that actually aren't fixed at the cognitive level. You haven't specified an algorithm or flow graph at that level. Another way of looking at this is that in contrast to a classical system, where the last thing you want to have is noise in your implementation (i.e., you want to protect the system from noise) in a connectionist implementation you plan on exploiting noise. You want the noise to be there because it is actually going to be magnified or amplified in ways that are going to effect the actual transitions described at the cognitive level.

This becomes clear if you consider the hidden units in a connectionist network—such as those in the diagrams in chapter 4 of *The Future of Folk Psychology*. As Ramsey, Stich, and Garon note, if you subject those hidden units to careful statistical analysis (it is made easier if you view the results in one of Geoffrey Hinton's lovely diagrams showing which nodes are active under which circumstances), you can discover that a certain node is always ON whenever the subject is (let us say) dogs, and never (or very weakly) ON when the subject is cats, whereas another node is ON for cats and not ON for dogs. Other nodes, however, seem to have no interpretation at all. They have no semantics; they're just there. As far as semantics is concerned, they are just noise; sometimes they are strongly active and at other times weak, but these times don't seem to match up with any category of interest. As many skeptics about connectionism have urged, the former sorts of nodes are plausibly labeled the DOG node and the CAT node and so forth, and so it is tempting to say that we have symbols after all. Connectionism turns out to be just a disguised version of good old-fashioned, symbol-manipulating AI! Plausible as this is (and there must be *some* truth to the idea that certain nodes should be viewed as semantic specialists), there is another fact about such networks that undercuts the skeptics' claim in a most interesting way. The best reason for *not* calling the dog-active node the dog symbol is that you can "kill" or disable that node and the system will go right on discriminating dogs, remembering about dogs, and so forth, with at most a slight degradation in performance. It turns out, in other words, that all those other "noisy" nodes were carrying some of the load. What is more, if you keep the "symbol" nodes alive and kill the other, merely noisy nodes, the system *doesn't* work.

The point about this that seems to me most important is that at the computational level in a connectionist system, no distinction is made between symbols and nonsymbols. All are treated exactly alike at that level. The computational mechanism doesn't have to know which ones are the symbols. They are all the same. Some of them *we* (at a higher level) can see take on a role rather like symbols, but this is not a feature that makes a difference at the computational level. That is a very nice property. It's a property that is entirely contrary to the spirit of GOFAI, where the distinction between symbol and nonsymbol makes all the computational difference in the world.

Having offered my praise, let me turn to what worries me about connectionism. Both connectionist chapters exhibit connectionist networks which have input nodes, output nodes, and hidden units, but all their discussion is about the hidden units. We should pause to worry about the fact that some of the input units (for instance) look much too Fodorian. It looks indeed as if there is a language of thought being used to input *Dogs have fur* across the bottom of the system, for instance. It looks as if the inputs are organized into something altogether too much like Fodorian propositions. Could it be that the only reason we aren't seeing the language of thought was that we aren't looking at the much larger cognitive systems of which these bits of memory are just small subsystems?

This worry is analogous to a concern one can have about very traditional AI systems. For instance, Hector Levesque (1984) has described a knowledge representation system (in AI) with some lovely properties, but one of its *un*lovely properties is that there is only one way of putting something into the knowledge base, and there is only one thing the knowledge base can do. Everything goes in by an operation called TELL followed by a statement in the predicate calculus; the only thing the system can do is permit itself to be subjected to an ASK operation. I submit that any model of knowledge which can be updated or enriched only by writing a proposition using the TELL function and which can be used only by extracting from it a proposition via the ASK function is a hopelessly Fodorian sententialist model of a robust knowledge system.

But for all that the connectionist chapters show us, that is what we have in their connectionist models too. We have a memory for which there is a TELL and an ASK defined. No other way of tweaking it, or utilizing it, or updating it has yet been defined. This is a serious charge, which I should try to defend with a more specific example. Here, finally, is one more little experiment concerning the structure of human memory. The claim I want to substantiate by it is that what the connectionists have offered us is not an architecture for memory but at best an architecture for maybe a little subcomponent of memory. When we start making the memory more realistic, we are going to have to add some architectural details that will require some quite different principles.

Here are some questions—personal questions about your own memory—which you should attempt to answer as quickly as you can:

Have you ever danced with a movie star?

Have you ever been introduced to a white-haired lady whose first name begins with V?

Have you ever driven for more than seven miles behind a blue Chevrolet?

Most people have a swift yes or no answer to the first question, and draw a blank on the others. Imagine how different their responses would be to the following:

Have you ever been introduced to a green-haired lady whose first name begins with V?

Have you ever driven for more than seven miles behind a pink Rolls Royce?

First of all, according to anybody's theory of memory it is false that you have stored as Fodorian sentences: "I have never danced with a movie star," "I have never driven more than seven miles behind a pink Rolls Royce," and so forth, because that would lead to combinatorial explosion. Think of all the things you've never done, and know you've never done.

Any remotely sane theory of how you answer these questions has to be one which works this way: When you hear the question, it provokes your memory and either it succeeds in tweaking a recollection of an event meeting the condition or it doesn't. In the case of the first proposition, if no recollection comes back, you draw the meta-conclusion that *had you ever done it, you would now be recalling it* and since you are not now recalling it, the chances are that you never have danced with a movie star. The parallel meta-conclusion, however, is simply not plausible in the third case, because there is no reason to suppose that had you ever driven seven miles behind a blue Chevy, you would now be recalling it. In order to make sense of this very simple, robust feature of human memory, we have to suppose that human memory is organized in such a fashion that you can unconsciously assess the likelihood that the failure of your memory to produce a recollection for you is a sign—it can be treated on this occasion as a premise or datum—from which you unconsciously "infer" the conclusion: "I've never done that." That shows a complexity far beyond ASK and TELL that we can establish quite clearly as a feature of human memory. So a good cognitive psychology will have to model that. How can I build a model of human memory that has that rather nifty, easily demonstrated property? Nobody in *non*connectionist cognitive psychology has a good model of that, so far as I know, but then neither do the connectionists.

And until the connectionists can show that their marvelous new fabrics can be fashioned into larger objects exhibiting some of these molar properties of human psychology, we should temper our enthusiasm.

5   Real Patterns[1]

Although this essay is already highly accessible in the pages of the Journal of Philosophy, *it is utterly central to my thinking, and the arguments in it do not appear in any of my recent books, so I thought it must be included here. The discussion of varieties of realism continues in several essays, and in my lengthy reply to critics, "Get Real," in the special issue of* Philosophical Topics *(1994,* **22**, *1 and 2) devoted to my work.*

Are there really beliefs? Or are we learning (from neuroscience and psychology, presumably) that, strictly speaking, beliefs are figments of our imagination, items in a superseded ontology? Philosophers generally regard such ontological questions as admitting just two possible answers: either beliefs exist or they don't. There is no such state as quasi-existence; there are no stable doctrines of semirealism. Beliefs must either be vindicated along with the viruses or banished along with the banshees. A bracing conviction prevails, then, to the effect that when it comes to beliefs (and other mental items) one must be either a realist or an eliminative materialist.

1   Realism about Beliefs

This conviction prevails in spite of my best efforts over the years to undermine it with various analogies: are *voices* in your ontology? (Dennett, 1969, chap. 1) Are *centers of gravity* in your ontology? (Dennett, 1981a)

Originally appeared in *Journal of Philosophy*, LXXXVIII (1), Jan. 1991, pp. 27–51.
1. Thanks to Kathleen Akins, Akeel Bilgrami, Donald Davidson, Barbara Hannan, Douglas Hofstadter, Norton Nelkin, W.V.O. Quine, Richard Rorty, George Smith, Peter Suber, Stephen White, and the MIT / Tufts philosophy of psychology discussion group for the discussions that provoked and shaped this paper.

It is amusing to note that my analogizing beliefs to centers of gravity
has been attacked from both sides of the ontological dichotomy, by
philosophers who think it is simply obvious that centers of gravity are
useful fictions, and by philosophers who think it is simply obvious that
centers of gravity are perfectly real:

The trouble with these supposed parallels . . . is that they are all strictly speaking *false,* although they are no doubt useful simplifications for many purposes.
It is false, for example, that the gravitational attraction between the Earth and
the Moon involves two point masses; but it is a good enough first approximation for many calculations. However, this is not at all what Dennett really
wants to say about intentional states. For he insists that to adopt the intentional
stance and interpret an agent as acting on certain beliefs and desires is to discern a pattern in his actions which is genuinely there (a pattern which is missed
if we instead adopt a scientific stance): Dennett certainly does not hold that
the role of intentional ascriptions is merely to give us a useful approximation
to a truth that can be more accurately expressed in non-intentional terms.
(Smith, 1988, p. 22)

Compare this with Dretske's equally confident assertion of realism:

I am a realist about centers of gravity. . . . The earth obviously exerts a gravitational attraction on *all* parts of the moon—not just its center of gravity. The
resultant force, a vector sum, acts through a point, but this is something quite
different. One should be very clear about what centers of gravity are *before*
deciding whether to be literal about them, *before* deciding whether or not to
be a center-of-gravity realist (Dretske, 1988, p. 511–512).

Dretske's advice is well taken. What are centers of gravity? They
are mathematical points—abstract objects or what Hans Reichenbach
called *abstracta*—definable in terms of physical forces and other properties. The question of whether abstract objects are real—the question
of whether or not "one should be a realist about them"—can take two
different paths, which we might call the metaphysical and the scientific.
The metaphysical path simply concerns the reality or existence of abstract objects generally, and does not distinguish them in terms of their
scientific utility. Consider, for instance, the *center of population* of the
United States. I define this as the mathematical point at the intersection
of the two lines such that there are as many inhabitants north as south
of the latitude, and as many inhabitants east as west of the longitude.
This point is (or can be) just as precisely defined as the center of gravity
or center of mass of an object. (Since these median strips might turn
out to be wide, take the midline of each strip as the line; count as inhabitants all those within the territorial waters and up to twenty miles in

altitude—orbiting astronauts don't count—and take each inhabitant's navel to be the determining point, etc.) I do not know the center of population's current geographic location, but I am quite sure it is west of where it was ten years ago. It jiggles around constantly, as people move about, taking rides on planes, trains and automobiles, etc. I doubt that this abstract object is of any value at all in any scientific theory, but just in case it is, here is an even more trivial abstract object: Dennett's lost sock center: the point defined as the center of the smallest sphere that can be inscribed around all the socks I have ever lost in my life.

These abstract objects have the same metaphysical status as centers of gravity. Is Dretske a realist about them all? Should we be? I don't intend to pursue this question, for I suspect that Dretske is—and we should be—more interested in the scientific path to realism: centers of gravity are real because they are (somehow) *good* abstract objects. They deserve to be taken seriously, learned about, used. If we go so far as to distinguish them as *real* (contrasting them, perhaps, with those abstract objects that are *bogus*), that is because we think they serve in perspicuous representations of real forces, "natural" properties, and the like. This path brings us closer, in any case, to the issues running in the debates about the reality of beliefs.

I have claimed that beliefs are best considered to be abstract objects rather like centers of gravity. Smith considers centers of gravity to be useful fictions while Dretske considers them to be useful (and hence?) real abstractions, and each takes his view to constitute a criticism of my position. The optimistic assessment of these opposite criticisms is that they cancel each other out; my analogy must have hit the nail on the head. The pessimistic assessment is that more needs to be said to convince philosophers that a mild and intermediate sort of realism is a positively attractive position, and not just the desperate dodge of ontological responsibility it has sometimes been taken to be. I have just such a case to present, a generalization and extension of my earlier attempts, via the concept of a *pattern*. My aim on this occasion is not so much to prove that my intermediate doctrine about the reality of psychological states is right, but just that it is quite possibly right, because a parallel doctrine is demonstrably right about some simpler cases.

We use folk psychology—interpretation of each other as believers, wanters, intenders, and the like—to predict what people will do next. Prediction isn't the only thing we care about, of course. Folk psychology helps us understand and empathize with others, organize our memories, interpret our emotions, and flavor our vision in a thousand ways, but at the heart of all these is the enormous predictive leverage of folk psychology. Without its predictive power, we could have no interpersonal projects or relations at all; human activity would be just so much Brownian motion; we would be baffling ciphers to each other and to ourselves—we could not even conceptualize our own flailings. In what follows I will concentrate always on folk-psychological prediction, not because I make the mistake of ignoring all the other interests we have in people aside from making bets on what they will do next, but because I claim that our power to *interpret* the actions of others depends on our power—seldom explicitly exercised—to predict them.[2]

Where utter patternlessness or randomness prevails, nothing is predictable. The success of folk-psychological prediction, like the success of any prediction, depends on there being some order or pattern in the world to exploit. Exactly where in the world does this pattern exist? What is the pattern a pattern *of?* (Nelkin, 1994). Some have thought, with Fodor, that the pattern of belief must in the end be a pattern of structures in the brain, formulae written in the language of thought. Where else could it be? Gibsonians might say the pattern is "in the light"—and Quinians (such as Davidson and I) could almost agree: the pattern is discernible in agents' (observable) behavior when we subject it to "radical interpretation" (Davidson) "from the intentional stance" (Dennett).

When are the elements of a pattern real and not merely apparent? Answering this question will help us resolve the misconceptions that have led to the proliferation of "ontological positions" about beliefs, the different grades or kinds of realism. I will concentrate on five salient exemplars arrayed in the space of possibilities: Fodor's industrial strength Realism (he writes it with a capital "R"); Davidson's regular strength realism; my mild realism; Rorty's milder-than-mild irrealism, according to which the pattern is *only* in the eyes of the beholders, and

---

2. R.A. Sharpe (1989, pp. 233–240) takes me to task on this point, using examples from Proust to drive home the point that "Proust draws our attention to possible lives and these possible lives are various. But in none of them is prediction of paramount importance." (p.240) I agree. I also agree that what makes people interesting (in novels and in real life) is precisely their unpredictability. But that unpredictability is only interesting against the backdrop of routine predictability on which all interpretation depends. As I note in *The Intentional Stance* (p. 79) in response to a similar objection of Fodor's, the same is true of chess: the game is interesting only because of the unpredictability of one's opponent, but that is to say: the intentional stance can usually eliminate *only* ninety percent of the legal moves.

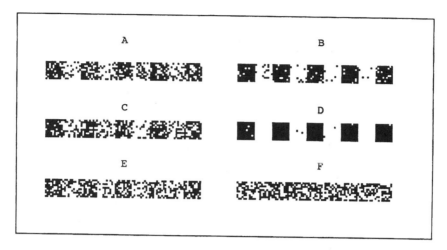

Figure 5.1

Paul Churchland's eliminative materialism, which denies the reality of beliefs altogether.

In what follows, I will assume that these disagreements all take place within an arena of common acceptance of what Arthur Fine calls NOA, the natural ontological attitude (Fine, 1986; see esp. p. 153n, and his comments there on Rorty, which I take to be consonant with mine here). That is, I take the interest in these disagreements to lie not in differences of opinion about the ultimate metaphysical status of physical things or abstract things (e.g., electrons or centers of gravity), but in differences of opinion about whether beliefs and other mental states are, shall we say, *as real as* electrons or centers of gravity. I want to show that mild realism is the doctrine that makes the most sense when what we are talking about is real patterns, such as the real patterns discernible from the intentional stance (Dennett, 1987, pp. 38–42, "Real Patterns, deeper fact, and empty questions").

In order to make clear the attractions and difficulties of these different positions about patterns, I will apply them first to a much simpler, more readily visualized, and uncontroversial sort of pattern.

2 The Reality of Patterns

Consider the six objects in figure 5.1 (which I will call *frames*).

We can understand a frame to be a finite subset of data, a window on an indefinitely larger world of further data. In one sense A–F all display different patterns; if you look closely you will see that no two frames are exactly alike ("atom-for-atom replicas," if you like). In another sense, A–F all display the same pattern; they were all made by the same basic process, a printing of ten rows of ninety dots, ten black dots followed by ten white dots, etc. The overall effect is to create five equally spaced vertical black bars in the window. I take it that this pattern, which I will dub *bar-code,* is a real pattern if anything is. But some random (actually pseudo-random) "noise" has been allowed to interfere with the actual printing: The noise ratio is as follows:

A: 25%   B: 10%
C: 25%   D: 1%
E: 33%   F: 50%

It is impossible to see that F is not purely (pseudo-) random noise; you will just have to take my word for it that it was actually generated by the same program that generated the other five patterns; all I changed was the noise ratio.

Now what does it mean to say that a pattern in one of these frames is real, or that it is really there? Given our privileged information about how these frames were generated, we may be tempted to say that there is a single pattern in all six cases—even in F, where it is "indiscernible." But I propose that the self-contradictory air of "indiscernible pattern" should be taken seriously. We may be able to make some extended, or metaphorical, sense of the idea of indiscernible patterns (or invisible pictures or silent symphonies), but in the root case a pattern is "by definition" a candidate for pattern *recognition.* (It is this loose but unbreakable link to observers or perspectives, of course, that makes "pattern" an attractive term to someone perched between instrumentalism and industrial strength Realism.)

Fortunately, there is a standard way of making these intuitions about the discernibility-in-principle of patterns precise. Consider the task of transmitting information about one of the frames from one place to another. How many bits of information will it take to transmit each frame? The least efficient method is simply to send the "bit map," which identifies each dot *seriatim* ("dot one is black, dot two is white, dot three is white, . . ."). For a black-and-white frame of 900 dots (or pixels, as they are called), the transmission requires 900 bits. Sending the bit map is in effect verbatim quotation, accurate but inefficient. Its most important virtue is that it is equally capable of transmitting any pattern or any particular instance of utter patternlessness.

Gregory Chaitin's (1975, pp. 47–52)valuable definition of mathematical randomness invokes this idea. A series (of dots or numbers or whatever) is random if and only if the information required to describe (transmit) the series accurately is *incompressible:* nothing shorter than the verbatim bit map will preserve the series. Then a series is not random—has a pattern—if and only if there is some more efficient way of describing it.[3] Frame D, for instance, can be described as "ten rows of ninety: ten black followed by ten white, etc., *with the following exceptions:* dots 57, 88, ..." This expression, suitably encoded, is much shorter than 900 bits long. The comparable expressions for the other frames will be proportionally longer, since they will have to mention, verbatim, more exceptions, and the degeneracy of the "pattern" in F is revealed by the fact that its description in this system will be no improvement over the bit map—in fact it will tend on average to be trivially longer, since it takes some bits to describe the pattern that is then obliterated by all the exceptions.

Of course there are bound to be other ways of describing the evident patterns in these frames, and some will be more efficient than others—in the precise sense of being systematically specifiable in less bits.[4] Any such description, if an improvement over the bit map, is the description of a real pattern in the data.[5]

---

3. More precisely: "A series of numbers is random if the smallest algorithm capable of specifying it to a computer has about the same number of bits of information as the series itself" (Chaitin, 1975, p. 48). This is what explains the fact that the "random number generator" built into most computers is not really properly named, since it is some function describable in a few bits (a little subroutine that is called for some output whenever a program requires a "random" number or series). If I send you the description of the pseudo-random number generator on my computer, you can use it to generate exactly the same infinite series of random-seeming digits.

4. Such schemes for efficient description, called compression algorithms, are widely used in computer graphics for saving storage space. They break the screen into uniformly colored regions, for instance, and specify region boundaries (rather like the "paint by numbers" line drawings sold in craft shops). The more complicated the picture on the screen, the longer the compressed description will be; in the worst case (a picture of confetti randomly sprinkled over the screen) the compression algorithm will be stumped, and can do no better than a verbatim bit map.

5. What about the "system" of pattern description that simply baptizes frames with proper names (A through F, in this case) and tells the receiver which frame is up by simply sending "F"? This looks much shorter than the bit map until we consider that such a description must be part of an entirely general system. How many proper names will we need to name all possible 900–dot frames? Trivially, the 900–bit binary number, 11111111. . . . To send the "worst-case" proper name will take exactly as many bits as sending the bit map. This confirms our intuition that proper names are maximally inefficient ways of couching generalizations ("Alf is tall and Bill is tall and. . . .").

Consider bar-code, the particular pattern seen in A–E, and almost perfectly instantiated in D. *That* pattern is quite readily discernible to the naked human eye in these presentations of the data, because of the particular pattern-recognition machinery hard-wired in our visual systems—edge detectors, luminance detectors, and the like. But the very same data (the very same streams of bits) presented in some other format might well yield no hint of pattern to us, especially in the cases where bar-code is contaminated by salt and pepper, as in frames A through C. For instance, if we broke the 900–bit series of frame B into 4–bit chunks, and then translated each of these into hexadecimal notation, one would be hard pressed indeed to tell the resulting series of hexadecimal digits from a random series, since the hexadecimal chunking would be seriously out of phase with the decimal pattern—and hence the "noise" would not "stand out" as noise. There are myriad ways of displaying any 900–bit series of data points, and not many of them would inspire us to concoct an efficient description of the series. Other creatures with different sense organs, or different interests, might readily perceive patterns that were imperceptible to us. The patterns would be *there* all along, but just invisible to *us*.

The idiosyncracy of perceivers' capacities to discern patterns is striking. Visual patterns with axes of vertical symmetry stick out like sore thumbs for us, but if one simply rotates the frame a few degrees, the symmetry is often utterly beyond noticing. And the "perspectives" from which patterns are "perceptible" are not restricted to variations on presentation to the sense modalities. Differences in knowledge yield striking differences in the capacity to pick up patterns. Expert chess players can instantly perceive (and subsequently recall with high accuracy) the total board position in a real game, but are much worse at recall if the same chess pieces are randomly placed on the board, even though to a novice both boards are equally hard to recall (de Groot, 1965). This should not surprise anyone who considers that an expert speaker of English would have much less difficulty perceiving and recalling

The frightened cat struggled to get loose.

than

Te ser.iogsehnde t srugfsalde go tgtt ole

which contains the same pieces, now somewhat disordered. Expert chess players, unlike novices, not only know how to *play* chess; they know how to *read* chess—how to see the patterns at a glance.

A pattern exists in some data—is real—if *there is* a description of the data that is more efficient than the bit map, whether or not anyone can concoct it. Compression algorithms, as general-purpose pattern-describers, are efficient ways of transmitting exact copies of frames, such as A–F, from one place to another, but our interests often favor a somewhat different goal: transmitting *inexact* copies that nevertheless preserve "the" pattern that is important to us. For some purposes, we need not list the exceptions to bar-code, but only transmit the information that the pattern is bar-code with $n\%$ noise. Following this strategy, frames A and C, though discernibly different under careful inspection, count as *the same pattern,* since what matters to us is that the pattern is bar-code with 25% noise, and we don't care which particular noise occurs, only that it occurs.

Sometimes we are interested in not just ignoring the noise, but eliminating it, improving the pattern in transmission. Copy-editing is a good example. Consider the likely effect thes santince wull hive hod on tha cupy adutor whu preparis thas monescrupt fur prunteng. *My* interest in this particular instance is that the "noise" be transmitted, not removed, though I actually don't care exactly *which* noise is there.

Here then are three different attitudes we take at various times toward patterns. Sometimes we care about exact description or reproduction of detail, at whatever cost. From this perspective, a real pattern in frame A is *bar-code with the following exceptions: 7, 8, 11, ...* At other times we care about the noise, but not where in particular it occurs. From this perspective, a real pattern in frame A is *bar-code with 25% noise.* And sometimes, we simply tolerate or ignore the noise. From this perspective, a real pattern in frame A is simply: *bar-code.* But is bar-code really there in frame A? I am tempted to respond: Look! You can see it with your own eyes. But there is something more constructive to say as well.

When two individuals confront the same data, they may perceive different patterns in it, but since we can have varied interests and perspectives, these differences do not all count as disagreements. Or in any event they should not. If Jones sees pattern α (with $n\%$ noise) and Brown sees pattern β (with $m\%$ noise) there may be no ground for determining that one of them is right and the other wrong. Suppose they are both using their patterns to bet on the next datum in the series. Jones bets according to the "pure" pattern α, but budgets for $n\%$ errors when he looks for odds. Brown does likewise, using pattern (. If both patterns are real, they will both get rich. That is to say, so long as they use their expectation of deviations from the "ideal" to temper their odds policy, they will do better than chance—perhaps very much better.

Now suppose they compare notes. Suppose that α is a simple, easy-to-calculate pattern, but with a high noise rate—for instance, suppose α is bar-code as it appears in frame E. And suppose that Brown has found some periodicity or progression in the "random" noise that Jones just tolerates, so that β is a much more complicated description of pattern-superimposed-on-pattern. This permits Brown to do better than chance, we may suppose, at predicting when the "noise" will come. As a result, Brown budgets for a lower error rate—say only 5%. "What you call noise, Jones, is actually pattern," Brown might say. "Of course there is still *some* noise in my pattern, but my pattern is better— more real—than yours! Yours is actually just a mere appearance." Jones might well reply that it is all a matter of taste; he notes how hard Brown has to work to calculate predictions, and points to the fact that he is getting just as rich (or maybe richer) by using a simpler, sloppier system and making more bets at good odds than Brown can muster. "My pattern is perfectly real—look how rich I'm getting. If it were an illusion, I'd be broke."

This crass way of putting things—in terms of betting and getting rich—is simply a vivid way of drawing attention to a real, and far from crass, tradeoff that is ubiquitous in nature, and hence in folk psychology. Would we prefer an extremely compact pattern description with a high noise ratio or a less compact pattern description with a lower noise ratio? Our decision may depend on how swiftly and reliably we can discern the simple pattern, how dangerous errors are, how much of our resources we can afford to allocate to detection and calculation. These "design decisions" are typically not left to us to make by individual and deliberate choices; they are incorporated into the design of our sense organs by genetic evolution, and into our culture by cultural evolution. The product of this design evolution process is what Sellars calls our *manifest image* (Sellars, 1963), and it is composed of folk physics, folk psychology, and the other pattern-making perspectives we have on the buzzing blooming confusion that bombards us with data. The ontology generated by the manifest image has thus a deeply pragmatic source.[6]

---

6. William Wimsatt (1980, pp. 287–329) offers a nice example (p.296): while the insectivorous bird tracks individual insects, the anteater just averages over the ant-infested area; one might say that while the bird's manifest image quantifies over insects, "ant" is a

Do these same pragmatic considerations apply to the scientific image, widely regarded as the final arbiter of ontology? Science is supposed to carve nature at the joints—at the *real* joints, of course. Is it permissible in science to adopt a carving system so simple that it makes sense to tolerate occasional misdivisions and consequent mispredictions? It happens all the time. The ubiquitous practice of using idealized models is exactly a matter of trading off reliability and accuracy of prediction against computational tractability. A particularly elegant and handy oversimplification may under some circumstances be irresistible. The use of Newtonian rather than Einsteinian mechanics in most mundane scientific and engineering calculations is an obvious example. A tractable oversimplification may be attractive even in the face of a high error rate; considering inherited traits to be carried by single genes "for" those traits is an example; considering agents in the marketplace to be perfectly rational self-aggrandizers with perfect information is another.

3   Patterns in Life

The time has come to export these observations about patterns and reality to the controversial arena of belief attribution. The largish leap we must make is nicely expedited by pausing at a stepping stone example midway between the world of the dot frames and the world of folk psychology: John Horton Conway's Game of Life. In my opinion, every philosophy student should be held responsible for an intimate acquaintance with the Game of Life. It should be considered an essential tool in every thought-experimenter's kit, a prodigiously versatile generator of philosophically important examples and thought experiments of admirable clarity and vividness. In *The Intentional Stance,* I briefly exploited it to make a point about the costs and benefits of risky prediction from the intentional stance (1987, pp. 37–39), but I have since learned that I presumed too much familiarity with the underlying ideas. Here, then, is a somewhat expanded basic introduction to Life.[7]

---

mass term for anteaters. See the discussion of this and related examples in my *Elbow Room* (1984d), pp. 108–110.

7. Martin Gardner introduced the Game of Life to a wide audience in two columns in *Scientific American* in October, 1970, and February, 1971. Poundstone (1985) is an excellent exploration of the game and its philosophical implications. The two figures above are reproduced from Poundstone's book, with kind permission from the author and publisher.

Life is played on a two-dimensional grid, such as a checkerboard or
a computer screen; it is not a game one plays to win; if it is a game at
all, it is solitaire. The grid divides space into square cells, and each cell
is either ON or OFF at each moment. Each cell has eight neighbors: the
four adjacent cells north, south, east, and west, and the four diagonals:
northeast, southeast, southwest, and northwest. Time in the Life world
is also discrete, not continuous; it advances in ticks, and the state of
the world changes between each tick according to the following rule:

Each cell, in order to determine what to do in the next instant, counts how
many of its eight neighbors is ON at the present instant. If the answer is exactly
two, the cell stays in its present state (ON or OFF) in the next instant. If the
answer is exactly three, the cell is ON in the next instant whatever its current
state. Under all other conditions the cell is OFF.

The entire physics of the Life world is captured in that single, unex-
ceptioned law. (While this is the fundamental law of the "physics" of
the Life world, it helps at first to conceive this curious physics in biological terms: think of cells going ON as births, cells going OFF as deaths,
and succeeding instants as generations. Either overcrowding [more
than three inhabited neighbors] or isolation [less than two inhabited
neighbors] leads to death.) By the scrupulous application of this single
law, one can predict with perfect accuracy the next instant of any configuration of ON and OFF cells, and the instant after that, and so forth.
In other words, the Life world is a toy world that perfectly instantiates
Laplace's vision of determinism: given the state description of this
world at an instant, we finite observers can perfectly predict the future
instants by the simple application of our one law of physics. Or, in my
terms, when we adopt the physical stance toward a configuration in
the Life world, our powers of prediction are perfect: there is no noise,
no uncertainty, no probability less than one. Moreover, it follows from
the two-dimensionality of the Life world that nothing is hidden from
view. There is no backstage; there are no hidden variables; the unfolding of the physics of objects in the Life world is directly and completely visible.

There are computer simulations of the Life world in which one can
set up configurations on the screen and then watch them evolve according to the single rule. In the best simulations, one can change the
scale of both time and space, alternating between close-up and bird's-
eye view. A nice touch added to some color versions is that ON cells
(often just called pixels) are color-coded by their age; they are born

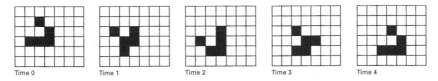

Time 0   Time 1   Time 2   Time 3   Time 4

Figure 5.2

blue, let us say, and then change color each generation, moving through green to yellow to orange to red to brown to black and then staying black unless they die. This permits one to see at a glance how old certain patterns are, which cells are co-generational, where the birth action is, and so forth.[8]

One soon discovers that some simple configurations are more interesting than others. In addition to those configurations that never change—the "still lifes" such as four pixels in a square—and those that evaporate entirely—such as any long diagonal line segment, whose two tail pixels die of isolation each instant until the line disappears entirely—there are configurations with all manner of periodicity. Three pixels in a line make a simple flasher, which becomes three pixels in a column in the next instant, and reverts to three in a line in the next, ad infinitum, unless some other configuration encroaches. Encroachment is what makes Life interesting: among the periodic configurations are some that swim, amoeba-like, across the plane. The simplest is the glider, the five-pixel configuration shown taking a single stroke to the southeast in figure 5.2.

Then there are the eaters, the puffer trains and space rakes, and a host of other aptly named denizens of the Life world that emerge in the ontology of a new level, analogous to what I have called the design level. This level has its own language, a transparent foreshortening of the tedious descriptions one could give at the physical level. For instance:

An eater can eat a glider in four generations. Whatever is being consumed, the basic process is the same. A bridge forms between the eater and its prey. In the next generation, the bridge region dies from overpopulation, taking a bite out of both eater and prey. The eater then repairs itself. The prey usually cannot. If the remainder of the prey dies out as with the glider, the prey is consumed. (Poundstone, 1985, p. 38)

---

8. Poundstone (1985) provides simple BASIC and IBM-PC assembly language simulations you can copy for your own home computer, and describes some of the interesting variations.

Note that there has been a distinct ontological shift as we move between levels; whereas at the physical level there is no motion, and the only individuals, cells, are defined by their fixed spatial location, at this design level we have the motion of persisting objects; it is one and the same glider that has moved southeast in figure 5.2, changing shape as it moves, and there is one less glider in the world after the eater has eaten it in figure 5.3. (Here is a warming up exercise for what is to follow: should we say that there is *real* motion in the Life world, or only *apparent* motion? The flashing pixels on the computer screen are a paradigm case, after all, of what a psychologist would call apparent motion. Are there *really* gliders that move, or are there just patterns of cell state that move? And if we opt for the latter, should we say at least that these moving patterns are real?)

Notice too that at this level one proposes generalizations that require "usually" or "provided nothing encroaches" clauses. Stray bits of debris from earlier events can "break" or "kill" one of the objects in the ontology at this level; their *salience as real things* is considerable, but not guaranteed. To say that their salience is considerable is to say that one can, with some small risk, ascend to this design level, adopt its ontology, and proceed to predict—sketchily and riskily—the behavior of larger configurations or systems of configurations, without bothering to compute the physical level. For instance, one can set oneself the task of designing some interesting supersystem out of the "parts" that the design level makes available. Surely the most impressive triumph of this design activity in the Life world is the proof that a working model of a universal Turing machine can in principle be constructed in the Life plane! Von Neumann had already shown that in principle a two-dimensional universal Turing machine could be constructed out of cellular automata, so it was "just" a matter of "engineering" to show how, in principle, it could be constructed out of the simpler cellular automata defined in the Life world. Glider streams can

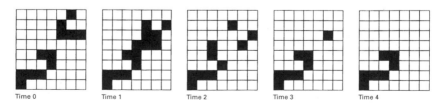

Time 0   Time 1   Time 2   Time 3   Time 4

Figure 5.3

provide the tape, for instance, and the tape-reader can be some huge assembly of still-lifes, eaters, gliders, and other bits and pieces. What does it look like? Poundstone calculates that the whole construction, a self-reproducing machine incorporating a universal Turing machine, would be on the order of 10^{13} pixels.

Displaying a 10^{13}–pixel pattern would require a video screen about 3 million pixels across at least. Assume the pixels are 1 millimeter square (which is very high resolution by the standards of home computers). Then the screen would have to be 3 kilometers (about two miles) across. It would have an area about six times that of Monaco.
  Perspective would shrink the pixels of a self-reproducing pattern to invisibility. If you got far enough away from the screen so that the entire pattern was comfortably in view, the pixels (and even the gliders, eaters and guns) would be too tiny to make out. A self-reproducing pattern would be a hazy glow, like a galaxy. (Poundstone, 1985, pp. 227–228)

Now since the universal Turing machine can compute any computable function, it can play chess—simply by mimicking the program of any chess-playing computer you like. Suppose, then, that such an entity occupies the Life plane, playing chess against itself. Looking at the configuration of dots that accomplishes this marvel would almost certainly be unilluminating to anyone who had no clue that a configuration with such powers could exist. But from the perspective of one who had the hypothesis that this huge array of black dots was a chess-playing computer, enormously efficient ways of predicting the future of that configuration are made available. As a first step one can shift from an ontology of gliders and eaters to an ontology of symbols and machine states, and, adopting this higher design stance toward the configuration, predict its future *as* a Turing machine. As a second and still more efficient step, one can shift to an ontology of chess board positions, possible chess moves, and the grounds for evaluating them; then, adopting the intentional stance toward the configuration, one can predict its future *as* a chess player performing intentional actions—making chess moves and trying to achieve checkmate. Once one has fixed on an interpretation scheme, permitting one to say which configurations of pixels count as which symbols (either, at the Turing machine level, the symbols "0" or "1," say, or at the intentional level, "QxBch" and the other symbols for chess moves), one can use the interpretation scheme to predict, for instance, that the next configuration to emerge from the galaxy will be such-and-such a glider stream (the symbols for "RxQ," say). There is risk involved in either case, because the chess program being run on the Turing machine may be far from perfectly rational, and, at a different level, debris may wander onto the scene and "break" the Turing machine configuration before it finishes the game.

In other words, real but (potentially) noisy patterns abound in such a configuration of the Life World, there for the picking up if only we are lucky or clever enough to hit on the right perspective. They are not *visual* patterns but, one might say, *intellectual* patterns. Squinting or twisting the page is not apt to help, while posing fanciful interpretations (or what W. V. O. Quine would call "analytical hypotheses") may uncover a goldmine. The opportunity confronting the observer of such a Life world is analogous to the opportunity confronting the cryptographer staring at a new patch of cipher text, or the opportunity confronting the Martian, peering through a telescope at the Superbowl Game. If the Martian hits on the intentional stance—or folk psychology—as the right level to look for pattern, shapes will readily emerge through the noise.

4   The Reality of Intentional Patterns

The scale of compression when one adopts the intentional stance toward the two-dimensional chess-playing computer-galaxy is stupendous: it is the difference between figuring out in your head what white's most likely (best) move is versus calculating the state of a few trillion pixels through a few hundred thousand generations. But the scale of the savings is really no greater in the Life world than in our own. Predicting that someone will duck if you throw a brick at him is easy from the folk psychological stance; it is and will always be intractable if you have to trace the photons from brick to eyeball, the neurotransmitters from optic nerve to motor nerve, and so forth.

For such vast computational leverage one might be prepared to pay quite a steep price in errors, but in fact one belief that is shared by all of the representatives on the spectrum I am discussing is that "folk psychology" provides a description system that permits highly reliable prediction of human (and much nonhuman) behavior.[9] They differ in

---

9. To see that the opposite poles share this view, see Fodor (1987), chapter 1, "Introduction: the Persistence of the Attitudes, " and Churchland (1979), especially p. 100: "For the P-theory [folk psychology] is in fact a marvelous intellectual achievement. It gives its possessor an explicit and systematic insight into the behaviour, verbal and otherwise, of some of the most complex agents in the environment, and its overall prowess in that

the explanations they offer of this predictive prowess, and the implications they see in it about "realism."

For Fodor, an industrial strength Realist, beliefs and their kin would not be real unless the pattern dimly discernible from the perspective of folk psychology could also be discerned (more clearly, with less noise) as a pattern of structures in the brain. The pattern would have to be discernible from the different perspective provided by a properly tuned *syntactoscope* aimed at the purely formal (nonsemantic) features of Mentalese terms written in the brain. For Fodor, the pattern seen through the noise by everyday folk psychologists would tell us nothing about reality, unless it, and the noise, had the following sort of explanation: what we discern from the perspective of folk psychology is the net effect of two processes: an ulterior, hidden process wherein the pattern exists quite pure, overlaid, and partially obscured by various intervening sources of noise: performance errors, observation errors, and other more or less random obstructions. He might add that the interior belief-producing process was in this respect *just* like the process responsible for the creation of frames A–F. If you were permitted to peer behind the scenes at the program I devised to create the frames, you would see, clear as a bell, the perfect bar-code periodicity, with the noise thrown on afterwards like so much salt and pepper.

This is often the explanation for the look of a data set in science, and Fodor may think that it is either the only explanation that can ever be given, or at any rate the only one that makes any sense of the success of folk psychology. But the rest of us disagree. As G. E. M. Anscombe put it in her pioneering exploration of intentional explanation, "if Aristotle's account [of reasoning using the practical syllogism] were supposed to describe actual mental processes, it would in general be quite absurd. The interest of the account is that it describes an order which is there whenever actions are done with intentions . . ." (Anscombe, 1957, p. 80).

But how *could* the order be there, so visible amidst the noise, if it were not the direct outline of a concrete orderly process in the background? Well, it *could* be there thanks to the statistical effect of very many concrete minutiae producing, as if by a hidden hand, an approximation of the "ideal" order. Philosophers have tended to ignore a variety of regularity intermediate between the regularities of planets and

---

respect remains unsurpassed by anything else our considerable theoretical efforts have produced."

other objects "obeying" the laws of physics and the regularities of rule-following (that is, rule-*consulting*) systems.[10] These intermediate regularities are those that are preserved under selection pressure: the regularities dictated by principles of good design and hence homed in on by self-designing systems. That is, a "rule of thought" may be much more than a mere regularity; it may be a *wise* rule, a rule one would design a system by if one were a system designer, and hence a rule one would expect self-designing systems to "discover" in the course of settling into their patterns of activity. Such rules no more need be explicitly represented than do the principles of aerodynamics honored in the design of birds' wings.[11]

The contrast between these different sorts of pattern-generation processes can be illustrated. The frames in figure 5.1 were created by a hard-edged process (ten black, ten white, ten black, . . .) obscured by noise, while the frames in figure 5.4 were created by a process almost the reverse of that: the top frame shows a pattern created by a normal distribution of black dots around means at $x = 10, 30, 50, 70,$ and 90 (rather like Mach bands or interference fringes); the middle and bottom frames were created by successive applications of a very simple contrast-enhancer applied to the top frame: a vertical slit "window" is thrown randomly onto the frame; the pixels in the window vote, and majority rules. This gradually removes the salt from the pepper and

---

10. A notable early exception is Wilfrid Sellars (1954, pp. 204–228) who discussed the importance of just this sort of regularity. See especially the subsection of this classic paper, entitled "Pattern Governed and Rule Obeying Behavior, " reprinted in Sellars (1963, pp. 324–327).

11. Several interpreters of a draft of this article have supposed that the conclusion I am urging here is that beliefs (or their contents) are *epiphenomena* having no causal powers, but this is a misrepresentation traceable to a simplistic notion of causation. If one finds a predictive pattern of the sort just described one has ipso facto discovered a causal power—a difference in the world that makes a subsequent difference testable by standard empirical methods of variable manipulation. Consider the crowd-drawing power of a sign reading "Free Lunch" placed in the window of a restaurant, and compare its power in a restaurant in New York to its power in a restaurant in Tokyo. The intentional level is obviously the right level at which to predict and explain such causal powers; the sign more reliably produces a particular belief in one population of perceivers than in the other, and variations in the color of typography of the sign are not as predictive of variations in crowd-drawing power as are variations in (perceivable) meaning. The fact that the regularities on which these successful predictions are based are efficiently capturable (only) in intentional terms and are not derived from "covering laws" does not show that the regularities are not "causal"; it just shows that philosophers have often relied on pinched notions of causality derived from exclusive attention to a few examples drawn from physics and chemistry. George Smith has pointed out to me that here I am echoing Aristotle's claim that his predecessors had ignored final causes.

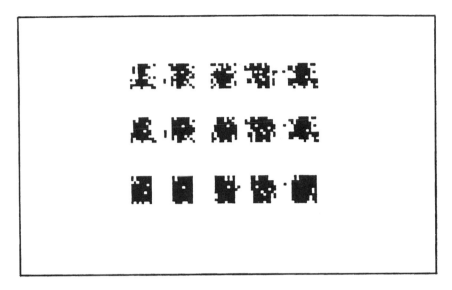

Figure 5.4

the pepper from the salt, creating "artifact" edges such as those discernible in the bottom frame. The effect would be more striking at a finer pixel scale, where the black merges imperceptibly through greys to white but I chose to keep the scale at the ten-pixel period of bar-code.

I do not mean to suggest that it is impossible to tell the patterns in figure 5.4 from the patterns in figure 5.1. Of course it is possible; for one thing, the process that produced the frames in figure 5.1 will almost always show edges at exactly 10, 20, 30, . . . and almost never at 9, 11, 19, 21, . . . while there is a higher probability of these "displaced" edges being created by the process of figure 5.4 (as a close inspection of figure 5.4 reveals). Fine tuning could of course reduce these probabilities, but that is not my point. My point is that *even if* the evidence is substantial that the discernible pattern is produced by one process rather than another, it can be rational to ignore those differences and use the simplest pattern-description (e.g., *bar-code*) as one's way of organizing the data.

Fodor and others have claimed that an interior language of thought is the best explanation of the hard edges visible in "propositional attitude psychology." Churchland and I have offered an alternative explanation of these edges, an explanation for which the process that produced the frames in figure 5.4 is a fine visual metaphor. The process that produces the data of folk psychology, we claim, is one in which the multidimensional complexities of the underlying processes are projected *through linguistic behavior,* which creates an appearance of definiteness and precision, thanks to the discreteness of words.[12] As Churchland puts it, a person's declarative utterance is a "one-dimensional *projection*—through the compound lens of Wernicke's and Broca's areas onto the idiosyncratic surface of the speaker's language—a one-dimensional projection of a four- or five-dimensional 'solid' that is an element in his true kinematic state." (Churchland, 1981, p. 85)

Fodor's industrial strength Realism takes beliefs to be things in the head—just like cells and blood vessels and viruses. Davidson and I both like Churchland's alternative idea of propositional attitude statements as indirect "measurements" of a reality diffused in the behavioral dispositions of the brain (and body).[13] We think beliefs are quite real enough to call real just so long as belief-talk measures these complex behavior-disposing organs as predictively as it does. What do we disagree about? As John Haugeland has pointed out, Davidson is more of a realist than I am,[14] and I have recently tracked down the source of this disagreement to a difference of opinion we have about the status of Quine's principle of indeterminacy of translation, which we both accept.

For Davidson, the principle is not the shocker it is often taken to be; in fact it is well nigh trivial—the two different translation manuals between which no fact of the matter decides are like two different scales for measuring temperature.

We know there is no contradiction between the temperature of the air being 32° fahrenheit and 0° celsius; there is nothing in this "relativism" to show that the properties being measured are not "real." Curiously, though, this conclusion has repeatedly been drawn. . . . Yet in the light of the considerations put forward here, this comes to no more than the recognition that more than one set of one person's utterances might be equally successful in capturing the contents of someone else's thoughts or speech. Just as numbers can capture all the empirically significant relations among weights or temperatures in infinitely many ways, so one person's utterances can capture all the significant features of another person's thoughts and speech in different ways. This fact does not

---

12. See my discussion of the distinction between beliefs and (linguistically infected) *opinions;* in (1978a, ch. 16), and in "The Illusions of Realism" (1987, pp. 110–116).

13. Churchland introduces the idea in (1979, pp. 100–107). My adoption of the idea was in "Beyond Belief" (1982a). Davidson's guarded approval is expressed in "What is Present to the Mind?" presented at the SOFIA meeting in Buenos Aires, August, 1989.

14. See the discussion of Haugeland's views in the last chapter of Dennett (1987), "Mid-Term Examination: Compare and Contrast, " pp. 348–349.

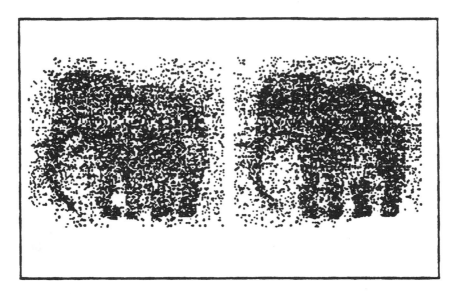

Figure 5.5

challenge the "reality" of the attitudes or meanings thus reported. (Davidson, 1991, pp. 210–211)

On Davidson's view, no substantive disagreements emerge from a comparison of the two description schemes, and so they can quite properly be viewed as competing descriptions of the same reality.

I think this is a flawed analogy. A better one is provided by the example of "rival" descriptions of patterns-with-noise. Consider two rival intentional interpretations of a single individual; they agree on the general shape of this individual's collection of beliefs (and desires, etc.), but because of their different idealizations of the pattern, they do not agree point-for-point. Recalling a famous analogy of Quine's[15] and extending it beyond radical translation to radical interpretation (as Davidson and I both wish to do), we get the image in figure 5.5.

To the left we see Brown's intentional interpretation of Ella; to the right, Jones's interpretation. Since these are intentional interpretations, the pixels or data points represent beliefs and so forth, not (for instance) bits of bodily motion or organs or cells or atoms, and since these are

15. "Different persons growing up in the same language are like different bushes trimmed and trained to take the shape of identical elephants. The anatomical details of twigs and branches will fulfill the elephantine form differently from bush to bush, but the overall outward results are the same." (Quine, 1960, p. 8).

rival intentional interpretations of a single individual, the patterns discerned are not statistical averages (e.g., "Democrats tend to favor welfare programs") but personal cognitive idiosyncracies (e.g., "She thinks she should get her queen out early"). Some of the patterns may indeed be simple observed periodicities (e.g., "Ella wants to talk about football on Mondays") but we are to understand the pattern to be what Anscombe called the "order which is there" in the rational coherence of a person's set of beliefs, desires, and intentions.

Notice that here the disagreements can be substantial—at least before the fact: when Brown and Jones make a series of predictive bets, they will not always make the same bet. They may *often* disagree on what, according to their chosen pattern, will happen next. To take a dramatic case, Brown may predict that Ella will decide to kill herself; Jones may disagree. This is not a trivial disagreement of prediction, and in principle this momentous a difference may emerge in spite of the overall consonance of the two interpretations.

Suppose, then, that Brown and Jones make a series of predictions of Ella's behavior, based on their rival interpretations. Consider the different categories that compose their track records. First, there are the occasions where they agree and are right. Both systems look good from the vantage point of these successes. Second, there are the occasions where they agree and are wrong. Both chalk it up to noise, take their budgeted loss and move on to the next case. But there will also be the occasions where they disagree, where their systems make different predictions, and in these cases sometimes (but not always) one will win and the other lose. (In the real world, predictions are not always from among binary alternatives, so in many cases they will disagree and both be wrong). When one wins and the other loses, it will look to the myopic observer as if one "theory" has scored a serious point against the other, but when one recognizes the possibility that both may chalk up such victories, and that there may be no pattern in the victories that permits either one to improve his theory by making adjustments, one sees that local triumphs may be insufficient to provide any ground in reality for declaring one account a closer approximation of the truth.

Now some might think this situation is *always* unstable; eventually one interpretation is bound to ramify better to new cases, or be deducible from some larger scheme covering other data, etc. That might be true in many cases, but—and this, I think, is the central point of Quine's indeterminacy thesis—it need not be true in all. *If* the strategy of intentional stance description is, as Quine says, a "dramatic idiom" in which there is ineliminable use of idealization, and if Fodor's industrial strength Realism is thus not the correct explanation of the reliable "visibility" of the pattern, such radical indeterminacy is a genuine and stable possibility.

This indeterminacy will be most striking in such cases as the imagined disagreement over Ella's suicidal mindset. If Ella does kill herself, is Brown shown to have clearly had the better intentional interpretation? Not necessarily. When Jones chalks up his scheme's failure in this instance to a bit of noise, this is no more ad hoc or unprincipled than the occasions when Brown was wrong about whether Ella would order the steak not the lobster, and chalked those misses up to noise. This is not at all to say that an interpretation can never be shown to be just wrong; there is plenty of leverage within the principles of intentional interpretation to refute particular hypotheses—for instance, by forcing their defense down the path of Pickwickian explosion ("You see, she didn't believe the gun was loaded because she thought that those bullet-shaped things were chocolates wrapped in foil, which was just a fantasy that occurred to her because . . ."). It *is* to say that there could be two interpretation schemes that were reliable and compact predictors over the long run, but which nevertheless disagreed on crucial cases.

It might seem that in a case as momentous as Ella's intention to kill herself, a closer examination of the details just prior to the fatal moment (if not at an earlier stage) would have to provide additional support for Brown's interpretation at the expense of Jones' interpretation. After all, there would be at least a few seconds—or a few hundred milliseconds—during which Ella's decision to pull the trigger got implemented, and during that brief period, at least, the evidence would swing sharply in favor of Brown's interpretation. That is no doubt true, and it is *perhaps* true that had one gone into enough detail earlier, all this last-second detail could have been predicted—but to have gone into *those* details earlier would have been to drop down from the intentional stance to the design or physical stances. From the intentional stance these determining considerations would have been invisible to both Brown and Jones, who were both prepared to smear over such details as noise in the interests of more practical prediction. Both interpreters concede that they will make false predictions, and moreover, that when they make false predictions there are apt to be harbingers of misprediction in the moments during which the dénouement unfolds. Such a brief swing does not constitute refutation of the interpretation, any more than the upcoming misprediction of behavior does.

How, then, does this make me less of a realist than Davidson? I see that there could be two different systems of belief attribution to an individual that differed *substantially* in what they attributed—even in yielding substantially different predictions of the individual's future behavior—and yet where no deeper fact of the matter could establish that one was a description of the individual's *real* beliefs and the other not. In other words, there could be two different, but equally real, patterns discernible in the noisy world. The rival theorists would not even agree on which parts of the world were pattern and which were noise, and yet nothing deeper would settle the issue.[16] The choice of a pattern would indeed be up to the observer, a matter to be decided on idiosyncratic pragmatic grounds. I myself do not see any feature of Davidson's position that would be a serious obstacle to his shifting analogies and agreeing with me. But then he would want to grant that indeterminacy is not such a trivial matter after all.[17]

What then is Rorty's view on these issues? Rorty wants to deny that any brand of "realism" could *explain* the (apparent?) success of the intentional stance. But since we have already joined Arthur Fine and set aside the "metaphysical" problem of realism, Rorty's reminding us of this only postpones the issue. Even someone who has transcended the scheme / content distinction and has seen the futility of correspondence theories of truth must accept the fact that *within* the natural ontological attitude we sometimes explain success by correspondence: one does better navigating off the coast of Maine when one uses an up-to-date nautical chart than one does when one uses a road map of Kansas. Why? Because the former accurately represents the hazards, markers, depths, and coastlines of the Maine coast, and the latter does not. Now why does one do better navigating the shoals of interpersonal relations using folk psychology than using astrology? Rorty might hold that the predictive "success" we folk-psychology-players relish is itself an arti-

---

16. Cf. "The Abilities of Men and Machines" in Dennett (1978a), where I discuss two people who agree exactly on the future behavior of some artifact, but impose different Turing machine interpretations of it. On both interpretations the machine occasionally "makes errors" but the two interpreters disagree about which cases are the errors. (They disagree about which features of the object's behavior count as signal and which as noise.) Which Turing machine is it really? This question has no answer.

17. Andrej Zabludowski (1989, pp. 35–64) seems to me to have overlooked this version of indeterminacy in "On Quine's Indeterminacy Doctrine."

fact, a mutual agreement engendered by the egging-on or consensual support we who play this game provide each other. He would grant that the game has no rivals in popularity, due—in the opinion of the players—to the power it gives them to understand and anticipate the animate world. But he would refuse to endorse this opinion. How, then, would he distinguish this popularity from the popularity among a smaller coterie of astrology?[18] It is undeniable that astrology provides its adherents with a highly articulated system of patterns that they *think* they see in the events of the world. The difference, however, is that no one has ever been able to get rich by betting on the patterns, but only by selling the patterns to others.

Rorty would have to claim that this is not a significant difference; the rest of us, however, find abundant evidence that our allegiance to folk psychology as a predictive tool can be defended in coldly objective terms. We agree that there is a real pattern being described by the terms of folk psychology. What divides the rest of us is the nature of the pattern, and the ontological implications of that nature.

Let us finally consider Churchland's eliminative materialism from this vantage point. As already pointed out, he is second to none in his appreciation of the power, to date, of the intentional stance as a strategy of prediction. Why does he think that it is nevertheless doomed to the trash heap? Because he anticipates that neuroscience will eventually— perhaps even soon—discover a pattern that is so clearly superior to the noisy pattern of folk psychology that everyone will readily abandon the former for the latter (except, perhaps, in the rough-and-tumble of daily life). This might happen, I suppose. But Churchland here is only playing a hunch, a hunch which should not be seen to gain plausibility from reflections on the irresistible forward march of science. For it is not enough for Churchland to suppose that in principle, neuroscientific levels of description will explain more of the variance, predict more of the "noise" that bedevils higher levels. This is of course bound to be true in the limit—if we descend all the way to the neurophysiological "bit map." But as we have seen, the trade-off between ease of use and immunity from error for such a cumbersome system may make it profoundly unattractive.[19] If the "pattern" is scarcely an improvement over the bit map, talk of eliminative materialism will fall on deaf

18. Cf. my comparison of "the astrological stance" to the intentional stance, (1987, p. 16).
19. As I have put it, physical stance predictions trump design stance predictions which trump intentional stance predictions—but one pays for the power with a loss of portability and a (usually unbearable) computational cost.

ears—just as it does when radical eliminativists urge us to abandon our ontological commitments to tables and chairs. A truly general-purpose, robust system of pattern-description more valuable than the intentional stance is not an impossibility, but anyone who wants to bet on it might care to talk to me about the odds they'll take.

What does all this show? Not that Fodor's industrial strength Realism must be false, and not that Churchland's eliminative materialism must be false, but just that both views are gratuitously strong forms of materialism—presumptive theses way out in front of the empirical support they require. Rorty's view errs in the opposite direction, ignoring the impressive empirical track record that distinguishes the intentional stance from the astrological stance. Davidson's intermediate position, like mine, ties reality to the brute existence of pattern, but Davidson has overlooked the possibility of two or more *conflicting* patterns being superimposed on the same data—a more radical indeterminacy of translation than he had supposed possible. Now, once again, is the view I am defending here a sort of instrumentalism or a sort of realism? I think that the view itself is clearer than either of the labels, so I will leave that question to anyone who stills find illumination in them.

6

Julian Jaynes's Software Archeology

Many of the factual claims advanced in Julian Jaynes's 1976 cult classic, The Origins of Consciousness in the Breakdown of the Bicameral Mind, *are false. Many were no doubt known to be false in 1976 (by researchers more up-to-the-minute than Jaynes), and many more were at best known to be unknowable — now and probably forever. How could one take such a book seriously? Because it asked some very good questions that had never been properly asked before and boldly proposed answers to them. As I say at the close of this essay, if Jaynes's answers are to be discarded (and I think most of them are), we will simply have to find better answers, enlightened by his pioneering project. My 1991 book,* Consciousness Explained, *is just such an attempt. This essay was composed for a symposium on Jaynes's book organized by the psychologist Sandra Witelson and held at McMaster University in Hamilton, Ontario, in November of 1983. The other participants were Jonathan Miller, the British polymath (television presenter, opera producer/director, physician, comedian, . . .), George Ojemann, the American neurosurgeon, and Jaynes himself. The taped discussions were transcribed and lightly edited into the form in which they were published.*

What a philosopher would usually do on an occasion like this is to begin to launch into a series of devastating arguments, criticisms, and counterexamples, and I am not going to do that today, because in this instance I don't think it would be very constructive. I think first it is very important to understand Julian Jaynes's project, to see a little bit more about what the whole shape of it is, and delay the barrage of nitpicking objections and criticisms until we have seen what the edifice as a whole is. After all, on the face of it, it is preposterous, and I have found that in talking with other philosophers my main task is to con-

Originally appeared in *Canadian Psychology*, 27, 1986, pp. 149–154.

vince them to take it seriously when they are very reluctant to do this. I take it very seriously, so I am going to use my time to try to describe what I take the project to be. Perhaps Julian will disavow the version of Julian Jaynes I am going to present, but at least the version I am going to present is one that I take very seriously.

Now, another thing that philosophers usually do on these occasions is demand definitions of consciousness, of mind, and of all the other terms. I am not going to do that either, because I don't think that would be constructive at this point. If I thought I could bring his entire project crashing down with one deft demand for an impossible definition, I would do it, but I don't think so.

Perhaps this is an autobiographical confession: I am rather fond of his way of using these terms; I rather like his way of carving up consciousness. It is in fact very similar to the way that I independently decided to carve up consciousness some years ago.

So what then is the project? The project is, in one sense, very simple and very familiar. It is bridging what he calls the "awesome chasm" between mere inert matter and the inwardness, as he puts it, of a conscious being. Consider the awesome chasm between a brick and a bricklayer. There isn't, in Thomas Nagel's (1974) famous phrase, anything that it is like to be a brick. But there is something that it is like to be a bricklayer, and we want to know what the conditions were under which there happened to come to be entities that it was like something to be in this rather special sense. That is the story, the developmental, evolutionary, historical story that Jaynes sets out to tell.

Now, if we are going to tell this story at all, obviously we are going to have to stretch our imaginations some, because if we think about it in our habitual ways, without trying to stretch our imaginations, we just end up with a blank: it is just incomprehensible. Sherry Turkle (1984), in her new book about computers, *The Second Self*, talks about the reactions small children have to computer toys when they open them up and look inside. What they see is just an absurd little chip and a battery and that's all. They are baffled at how *that* could possibly do what they have just seen the toy do. Interestingly, she says they look at the situation, scratch their heads for a while, and then they typically say very knowingly, "It's the battery!" (A grown-up version of the same fallacy is committed by the philosopher John Searle, 1980, when he, arriving at a similar predicament, says: "It's the mysterious causal powers of the brain that explain consciousness.") Suddenly facing the absurdly large gap between what we know from the inside

about consciousness and what we see if we take off the top of somebody's skull and look in can provoke such desperate reactions. When
we look at a human brain and try to think of it as the seat of all that
mental activity, we see something that is just as incomprehensible as
the microchip is to the child when she considers it to be the seat of all
the fascinating activity that she knows so well as the behavior of the
simple toy.

Now, if we are going to do this work at all, if we are going to try
to fill this gap, we are going to have to talk about consciousness, because that is what is at one edge of this large terrain. It is fascinating
to me to see how reluctant, how uncomfortable, most scientifically
minded people are in talking about consciousness. They realize that
some day they will have to talk about consciousness—unless they are
going to do what the behaviorists tried so unconvincingly to do, just
dismiss the problem as not really there. If you can't quite face "feigning
anesthesia" for the rest of your days, you are going to have to admit
that consciousness is a phenomenon that needs explaining. We are going to have to talk about the ephemeral, swift, curious, metaphorical
features of consciousness.

Many people say: "Some day, but not yet. This enterprise is all just
premature." And others say: "Leave it to the philosophers (and look
what a mess they make of it)." I want to suggest that it is not premature,
that in fact there is no alternative but to start looking as hard as we
can at consciousness first. If we don't look at consciousness and get
clear about what the destination is, and instead try to work our way
up by just thinking about how the brain is put together, we won't know
where we are trying to get to from where we are and we will be hopelessly lost. This is commonly referred to as the defense of the top-down
strategy, and in looking at Jaynes's book again this morning I find that
in his introduction he has one of the clearest and most perspicuous
defenses of the top-down approach that I have ever come across:

We can only know in the nervous system what we have known in behavior
first. Even if we had a complete wiring diagram of the nervous system, we
still would not be able to answer our basic question. Though we knew the
connections of every tickling thread of every single axon and dendrite in every
species that ever existed, together with all its neurotransmitters and how they
varied in its billions of synapses of every brain that ever existed, we could
still never—*not ever*—from a knowledge of the brain alone know if that brain
contained a consciousness like our own. We first have to start from the top,
from some conception of what consciousness is, from what our own introspection is. (Jaynes, 1976, p. 18)

When I try to make this idea clear to other people I sometimes use a somewhat threadbare analogy with computers. If you want to know what a chess-playing computer does, forget about trying to understand it from the bottom up. If you don't understand the conceptual domain in which the topic is chess—moves and strategy—you'll never make sense of what happens by building up from an analysis of the registers and logico-arithmetic operations in the central processing unit. (I am going to put this comparison with computers to a number of other uses in talking about Jaynes's work.)

If we are going to use this top-down approach, we are going to have to be bold. We are going to have to be speculative, but there is good and bad speculation, and this is not an unparalleled activity in science. An area of great fascination in science is the speculative hypothesis-spinning about the very origins of life, of the first self-replicating creatures, in the primordial soup. That sort of research has to be speculative; there simply are no data imaginable anywhere in the world today, nor are there experiments that could tease out with any certainty how that process began, but if you let your imaginations wander and start speculating about how it might have begun, you can put together some pretty interesting stories. Soon you can even begin to test some of them. Although I know that this enterprise is looked askance upon by many hardheaded scientists, it is certainly one that I would defend as a valuable part of our scientific enterprise more largely seen.

The dangers of this top-down approach of course are many. Speculation is guided largely by plausibility, and plausibility is a function of our knowledge, but also of our bad habits, misconceptions, and bits of ignorance, so when you make a mistake it tends to be huge and embarrassing. That's the price you pay in playing this game. Some people have no taste for this, but we really can't do without it. Those scientists who have no taste for this sort of speculative exercise will just have to stay in the trenches and do without it, while the rest of us risk embarrassing mistakes and have a lot of fun.

Consider the current controversy in biology between the adaptationists and their critics Stephen J. Gould and Richard Lewontin (1979) at Harvard. Gould and Lewontin shake an angry and puritanical finger at the adaptationists for their "just-so stories," their "panglossian" assumptions, their willingness to engage in speculation where the only real test seems to be how imaginative you can be and how plausible a story you can tell. But see Dennett (1983a). One of the responses that one can make is that there is no alternative; the fossil record is simply not going to provide enough information to provide a rigorous, bottom-up, scientific account of all the important moments in the evolution of species. The provable history has to be embellished and extrapolated with a good deal of adaptationists' thinking. What we need is a *just-so story*. This term comes, of course, from Kipling and is used as a term of abuse by Gould and Lewontin, but I am happy to say that some of those who are unblushing adaptationists have simply adopted it. They say, in effect: "That's right; what we are doing is telling just-so stories, and just-so stories have a real role to play in science."

Now, when Julian Jaynes tells his story he doesn't say that it is a just-so story. He doesn't say it is just a sort of guess at how it might have been. He claims to be telling the historical truth as best as he can figure it out.

But he is also clever enough to realize that if he doesn't have the details just right, then some other story which is in very important respects rather like it must be true. So the whole account is put together by a rather interesting amalgam of aprioristic thinking about *how it had to be*, historical sleuthing, and inspired guesswork. He uses aprioristic reasoning to establish that we have to have traveled from point A to point B by *some* route—where and when the twists come is an interesting empirical question. He flavors and deepens and constrains his aprioristic thinking about how it had to be with whatever he can find about how it was and he lets his imagination go as fertile as he can and clutches at whatever straws he can find in the "fossil record."

Now, it is good to be "modular" when you do this sort of theorizing, and Jaynes's account is remarkably modular. On page 221 of his book he presents a summary of seven factors which go into his account: (1) the weakening of the auditory by the advent of writing; (2) the inherent fragility of hallucinatory control; (3) the unworkableness of gods in the chaos of historical upheaval; (4) the positing of internal cause in the observation of difference in others; (5) the acquisition of narratization from epics; (6) the survival value of deceit; and (7) a modicum of natural selection.

He has given us seven factors in this passage, and I think he would agree that you could throw out any one of them and replace it with something that simply did the same work but was historically very different; his theory would survive otherwise quite intact. Moreover, there are many details in his theory which are, as he has noted today, optional. There are ideas which are plausible, indications of the detailed way that his account *might* run, but if they turn out to be wrong they can be jettisoned with small damage to the fabric of the whole theory.

I will just mention a few that are favorites of mine. He claims, for example, that there is a little evidence to suggest that in the period when bicameral people and conscious people coexisted, there was a policy of killing obdurately bicameral children, which may in fact have hastened the demise of the bicameral type. This possible policy of "eugenics" may have given the *cultural* evolutionary process he is describing a biological (or genetic) boost, speeding up the process. You don't need it (to make the just-so story work), but there is a little evidence to suggest something like that might have happened.

Another of his optional modules is the idea that the reason that the Greeks placed the mind in the breast (in the "heart") is that when you have to make decisions you go into a stressful state which makes you breathe harder and may even make your pulse quicken. You notice the turmoil in your breast and this leads to a localization fallacy. Jaynes suggests that's why some of the Greek terms for mind have their roots as it were in the chest instead of in the head. That might be true. It might not, but it's another of the optional modules.

I don't know if Jaynes would agree with me about how much optionality there is in his system. The module I would be most interested in simply discarding is the one about hallucinations. Now you might think that if you throw out his account of hallucinations you haven't got much left of Jaynes's theory, but in fact I think you would, although he would probably resist throwing that part away.

This, then, is why I think it is a mistake, as I said at the outset, simply to bash away at the weakest links in sight, because the weakest links are almost certainly not correct—but also not critical to the enterprise as a whole.

I want to turn now to an explanation of what I find most remarkable about Julian Jaynes's just-so story, by comparing it with another (and this was in fact touched upon by one of the earlier questions). In the seventeenth century Thomas Hobbes (1651) asked himself where morality came from. If you look at what he called the state of nature—if you look at animals in the wild, at lions hunting and killing wildebeests, for instance—there is no morality or immorality to be seen there at all. There is no good or evil. There is killing, there is pain, but there is no "ought," there is no right, there is no wrong, there is no sin. But then look at us; here we see the institution of morality permeating the entire fabric of our lives. How did we get from there to here? Hobbes had the same sort of problem as the problem that Jaynes is facing, and his answer of course was a famous just-so story. Back in the old days, he says, man lived in the state of nature and his life was "solitary, poor, nasty, brutish and short." Then there was a sort of crisis and people got together in a group and they formed a covenant or compact, and out of this morality was born. Right and wrong came into existence as a consequence of that social contract.

Now, as history, it is absurd. Hobbes didn't think otherwise. His just-so story was quite obviously a thought experiment, a rational reconstruction or idealization. The last thing Hobbes would have done would have been to look through cuneiform records to see exactly when this particular momentous occasion happened.

But now consider the following objection to Hobbes's account, but first applied to Julian Jaynes's work. In a review of Jaynes's book some years ago, Ned Block (1981) said the whole book made one great crashing mistake, what we sometimes call a "use-mention" error: confusing a phenomenon with either the name of the phenomenon or the concept of the phenomenon. Block claimed that even if everything that Jaynes said about historical events were correct, all he would have shown was not that *consciousness* arrived in 1400 B.C., but that the *concept of* consciousness arrived in 1400 B.C. People were conscious long before they had the concept of consciousness, Block declared, in the same way that there was gravity long before Newton ever hit upon the concept of gravity. The whole book in Block's view was simply a great mistake. Concept does not equal phenomenon. You can't ride the concept of the horse!

Well, now, has Jaynes made that mistake? Let's ask if Hobbes made the same mistake. Hobbes says that morality came into existence out of the social contract. Now one might say, "What a stupid mistake Hobbes has made! Maybe the *concepts* of right and wrong didn't exist before the contract of which he speaks, but certainly right and wrong themselves did. That is, people did things that were nasty and evil before they had the concepts of it."

Right and wrong, however, are parts of morality, a peculiar phenomenon that *can't* predate a certain set of concepts, including the concepts of right and wrong. The phenomenon is *created* in part by the arrival on the scene of a certain set of concepts. It is not that animals just haven't noticed that they are doing things that are evil and good. Lacking the concept, they are not doing anything right or wrong; there isn't any evil or good in their world. It's only once you get in a certain conceptual environment that the phenomenon of right and wrong, the phenomenon of morality, exists at all.

Now, I take Jaynes to be making a similarly exciting and striking move with regard to consciousness. To put it really somewhat paradoxically, you can't have consciousness until you have the concept of consciousness. In fact he has a more subtle theory than that, but that's the basic shape of the move.

These aren't the only two phenomena, morality and consciousness, that work this way. Another one that Jaynes mentions is history, and at first one thinks, "Here's another use-mention error!" At one point in the book Jaynes suggests that history was invented or discovered just a few years before Herodotus, and one starts to object that of course there was history long before there were historians, but then one realizes that in a sense Jaynes is right. Is there a *history* of lions and antelopes? Just as many years have passed for them as for us, and things have happened to them, but it is very different. Their passage of time has not been conditioned by their recognition of the transition, it has not been conditioned and tuned and modulated by any reflective consideration of that very process. So history itself, our *having* histories, is in part a function of our recognizing that very fact. Other phenomena in this category are obvious: you can't have baseball before you have the concept of baseball, you can't have money before you have the concept of money.

I have used up as much time as I should use, but I am going to say a few more words. If you want to pursue the interesting idea that consciousness postdates the arrival of a certain set of concepts, then of course you have to have in your conceptual armamentarium the idea that concepts themselves can be preconscious, that concepts do not require consciousness. Many have held that there is no such thing as the unconscious wielding of concepts, but Jaynes's account of the origins of consciousness depends on the claim that an elaboration of a conceptual scheme under certain social and environmental pressures was the *precondition* for the emergence of consciousness as we know it. This is, to my mind, the most important claim that Jaynes makes in his book. As he puts it, "The bee has a concept of the flower," but not a conscious concept. We have a very salient theoretical role for something which we might as well call concepts, but if you don't like it we can call them schmoncepts, concept-like things that you don't have to be conscious to have.

For instance, computers have them. They are not conscious—yet—but they have lots of concepts, and in fact one way of viewing artificial intelligence is as the attempt to design conceptual systems for those computers to use. In fact this is the way people in artificial intelligence talk all the time. For instance, they may note that they have to give a robot *some concept* of an obstacle so that it can recognize this and that as an obstacle in its environment. Having figured out what concepts to give the robot or the computer, you do some fancy software design, and then you say: Here's how we have realized the concept of *causation,* or *obstacle,* or *the passage of time,* or *other sources of information* or whatever. The idea of unconscious concepts is, as a computer scientist would say, a "winning" idea, and if it is hard for you to get used to it, then at least my recommendation (along with Jaynes) would be: try harder because it is a very useful idea.

After all, one way of casting this whole question (the way that I usually think about it) is not "How do we get from the bricks, amoebas, and then apes to us?" but "How in the world could you ever make a conscious automaton, how could you make a conscious robot?" The answer, I think, is not to be found in hypotheses about hardware particularly, but in software. What you want to do is design the software in such a way that the system has a certain set of concepts. If you manage to endow the system with the right sort of concepts, you create one of those *logical spaces* that Jaynes talks about.

This in fact is a ubiquitous way of talking in the field of Artificial Intelligence. Consider for instance the idea of LISP. LISP is a programming language. Once you have LISP, your whole vision of how a computer is put together, and what you can do with it, changes dramatically. All sorts of things become possible that weren't possible before. Logical spaces are created that didn't exist before and you could never find them in the hardware. Such a logical space is not in the hardware, it is not in the "organs": it is purely at the software level. Now Jaynes, in his largest and most dispensable optional module, ties his entire theory to the structure of the brain and I am fascinated to know whether there is anything in that. But I am quite content to jettison the whole business, because what I think he is really talking about is a software characterization of the mind, at the level, as a computer scientist would say, of a *virtual machine.*

The underlying hardware of the brain is just the same now as it was thousands of years ago (or it may be just the same), but what had to happen was that the environment had to be such as to encourage the development, the emergence, of certain concepts, certain software, which then set in motion some sort of chain reaction. Jaynes is saying that when the right concepts settled into place in the preconscious "minds" of our ancestors, there was a sort of explosion, like the explosion in computer science that happens when you invent something like LISP. Suddenly you discover a new logical space, where you get the sorts of different behaviors, the sorts of new powers, the sorts of new problems that we recognize as having the flavor of human consciousness.

Of course, if that is what Jaynes's theory really is, it is no wonder he has to be bold in his interpretation of the tangible evidence, because this isn't just archeology he is doing: this is *software archeology,* and software doesn't leave much of a fossil record. Software, after all, is just concepts. It is abstract and yet, of course, once it is embodied it has very real effects. So if you want to find a record of major "software" changes in archeological history, what are you going to have to look at? You are going to have to look at the "printouts," but they are very indirect. You are going to have to look at texts, and you are going to have to look at the pottery shards and figurines as Jaynes does, because that is the only place you are going to find any trace. Now, of course, maybe the traces are just gone, maybe the "fossil record" is simply not good enough.

Jaynes's idea is that for us to be the way we are now, there has to have been a revolution—almost certainly not an *organic* revolution, but a *software* revolution—in the organization of our information processing system, and that has to have come *after* language. That, I think, is an absolutely wonderful idea, and if Jaynes is completely wrong in the details, that is a darn shame, but something like what he proposes has to be right; and we can start looking around for better modules to put in the place of the modules that he has already given us.

7

Real Consciousness

Many critics have raised questions and objections about the theory of con-
sciousness that Marcel Kinsbourne and I call the Multiple Drafts Model.
I have often responded in print (Dennett, 1993a, c, d, f, 1994b, Dennett and
Kinsbourne, 1994), but those essays need their targets beside them for compre-
hension. In this and the following essay, some of the most persistent criticisms
are distilled and responded to.

In *Consciousness Explained* (Dennett, 1991a), I put forward a rather detailed empirical theory of consciousness, together with an analysis of
the implications of that theory for traditional philosophical treatments
of consciousness. In the critical response to the book, one of the common themes has been that my theory is not a "realist" theory, but
rather an eliminativist or verificationist denial, in one way or another,
of the very reality of consciousness. Here I will draw together a number
of those threads, and my responses to them.[1]

It is clear that your consciousness of a stimulus is not simply a matter
of its arrival at some peripheral receptor or transducer; most of
the impingements on our end-organs of sense never reach consciousness, and those that do become elements of our conscious experience
somewhat after their arrival at your peripheries. To put it with bizarre
vividness, a live, healthy eyeball disconnected from its brain is not a
seat of visual consciousness—or at least that is the way we are accus-
tomed to think of these matters. The eyes and ears (and other end-
organs) are entry points for raw materials of consciousness, not the
sites themselves of conscious experiences. So visual consciousness

---

Originally appeared in Revonsuo, A., and Kamppinen, M., eds., *Consciousness in Philoso-*
phy and Cognitive Neuroscience (Hillsdale, NJ: Lawrence Erlbaum, 1994), pp. 55–63.
1. This paper draws on Dennett and Kinsbourne (1992a), and Dennett, (1993c, 1993d,
1995a).

must happen *in between* the eyeball and the mouth—to put it crudely. Where?

To bring out what the problem is, let me pose an analogy: You go to the racetrack and watch three horses, Able, Baker, and Charlie, gallop around the track. At pole 97 Able leads by a neck, at pole 98 Baker, at pole 99 Charlie, but then Able takes the lead again, and then Baker and Charlie run neck and neck for awhile, and then, eventually all the horses slow down to a walk and are led off to the stable. You recount all this to a friend, who asks "Who won the race?" and you say, well, since there was no finish line, there's no telling. It wasn't a real race, you see, with a finish line. First one horse led and then another, and eventually they all stopped running.

The event you witnessed was not a real race, but it was a real event— not some mere illusion or figment of your imagination. Just what kind of an event to call it is perhaps not clear, but whatever it was, it was as real as real can be.

Now consider a somewhat similar phenomenon. You are presented with some visual stimuli, A followed by B, which provoke various scattered chains of events through your brain. First the chain of events initiated by A dominates cortical activity in some regions, and then chain B takes over, and then perhaps some chain C, produced by an interaction between chain A and B, enjoys a brief period of dominance, to be followed by a resurgence of chain A. Then eventually all three (or more) chains of events die out, leaving behind various traces in memory. Someone asks you: Which stimulus did you become conscious of first: A or B (or C)?

If Descartes's view of consciousness were right, there would be a forthright way of telling. Descartes held that for an event to reach consciousness, it had to pass through a special gateway—which we might call the Cartesian bottleneck or turnstile—which Descartes located in the pineal gland or epiphysis. But everybody knows that Descartes was wrong. Not only is the pineal gland not the fax machine to the soul; it is not the Oval Office of the brain. It is not the "place where it all comes together" for consciousness, nor does any other place in the brain fit this description. I call this mythic place in the brain where it all comes together (and where the order of arrival determines the order of consciousness) the Cartesian Theater. There is no Cartesian Theater in the brain. That is a fact. Besides, if there were, what could happen there? Presumably, we care about consciousness because it matters what happens in our conscious lives—for instance, pains that never become conscious are either not pains at all, or if they are, they are not the sort that cause us suffering (such as the pains that keep us from sleeping in contorted positions or those unfortunates congenitally insensitive to pain.) But if what happens in consciousness matters, surely it must make a difference—something must get done because of what happened there. However, if all the important work gets done *at a point* (or just within the narrow confines of the pea-sized pineal gland), how does the rest of the brain play a role in it?

All the work that was dimly imagined to be done in the Cartesian Theater has to be done somewhere, and no doubt it is distributed around in the brain. This work is largely a matter of responding to the "given" by *taking* it—by responding to it with one interpretive judgment or another. This corner must be turned somehow by any model of observation. On the traditional view, all the taking is deferred until the raw given, the raw materials of stimulation, have been processed in various ways. Once each bit is "finished," it can enter consciousness and be appreciated for the first time. As C. S. Sherrington (1934) put it, "The mental action lies buried in the brain, and in that part most deeply recessed from the outside world that is furthest from input and output."

In the Multiple Drafts Model developed by Marcel Kinsbourne and me (Dennett, 1991a; Dennett and Kinsbourne, 1992b), this single unified taking is broken up in cerebral space and real time. We suggest that the judgmental tasks are fragmented into many distributed moments of micro-taking (Damasio, 1989; Kinsbourne, 1988). The novelty lies in how we develop the implications of this fragmentation.

It may seem at first as if we are stuck with only three alternatives:

1. Each of these distributed micro-takings is an episode of unconscious judgment, and the consciousness of the taken element must be deferred to some later process (what we call the Stalinesque show trial in a Cartesian Theater). But then how long must each scene wait, pending potential revision, before the curtain rises on it?

2. Each of these distributed micro-takings is an episode of conscious judgment (multiple minicinemas). But then why don't we all have either a kaleidoscopic and jumbled "stream of consciousness" or (if these distributed micro-takings are not "co-conscious") a case of "multiple selves"? Is our *retrospective* sense of unified, coherent consciousness

just the artifact of an Orwellian historian's tampering with memory? As several commentators have asked, how can the manifest coherence, seriality, or unity of conscious experience be explained?

3. Some of the distributed micro-takings are conscious and the rest are not. The problem then becomes: Which special property distinguishes those that are conscious, and how do we clock the onset of their activity? And, of course, because distributed microtakings may occur slightly "out of order," what "mechanism" serves to unify the scattered micro-takings that *are* conscious, and in each case, does it operate before or after the onset of consciousness (i.e., which phenomena are Orwellian and which are Stalinesque)?

Our view is that there is a yet a fourth alternative:

4. The creation of conscious experience is not a batch process but a continuous process. The micro-takings have to interact. A micro-taking, as a sort of judgment or decision, can't just be inscribed in the brain in isolation; it has to have its consequences—for guiding action and modulating further micro-judgments made "in its light," creating larger fragments of what we call narrative. However it is accomplished in particular cases, the interaction of micro-takings has the effect that a modicum of coherence is maintained, with discrepant elements dropping out of contention, and without the assistance of a Master Judge. Because there is no Master Judge, there is no *further* process of being-appreciated-in-consciousness, so the question of *exactly* when a particular element was *consciously* (as opposed to unconsciously) taken admits no nonarbitrary answer.

So there is a sort of stream of consciousness, with swirls and eddies, but—and this is the most important "architectural" point of our model—*there is no bridge over the stream.* Those of you familiar with A. A. Milne and Winnie the Pooh will appreciate the motto: "You can't play Pooh-sticks with consciousness."

As "realists" about consciousness, we believe that there has to be something—some property K—that distinguishes conscious events from nonconscious events. Consider the following candidate for property K: A contentful event becomes conscious if and when it *becomes part of a temporarily dominant activity in the cerebral cortex* (Kinsbourne, 1988, and in preparation). This is deliberately general and undetailed, and it lacks any suggestion of a threshold. How long must participation in this dominance last, and how intense or exclusive does this dominance need to be, for an element to be conscious? There is no suggestion of a principled answer. Such a definition of property K meets the minimal demands of "realism," but threatens the presumed distinction between Orwellian and Stalinesque revisions. Suppose some contentful element briefly flourishes in such a dominant pattern, but fades before leaving a salient, reportable trace on memory. (A plausible example would be the representation of the first stimulus in a case of metacontrast—a phenomenon described in detail in Dennett, 1991a, and Dennett and Kinsbourne, 1992b). Would this support an Orwellian or a Stalinesque model? If the element participated for "long enough," it would be "in consciousness" even if it never was properly remembered (Orwell), but if it faded "too early," it would never quite make it into the privileged category, even if it left some traces in memory (Stalin). But how long is long enough? There is no way of saying. No discontinuity divides the cases in two.

The analogy with the horse race that wasn't a horse race after all should now be manifest. Commentators on our theory generally agree with us that (a) the time of representing should not be confused with the time represented, and (b) there is no privileged place within the brain "where it all comes together." They do not all agree with us, however, that it follows from (a) and (b) that the Orwellian/Stalinesque distinction must break down at some scale of temporal resolution, leaving no fact of the matter about whether one is remembering misexperiences or mis-remembering experiences. Here, some claim, we have gone overboard, lapsing into "verificationism" or "eliminativism" or "antirealism" or some other gratuitously radical position. This is curious, for we consider our position to be unproblematically "realist" and materialist: Conscious experiences are real events occurring in the real time and space of the brain, and hence they are clockable and locatable within the appropriate limits of precision for real phenomena of their type. (For an extended defense of this version of realism, see chap. 5 of this volume.) Certain sorts of questions one might think it appropriate to ask about them, however, have no answers, because these questions presuppose inappropriate—unmotivatable—temporal and spatial boundaries that are more fine-grained than the phenomena admit.

In the same spirit we are also realists about the British Empire—it really and truly existed, in the physical space and time of this planet—but, again, we think that certain sorts of questions about the British Empire have no answers, simply because the British Empire was nothing *over and above* the various institutions, bureaucracies, and individuals that composed it. The question "Exactly when did the British Empire become informed of the truce in the War of 1812?" cannot be answered. The most that can be said is, "Sometime between December 24, 1814 and mid-January, 1815." The signing of the truce was one official, intentional act of the Empire, but the later participation by the British forces in the Battle of New Orleans was another, and it was an act performed under the assumption that no truce had been signed. Even if we can give precise times for the various moments at which various officials of the Empire became informed, no one of these moments can be singled out—except arbitrarily—as the time the Empire itself was informed. Similarly, since you are nothing over and above the various subagencies and processes in your nervous system that compose you, the following sort of question is always a trap: "Exactly when did I (as opposed to various parts of my brain) become informed (aware, conscious) of some event?" Conscious experience, in our view, is a succession of states *constituted by* various processes occurring in the brain, and not something over and above these processes that is *caused by* them.

The idea is still very compelling, however, that "realism" about consciousness guarantees that certain questions have answers (even if they are currently unknowable), and I have recently been fielding a variety of objections on that theme. Michael Lockwood, a commentator who is happy to declare himself to be a Cartesian materialist, nicely summed up the intuition that I am calling in question. "Consciousness," he said, with an air of enunciating something almost definitional in its status, "is the leading edge of perceptual memory" (Lockwood, 1993, p. 60).

" 'Edge'?" I retorted. "What makes you think there is an edge?" Consider what must be the case if there is no such edge. The *only* difference between the Orwellian and Stalinesque treatment of any phenomenon is whether or not the editing or adjustment or tampering occurs before or after a presumed *moment of onset of consciousness* for the contents in question. The distinction can survive only if the debut into consciousness for some content is at least as accurately timable as the events of micro-taking (the binding, revising, interpreting, etc.) whose order relative to the onset of consciousness defines the two positions. If the onset of consciousness is not so sharply marked, the difference between pre-presentation Stalinesque revision and post-presentation Orwellian revision disappears, and is restorable only by arbitrary fiat.

This is not verificationism in any contentious sense. Another analogy will make this clear. Andy Warhol anticipated a future in which each person would be famous for fifteen minutes. What he nicely captured in this remark was a reductio ad absurdum of a certain (imaginary) concept of fame. Would that be *fame?* Has Warhol described a logically possible world? If we pause to think about his example more carefully than usual, we see that what makes the remark funny is that he has stretched something beyond the breaking point. It is true, no doubt, that thanks to the mass media, fame can be conferred on an anonymous citizen almost instantaneously (Rodney King comes to mind), and thanks to the fickleness of public attention, fame can evaporate almost as fast. But Warhol's rhetorical exaggeration of this fact carries us into the absurdity of Wonderland. We have yet to see an instance of some-one being famous for just fifteen minutes, and in fact we never will. Let some one citizen be viewed for fifteen minutes by hundreds of millions of people, and then—unlike Rodney King—be utterly forgot-ten. To call that fame would be to misuse the term (ah yes, an "ordinary language" move, and a good one, if used with discretion).

If that is not obvious, then let me raise the ante: could a person be famous—not merely attended-to-by-millions-of-eyes, but famous—for five seconds? Every day there are in fact hundreds if not thousands of people who pass through the state of being viewed, for a few seconds, by millions of people. Consider the evening news on television, pre-senting a story about the approval of a new drug. Accompanying Dan Rather's voice-over, an utterly anonymous nurse is seen (by millions) plunging a hypodermic into the arm of an utterly anonymous patient. Now that's fame—right? Of course not. Being seen on television and being famous are different sorts of phenomena; the former has techno-logically sharp edges that the latter entirely lacks.

What I have argued, in my attack on the Cartesian theater, is that being an item in consciousness is *not at all* like being on television; it is, rather, a species of mental fame—almost literally. Consciousness is cerebral celebrity—nothing more and nothing less. Those contents are conscious that persevere, that monopolize resources long enough to achieve certain typical and "symptomatic" effects—on memory, on the control of behavior and so forth. Not every content can be famous, for in such competitions there must be more losers than winners. And un-like the world of sports, winning is everything. There are no higher honors to be bestowed on the winners, no Hall of Fame to be inducted into. In just the way that a Hall of Fame is a redundant formality (if you are already famous, election is superfluous, and if you are not, election probably won't make the difference), there is no induction or transduction into consciousness beyond the influence already secured by winning the competition and thereby planting lots of hooks into the ongoing operations of the brain.

Instantaneous fame is a disguised contradiction in terms, and it follows from my proposed conception of what consciousness is that an instantaneous flicker of consciousness is also an incoherent notion. Those philosophers who see me as underestimating the power of future research in neuroscience when I claim that no further discoveries from that quarter could establish that there was indeed a heretofore undreamt-of variety of evanescent—but genuine—consciousness might ask themselves if I similarly undervalue the research potential of sociology when I proclaim that it is inconceivable that sociologists could discover that Andy Warhol's prediction had come true. This could only make sense, I submit, to someone who is still covertly attached to the idea that consciousness (or fame) is the sort of semi-mysterious property that might be discovered to be present by the telltale ticking of the phenomenometer or famometer (patent pending!)[2]

Consider a question nicely parallel to the Orwell-Stalin stumpers I declare to be vacuous: did Jack Ruby become famous before Lee Harvey Oswald died? Hmm. Well, hundreds of millions witnessed him

---

2. Owen Flanagan (1992), esp. pp. 14–15, pp. 82–83, has made the claim in detail. He supposes, for instance, that the 40-hertz phase-locked oscillation championed by Singer, von der Malsburg, and others, and suggested by Crick and Koch as a key mechanism in consciousness, might serve as the missing ingredient that could trump my short-sighted verificationism. "Never say never, " he advises me. Well, now that neuroscience's love affair with 40-hertz is beginning to cool off (because of problems that were always inherent in the idea—people were asking too much of it), let's look more closely at the prospects. If Crick and Koch are taken to be proposing a mechanism for *securing cerebral celebrity*—the underlying mechanism by which some contents win and others lose in competition—then they are not offering a rival view, but merely specifying details I left blank in my sketch. Ignore the problems and suppose they are right (I would love to have an account of the detailed mechanisms, after all). Notice that it is logically impossible for a 40-hertz oscillation mechanism to resolve temporal onset questions below the two-pulse minimum of 25 milliseconds, and any plausible competition-for-entrainment model would surely require considerably more time—moving us inexorably into a window of indeterminacy of the size I postulated: several hundred milliseconds. Alternatively, if Flanagan supposes that Crick and Koch are claiming that 40-hertz entrainment *causes a subsequent state-change* (which could be an instantaneous transduction into some new medium, for instance), then he is simply insisting on the very concept of consciousness I am challenging—that consciousness requires entrance into a "charmed circle."

shooting Oswald on "live" television, and certainly he *subsequently* became famous, but did his fame begin at the instant his gun-toting arm
hove into view, while Oswald was still alive and breathing? I for one
do not think there is any fact we don't already know that could conceivably shed light on this question of event ordering.

The familiar ideas die hard. It has seemed obvious to many that consciousness is—must be—rather like an inner light shining, or rather
like television, or rather like a play or movie presented in the Cartesian
Theater. If they were right, then consciousness would have to have
certain features that I deny it to have. But they are simply wrong. When
I point this out I am not denying the reality of consciousness at all; I
am just denying that consciousness, real consciousness, is like what
they think it is like.

8   Instead of Qualia[1]

Owen Flanagan (1992) begins his chapter on qualia by noting that I say there are no such things as qualia. He objects: "This is a bad idea. Qualia are for real" (p. 61). At the end of that chapter, having defended a view that is in most regards consonant with mine, he says "To conclude: there are no qualia in Dennett's contentious sense, but there are qualia" (p. 85). He agrees with me after all: there are no qualia in the "contentious" sense in which I used the term. The contentious sense anchors the term to the presumed possibility of "inverted qualia" and "absent qualia." Another philosopher who (almost) agrees with me about this is David Chalmers: "It is therefore extremely implausible that absent qualia and inverted qualia are possible" (Chalmers, 1995, p. 98). Since "qualia" is a bit of philosophers' jargon, not an everyday word, I think it is appropriate to use it in the "contentious" sense that most philosophers have favored. In that sense, there are no qualia. There is no other sense that has a clear and agreed-upon meaning, so I have recommended abandoning the word, but I seem to have lost that battle (Dennett, 1995b).

Philosophers have adopted various names for the things in the beholder (or properties of the beholder) that have been supposed to provide a safe home for the colors and the rest of the properties that have been banished from the "external" world by the triumphs of physics: *raw feels, sensa, phenomenal qualities, intrinsic properties of conscious experiences, the qualitative content of mental states* and, of course, *qualia*, the term I will use. There are subtle differences in how these terms have been defined, but I'm going to ride roughshod over them. I deny that there are *any* such properties. But I agree wholeheartedly that there seem to be.

Originally appeared in Revensuo, A., and Kamppinen, M., eds., *Consciousness in Philosophy and Cognitive Science* (Hillsdale, NJ: Lawrence Erlbaum, 1994), pp. 129–139.
1. Portions of this chapter are drawn from Dennett 1991a, 1991b.

There seem to be qualia, because it really does seem as if science has shown us that the colors can't be out there, and hence must be in here. Moreover, it seems that what is in here can't *just* be the judgments we make when things seem colored to us. Don't our internal discriminative states *also* have some special "intrinsic" properties, the subjective, private, ineffable properties that constitute *the way things look to us* (sound to us, smell to us, etc.)? Those additional properties would be the qualia, and before looking at the arguments philosophers have devised in an attempt to *prove* that there are these additional properties, I will try to remove the motivation for believing in these properties in the first place, by finding alternative explanations for the phenomena that seem to demand them. Then the systematic flaws in the attempted proofs will be readily visible.

An excellent introductory book on the brain contains the following passage: " 'Color' as such does not exist in the world; it exists only in the eye and brain of the beholder. Objects reflect many different wavelengths of light, but these light waves themselves have no color" (Ornstein and Thompson, 1984).

This is a good stab at expressing the common wisdom, but notice that taken strictly and literally, it cannot be what the authors mean, and it cannot be true. Color, they say, does not exist "in the world" but only in the "eye and brain" of the beholder. But the eye and brain of the beholder are in the world, just as much parts of the physical world as the objects seen by the observer. And like those objects, the eye and brain are colorful. Eyes can be blue or brown or green, and even the brain is made not *just* of grey (and white) matter: in addition to the *substantia nigra* (the black stuff) there is the *locus ceruleus* (the blue place). But, of course, the colors that are "in the eye and brain of the beholder" in *this* sense are not what the authors are talking about. What makes anyone think there is color in any other sense?

The common wisdom is that modern science has removed the color from the physical world, replacing it with colorless electromagnetic radiation of various wavelengths, bouncing off surfaces that variably reflect and absorb that radiation—due to what Locke and Boyle called their secondary qualities, dispositional powers composed of their basic, or primary qualities. It may look as if the color is *out there*, but it isn't. It's *in here*. It seems to follow that what is *in here* is both necessarily conscious (otherwise it isn't all the way "in") and necessarily "qualitative" (otherwise color would be utterly missing in the world). Locke's way of defining secondary qualities has become part of the standard layperson's interpretation of science, and it has its virtues, but it also gives hostages: the things produced in the mind. The secondary quality *red*, for instance, was for Locke the dispositional property or power of certain surfaces of physical objects, thanks to their microscopic textural features, to produce in us the *idea of red* whenever light was reflected off those surfaces into our eyes. The power in the external object is clear enough, it seems, but what kind of a thing is an idea of red? Is it, like a beautiful gown of blue, *colored*—in some sense? Or is it, like a beautiful discussion of purple, just *about* a color, without itself being colored at all? This opens up possibilities, but how could an idea be just *about* a color (e.g., the color red) if nothing anywhere *is* red— "intrinsically"?

This reasoning is confused. What science has actually shown us is just that the light-reflecting properties of objects—their secondary qualities—cause creatures to go into various discriminative states, underlying a host of innate dispositions and learned habits of varying complexity. And what are the properties of these "internal" states? Here we can indeed play Locke's card a second time: These discriminative states of observers' brains have various primary properties (their mechanistic properties due to their connections, the excitation states of their elements, etc.), and in virtue of these primary properties, they too have various secondary, merely dispositional properties. In human creatures with language, for instance, these discriminative states often eventually dispose the creatures to express verbal judgments alluding to the "color" of various things. The semantics of these statements makes it clear what colors supposedly are: reflective properties of the surfaces of objects, or of transparent volumes (the pink ice cube, the shaft of limelight). And that is just what colors are in fact—though saying just *which* reflective properties they are is tricky.

Don't our internal discriminative states *also* have some special "intrinsic" properties, the subjective, private, ineffable properties that constitute *the way things look to us* (sound to us, smell to us, etc.)? No. The dispositional properties of those discriminative states already suffice to explain *all* the effects: the effects on both peripheral behavior (saying "Red!" stepping the brake, etc.) and "internal" behavior (judging "Red!" seeing something *as* red, reacting with uneasiness or displeasure if, say, red things upset one). Any additional "qualitative" properties or qualia would thus have no positive role to play in *any* explanations, nor are they somehow vouchsafed to us "directly" in intuition. Qualitative properties that are intrinsically conscious are a myth, an artifact of misguided theorizing, not anything given pretheoretically.

We do have a need, as David Rosenthal (1991a) has shown, for properties of discriminative states that are in one sense independent of consciousness, and that can be for that very reason informatively cited in explanations of particular contents of our consciousness. These properties are partially, but not entirely, independent of consciousness. We may call such properties *lovely* properties as contrasted with *suspect* properties. Someone could be lovely who had never yet, as it happened, been observed by any observer of the sort who would find her lovely, but she could not—as a matter of logic—be a suspect until someone actually suspected her of something. Particular instances of lovely qualities (such as the quality of loveliness) can be said to exist as Lockean dispositions prior to the moment (if any) where they exercise their power over an observer, producing the defining effect therein. Thus some unseen woman (self-raised on a desert island, I guess) could be genuinely lovely, having the dispositional power to affect normal observers of a certain class in a certain way, in spite of never having the opportunity to do so. But lovely qualities cannot be defined independently of the proclivities, susceptibilities, or dispositions of a class of observers. Actually, that is a bit too strong. Lovely qualities *would* not be defined—there would be no point in defining *them*, in contrast to all the other logically possible gerrymandered properties—independently of such a class of observers. So while it might be logically possible ("in retrospect" one might say) to gather color property instances together by something like brute force enumeration, the reasons for singling out such properties (for instance, in order to explain certain causal regularities in a set of curiously complicated objects) depend on the existence of the class of observers.

Are elephant seals[2] lovely? Not to us. It is hard to imagine an uglier creature. What makes an elephant seal lovely to another elephant seal is not what makes a woman lovely to another human being, and to call some as-yet-unobserved woman lovely who, as it happens, would mightily appeal to elephant seals would be to abuse both her and the term. It is only by reference to human tastes, which are contingent and indeed idiosyncratic features of the world, that the property of loveliness (-to-a-human-being) can be identified.

---

2. In Dennett 1991a and 1991b, I misremembered the name of this amazing beast, whose antics I watched on the California coast in 1980—I called them sea elephants. No one has yet bothered to correct me on that, so I correct myself.

On the other hand, suspect qualities (such as the property of being a suspect) are understood in such a way as to presuppose that any instance of the property has already had its defining effect on at least one observer. You may be eminently worthy of suspicion—you may even be obviously guilty—but you can't be a suspect until someone actually suspects you. The tradition that Rosenthal is denying would have it that "sensory qualities" are suspect properties—their *esse* is in every instance *percipi*. Just as an unsuspected suspect is no suspect at all, so an unfelt pain is supposedly no pain at all. But, for the reasons Rosenthal adduces, this is exactly as unreasonable as the claim that an unseen object cannot be colored. He claims, in effect, that sensory qualities should rather be considered lovely properties—like Lockean secondary qualities generally. Our intuition that the as-yet-unobserved emerald in the middle of the clump of ore is *already* green does not have to be denied, even though its being green is not a property it can be said to have "intrinsically." This is easier to accept for some secondary qualities than for others. That the sulphurous fumes spewed forth by primordial volcanos were yellow seems somehow more objective than that they stank, but so long as what we mean by "yellow" is what *we* mean by "yellow," the claims are parallel. For suppose some primordial earthquake cast up a cliff face exposing the stripes of hundreds of chemically different layers to the atmosphere. Were those stripes *visible*? We must ask to whom. Perhaps some of them would be visible to us and others not. Perhaps some of the invisible stripes would be visible to pigeons (with their tetrachromat color vision), or to creatures who saw in the infrared or ultraviolet part of the electromagnetic spectrum. For the same reason one cannot meaningfully ask whether the difference between emeralds and rubies is a visible difference without specifying the vision system in question.

The same moral should be drawn about the sensory qualities Rosenthal attributes to mental (or cerebral) states. Like Lockean secondary qualities in general, they are equivalence classes of complexes of primary qualities of those states and thus can exist independently of any observer, but because the equivalence classes of different complexes that compose the property are gathered by their characteristic effect on normal observers, it makes no sense to single them out as properties in the absence of the class of observers. There wouldn't be colors at all if there were no observers with color vision, and there wouldn't be pains at all if there were no subjects capable of conscious experience of pains, but that does not make either colors or pains into suspect properties.

Rosenthal (in a personal communication) asks whether this is not too strong. Why should the existence of pains require subjects capable of conscious experience of pains, as opposed simply to subjects capable of having nonconscious pains? Fair question, and his implied point is a good one—except for what amounts, in the end, to a lexical quandary, which can be brought out by considering the parallel with color. There is nothing except the specific effects *on normal human beings* that demarcates the boundaries of the "visible spectrum." Infrared and ultraviolet radiation does not count as subserving color vision (at least according to a sort of purist definitional taste) even in creatures who respond to it in the ways we respond to the humanly visible spectrum. "Yes, it's *like* color vision, but it isn't *color* vision," someone might insist. "Color vision is vision whose proper objects are (only) red through violet." Now imagine that we confront a set of primary property complexes as candidates for the secondary property of pain, and suppose it is a somewhat enlarged set (it includes infrapain and ultrapain, in effect), including outlying cases of which we human beings would never be conscious (but which have the sorts of effects on variant human beings that paradigmatic pains have on us, etc.). Would those be pains? There would certainly be a property which was the property picked out by *that* set, but would it be pain? (Not a terribly interesting question.)

I claim, then, that sensory qualities are nothing other than the dispositional properties of cerebral states to produce certain further effects in the very observers whose states they are. It is no objection to declare that it just seems obvious that our mental states really do have intrinsic properties over and above their dispositional properties. (If this were a good argument, it would be a good argument against the original distinction, by Locke, Boyle, and others, between primary and secondary qualities, for it certainly "seems obvious" that physical objects have their color properties "intrinsically"—just look at them!) It does indeed appear to us as if we somehow enjoy, in our minds, some sort of direct and intimate access to "intrinsic" properties of our conscious states, but as Rosenthal observes, "We need not preserve the 'element of truth' in erroneous common-sense intuitions when we become convinced that these intuitions reflect how things appear, rather than how they really are" (Rosenthal, 1991a, p. 27).

The prima facie case for the common conviction that qualia are needed over and above the various "merely dispositional" properties of our cerebral states can be dramatized—and then exploded—by an example. We can compare the colors of things in the world by putting them side by side and looking at them, to see what judgment we reach, but we can also compare the colors of things by just recalling or imagining them "in our minds." Is the standard red of the stripes on the American flag the same red as, or is it darker or lighter or brighter or more or less orange than, the standard red of Santa Claus's suit (or a British pillar box or the Soviet red star)? (If no two of these standards are available in your memory, try a different pair, such as Visa-card-blue and sky blue, or billiard-table-felt-green and Granny-Smith-apple-green, or lemon-yellow and butter-yellow.) We are able to make such comparisons "in our minds' eyes," and when we do, we somehow make something happen in us that retrieves information from memory and permits us to compare, in conscious experience, the colors of the standard objects as we remember them (as we take ourselves to remember them, in any case). Some of us are better at this than others, no doubt, and many of us are not very confident in the judgments we reach under such circumstances. That is why we take home paint samples, or take fabric samples to the paint store, so that we can put side by side in the external world instances of the two colors we wish to compare.

When we do make these comparisons "in our minds' eyes," what happens? It surely *seems* as if we confront in the most intimate way imaginable some intrinsic subjective color properties of the mental objects we compare, but before trying to figure out what happens in us, let us look at a deliberately oversimplified version of a parallel question: What would go on inside a color-detecting robot given the same sort of task?

Figure 8.1 shows our robot, with a color TV camera feeding its signal into a sort of color CAD system, which digitizes the images, color-coding each frame. No information is lost. Going to digital from analog simply makes for greater fidelity (as in the case of compact discs), and ease of explanation in the thought experiment. Let's suppose the computer can discriminate 1024 colors, numbered from 0 to 1023 (or in binary, from 0000000000 to 1111111111. (It also codes, for every number, a saturation number between, say, 0 and 127, and a brightness [or grey scale] between 0 [black] and 15 [white].) Every value of these three variables is associated with a particular hue, intensity, and brightness, and to add a human touch, we can imagine the colors being assigned numbers not just in an orderly fashion, but in the particular sort of order that human color vision would provide, with its red-green-blue

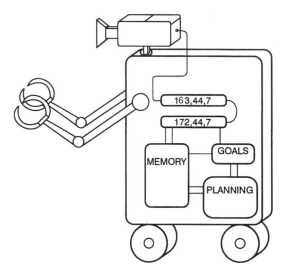

Figure 8.1

(RGB) sensors in the retina, feeding into an opponent-process system (which gives us the "complementary colors" of afterimages). This is also easy to do, since there are off-the-shelf converters that recode the standard television scheme into the RGB system that computers use, in mimicry of the red-green-blue poles of maximal sensitivity in human vision. With our coding system in place, simple arithmetic operations will preserve simple "psychophysical" effects: Plus-1 for brightness will take us to the nearest distinguishable shade of the same color, just changing its grey-scale value; minus-1 in hue changes the hue in the counterclockwise direction by one step, leaving saturation and brightness the same, and so forth.

Now suppose we place a color picture of Santa Claus in front of it and ask it whether the red in the picture is deeper than the red of the American flag (something it has already stored in its memory). This is what it would do: retrieve its representation of Old Glory from memory, and locate the red stripes (they are labeled "163, 44, 7" in its diagram). It would then compare this red to the red of the Santa Claus suit in the picture in front of its camera, which happens to be transduced by its color graphics system as 172, 44, 7. It would compare the two reds *by subtracting 163 from 172 and getting 9,* which it would interpret, let's say, as showing that Santa Claus red seems somewhat deeper—toward crimson—than American flag red.

This story is deliberately oversimple, to dramatize the assertion I wish to make: We have not yet been shown a difference of any theoretical importance between the robot's way of performing this task and our own. The robot does not perform its comparison by rendering colored representations and comparing their spectral properties, and neither do we. Nothing red, white, or blue happens in your brain when you conjure up an American flag, but no doubt something happens that has three physical variable clusters associated with it—one for red, one for white, and one for blue, and it is by some "mechanical" comparison of the values of those variables with "stored" values of the same variables in memory that you come to be furnished with an opinion about the relative shades of the seen and remembered colors. So while voltages in memory registers is surely not the way your brain represents colors, it will do as a stand-in for the unknown cerebral variables. In other words, so far we have been given no reason to deny that the discriminative states of the robot have content in just the same way, and for just the same reasons, as the discriminative brain states I have put in place of Locke's ideas.

But perhaps the example is misleading because of a lack of detail. Let's add some realistic touches. Each color in the robot's coded color space may be supposed to be cross-linked in the robot's memory systems with many earlier events in its "experience"—some of them positive, some negative, some directly, some indirectly. Let's make up a few possibilities. Since it's an IBM computer, let's suppose, its designers have cleverly programmed in an innate preference for Big Blue. Any time Big Blue (477, 51, 5) comes in, it activates the "Hurrah for IBM!" modules, which—if nothing else is going on—tend to get expressed in one way or another: Under extreme conditions, the robot will begin to sing the praises of IBM, out loud. Under other conditions, the robot, if offered a choice, will prefer to rest in a Big Blue room, will exchange an orange extension cord for a Big Blue one, and so forth. And, since there are plenty of other shades of blue, these near misses will also tend to activate these IBM centers, though not as strongly.

Other colors will activate other routines (or subsystems, or modules, or memory clusters). In fact, every color gets assigned a host of disposition-provoking powers, most of which, of course, remain all but invisible in various slight reorganizations of its internal states. The effects may be supposed to be cumulative and associative or ancestral: A certain shade of rosy orange (950, 31, 3 let's say) reminds the robot of its task of turning on the porch light at sunset every night—a task long

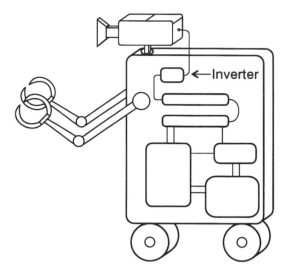

Figure 8.2

ago discontinued, but still in memory—and this activation of memory reminds the robot of the time it broke the light switch, shortcircuiting the whole house, and of the ensuing furor, the points subtracted from its good-designedness rating (a number that fluctuates up and down as the robot goes about its tasks, and having the effect, when it is diminishing rapidly, of causing major choatic reorganizations of its priority settings), and so forth.

In short, when a color is discriminated by the robot, the number doesn't *just* get stored away inertly in some register. It has a cascade of further effects, changing as a function of time and context.

Now along come the evil neurosurgeons—only these are computer scientists—and they do something ridiculously simple: They insert a little routine early in the system that subtracts each color's hue number from 1023, and sends on the balance!

Spectrum inversion! But to get the shocking effect, they have to make the change early, before the numbers begin cascading their effects through the memory (as in figure 8.2). If there is a central port, *after* the determination of color perception is accomplished and *before* all the effects, we have a place where we can locate the qualia of the system. An inversion there will throw the system into bizarre behavior. It lunges for the bright yellow extension cord, and pale green light reminds it of that unhappy episode with the light switch.

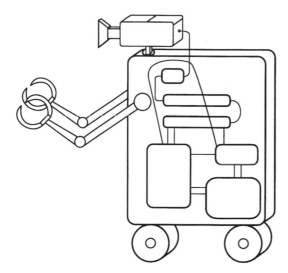

Figure 8.3

But if some other computer scientists come along and also invert the numbers-for-colors throughout memory, the robot will behave in every way exactly the way it did before. It will be a functional duplicate. But whereas Big Blue used to be registered by the hue number 477, now it is registered by the number 546, and so forth. Are the qualia still inverted? Well the numbers are. And this would be detectable trivially by a direct examination of the contents of each register—robot B could be distinguished from robot A, its presurgical twin, by the different voltage patterns used for each number. But lacking the capacity for such direct inspection, the robots would be unable to detect any differences in their own color behavior or "experience," and robot B would be oblivious to the switch from its earlier states. It would *have* to be oblivious to it, unless there were some leftover links to the old dispositional states which it could use for leverage—for identifying, to itself, the way things used to be.

But note that our spectrum inversion fantasy in the robot depends crucially on there being a central place from which all "subjective" color-effects flow. It is the value *in that register* that determines which color something "seems to be" to the robot. But what if there is no such central depot or clearing house? What if the various effects on memory and behavior start to diverge right from the tv-camera's signal (as in figure 8.3), utilizing different coding systems for different purposes, so that no single variable's value counts as the subjective effect of the perceived color?

Then the whole idea of qualia inversion becomes undefinable for the system. And that is precisely the situation we now know to exist in human perception. For instance, in some cases of cerebral achromatopsia, patients can see color boundaries in the absence of luminance or brightness boundaries, but cannot identify the colors that make the boundaries! (It is not that they claim to "see in black and white" either—they confidently name the colors, and have no complaint about their color vision at all—but their naming is at chance!)

The whole idea of qualia, as understood by *pholk* psychologists— that is, by philosophers who have massaged each others intuitions with a host of intuition pumps—is predicated on the mistaken idea that there is, there must be, such a central registration medium for subjectivity. Tradition has tacitly supposed that there is, but there is not. It's as simple as that.

9

The Practical Requirements for Making a Conscious Robot

In 1993, Rodney Brooks and Lynn Andrea Stein at the AI Lab at MIT invited me to join them as a subcontractor on a large grant proposal to build a humanoid robot, Cog. We didn't get the major grant, and are still looking for the bulk of the funding, but the project has struggled along remarkably well in dire straits. This essay introduces Cog, and concentrates on some of the philosophical implications. There are many important issues addressed by the Cog project; for the latest news, consult Cog's Web page, http://www.ai.mit.edu/projects/cog/.

Summary

Arguments about whether a robot could ever be conscious have been conducted up to now in the factually impoverished arena of what is "possible in principle." A team at MIT, of which I am a part, is now embarking on a long-term project to design and build a humanoid robot, Cog, whose cognitive talents will include speech, eye-coordinated manipulation of objects, and a host of self-protective, self-regulatory and self-exploring activities. The aim of the project is not to make a conscious robot, but to make a robot that can interact with human beings in a robust and versatile manner in real time, take care of itself, and tell its designers things about itself that would otherwise be extremely difficult if not impossible to determine by examination. Many of the details of Cog's "neural" organization will parallel what is known (or presumed known) about their counterparts in the human brain, but the intended realism of Cog as a model is relatively coarse-grained, varying opportunistically as a function of what we think we know,

Originally appeared in *Philosophical Transactions of the Royal Society*, A349, 1994, pp. 133–146.

what we think we can build, and what we think doesn't matter. Much of what we think will of course prove to be mistaken; that is one advantage of real experiments over thought experiments.

1   Are Conscious Robots Possible "In Principle"?

It is unlikely, in my opinion, that anyone will ever make a robot that is conscious in just the way we human beings are. Presumably that prediction is less interesting than the reasons one might offer for it. They might be deep (conscious robots are in some way "impossible in principle") or they might be trivial (for instance, conscious robots might simply cost too much to make). Nobody will ever synthesize a gall bladder out of atoms of the requisite elements, but I think it is uncontroversial that a gall bladder is nevertheless "just" a stupendous assembly of such atoms. Might a conscious robot be "just" a stupendous assembly of more elementary artifacts—silicon chips, wires, tiny motors and cameras—or would any such assembly, of whatever size and sophistication, have to leave out some special ingredient that is requisite for consciousness?

Let us briefly survey a nested series of reasons someone might advance for the impossibility of a conscious robot:

1. Robots are purely material things, and consciousness requires immaterial mind-stuff. (Old-fashioned dualism.)

It continues to amaze me how attractive this position still is to many people. I would have thought a historical perspective alone would make this view seem ludicrous: over the centuries, every *other* phenomenon of initially "supernatural" mysteriousness has succumbed to an uncontroversial explanation within the commodious folds of physical science. Thales, the pre-Socratic protoscientist, thought the loadstone had a soul, but we now know better; magnetism is one of the best understood of physical phenomena, strange though its manifestations are. The "miracles" of life itself, and of reproduction, are now analyzed into the well-known intricacies of molecular biology. Why should consciousness be any exception? Why should the brain be the only complex physical object in the universe to have an interface with another realm of being? Besides, the notorious problems with the supposed transactions at that dualistic interface are as good as a reductio ad absurdum of the view. The phenomena of consciousness are an admittedly dazzling lot, but I suspect that dualism would never be seriously considered if there weren't such a strong undercurrent of desire to protect the mind from science, by supposing it composed of a stuff that is in principle uninvestigatable by the methods of the physical sciences.

But if you are willing to concede the hopelessness of dualism, and accept some version of materialism, you might still hold:

2. Robots are inorganic (by definition), and consciousness can exist only in an organic brain.

Why might this be? Instead of just hooting this view off the stage as an embarrassing throwback to old-fashioned vitalism, we might pause to note that there is a respectable, if not very interesting, way of defending this claim. Vitalism is deservedly dead; as biochemistry has shown in matchless detail, the powers of organic compounds are themselves all mechanistically reducible and hence mechanistically reproducible at one scale or another in alternative physical media; but it is conceivable—if unlikely—that the sheer speed and compactness of biochemically engineered processes in the brain are in fact unreproducible in other physical media (Dennett, 1987, pp. 323–337). So there might be straightforward reasons of engineering that showed that any robot that could not make use of organic tissues of one sort or another within its fabric would be too ungainly to execute some task critical for consciousness. If making a conscious robot were conceived of as a sort of sporting event—like the America's Cup—rather than a scientific endeavor, this could raise a curious conflict over the official rules. Team A wants to use artificially constructed organic polymer "muscles" to move its robot's limbs, because otherwise the motor noise wreaks havoc with the robot's artificial ears. Should this be allowed? Is a robot with "muscles" instead of motors a robot within the meaning of the act? If muscles are allowed, what about lining the robot's artificial retinas with genuine organic rods and cones instead of relying on relatively clumsy color-tv technology?

I take it that no serious scientific or philosophical thesis links its fate to the fate of the proposition that a *protein-free* conscious robot can be made, for example. The standard understanding that a robot shall be made of metal, silicon chips, glass, plastic, rubber, and such, is an expression of the willingness of theorists to bet on a simplification of the issues: their conviction is that the crucial functions of intelligence can be achieved by one high-level simulation or another, so that it would be no undue hardship to restrict themselves to these materials, the readily available cost-effective ingredients in any case. But if somebody were to invent some sort of cheap artificial neural network fabric that could usefully be spliced into various tight corners in a robot's control system, the embarrassing fact that this fabric was made of organic molecules would not and should not dissuade serious roboticists from using it; and simply taking on the burden of explaining to the uninitiated why this did not constitute "cheating" in any important sense.

I have discovered that some people are attracted by a third reason for believing in the impossibility of conscious robots.

3. Robots are artifacts, and consciousness abhors an artifact; only something natural, born not manufactured, could exhibit genuine consciousness.

Once again, it is tempting to dismiss this claim with derision, and in some of its forms, derision is just what it deserves. Consider the general category of creed we might call *origin essentialism:* only wine made under the direction of the proprietors of Chateau Plonque counts as genuine Chateau Plonque; only a canvas every blotch on which was caused by the hand of Cézanne counts as a genuine Cézanne; only someone "with Cherokee blood" can be a real Cherokee. There are perfectly respectable reasons, eminently defensible in a court of law, for maintaining such distinctions, so long as they are understood to be protections of rights growing out of historical processes. If they are interpreted, however, as indicators of "intrinsic properties" that set their holders apart from their otherwise indistinguishable counterparts, they are pernicious nonsense. Let us dub *origin chauvinism* the category of view that holds out for some mystic difference (a difference of value, typically) due *simply* to such a fact about origin. Perfect imitation Chateau Plonque is exactly as good a wine as the real thing, counterfeit though it is, and the same holds for the fake Cézanne, if it is really indistinguishable by experts. And of course no person is intrinsically better or worse in any regard just for having or not having Cherokee (or Jewish, or African) "blood."

And to take a threadbare philosophical example, an atom-for-atom duplicate of a human being, an artifactual counterfeit of you, let us say, might not *legally* be you, and hence might not be entitled to your belongings, or deserve your punishments, but the suggestion that such a being would not be a feeling, conscious, alive *person* as genuine as any born of woman is preposterous nonsense, all the more deserving of our ridicule because if taken seriously it might seem to lend credibility to the racist drivel with which it shares a bogus intuition.

If consciousness abhors an artifact, it cannot be because being born gives a complex of cells a property (aside from that historic property itself) that it could not otherwise have "in principle." There might, however, be a question of practicality. We have just seen how, as a matter of exigent practicality, it could turn out after all that organic materials were needed to make a conscious robot. For similar reasons, it could turn out that any conscious robot had to be, if not born, at least the beneficiary of a longish period of infancy. Making a fully equipped conscious adult robot might just be too much work. It might be vastly easier to make an initially unconscious or nonconscious infant robot and let it "grow up" into consciousness, more or less the way we all do. This hunch is not the disreputable claim that a certain sort of historic process puts a mystic stamp of approval on its product, but the more interesting and plausible claim that a certain sort of process is the only practical way of designing all the things that need designing in a conscious being.

Such a claim is entirely reasonable. Compare it to the claim one might make about the creation of Steven Spielberg's film, *Schindler's List:* It could not have been created entirely by computer animation, without the filming of real live actors. This impossibility claim must be false "in principle," since every frame of that film is nothing more than a matrix of gray-scale pixels of the sort that computer animation can manifestly create, at any level of detail or realism you are willing to pay for. There is nothing mystical, however, about the claim that it would be practically impossible to render the nuances of that film by such a bizarre exercise of technology. How much easier it is, practically, to put actors in the relevant circumstances, in a concrete simulation of the scenes one wishes to portray, and let them, via ensemble activity and re-activity, provide the information to the cameras that will then fill in all the pixels in each frame. This little exercise of the imagination helps to drive home just how much information there is in a "realistic" film, but even a great film, such as *Schindler's List,* for all its complexity, is a simple, noninteractive artifact many orders of magnitude less complex than a conscious being.

When robot makers have claimed in the past that in principle they could construct "by hand" a conscious robot, this was a hubristic overstatement analogous to what Walt Disney might once have proclaimed: that his studio of animators could create a film so realistic that no one would be able to tell that it was a cartoon, not a "live action" film. What Disney couldn't do in fact, computer animators still cannot do, but perhaps only for the time being. Robot makers, even with the latest high-tech innovations, also fall far short of their hubristic goals, now and for the foreseeable future. The comparison serves to expose the likely source of the outrage so many skeptics feel when they encounter the manifestos of the Artificial Intelligencia. Anyone who seriously claimed that *Schindler's List* could in fact have been made by computer animation could be seen to betray an obscenely impoverished sense of what is conveyed in that film. An important element of the film's power is the fact that it *is* a film made by assembling human actors to portray those events, and that it is not actually the newsreel footage that its black-and-white format reminds you of. When one juxtaposes in one's imagination a sense of what the actors must have gone through to make the film with a sense of what the people who actually lived the events went through, this reflection sets up reverberations in one's thinking that draw attention to the deeper meanings of the film. Similarly, when robot enthusiasts proclaim the likelihood that they can simply *construct* a conscious robot, there is an understandable suspicion that they are simply betraying an infantile grasp of the subtleties of conscious life. (I hope I have put enough feeling into that condemnation to satisfy the skeptics.)

But however justified that might be in some instances as an ad hominem suspicion, it is simply irrelevant to the important theoretical issues. Perhaps no cartoon could be a great film, but they are certainly real films, and some are indeed good films; if the best the roboticists can hope for is the creation of some crude, cheesy, second-rate, artificial consciousness, they still win. Still, it is not a foregone conclusion that even this modest goal is reachable. If you want to have a defensible reason for claiming that no conscious robot will ever be created, you might want to settle for this.

4. Robots will always just be much too simple to be conscious.

After all, a normal human being is composed of trillions of parts (if we descend to the level of the macromolecules), and many of these rival in complexity and design cunning the fanciest artifacts that have ever been created. We consist of billions of cells, and a single human cell contains within itself complex "machinery" that is still well beyond the artifactual powers of engineers. We are composed of thousands of different kinds of cells, including thousands of different species of symbiont visitors, some of whom might be as important to our consciousness as others are to our ability to digest our food! If all that complexity were needed for consciousness to exist, then the task of making a single conscious robot would dwarf the entire scientific and engineering resources of the planet for millennia. And who would pay for it?

If no other reason can be found, this may do to ground your skepticism about conscious robots in your future, but one shortcoming of this last reason is that it is scientifically boring. If this is the only reason there won't be conscious robots, then consciousness isn't that special, after all. Another shortcoming with this reason is that it is dubious on its face. Everywhere else we have looked, we have found higher-level commonalities of function that permit us to substitute relatively simple bits for fiendishly complicated bits. Artificial heart valves work really very well, but they are orders of magnitude simpler than organic heart valves, heart valves born of woman or sow, you might say. Artificial ears and eyes that will do a serviceable (if crude) job of substituting for lost perceptual organs are visible on the horizon, and anyone who doubts they are possible in principle is simply out of touch. Nobody ever said a prosthetic eye had to see as keenly, or focus as fast, or be as sensitive to color gradations as a normal human (or other animal) eye in order to count as an eye. If an eye, why not an optic nerve (or acceptable substitute thereof), and so forth, all the way in?

Some (Searle, 1992; Mangan, 1993) have supposed, most improbably, that this proposed regress would somewhere run into a nonfungible medium of consciousness, a part of the brain that could not be substituted on pain of death or zombiehood. Once the implications of that view are spelled out (Dennett, 1993a, 1993e), one can see that it is a nonstarter. There is no reason at all to believe that some one part of the brain is utterly irreplaceable by prosthesis, provided we allow that some crudity, some loss of function, is to be expected in most substitutions of the simple for the complex. An artificial brain is, on the face of it, as "possible in principle" as an artificial heart, just much, much harder to make and hook up. Of course once we start letting crude forms of prosthetic consciousness—like crude forms of prosthetic vision or hearing—pass our litmus tests for consciousness (whichever tests we favor) the way is open for another boring debate, over whether the phenomena in question are too crude to count.

2   The Cog Project: A Humanoid Robot

A much more interesting tack to explore, in my opinion, is simply to
set out to make a robot that is theoretically interesting independent of
the philosophical conundrum about whether it is conscious. Such a
robot would have to perform a lot of the feats that we have typically
associated with consciousness in the past, but we would not need to
dwell on that issue from the outset. Maybe we could even learn something interesting about what the truly hard problems are without ever
settling any of the issues about consciousness.

Such a project is now underway at MIT. Under the direction of Rodney Brooks and Lynn Andrea Stein of the AI Lab, a group of bright,
hard-working young graduate students are laboring as I speak to create
Cog, the most humanoid robot yet attempted, and I am happy to be a
part of the Cog team. Cog is just about life-size, about the size of a
human adult. Cog has no legs, but lives bolted at the hips, you might
say, to its stand. It has two human-length arms, however, with somewhat simple hands on the wrists. It can bend at the waist and swing
its torso, and its head moves with three degrees of freedom just about
the way yours does. It has two eyes, each equipped with both a foveal
high-resolution vision area and a low-resolution wide-angle parafoveal
vision area, and these eyes saccade at almost human speed. That is,
the two eyes can complete approximately three fixations a second,
while you and I can manage four or five. Your foveas are at the center
of your retinas, surrounded by the grainier low-resolution parafoveal
areas; for reasons of engineering simplicity, Cog's eyes have their foveas mounted above their wide-angle vision areas.

This is typical of the sort of compromise that the Cog team is willing
to make. It amounts to a wager that a vision system with the foveas
moved out of the middle can still work well enough not to be debilitat-
ing, and the problems encountered will not be irrelevant to the problems encountered in normal human vision. After all, nature gives us
examples of other eyes with different foveal arrangements. Eagles, for
instance, have two different foveas in each eye. Cog's eyes won't give
it visual information exactly like that provided to human vision by
human eyes (in fact, of course, it will be vastly degraded), but the wager is that this will be plenty to give Cog the opportunity to perform
impressive feats of hand-eye coordination, identification, and search.
At the outset, Cog will not have color vision.

Since its eyes are video cameras mounted on delicate, fast-moving
gimbals, it might be disastrous if Cog were inadvertently to punch it-

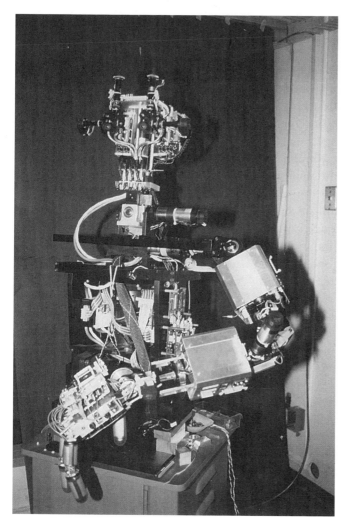

Figure 9.1
Cog, a pre-natal portrait

self in the eye, so part of the hard-wiring that must be provided in advance is an "innate" if rudimentary "pain" or "alarm" system to serve roughly the same protective functions as the reflex eye-blink and pain-avoidance systems hard-wired into human infants.

Cog will not be an adult at first, in spite of its adult size. It is being designed to pass through an extended period of artificial infancy, during which it will have to learn from experience, experience it will gain in the rough-and-tumble environment of the real world. Like a human infant, however, it will need a great deal of protection at the outset, in spite of the fact that it will be equipped with many of the most crucial safety-systems of a living being. It has limit switches, heat sensors, current sensors, strain gauges, and alarm signals in all the right places to prevent it from destroying its many motors and joints. It has enormous "funny bones"; motors sticking out from its elbows in a risky way. These will be protected from harm not by being shielded in heavy armor, but by being equipped with patches of exquisitely sensitive piezo-electric membrane "skin" which will trigger alarms when they make contact with anything. The goal is that Cog will quickly learn to keep its funny bones from being bumped: If Cog cannot learn this in short order, it will have to have this high-priority policy hard-wired in. The same sensitive membranes will be used on its fingertips and elsewhere, and, like human tactile nerves, the meaning of the signals sent along the attached wires will depend more on what the central control system makes of them than on their intrinsic characteristics. A gentle touch, signalling sought-for contact with an object to be grasped, will not differ, as an information packet, from a sharp pain, signalling a need for rapid countermeasures. It all depends on what the central system is designed to do with the packet, and this design is itself indefinitely revisable; something that can be adjusted either by Cog's own experience or by the tinkering of Cog's artificers.

One of its most interesting "innate" endowments will be software for visual face recognition. Faces will "pop out" from the background of other objects as items of special interest to Cog. It will further be innately designed to want to keep its mother's face in view, and to work hard to keep mother from turning away. The role of "mother" has not yet been cast, but several of the graduate students have been tentatively tapped for this role. Unlike a human infant, of course, there is no reason why Cog can't have a whole team of mothers, each of whom is innately distinguished by Cog as a face to please if possible. Clearly, even if Cog really does have a *Lebenswelt*, it will not be the same as *ours*.

Decisions have not yet been reached about many of the candidates for hard-wiring or innate features. Anything that can learn must be initially equipped with a great deal of unlearned design. That is no longer an issue; no tabula rasa could ever be impressed with knowledge from experience. But it is also not much of an issue which features ought to be innately fixed, for there is a convenient trade-off. I haven't mentioned yet that Cog will actually be a multigenerational series of ever improved models (if all goes well!), but of course that is the way any complex artifact gets designed. Any feature that is not innately fixed at the outset, but does get itself designed into Cog's control system through learning, can then often be lifted whole (with some revision, perhaps) into Cog-II, as a new bit of innate endowment designed by Cog itself—or rather by Cog's history of interactions with its environment. So even in cases in which we have the best of reasons for thinking that human infants actually come innately equipped with pre-designed gear, we may choose to try to get Cog to learn the design in question, rather than be born with it. In some instances, this is laziness or opportunism—we don't really know what might work well, but maybe Cog can train itself up. This insouciance about the putative nature / nurture boundary is already a familiar attitude among neural net modelers, of course. Although Cog is not specifically intended to demonstrate any particular neural net thesis, it should come as no surprise that Cog's nervous system is a massively parallel architecture capable of simultaneously training up an indefinite number of special-purpose networks or circuits, under various regimes.

How plausible is the hope that Cog can retrace the steps of millions of years of evolution in a few months or years of laboratory exploration? Notice first that what I have just described is a variety of Lamarckian inheritance that no organic lineage has been able to avail itself of. The acquired design innovations of Cog can be immediately transferred to Cog-II, a speed-up of evolution of tremendous, if incalculable, magnitude. Moreover, if you bear in mind that, unlike the natural case, there will be a team of overseers ready to make patches whenever obvious shortcomings reveal themselves, and to jog the systems out of ruts whenever they enter them, it is not so outrageous a hope, in our opinion. But then, we are all rather outrageous people.

One talent that we have hopes of teaching to Cog is a rudimentary capacity for human language. And here we run into the fabled innate language organ or Language Acquisition Device (LAD) made famous by Noam Chomsky. Is there going to be an attempt to build an innate LAD for our Cog? No. We are going to try to get Cog to build language the hard way, the way our ancestors must have done, over thousands of generations. Cog has ears (four, because it's easier to get good localization with four microphones than with carefully shaped ears like ours!) and some special-purpose signal-analyzing software is being developed to give Cog a fairly good chance of discriminating human speech sounds, and probably the capacity to distinguish different human voices. Cog will also have to have speech synthesis hardware and software, of course, but decisions have not yet been reached about the details. It is important to have Cog as well-equipped as possible for rich and natural interactions with human beings, for the team intends to take advantage of as much free labor as it can. Untrained people ought to be able to spend time—hours if they like, and we rather hope they do—trying to get Cog to learn this or that. Growing into an adult is a long, time-consuming business, and Cog—and the team that is building Cog—will need all the help it can get.

Obviously this will not work unless the team manages somehow to give Cog a motivational structure that can be at least dimly recognized, responded to, and exploited by naive observers. In short, Cog should be as human as possible in its wants and fears, likes and dislikes. If those anthropomorphic terms strike you as unwarranted, put them in scare-quotes or drop them altogether and replace them with tedious neologisms of your own choosing: Cog, you may prefer to say, must have *goal-registrations* and *preference-functions* that map in rough isomorphism to human desires. This is so for many reasons, of course. Cog won't work at all unless it has its act together in a daunting number of different regards. It must somehow delight in learning, abhor error, strive for novelty, recognize progress. It must be vigilant in some regards, curious in others, and deeply unwilling to engage in self-destructive activity. While we are at it, we might as well try to make it crave human praise and company, and even exhibit a sense of humor.

Let me switch abruptly from this heavily anthropomorphic language to a brief description of Cog's initial endowment of information-processing hardware. The computer-complex that has been built to serve as the development platform for Cog's artificial nervous system consists of four backplanes, each with 16 nodes; each node is basically a Mac-II computer—a 68332 processor with a megabyte of RAM. In other words, you can think of Cog's brain as roughly equivalent to sixty-four Mac-IIs yoked in a custom parallel architecture. Each node is itself a multiprocessor, and instead of running Mac software, they all run a special version of parallel Lisp developed by Rodney Brooks, and called, simply, "L." Each node has an interpreter for L in its ROM, so it can execute L files independently of every other node.

Each node has six assignable input-output ports, in addition to the possibility of separate i-o (input-output) to the motor boards directly controlling the various joints, as well as the all-important i-o to the experimenters' monitoring and control system, the Front End Processor or FEP (via another unit known as the Interfep). On a bank of separate monitors, one can see the current image in each camera (two foveas, two parafoveas), the activity in each of the many different visual processing areas, or the activities of any other nodes. Cog is thus equipped at birth with the equivalent of chronically implanted electrodes for each of its neurons; all its activities can be monitored in real time, recorded, and debugged. The FEP is itself a Macintosh computer in more conventional packaging. At startup, each node is awakened by a FEP call that commands it to load its appropriate files of L from a file server. These files configure it for whatever tasks it has currently been designed to execute. Thus the underlying hardware machine can be turned into any of a host of different virtual machines, thanks to the capacity of each node to run its current program. The nodes do not make further use of disk memory, however, during normal operation. They keep their transient memories locally, in their individual megabytes of RAM. In other words, Cog stores both its genetic endowment (the virtual machine) and its long-term memory on disk when it is shut down, but when it is powered on, it first configures itself and then stores all its short term memory distributed one way or another among its sixty-four nodes.

The space of possible virtual machines made available and readily explorable by this underlying architecture is huge, of course, and it covers a volume in the space of all computations that has not yet been seriously explored by artificial intelligence researchers. Moreover, the space of possibilities it represents is manifestly much more realistic as a space to build brains in than is the space heretofore explored, either by the largely serial architectures of GOFAI ("Good Old Fashioned AI," Haugeland, 1985), or by parallel architectures simulated by serial machines. Nevertheless, it is arguable that every one of the possible virtual machines executable by Cog is minute in comparison to a real human brain. In short, Cog has a tiny brain. There is a big wager being made: the parallelism made possible by this arrangement will be sufficient to provide real-time control of importantly humanoid activities occurring on a human timescale. If this proves to be too optimistic by as little as an order of magnitude, the whole project will be forlorn, for the motivating insight for the project is that by confronting and solving *actual, real time* problems of self-protection, hand-eye coordination, and interaction with other animate beings, Cog's artificers will discover the *sufficient* conditions for higher cognitive functions in general—and maybe even for a variety of consciousness that would satisfy the skeptics.

It is important to recognize that although the theoretical importance of having a body has been appreciated ever since Alan Turing (1950) drew specific attention to it in his classic paper, "Computing Machines and Intelligence," within the field of Artificial Intelligence there has long been a contrary opinion that robotics is largely a waste of time, money, and effort. According to this view, whatever deep principles of organization make cognition possible can be as readily discovered in the more abstract realm of pure simulation, at a fraction of the cost. In many fields, this thrifty attitude has proven to be uncontroversial wisdom. No economists have asked for the funds to implement their computer models of markets and industries in tiny robotic Wall Streets or Detroits, and civil engineers have largely replaced their scale models of bridges and tunnels with computer models that can do a better job of simulating all the relevant conditions of load, stress, and strain. Closer to home, simulations of ingeniously oversimplified imaginary organisms foraging in imaginary environments, avoiding imaginary predators and differentially producing imaginary offspring are yielding important insights into the mechanisms of evolution and ecology in the new field of Artificial Life. So it is something of a surprise to find this AI group conceding, in effect, that there is indeed something to the skeptics' claim (see, e.g., Dreyfus and Dreyfus, 1986) that genuine embodiment in a real world is crucial to consciousness. Not, I hasten to add, because genuine embodiment provides some special vital juice that mere virtual-world simulations cannot secrete, but for the more practical reason—or hunch—that unless you saddle yourself with all the problems of making a concrete agent take care of itself in the real world, you will tend to overlook, underestimate, or misconstrue the deepest problems of design.

Besides, as I have already noted, there is the hope that Cog will be able to design itself in large measure, learning from infancy, and building its own representation of its world in the terms that it innately understands. Nobody doubts that any agent capable of interacting intelligently with a human being on human terms must have access to literally millions if not billions of logically independent items of world knowledge. Either these must be hand-coded individually by human programmers—a tactic being pursued, notoriously, by Douglas Lenat (Lenat and Guha, 1990) and his CYC team in Dallas—or some way must be found for the artificial agent to learn its world knowledge from (real) interactions with the (real) world. The potential virtues of this shortcut have long been recognized within AI circles (see, e.g., Waltz, 1988). The unanswered question is whether taking on the task of solving the grubby details of real-world robotics will actually permit one to finesse the task of hand-coding the world knowledge. Brooks, Stein, and their team—myself included—are gambling that it will.

At this stage of the project, most of the problems being addressed would never arise in the realm of pure, disembodied AI. How many separate motors might be used for controlling each hand? They will have to be mounted somehow on the forearms. Will there then be room to mount the motor boards directly on the arms, close to the joints they control, or would they get in the way? How much cabling can each arm carry before weariness or clumsiness overcome it? The arm joints have been built to be compliant—springy, like your own joints. This means that if Cog wants to do some fine-fingered manipulation, it will have to learn to "burn" some of the degrees of freedom in its arm motion by temporarily bracing its elbows or wrists on a table or other convenient landmark, just as you would do. Such compliance is typical of the mixed bag of opportunities and problems created by real robotics. Another is the need for self-calibration or recalibration in the eyes. If Cog's eyes jiggle away from their preset aim, thanks to the wear and tear of all that sudden saccading, there must be ways for Cog to compensate, short of trying continually to adjust its camera-eyes with its fingers. Software designed to tolerate this probable sloppiness in the first place may well be more robust and versatile in many other ways than software designed to work in a more "perfect" world.

Earlier I mentioned a reason for using artificial muscles, not motors, to control a robot's joints, and the example was not imaginary. Brooks is concerned that the sheer noise of Cog's skeletal activities may seriously interfere with the attempt to give Cog humanoid hearing. There is research underway at the AI Lab to develop synthetic electro-mechanical muscle tissues, which would operate silently as well as being more compact, but this will not be available for early incarnations of Cog. For an entirely different reason, thought is being given to the option of designing Cog's visual control software *as if* its eyes were moved by muscles, not motors, building in a software interface that amounts to giving Cog a set of *virtual* eye-muscles. Why might this extra complication in the interface be wise? Because the "opponent-process" control system exemplified by eye-muscle controls is apparently a deep and ubiquitous feature of nervous systems, involved in control of attention generally and disrupted in such pathologies as uni-lateral neglect. If we are going to have such competitive systems at higher levels of control, it might be wise to build them in "all the way down," concealing the final translation into electric-motor-talk as part of the backstage implementation, not the model.

Other practicalities are more obvious, or at least more immediately evocative to the uninitiated. Three huge red "emergency kill" buttons have already been provided in Cog's environment, to ensure that if Cog happens to engage in some activity that could injure or endanger a human interactor (or itself), there is a way of getting it to stop. But what is the appropriate response for Cog to make to the kill button? If power to Cog's motors is suddenly shut off, Cog will slump, and its arms will crash down on whatever is below them. Is this what we want to happen? Do we want Cog to drop whatever it is holding? What should "Stop!" *mean* to Cog? This is a real issue about which there is not yet any consensus.

There are many more details of the current and anticipated design of Cog that are of more than passing interest to those in the field, but on this occasion, I want to address some overriding questions that have been much debated by philosophers, and that receive a ready treatment in the environment of thought made possible by Cog. In other words, let's consider Cog merely as a prosthetic aid to philosophical thought experiments, a modest but by no means negligible role for Cog to play.

3 Three Philosophical Themes Addressed

A recent criticism of "strong AI" that has received quite a bit of atten-tion is the so-called problem of symbol grounding (Harnad, 1990). It is all very well for large AI programs to have data structures that *pur-port* to refer to Chicago, milk, or the person to whom I am now talking, but such imaginary reference is not the same as real reference, ac-cording to this line of criticism. These internal "symbols" are not prop-erly "grounded" in the world, and the problems thereby eschewed by pure, nonrobotic AI are not trivial or peripheral. As one who discussed, and ultimately dismissed, a version of this problem many years ago (Dennett, 1969, p. 182ff), I would not want to be interpreted as now abandoning my earlier view. I submit that Cog moots the problem of symbol grounding, without having to settle its status as a criticism of "strong AI." Anything in Cog that might be a candidate for symbolhood will automatically be grounded in Cog's real predicament, as surely as its counterpart in any child, so the issue doesn't arise, except as a practical problem for the Cog team, to be solved or not, as fortune dictates. If the day ever comes for Cog to comment to anybody about Chicago, the question of whether Cog is in any position to do so will arise for exactly the same reasons, and be resolvable on the same considerations, as the parallel question about the reference of the word "Chicago" in the idiolect of a young child.

Another claim that has often been advanced, most carefully by Haugeland (1985), is that nothing could properly "matter" to an artificial intelligence, and mattering (it is claimed) is crucial to consciousness. Haugeland restricted his claim to traditional GOFAI systems, and left robots out of consideration. Would he concede that something could matter to Cog? The question, presumably, is how seriously to weigh the import of the quite deliberate decision by Cog's creators to make Cog as much as possible responsible for its own welfare. Cog will be equipped with some innate but not at all arbitrary preferences, and hence provided of necessity with the concomitant capacity to be "bothered" by the thwarting of those preferences, and "pleased" by the furthering of the ends it was innately designed to seek. Some may want to retort: "This is not *real* pleasure or pain, but merely a simulacrum." Perhaps, but on what grounds will they defend this claim? Cog may be said to have quite crude, simplistic, one-dimensional pleasure and pain, cartoon pleasure and pain if you like, but then the same might also be said of the pleasure and pain of simpler organisms— clams or houseflies, for instance. Most, if not all, of the burden of proof is shifted by Cog, in my estimation. The reasons for saying that something *does* matter to Cog are not arbitrary; they are exactly parallel to the reasons we give for saying that things matter to us and to other creatures. Since we have cut off the dubious retreats to vitalism or origin chauvinism, it will be interesting to see if the skeptics have any good reasons for declaring Cog's pains and pleasures not to matter— at least to it, and for that very reason, to us as well. It will come as no surprise, I hope, that more than a few participants in the Cog project are already musing about what obligations they might come to have to Cog, over and above their obligations to the Cog team.

Finally, J. R. Lucas has raised the claim (Lucas, 1994) that if a robot were really conscious, we would have to be prepared to believe it about its own internal states. I would like to close by pointing out that this is a rather likely reality in the case of Cog. Although equipped with an optimal suite of monitoring devices that will reveal the details of its inner workings to the observing team, Cog's own pronouncements could very well come to be a more trustworthy and informative source of information on what was really going on inside it. The information visible on the banks of monitors, or gathered by the gigabyte on hard disks, will be at the outset almost as hard to interpret, even by Cog's own designers, as the information obtainable by such "third-person" methods as MRI and CT scanning in the neurosciences. As the observers refine their models, and their understanding of their models, their authority as interpreters of the data may grow, but it may also suffer eclipse. Especially since Cog will be designed from the outset to redesign itself as much as possible, there is a high probability that the designers will simply lose the standard hegemony of the artificer ("I made it, so I know what it is supposed to do, and what it is doing now!"). Into this epistemological vacuum Cog may very well thrust itself. In fact, I would gladly defend the conditional prediction: *if* Cog develops to the point where it can conduct what appear to be robust and well-controlled conversations in something like a natural language, it will certainly be in a position to rival its own monitors (and the theorists who interpret them) as a source of knowledge about what it is doing and feeling, and why.

10

The Unimagined Preposterousness of Zombies: Commentary on Moody, Flanagan, and Polger

The explosion of interest in consciousness has led to the creation of several new journals, of which the most . . . ecumenical is Journal of Consciousness Studies. *It seemed an appropriate place to lay down the gauntlet about a topic that other journals would, quite appropriately, shun. It helps to have read the essays by Moody and Flanagan and Polger to which this is a reply, but one can get the point of my challenge without them. To date, several philosophers have told me that they plan to accept my challenge to offer a non-question-begging defense of zombies, but the only one I have seen so far involves postulating a "logically possible" but fantastic being — a descendent of Ned Block's Giant Lookup Table fantasy discussed in chapter 1. This entity, by its author's admission, "would no doubt undergo gravitational collapse and become a black hole before making his mark on either philosophy or haute cuisine" (Mulhauser, unpublished). I get the point, but I am not moved.*

Knock-down refutations are rare in philosophy, and unambiguous self-refutations are even rarer, for obvious reasons, but sometimes we get lucky. Sometimes philosophers clutch an insupportable hypothesis to their bosoms and run headlong over the cliff edge. Then, like cartoon characters, they hang there in midair, until they notice what they have done and gravity takes over. Just such a boon is the philosophers' concept of a zombie, a strangely attractive notion that sums up, in one leaden lump, almost everything that I think is wrong with current thinking about consciousness. Philosophers ought to have dropped the zombie like a hot potato, but since they persist in their embrace, this gives me a golden opportunity to focus attention on the most seductive error in current thinking.

Todd Moody's (1994) essay on zombies, and Owen Flanagan and

Originally appeared in *Journal of Consciousness Studies*, 2 (4), 1995, pp. 322–326.

Thomas Polger's (1995) commentary on it, vividly illustrate a point I have made before, but now want to drive home: when philosophers claim that zombies are conceivable, they invariably underestimate the task of conception (or imagination), and end up imagining something that violates their own definition. This conceals from them the fact that the philosophical concept of a zombie is sillier than they have noticed. Or to put the same point positively, the fact that they take zombies seriously can be used to show just how easy it is to underestimate the power of the "behaviorism" they oppose. Again and again in Moody's essay, he imagines scenarios to which he is not entitled. If, ex hypothesi, zombies are behaviorally indistinguishable from us normal folk, then they are really behaviorally indistinguishable! They say just what we say, they understand what they say (or, not to beg any questions, they understand$_z$ what they say), they believe$_z$ what we believe, right down to having beliefs$_z$ that perfectly mirror all our beliefs about inverted spectra, "qualia," *and every other possible topic of human reflection and conversation.* Flanagan and Polger point out several of Moody's imaginative lapses on these matters in careful detail, so I needn't belabor them. In any case, they follow trivially from the philosophical concept of a zombie.

Flanagan and Polger also fall in the very same trap, however. For instance, they say it is "highly unlikely—implausible to the extreme—that mentalistic vocabulary would evolve among Moody's zombies. But is it metaphysically, logically, or nomically impossible? No." Here getting it half right is getting it all wrong. It is *not at all* unlikely or implausible that mentalistic vocabulary would evolve among zombies. That must be conceded as part of the concession that zombies are "behavioral" twins of conscious beings; if it is likely that we conscious folks would develop mentalistic vocabulary, then it must be exactly as likely that zombies do. It is just such lapses as this one by Flanagan and Polger that feed the persistent mis-imagination of zombies and make them appear less preposterous than they are.

Some zombies *do* have an "inner life." In Dennett (1991a), I introduced the category of a *zimbo*, by definition a zombie equipped for higher-order reflective informational states (e.g., beliefs$_z$ about its other beliefs$_z$ and its other zombic states). This was a strategic move on my part, I hasten to add. Its point was to make a distinction within the imaginary category of zombies that would have to be granted by believers in zombies, and that could do all the work they imputed to consciousness, thereby showing either that their concept was subtly self-contradictory, since some zombies—zimboes—were conscious after all, or that their concept of consciousness was not tied to anything familiar and hence amounted to an illicit contrast: consciousness as a "player to be named later" or an undeclared wild card. As I pointed out when I introduced the term, zombies behaviorally indistinguishable from us are zimboes, capable of all the higher-order reflections we are capable of, because they are competent, ex hypothesi, to execute all the behaviors that, when we perform them, manifestly depend on our higher-order reflections. Only zimboes could pass a demanding Turing test, for instance, since the judge can ask as many questions as you like about what it was like answering the previous question, what it is like thinking about how to answer this question, and so forth. Zimboes think$_z$ they are conscious, think$_z$ they have qualia, think$_z$ they suffer pains—they are just "wrong" (according to this lamentable tradition), in ways that neither they nor we could ever discover!

According to Flanagan and Polger, there is still a difference between the inner lives of zombies and ours: theirs are merely "informationally sensitive" while ours are also "experientially sensitive." This contrast, drawn from Flanagan (1992) is ill conceived, so far as I can see. It apparently arises out of a self-induced illusion, a fallacy of subtraction. On this outing, it arises in Flanagan and Polger's brisk dismissal of my accounts of pain and lust. They concede that there is an uncontroversial evolutionary explanation of why there should be a peremptory (well-nigh irresistible) damage-alarm system, or a clarion call system in the case of sex, but, they ask, what about the evolutionary explanation of the conscious feelings themselves? They see me as failing to address (or address well) my own further questions about why the pains should hurt so much, or why (in our species) lust should be so . . . lusty. I had better spell out my view in a little more detail.

In creatures as cognitively complex as us (with our roughly inexhaustible capacity for meta-reflections and higher-order competitions between policies, meta-policies, etc.), the "blood-is-about-to-be-lost sensors" and their kin cannot *simply* be "hooked up to the right action paths" as Flanagan and Polger put it. These ancestral hookups, which serve quite well in simpler creatures, do exist in us as part of our innate wiring, but they can be overridden by a sufficiently potent coalition of competing drafts (in my Multiple Drafts Model). So it is that in us, there is an *informationally sensitive* tug-of-war, which leaves many traces, provokes many reflections (about the detailed awfulness of it all), permits many protocols (and poignant complaints), adjusts many behavioral propensities (such as desires to reform one's ways, or seek revenge), lays down many ("false") memories about the way the pain felt, etc. Notice that "experiential sensitivity" (whatever that might be) never comes into my account—the "conscious feelings themselves" get distributed around into the powers and dispositional effects of all the extra informational machinery—machinery lacking in the case of simple organisms. My account is entirely in terms of complications that naturally arise in the competitive interaction between elements in the Multiple Drafts Model. It would serve exactly as well as an account of the pain and lust systems in zimboes, who are so complex in their internal cognitive architecture that whenever there is a strong signal in either the pain or the lust circuitry, all these "merely informational" effects (and the effects of those effects, etc.), are engendered. That's why zimboes, too, wonder$_z$ why sex is so sexy for them (but not for simpler zombies, such as insects) and why their pains have to "hurt."

If you deny that zimboes would wonder such wonders, you contradict the definition of a zombie. Hark back to a point I made in *Brainstorms* (1978a) about what I called the beta-manifold of beliefs arising from having mental images. The game is over as soon as the zombie-defender grants—as the zombie-defender must on pain of self-contradiction—that there is no human belief (however much concerned with "phenomenal" topics) that does not have a zombic functional counterpart—a mere belief$_z$—which is behaviorally indistinguishable from that belief.

Notice what has happened. The contrast Flanagan and Polger would draw between zombies and us in regard to pain and sex, I draw between simple zombies and fancier zombies—zimboes. And I have offered a sketch of an evolutionary account of why this contrast would exist. (It is evolutionary in the extended sense that applies to systems that evolve within individual organisms during their lifetimes.) This responds directly to Flanagan and Polger's demand for an explanation from me of why *our* pains should hurt and why sex should strike *us* as so sexy. We are not just simple zombies, but zimboes, and zimboes, unlike insects and even most mammals, *do* find sex sexy, and *do* wonder about why pain has to hurt. Flanagan and Polger overlook this fact about zimboes, and hence mis-locate the contrast. "Why think," they ask, "even supposing that luna moth mating behavior is regulated by olfactory cues, that any advantage whatsoever is conferred by experienced odors that arouse lust over sensors that unconsciously pick up the airborne chemical cues indicating that it is time to mate?" But who says luna moths do experience lust? I see no reason to believe they do. If luna moths are zombies, they are not zimboes; they are simpler zombies. And indeed, to respond to Flanagan and Polger's question, there is no evolutionary reason at hand to suppose that their sex-drive is complicated by storms of lust. The experience of lust is the fate of fancier creatures—zimboes like us.

This mis-location of the issue by Flanagan and Polger gives illicit support to their claim that "experiential sensitivity" differs from mere "informational sensitivity" by encouraging (however unintendedly) the following fallacious train of thought (I have tested this on my students): zombies would pull their hands off hot stoves, and breed like luna moths, but they wouldn't be upset by memories or anticipations of pain, and they wouldn't be apt to engage in sexual fantasies. No. While all this might be true of simple zombies, zimboes would be exactly as engrossed by sexual fantasies as we are, and exactly as unwilling to engage in behaviors they anticipate to be painful. If you imagine them otherwise, you have just not imagined zombies correctly.

Flanagan and Polger compound this mistake when they go on to ask what the adaptive advantage of consciousness (as contrasted with mere "informational sensitivity") would be. It can't be "learning and plasticity," they argue, since learning and plasticity can go on without consciousness. It can go on in zimboes, for instance. I expect that they might concede that my story does succeed in explaining (in a sketchy and speculative way) why zimboes might evolve from simpler zombies, and what particular advantages (e.g., in learning and plasticity) their capacities for higher-order reflection might have. But they don't see this as even the beginnings of an evolutionary account of consciousness, since by their lights what zimboes have but simpler zombies lack is not consciousness at all, not "experiential sensitivity." What zimboes have, however, is the very sort of thing they were pointing to when they demanded from me an account of hurting pains and sexy feelings.

The question of adaptive advantage, however, is ill posed in the first place. If consciousness is (as I argue) not a single wonderful separable thing ("experiential sensitivity") but a huge complex of many different informational capacities that individually arise for a wide variety of reasons, there is no reason to suppose that "it" is something that stands in need of its own separable status as fitness-enhancing. It is not a separate organ or a separate medium or a separate talent.

To see the fallacy, consider the parallel question about what the adaptive advantage of *health* is. Consider "health inessentialism": for any bodily activity *b,* performed in any domain *d,* even if *we* need to be healthy to engage in it (e.g., pole vaulting, swimming the English Channel, climbing Mount Everest), it could in principle be engaged in by something that wasn't healthy at all. So what is health *for?* Such a mystery! But the mystery would arise only for someone who made the mistake of supposing that health was some *additional* thing that could be added or subtracted to the proper workings of all the parts. In the case of health we are not apt to make such a simple mistake, but there is a tradition of supposing just this in the case of consciousness. Supposing that by an act of stipulative imagination you can remove consciousness while leaving all cognitive systems intact—a quite standard but entirely bogus feat of imagination—is like supposing that by an act of stipulative imagination, you can remove health while leaving all bodily functions and powers intact. If you think you can imagine this, it's only because you are confusedly imagining some health-module that might or might not be present in a body. Health isn't that sort of thing, and neither is consciousness.

All I can do at this point is to reiterate my plea: consider the suggestion, once again, that when you've given an evolutionary account of the talents of zimboes, you've answered all the real questions about consciousness *because the putative contrast between zombies and conscious beings is illusory.* I know that many philosophers are sure that it is not illusory. I know that they are sure that *they* don't make such mistakes of imagination when they claim to conceive of zombies. Maybe they don't. But Moody does, as Flanagan and Polger show, and then they themselves do, as I have just shown. These two essays continue a tradition unbroken in my experience. That is, I have never seen an argument in support of the zombie distinction that didn't make a mistake of the imagination of this sort. This prevailing wind of mis-imagination undoubtedly provides ill-gotten support for the widespread conviction among the populace (reported, for instance, by David Chalmers) that there is an important difference between zombies and conscious beings. That is, those who believe in the distinction ought to grant me that even professional philosophers sometimes do fail to appreciate that these are *bad* reasons for believing in the distinction. The question I pose to them is whether there are any *good* reasons for believing in the distinction. My conviction is that the philosophical tradition of zombies would die overnight if philosophers ceased to mis-imagine them, but of course I cannot prove it a priori. We will just have to wait for some philosopher to write an essay in defense of zombies that doesn't commit any such misdirections, and see what happens.

To make sure the challenge is clear, let me review the burden and its attendant requirements. One must show that there is a difference between conscious beings and zombies, *and* one must show that one's demonstration of this difference doesn't depend on underestimating in the well-nigh standard way the powers of zombies. Here's a handy way of checking one's exercises of imagination: demonstrate that a parallel difference does *not* exist between zimboes and less fancy zombies. One may in this way ensure that one hasn't simply underestimated the power of zombies by imagining some crude non-zimbo zombie, rather than a zombie with all the "informational sensitivity" of us human beings.

In a thoughtful essay Joseph Levine (1994) deplores the ridicule to which I have subjected believers in zombies. This is a matter of some urgency for philosophers, since, as I say in "Get Real" (Dennett, 1994b—my reply to Levine and others), it is an embarrassment to our discipline that what is widely regarded among philosophers as a major theoretical controversy should come down to whether or not zombies (philosophers' zombies) are possible / conceivable. I deplore the bad image this gives to philosophy just as much as Levine does, but for the life of me, I can't see why a belief in zombies isn't simply ridiculous, and I'm going to go on comparing zombies to epiphenomenal gremlins and other such *prepostera* until some philosopher mounts a proper defense, showing that the belief in the possibility of zombies is somehow better supported than these other cases.

Again, let me clarify the challenge. It seems to me that postulating zombies is exactly as silly as postulating epiphenomenal gremlins, and so when a philosopher does it, I blush for the profession. Show me, please, why the zombie hypothesis deserves to be taken seriously, and I will apologize handsomely for having ridiculed those who think so. But I want to see an argument, and not just the nudges and mumbles I have provoked by this question in the past. Tradition doesn't cut it. "If you got to ask, you ain't never gonna get to know" doesn't cut it. "Everybody else believes in them" doesn't cut it. Calling me an instrumentalist or an operationalist or a behaviorist—as if these were obviously terms of censure—doesn't cut it. If the philosophical concept of zombies is so important, so useful, some philosopher ought to be able to say why in non-question-begging terms. I'll be curious to see if anybody can mount such a defense, but I won't be holding my breath.

II

Artificial Intelligence and Artificial Life

11

Cognitive Wheels:
The Frame Problem of AI

In 1969, John McCarthy, the mathematician who coined the term "Artificial Intelligence," joined forces with another AI researcher, Patrick Hayes, and coined another term, "the frame problem." It seemed to be a devil of a problem, perhaps even a mortal blow to the hopes of AI. It looked to me like a new philosophical or epistemological problem, certainly not an electronic or computational problem. What is the frame problem? In this essay I thought I was providing interested bystanders with a useful introduction to the problem, as well as an account of its philosophical interest, but some people in AI, including McCarthy and Hayes (who ought to know), thought I was misleading the bystanders. The real frame problem was not, they said, what I was talking about. Others weren't so sure. I myself no longer have any firm convictions about which problems are which, or even about which problems are really hard after all — but something is still obstreperously resisting solution, that's for sure. Happily, there are now three follow-up volumes that pursue these disagreements through fascinating thickets of controversy: The Robot's Dilemma *(Pylyshyn, 1987),* Reasoning Agents in a Dynamic World *(Ford and Hayes, 1991), and* The Robot's Dilemma Revisited *(Ford and Pylyshyn, 1996). If you read and understand those volumes you will understand just about everything anybody understands about the frame problem. Good luck.*

Once upon a time there was robot, named R1 by its creators. Its only task was to fend for itself. One day its designers arranged for it to learn that its spare battery, its precious energy supply, was locked in a room with a time bomb set to go off soon. R1 located the room and the key to the door, and formulated a plan to rescue its battery. There was

---

Originally appeared in Hookway, C., ed., *Minds, Machines and Evolution* (Cambridge: Cambridge University Press, 1984), pp. 129–151.

a wagon in the room, and the battery was on the wagon, and R1 hypothesized that a certain action which it called PULLOUT (WAGON, ROOM) would result in the battery being removed from the room. Straightway it acted, and did succeed in getting the battery out of the room before the bomb went off. Unfortunately, however, the bomb was also on the wagon. R1 *knew* that the bomb was on the wagon in the room, but didn't realize that pulling the wagon would bring the bomb out along with the battery. Poor R1 had missed that obvious implication of its planned act.

Back to the drawing board. "The solution is obvious," said the designers. "Our next robot must be made to recognize not just the intended implications of its acts, but also the implications about their side effects, by deducing these implications from the descriptions it uses in formulating its plans." They called their next model, the robot-deducer, R1D1. They placed R1D1 in much the same predicament that R1 had succumbed to, and as it too hit upon the idea of PULLOUT (WAGON, ROOM) it began, as designed, to consider the implications of such a course of action. It had just finished deducing that pulling the wagon out of the room would not change the color of the room's walls, and was embarking on a proof of the further implication that pulling the wagon out would cause its wheels to turn more revolutions than there were wheels on the wagon—when the bomb exploded.

Back to the drawing board. "We must teach it the difference between relevant implications and irrelevant implications," said the designers, "and teach it to ignore the irrelevant ones." So they developed a method of tagging implications as either relevant or irrelevant to the project at hand, and installed the method in their next model, the robot-relevant-deducer, or R2D1 for short. When they subjected R2D1 to the test that had so unequivocally selected its ancestors for extinction, they were surprised to see it sitting, Hamlet-like, outside the room containing the ticking bomb, the native hue of its resolution sicklied o'er with the pale cast of thought, as Shakespeare (and more recently Fodor) has aptly put it. "Do something!" they yelled at it. "I am," it retorted. "I'm busy ignoring some thousands of implications I have determined to be irrelevant. Just as soon as I find an irrelevant implication, I put it on the list of those I must ignore, and . . ." the bomb went off.

All these robot suffer from the *frame problem*.[1] If there is ever to be

---

1. The problem is introduced by John McCarthy and Patrick Hayes in their 1969 paper. The task in which the problem arises was first formulated in McCarthy 1960. I am grateful to Bo Dahlbohm, Pat Hayes, John Haugeland, John McCarthy, Bob Moore, and Zenon

a robot with the fabled perspicacity and real-time adroitness of R2D2, robot designers must solve the frame problem. It appears at first to be at best an annoying technical embarrassment in robotics, or merely a curious puzzle for the bemusement of people working in Artificial Intelligence (AI). I think, on the contrary, that it is a new, deep epistemological problem—accessible in principle but unnoticed by generations of philosophers—brought to light by the novel methods of AI, and still far from being solved. Many people in AI have come to have a similarly high regard for the seriousness of the frame problem. As one researcher has quipped, "We have given up the goal of designing an intelligent robot, and turned to the task of designing a gun that will destroy any intelligent robot that anyone else designs!"

I will try here to present an elementary, nontechnical, philosophical introduction to the frame problem, and show why it is so interesting. I have no solution to offer, or even any original suggestions for where a solution might lie. It is hard enough, I have discovered, just to say clearly what the frame problem is—and is not. In fact, there is less than perfect agreement in usage within the AI research community. McCarthy and Hayes, who coined the term, use it to refer to a particular, narrowly conceived problem about representation that arises only for certain strategies for dealing with a broader problem about real-time planning systems. Others call this broader problem the frame problem—"the whole pudding," as Hayes has called it (personal correspondence)—and this may not be mere terminological sloppiness. If "solutions" to the narrowly conceived problem have the effect of driving a (deeper) difficulty into some other quarter of the broad problem, we might better reserve the title for this hard-to-corner difficulty. With apologies to McCarthy and Hayes for joining those who would appropriate their term, I am going to attempt an introduction to the whole pudding, calling *it* the frame problem. I will try in due course to describe the narrower version of the problem, "the frame problem proper" if you like, and show something of its relation to the broader problem.

Pylyshyn for the many hours they have spent trying to make me understand the frame problem. It is not their fault that so much of their instruction has still not taken.

I have also benefited greatly from reading an unpublished paper, "Modeling Change—the Frame Problem, " by Lars-Erik Janlert, Institute of Information Processing, University of Umea, Sweden. It is to be hoped that a subsequent version of that paper will soon find its way into print, since it is an invaluable *vademecum* for any neophyte, in addition to advancing several novel themes. [This hope has been fulfilled: Janlert, 1987.—DCD, 1997]

Since the frame problem, whatever it is, is certainly not solved yet (and may be, in its current guises, insoluble), the ideological foes of AI such as Hubert Dreyfus and John Searle are tempted to compose obituaries for the field, citing the frame problem as the cause of death. In *What Computers Can't Do* (Dreyfus 1972), Dreyfus sought to show that AI was a fundamentally mistaken method for studying the mind, and in fact many of his somewhat impressionistic complaints about AI models and many of his declared insights into their intrinsic limitations can be seen to hover quite systematically in the neighborhood of the frame problem. Dreyfus never explicitly mentions the frame problem,[2] but is it perhaps the smoking pistol he was looking for but didn't quite know how to describe? Yes, I think AI can be seen to be holding a smoking pistol, but at least in its "whole pudding" guise it is everybody's problem, not just a problem for AI, which, like the good guy in many a mystery story, should be credited with a discovery, not accused of a crime.

One does not have to hope for a robot-filled future to be worried by the frame problem. It apparently arises from some very widely held and innocuous-*seeming* assumptions about the nature of intelligence, the truth of the most undoctrinaire brand of physicalism, and the conviction that it must be possible to explain how we think. (The dualist evades the frame problem—but only because dualism draws the veil of mystery and obfuscation over all the tough how-questions; as we shall see, the problem arises when one takes seriously the task of answering certain how-questions. Dualists inexcusably excuse themselves from the frame problem.) One utterly central—if not defining—feature of an intelligent being is that it can "look before it leaps." Better, it can *think* before it leaps. Intelligence is (at least partly) a matter of using well what you know—but for what? For improving the fidelity

---

2. Dreyfus mentions McCarthy (1960, pp. 213–214), but the theme of his discussion there is that McCarthy ignores the difference between a *physical state* description and a *situation* description, a theme that might be succinctly summarized: a house is not a home.

Similarly, he mentions ceteris paribus assumptions (in the Introduction to the Revised Edition, p. 56ff), but only in announcing his allegiance to Wittgenstein's idea that "whenever human behavior is analyzed in terms of rules, these rules must always contain a ceteris paribus condition." But this, even if true, misses the deeper point: the need for something like *ceteris paribus* assumptions confronts Robinson Crusoe just as ineluctably as it confronts any protagonist who finds himself in a situation involving human culture. The point is not, it seems, restricted to *Geisteswissenschaft* (as it is usually conceived); the "intelligent" robot on an (otherwise?) uninhabited but hostile planet faces the frame problem as soon as it commences to plan its days.

of your expectations about what is going to happen next, for planning, for considering courses of action, for framing further hypotheses with the aim of increasing the knowledge you will use in the future, so that you can preserve yourself, by letting your hypotheses die in your stead (as Sir Karl Popper once put it). The stupid—as opposed to ignorant—being is the one who lights the match to peer into the fuel tank,[3] who saws off the limb he is sitting on, who locks his keys in his car and then spends the next hour wondering how on earth to get his family out of the car.

But when we think before we leap, *how do we do it?* The answer seems obvious: an intelligent being learns from experience, and then uses what it has learned to guide expectations in the future. Hume explained this in terms of habits of expectation, in effect. *But how do the habits work?* Hume had a hand-waving answer—associationism—to the effect that certain transition paths between ideas grew more likely-to-be-followed as they became well worn, but since it was not *Hume's* job, surely, to explain in more detail the mechanics of these links, problems about how such paths could be put to good use—and not just turned into an impenetrable maze of untraversable alternatives—were not discovered.

Hume, like virtually all other philosophers and "mentalistic" psychologists, was unable to see the frame problem because he operated at what I call a purely semantic level, or a *phenomenological* level. At the phenomenological level, all the items in view are *individuated by their meanings.* Their meanings are, if you like, "given"—but this just means that the theorist helps himself to all the meanings he wants. In this way the semantic relation between one item and the next is typically plain to see, and one just assumes that the items behave as items with those meanings *ought* to behave. We can bring this out by concocting a Humean account of a bit of learning.

Suppose there are two children, both of whom initially tend to grab cookies from the jar without asking. One child is allowed to do this unmolested but the other is spanked each time she tries. What is the result? The second child learns not to go for the cookies. Why? Because she has had experience of cookie-reaching followed swiftly by spanking. What good does that do? Well, the *idea* of cookie-reaching becomes connected by a habit path to the idea of spanking, which in turn is

---

3. The example is from an important discussion of rationality by Christopher Cherniak, in "Rationality and the Structure of Memory" (1983).

connected to the idea of pain . . . so *of course* the child refrains. Why? Well, that's just the effect of that idea on that sort of circumstance. But why? Well, what else ought the idea of pain to do on such an occasion? Well, it might cause the child to pirouette on her left foot, or recite poetry or blink or recall her fifth birthday. But given what the idea of pain *means*, any of those effects would be absurd. True; now *how* can ideas be designed so that their effects are what they ought to be, given what they mean? Designing some internal thing—an idea, let's call it— so that it behaves vis-à-vis its brethren as if it meant *cookie* or *pain* is the only way of endowing that thing with that meaning; it couldn't mean a thing if it didn't have those internal behavioral dispositions.

That is the mechanical question the philosophers left to some dimly imagined future researcher. Such a division of labor might have been all right, but it is turning out that most of the truly difficult and deep puzzles of learning and intelligence get kicked downstairs by this move. It is rather as if philosophers were to proclaim themselves expert explainers of the methods of a stage magician, and then, when we ask them to explain how the magician does the sawing-the-lady-in-half trick, they explain that it is really quite obvious: the magician doesn't really saw her in half; he simply makes it appear that he does. "But how does he do *that?*" we ask. "Not our department," say the philosophers—and some of them add, sonorously: "Explanation has to stop somewhere."[4]

When one operates at the purely phenomenological or semantic level, where does one get one's data, and how does theorizing proceed? The term "phenomenology" has traditionally been associated with an introspective method—an *examination* of what is presented or given to consciousness. A person's phenomenology just was by definition the contents of his or her consciousness. Although this has been the ideology all along, it has never been the practice. Locke, for instance, may have thought his "historical, plain method" was a method of unbiased self-observation, but in fact it was largely a matter of disguised aprioristic reasoning about what ideas and impressions *had to be* to do the jobs they "obviously" did.[5] The myth that each of us can observe our

---

4. Note that on this unflattering portrayal, the philosophers might still be doing *some* valuable work; the wild goose chases one might avert for some investigator who had rashly concluded that the magician really did saw the lady in half and then miraculously reunite her. People have jumped to such silly conclusions, after all; many philosophers have done so, for instance.

5. See my 1982d, a commentary on Goodman (1982).

mental activities has prolonged the illusion that major progress could be made on the theory of thinking by simply reflecting carefully on our own cases. For some time now we have known better: we have conscious access to only the upper surface, as it were, of the multilevel system of information-processing that occurs in us. Nevertheless, the myth still claims its victims.

So the analogy of the stage magician is particularly apt. One is not likely to make much progress in figuring out *how* the tricks are done by simply sitting attentively in the audience and watching like a hawk. Too much is going on out of sight. Better to face the fact that one must either rummage around backstage or in the wings, hoping to disrupt the performance in telling ways; or, from one's armchair, think aprioristically about how the tricks *must* be done, given whatever is manifest about the constraints. The frame problem is then rather like the unsettling but familiar "discovery" that so far as armchair thought can determine, a certain trick we have just observed is flat impossible.

Here is an example of the trick. Making a midnight snack. How is it that I can get myself a midnight snack? What could be simpler? I suspect there is some sliced leftover turkey and mayonnaise in the fridge, and bread in the bread box—and a bottle of beer in the fridge as well. I realize I can put these elements together, so I concoct a childishly simple plan: I'll just go and check out the fridge, get out the requisite materials, and make myself a sandwich, to be washed down with a beer. I'll need a knife, a plate, and a glass for the beer. I forthwith put the plan into action and it works! Big deal.

Now of course I couldn't do this without knowing a good deal—about bread, spreading mayonnaise, opening the fridge, the friction and inertia that will keep the turkey between the bread slices and the bread on the plate as I carry the plate over to the table beside my easy chair. I also need to know about how to get the beer out of the bottle and into the glass.[6] Thanks to my previous accumulation of experience in the world, fortunately, I am equipped with all this worldly knowledge. Of course some of the knowledge I need *might* be innate. For instance, one trivial thing I have to know is that when the beer gets into the glass it is no longer in the bottle, and that if I'm holding the mayonnaise jar in my left hand I cannot also be spreading the mayonnaise with the knife in my left hand. Perhaps these are straightforward

---

6. This knowledge of physics is not what one learns in school, but in one's crib. See Hayes 1978, 1980.

implications—instantiations—of some more fundamental things that I was in effect *born knowing* such as, perhaps, the fact that if something is in one location it isn't also in another, different location; or the fact that two things can't be in the same place at the same time; or the fact that situations change as the result of actions. It is hard to imagine just how one could learn these facts from experience.

Such utterly banal facts escape our notice as we act and plan, and it is not surprising that philosophers, thinking phenomenologically *but introspectively*, should have overlooked them. But if one turns one's back on introspection, and just thinks "hetero-phenomenologically"[7] about the purely informational demands of the task—what *must* be known by any entity that can perform this task—these banal bits of knowledge rise to our attention. We can easily satisfy ourselves that no agent that did not *in some sense* have the benefit of information (that beer in the bottle is not in the glass, etc.) could perform such a simple task. It is one of the chief methodological beauties of AI that it makes one be a phenomenologist, one reasons about what the agent must "know" or figure out *unconsciously or consciously* in order to perform in various ways.

The reason AI forces the banal information to the surface is that the tasks set by AI start at zero: the computer to be programmed to simulate the agent (or the brain of the robot, if we are actually going to operate in the real, nonsimulated world), initially knows nothing at all "about the world." The computer is the fabled tabula rasa on which every required item must somehow be impressed, either by the programmer at the outset or via subsequent "learning" by the system.

We can all agree, today, that there could be no learning at all by an entity that faced the world at birth as a tabula rasa, but the dividing line between what is innate and what develops maturationally and what is actually learned is of less theoretical importance than one might have thought. While some information has to be innate, there is hardly any particular item that must be: an appreciation of *modus ponens*, perhaps, and the law of the excluded middle, and some sense of causality. And while some things we know must be learned—for example, that Thanksgiving falls on a Thursday, or that refrigerators keep food fresh—many other "very empirical" things could in principle be innately known—for example, that smiles mean happiness, or that un-

---

7. For elaborations of hetero-phenomenology, see Dennett 1978a, chapter 10, "Two Approaches to Mental Images," and Dennett 1982b. See also Dennett 1982a and 1991.

suspended, unsupported things fall. (There is some evidence, in fact, that there is an innate bias in favor of perceiving things to fall with gravitational acceleration).[8]

Taking advantage of this advance in theoretical understanding (if that is what it is), people in AI can frankly ignore the problem of learning (it seems) and take the shortcut of *installing* all that an agent has to "know" to solve a problem. After all, if God made Adam as an adult who could presumably solve the midnight snack problem ab initio, AI agent-creators can *in principle* make an "adult" agent who is equipped with worldly knowledge *as if* it had laboriously learned all the things it needs to know. This may of course be a dangerous shortcut.

The installation problem is then the problem of installing in one way or another all the information needed by an agent to plan in a changing world. It is a difficult problem because the information must be installed in a usable format. The problem can be broken down initially into the semantic problem and the syntactic problem. The semantic problem—called by Allan Newell the problem at the "knowledge level" (Newell, 1982)—is the problem of just what information (on what topics, to what effect) must be installed. The syntactic problem is what system, format, structure, or mechanism to use to put that information in.[9]

The division is clearly seen in the example of the midnight snack problem. I *listed* a few of the very many humdrum facts one needs to know to solve the snack problem, but I didn't mean to suggest that those facts are stored in me—or in any agent—piecemeal, in the form

---

8. Gunnar Johannsen has shown that animated films of "falling" objects in which the moving spots drop with the normal acceleration of gravity are unmistakably distinguished by the casual observer from "artificial" motions. I do not know whether infants have been tested to see if they respond selectively to such displays.

9. McCarthy and Hayes (1969) draw a different distinction between the "epistemological" and the "heuristic." The difference is that they include the question "In what kind of internal notation is the system's knowledge to be expressed?" in the epistemological problem (see p. 466), dividing off *that* syntactic (and hence somewhat mechanical) question from the procedural questions of the design of "the mechanism that on the basis of the information solves the problem and decides what to do."

One of the prime grounds for controversy about just which problem the frame problem is springs from this attempted division of the issue. For the answer to the syntactical aspects of the epistemological question makes a large difference to the nature of the heuristic problem. After all, if the syntax of the expression of the system's knowledge is sufficiently perverse, then in spite of the *accuracy* of the representation of that knowledge, the heuristic problem will be impossible. And some have suggested that the heuristic problem would virtually disappear if the world knowledge were felicitously couched in the first place.

of a long list of sentences explicitly declaring each of these facts for the benefit of the agent. That is of course one possibility, officially: it is a preposterously extreme version of the "language of thought" theory of mental representation, with each distinguishable "proposition" separately inscribed in the system. No one subscribes to such a view; even an encyclopedia achieves important economies of explicit expression via its organization, and a walking encyclopedia—not a bad caricature of the envisaged AI agent—must use different systemic principles to achieve efficient representation and access. We know trillions of things; we know that mayonnaise doesn't dissolve knives on contact, that a slice of bread is smaller that Mount Everest, that opening the refrigerator doesn't cause a nuclear holocaust in the kitchen.

There must be in us—and in any intelligent agent—some highly efficient, partly generative or productive system of representing—storing for use—all the information needed. Somehow, then, we must store many "facts" at once—where facts are presumed to line up more or less one-to-one with nonsynonymous declarative sentences. Moreover, we cannot realistically hope for what one might call a Spinozistic solution—a *small* set of axioms and definitions from which all the rest of our knowledge is deducible on demand—since it is clear that there simply are no entailment relations between vast numbers of these facts. (When we rely, as we must, on experience to tell us how the world is, experience tells us things that do not at all follow from what we have heretofore known.)

The demand for an efficient system of information storage is in part a space limitation, since our brains are not all that large, but more importantly it is a time limitation, for stored information that is not reliably accessible for use in the short real-time spans typically available to agents in the world is of no use at all. A creature that can solve any problem given enough time—say a million years—is not in fact intelligent at all. We live in a time-pressured world and must be able to think quickly before we leap. (One doesn't have to view this as an a priori condition on intelligence. One can simply note that we do in fact think quickly, so there is an empirical question about how we manage to do it.)

The task facing the AI researcher appears to be designing a system that can plan by using well-selected elements from its store of knowledge about the world it operates in. "Introspection" on how *we* plan yields the following description of a process: one envisages a certain situation (often very sketchily); one then imagines performing a certain act in that situation; one then "sees" what the likely outcome of that envisaged act in that situation would be, and evaluates it. What happens backstage, as it were, to permit this "seeing" (and render it as reliable as it is) is utterly inaccessible to introspection.

On relatively rare occasions we all experience such bouts of thought, unfolding in consciousness at the deliberate speed of pondering. These are the occasions in which we are faced with some novel and relatively difficult problem, such as: How can I get the piano upstairs? or Is there any way to electrify the chandelier without cutting through the plaster ceiling? It would be quite odd to find that one had to think *that* way (consciously and slowly) in order to solve the midnight snack problem. But the suggestion is that even the trivial problems of planning and bodily guidance that are beneath our notice (though in some sense we "face" them) are solved by similar processes. Why? I don't *observe* myself planning in such situations. This fact suffices to convince the traditional, introspective phenomenologist that no such planning is going on.[10] The hetero-phenomenologist, on the other hand, reasons that *one way or another* information about the objects in the situation, and about the intended effects and side effects of the candidate actions, *must* be used (considered, attended to, applied, appreciated). Why? Because otherwise the "smart" behavior would be sheer luck or magic. (Do we have any model for how such unconscious information-appreciation might be accomplished? The only model we have *so far* is conscious, deliberate information-appreciation. Perhaps, AI suggests, this is a good model. If it isn't, we are all utterly in the dark for the time being.)

We assure ourselves of the intelligence of an agent by considering counterfactuals: if I had been told that the turkey was poisoned, or the beer explosive, or the plate dirty, or the knife too fragile to spread mayonnaise; would I have acted as I did? If I were a stupid "automaton"—or like the *Sphex* wasp you "mindlessly" repeats her stereotyped burrow-checking routine till she drops[11]—I might infelicitously "go

---

10. Such observations also convinced Gilbert Ryle, who was, in an important sense, an introspective phenomenologist (and not a "behaviorist"). See Ryle 1949.

One can readily imagine Ryle's attack on AI: "And *how many* inferences do I perform in the course of preparing my sandwich? What syllogisms convince me that the beer will stay in the glass?" For a further discussion of Ryle's skeptical arguments and their relation to cognitive science, see my (1983b) "Styles of Representation."

11. "When the time comes for egg laying the wasp *Sphex* builds a burrow for the purpose and seeks out a cricket which she stings in such a way as to paralyze but not kill it. She drags the cricket into her burrow, lays her eggs alongside, closes the burrow, then flies away, never to return. In due course, the eggs hatch and the wasp grubs feed off the paralyzed cricket, which has not decayed, having been kept in the wasp equivalent of

through the motions" of making a midnight snack oblivious to the re-
calcitrant features of the environment.[12] But in fact, my midnight-
snack-making behavior is multifariously sensitive to current and background information about the situation. The only way it could be so
sensitive—runs the tacit hetero-phenomenological reasoning—is for it
to examine, or test for, the information in question. This information
manipulation may be unconscious and swift, and it need not (it *better*
not) consist of hundred or thousands of *seriatim* testing procedures, but
it must occur somehow, and its benefits must appear in time to help
me as I commit myself to action.

I may of course have a midnight snack routine, developed over the
years, in which case I can partly rely on it to pilot my actions. Such a
complicated "habit" would have to be under the control of a mechanism of some complexity, since even a rigid sequence of steps would
involve periodic testing to ensure that subgoals had been satisfied.
And even if I am an infrequent snacker, I no doubt have routines for
mayonnaise-spreading, sandwich-making, and getting something out
of the fridge, from which I could compose my somewhat novel activity.
Would such ensembles of routines, nicely integrated, suffice to solve
the frame problem for me, at least in my more "mindless" endeavors?
That is an open question to which I will return below.

It is important in any case to acknowledge at the outset, and remind
oneself frequently, that even very intelligent people do make mistakes;
we are not only not infallible planners, we are quite prone to overlook-
ing large and retrospectively obvious flaws in our plans. This foible
manifests itself in the familiar case of "force of habit" errors (in which
our stereotypical routines reveal themselves to be surprisingly insensi-

---

a deep freeze. To the human mind, such an elaborately organized and seemingly purposeful routine conveys a convincing flavor of logic and thoughtfulness—until more
details are examined. For example, the wasp's routine is to bring the paralyzed cricket
to the burrow, leave it on the threshold, go inside to see that all is well, emerge, and
then drag the cricket in. If, while the wasp is inside making her preliminary inspection
the cricket is moved a few inches away, the wasp, on emerging from the burrow, will
bring the cricket back to the threshold, but not inside, and will then repeat the prepara-
tory procedure of entering the burrow to see that everything is all right. If again the
cricket is removed a few inches while the wasp is inside, once again the wasp will move
the cricket up to the threshold and re-enter the burrow for a final check. The wasp never
thinks of pulling the cricket straight in. On one occasion, this procedure was repeated
forty times, always with the same result" (Wooldridge 1963).

This vivid example of a familiar phenomenon among insects is discussed by me in
Brainstorms, and in Douglas R. Hofstadter 1982.

12. See my 1982a: 58–59, on "Robot Theater."

tive to some portentous environmental changes while surprisingly sensitive to others). The same weakness also appears on occasion in cases
where we have consciously deliberated with some care. How often
have you embarked on a project of the piano-moving variety—in
which you've thought through or even "walked through" the whole
operation in advance—only to discover that you must backtrack or
abandon the project when some perfectly foreseeable but unforeseen
obstacle or unintended side effect loomed? If we smart folk seldom
actually paint ourselves into corners, it may not be because we plan
ahead so well as that we supplement our sloppy planning powers with
a combination of recollected lore (about fools who paint themselves
into corners, for instance) and frequent progress checks as we proceed.
Even so, we must know enough to call up the right lore at the right
time, and to recognize impending problems as such.

To summarize: we have been led by fairly obvious and compelling
considerations to the conclusion that an intelligent agent must engage
in swift information-sensitive "planning" which has the effect of producing reliable but not foolproof expectations of the effects of its actions. That these expectations are normally in force in intelligent
creatures is testified to by the startled reaction they exhibit when their
expectations are thwarted. This suggests a graphic way of characterizing the minimal goal that can spawn the frame problem: we want a
midnight-snack-making robot to be "surprised" by the trick plate, the
unspreadable concrete mayonnaise, the fact that we've glued the beer
glass to the shelf. To be surprised you have to have expected something
else, and in order to have expected the right something else, you have
to have *and use* a lot of information about the things in the world.[13]

The central role of expectation has led some to conclude that the

---

13. Hubert Dreyfus has pointed out that *not expecting x* does not imply *expecting y* (where
$x \neq y$), so one can be startled by something one didn't expect without its having to be
the case that one (unconsciously) expected something else. But this sense of *not expecting*
will not suffice to explain startle. What are the odds against your seeing an Alfa Romeo,
a Buick, a Chevrolet, and a Dodge parked in alphabetical order some time or other within
the next five hours? Very high, no doubt, all things considered, so I would not expect
you to expect this; I also would not expect you to be startled by seeing this unexpected
sight—except in the sort of special case where you had reason to expect something else
at that time and place.

Startle reactions are powerful indicators of cognitive state—a fact long known by the
police (and writers of detective novels). *Only* someone who expected the refrigerator to
contain Smith's corpse (say) would be startled (as opposed to mildly interested) to find
it to contain the rather unlikely trio: a bottle of vintage Chablis, a can of cat food, and
a dishrag.

frame problem is not a new problem at all, and has nothing particularly to do with planning actions. It is, they think, simply the problem of having good expectations about any future events, whether they are one's own actions, the actions of another agent, or mere happenings of nature. That is the problem of induction—noted by Hume and intensified by Goodman (Goodman 1965), but still not solved to anyone's satisfaction. We know today that the problem is a nasty one indeed. Theories of subjective probability and belief fixation have not been stabilized in reflective equilibrium, so it is fair to say that no one has a good, principled answer to the general question: given that I believe all *this* (have all this evidence), what *ought* I to believe as well (about the future, or about unexamined parts of the world)?

The reduction of one unsolved problem to another is some sort of progress, unsatisfying though it may be, but it is not an option in this case. The frame problem is not the problem of induction in disguise. For suppose the problem of induction were solved. Suppose—perhaps miraculously—that our agent has solved all its induction problems or had them solved by fiat; it believes, then, all the right generalizations from its evidence, and associates with all of them the appropriate probabilities and conditional probabilities. This agent, ex hypothesi, believes just what it ought to believe about all empirical matters in its ken, including the probabilities of future events. It might still have a bad case of the frame problem, for that problem concerns how to represent (so it can be *used*) all that hard-won empirical information—a problem that arises independently of the truth value, probability, warranted assertability, or subjective certainty of any of it. Even if you have excellent *knowledge* (and not mere belief) about the changing world, how can this knowledge be represented so that it can be efficaciously brought to bear?

Recall poor R1D1, and suppose for the sake of argument that it had perfect empirical knowledge of the probabilities of all the effects of all its actions that would be detectable by it. Thus it believes that with probability 0.7864, executing PULLOUT (WAGON, ROOM) will cause the wagon wheels to make an audible noise; and with probability 0.5, the door to the room will open in rather than out; and with probability 0.999996, there will be no live elephants in the room, and with probability 0.997 the bomb will remain on the wagon when it is moved. How is R1D1 to find this last, relevant needle in its haystack of empirical knowledge? A walking encyclopedia will walk over a cliff, for all its knowledge of cliffs and the effects of gravity, unless it is designed in such a fashion that it can find the right bits of knowledge at the right times, so it can plan its engagements with the real world.

The earliest work on planning systems in AI took a deductive approach. Inspired by the development of Robinson's methods of resolution theorem proving, designers hoped to represent all the system's "world knowledge" explicitly as axioms, and use ordinary logic—the predicate calculus—to deduce the effects of actions. Envisaging a certain situation S was modeled by having the system entertain a set of axioms describing the situation. Added to this were background axioms (the so-called frame axioms that give the frame problem its name) which describe general conditions and the general effects of every action type defined for the system. To this set of axioms the system would apply an action—by postulating the occurrence of some action A in situation S—and then deduce the effect of A in S, producing a description of the outcome situation S'. While all this logical deduction looks like nothing at all in our conscious experience, research on deductive approach could proceed on either or both of two enabling assumptions: the methodological assumption that psychological realism was a gratuitous bonus, not a goal, of "pure" AI, or the substantive (if still vague) assumption that the deductive processes described would somehow model the backstage processes beyond conscious access. In other words, either we don't do our thinking deductively in the predicate calculus but a robot might; or we do (unconsciously) think deductively in the predicate calculus. Quite aside from doubts about its psychological realism, however, the deductive approach has not been made to work—the proof of the pudding for any robot—except for deliberately trivialized cases.

Consider some typical frame axioms associated with the action type: *move x onto y.*

1. If $z \neq x$ and I move x onto y, then if z was on w before, then z is on w after

2. If x is blue before, and I move x onto y, then x is blue after

Note that (2), about being blue, is just one example of the many boring "no-change" axioms we have to associate with this action type. Worse still, note that a cousin of (2), also about being blue, would have to be associated with every other action-type—with *pick up x* and with *give x to y*, for instance. One cannot save this mindless repetition by postulating once and for all something like

3. If anything is blue, it stays blue

for that is false, and in particular we will want to leave room for the introduction of such action types as *paint x red*. Since virtually any aspect of a situation can change under some circumstance, this method requires introducing for each aspect (each predication in the description of S) an axiom to handle whether that aspect changes for each action type.

This representational profligacy quickly gets out of hand, but for some "toy" problems in AI, the frame problem can be overpowered to some extent by a mixture of the toyness of the environment and brute force. The early version of SHAKEY, the robot at S.R.I., operated in such a simplified and sterile world, with so few aspects it could worry about that it could get away with an exhaustive consideration of frame axioms.[14]

Attempts to circumvent this explosion of axioms began with the proposal that the system operate on the tacit assumption that nothing changes in a situation but what is explicitly asserted to change in the definition of the applied action (Fikes and Nilsson, 1971). The problem here is that, as Garrett Hardin once noted, you can't do just one thing. This was RI's problem, when it failed to notice that it would pull the bomb out with the wagon. In the explicit representation (a few pages back) of my midnight snack solution, I mentioned carrying the plate over to the table. On this proposal, my model of S' would leave the turkey back in the kitchen, for I didn't explicitly say the turkey would come along with the plate. One can of course patch up the definition of "bring" or "plate" to handle just this problem, but only at the cost of creating others. (Will a few more patches tame the problem? At what point should one abandon patches and seek an altogether new approach? Such are the methodological uncertainties regularly encountered in this field, and of course no one can responsibly claim in advance to have a good rule for dealing with them. Premature counsels of despair or calls for revolution are as clearly to be shunned as the dogged pursuit of hopeless avenues; small wonder the field is contentious.)

While one cannot get away with the tactic of supposing that one can do just one thing, it remains true that very little of what could (logically) happen in any situation does happen. Is there some way of falli-

---

14. This early feature of SHAKEY was drawn to my attention by Pat Hayes. See also Dreyfus (1972, p. 26). SHAKEY is put to quite a different use in Dennett (1982b).

bly marking the likely area of important side effects, and assuming the rest of the situation to stay unchanged? Here is where relevance tests seem like a good idea, and they may well be, but not within the deductive approach. As Minsky notes:

> Even if we formulate relevancy restrictions, logistic systems have a problem using them. In any logistic system, all the axioms are necessarily "permissive"— they all help to permit new inferences to be drawn. Each added axiom means more theorems; none can disappear. There simply is no direct way to add information to tell such a system about kinds of conclusions that should *not* be drawn! . . . If we try to change this by adding axioms about relevancy, we still produce all the unwanted theorems, plus annoying statements about their irrelevancy. (Minsky, 1981, p. 125)

What is needed is a system that genuinely *ignores* most of what it knows, and operates with a well-chosen portion of its knowledge at any moment. Well-chosen, but not chosen by exhaustive consideration. How, though, can you give a system *rules* for ignoring—or better, since explicit rule following is not the problem, how can you design a system that reliably ignores what it ought to ignore under a wide variety of different circumstances in a complex action environment?

John McCarthy calls this the *qualification problem,* and vividly illustrates it via the famous puzzle of the missionaries and the cannibals.

> Three missionaries and three cannibals come to a river. A rowboat that seats two is available. If the cannibals ever outnumber the missionaries on either bank of the river, the missionaries will be eaten. How shall they cross the river?
>
> Obviously the puzzler is expected to devise a strategy of rowing the boat back and forth that gets them all across and avoids disaster. . . .
>
> Imagine giving someone the problem, and after he puzzles for awhile, he suggests going upstream half a mile and crossing on a bridge. "What bridge?" you say. "No bridge is mentioned in the statement of the problem." And this dunce replies, "Well, they don't say there isn't a bridge." You look at the English and even at the translation of the English into first order logic, and you must admit that "they don't say" there is no bridge. So you modify the problem to exclude bridges and pose it again, and the dunce proposes a helicopter, and after you exclude that, he proposes a winged horse or that the others hang onto the outside of the boat while two row.
>
> You now see that while a dunce, he is an inventive dunce. Despairing of getting him to accept the problem in the proper puzzler's spirit, you tell him the solution. To your further annoyance, he attacks your solution on the grounds that the boat might have a leak or lack oars. After you rectify that omission from the statement of problem, he suggests that a sea monster may swim up the river and may swallow the boat. Again you are frustrated, and you look for a mode of reasoning that will settle his hash once and for all. (McCarthy, 1980, pp. 29–30)

What a normal, intelligent human being does in such a situation is to engage in some form of *nonmonotonic inference*. In a classical, monotonic logical system, *adding* premises never *diminishes* what can be proved from the premises. As Minsky noted, the axioms are essentially permissive, and once a theorem is permitted, adding more axioms will never invalidate the proofs of earlier theorems. But when we think about a puzzle or a real life problem, we can achieve a solution (and even prove that it is a solution, or even the only solution to *that* problem), and then discover our solution invalidated by the addition of a new element to the posing of the problem; For example, "I forgot to tell you—there are no oars" or "By the way, there's a perfectly good bridge upstream."

What such late additions show us is that, contrary to our assumption, other things weren't equal. We had been reasoning with the aid of a ceteris paribus assumption, and now our reasoning has just been jeopardized by the discovery that something "abnormal" is the case. (Note, by the way, that the abnormality in question is a much subtler notion than anything anyone has yet squeezed out of probability theory. As McCarthy notes, "The whole situation involving cannibals with the postulated properties cannot be regarded as having a probability, so it is hard to take seriously the conditional probability of a bridge given the hypothesis" [*ibid.*].)

The beauty of a ceteris paribus clause in a bit of reasoning is that one does not have to say exactly what it means. "What do you mean, 'other things being equal'? Exactly which arrangements of which other things count as being equal?" If one had to answer such a question, invoking the ceteris paribus clause would be pointless, for it is precisely in order to evade that task that one uses it. If one could answer that question, one wouldn't need to invoke the clause in the first place. One way of viewing the frame problem, then, is as the attempt to get a computer to avail itself of this distinctively human style of mental operation. There are several quite different approaches to nonmonotonic inference being pursued in AI today. They have in common only the goal of capturing the human talent for *ignoring* what should be ignored, while staying alert to relevant recalcitrance when it occurs.

One family of approaches, typified by the work of Marvin Minsky and Roger Schank (Minsky 1981; Schank and Abelson 1977), gets its ignoring-power from the attention-focussing power of stereotypes. The inspiring insight here is the idea that all of life's experiences, for all their variety, boil down to variations on a manageable number of stereotypic themes, paradigmatic scenarios—"frames" in Minsky's terms, "scripts" in Schank's.

An artificial agent with a well-stocked compendium of frames or scripts, appropriately linked to each other and to the impingements of the world via its perceptual organs, would face the world with an elaborate system of what might be called habits of attention and benign tendencies to leap to particular sorts of conclusions in particular sorts of circumstances. It would "automatically" pay attention to certain features in certain environments and assume that certain unexamined normal features of those environments were present. Concomitantly, it would be differentially alert to relevant divergences from the stereotypes it would always be "expecting."

Simulations of fragments of such an agent's encounters with its world reveal that in many situations it behaves quite felicitously and apparently naturally, and it is hard to say, of course, what the limits of this approach are. But there are strong grounds for skepticism. Most obviously, while such systems perform creditably when the world cooperates with their stereotypes, and even with *anticipated* variations on them, when their worlds turn perverse, such systems typically cannot recover gracefully from the misanalyses they are led into. In fact, their behavior in extremis looks for all the world like the preposterously counterproductive activities of insects betrayed by their rigid tropisms and other genetically hard-wired behavioral routines.

When these embarrassing misadventures occur, the system designer can improve the design by adding provisions to deal with the particular cases. It is important to note that in these cases, the system does not redesign itself (or learn) but rather must wait for an external designer to select an improved design. This process of redesign recapitulates the process of natural selection in some regards; it favors minimal, piecemeal, ad hoc redesign which is tantamount to a wager on the likelihood of patterns in future events. So in some regards it is faithful to biological themes.[15]

Several different sophisticated attempts to provide the representational framework for this deeper understanding have emerged from

---

15. In one important regard, however, it is dramatically unlike the process of natural selection, since the trial, error and selection of the process is far from blind. But a case can be made that the impatient researcher does nothing more than telescope time by such foresighted interventions in the redesign process.

the deductive tradition in recent years. Drew McDermott and Jon Doyle have developed a "nonmonotonic logic" (1980), Ray Reiter has a "logic for default reasoning" (1980), and John McCarthy has developed a system of "circumscription," a formalized "rule of conjecture that can be used by a person or program for 'jumping to conclusions' " (1980). None of these is, or is claimed to be, a complete solution to the problem of ceteris paribus reasoning, but they might be components of such a solution. More recently, McDermott (1982) has offered a "temporal logic for reasoning about processes and plans." I will not attempt to assay the formal strengths and weaknesses of these approaches. Instead I will concentrate on another worry. From one point of view, nonmonotonic or default logic, circumscription, and temporal logic all appear to be radical improvements to the mindless and clanking deductive approach, but from a slightly different perspective they appear to be more of the same, and at least as unrealistic as frameworks for psychological models.

They appear in the former guise to be a step toward greater psychological realism, for they take seriously, and attempt to represent, the phenomenologically salient phenomenon of common sense ceteris paribus "jumping to conclusions" reasoning. But do they really succeed in offering any plausible suggestions about how the backstage implementation of that conscious thinking is accomplished *in people*? Even if on some glorious future day a robot with debugged circumscription methods maneuvered well in a non-toy environment, would there be much likelihood that its constituent processes, *described at levels below the phenomenological*, would bear informative relations to the unknown lower-level backstage processes in human beings? To bring out better what my worry is, I want to introduce the concept of a *cognitive wheel*.

We can understand what a cognitive wheel might be by reminding ourselves first about ordinary wheels. Wheels are wonderful, elegant triumphs of technology. The traditional veneration of the mythic inventor of the wheel is entirely justified. But if wheels are so wonderful, why are there no animals with wheels? Why are no wheels to be found (functioning as wheels) in nature? First, the presumption of these questions must be qualified. A few years ago the astonishing discovery was made of several microscopic beasties (some bacteria and some unicellular eukaryotes) that have wheels of sorts. Their propulsive tails, long thought to be flexible flagella, turn out to be more or less rigid corkscrews, which rotate continuously, propelled by microscopic motors of sorts, complete with main bearings.[16] Better known, if less interesting for obvious reasons, are tumbleweeds. So it is not quite true that there are no wheels (or wheeliform designs) in nature.

Still, macroscopic wheels—reptilian or mammalian or avian wheels —are not to be found. Why not? They would seem to be wonderful retractable landing gear for some birds, for instance. Once the questions is posed, plausible reasons rush in to explain their absence. Most important, probably, are the considerations about the topological properties of the axle / bearing boundary that make the transmission of material or energy across it particularly difficult. How could the life-support traffic arteries of a living system maintain integrity across this boundary? But once that problem is posed, solutions suggest themselves; suppose the living wheel grows to mature form in a nonrotating, nonfunctional form, and is then hardened and sloughed off, like antlers or an outgrown shell, but not completely off: it then rotates freely on a lubricated fixed axle. Possible? It's hard to say. Useful? Also hard to say, especially since such a wheel would have to be freewheeling. This is an interesting speculative exercise, but certainly not one that should inspire us to draw categorical, a priori conclusions. It would be foolhardy to declare wheels biologically impossible, but at the same time we can appreciate that they are at least very distant and unlikely solutions to *natural* problems of design.

Now a cognitive wheel is simply any design proposal in cognitive theory (at any level from the purest semantic level to the most concrete level of "wiring diagrams" of the neurons) that is profoundly unbiological, however wizardly and elegant it is as a bit of technology.

Clearly this is a vaguely defined concept, useful only as a rhetorical abbreviation, as a gesture in the direction of real difficulties to be spelled out carefully. "Beware of postulating cognitive wheels" masquerades as good advice to the cognitive scientist, while courting vacuity as a maxim to follow.[17] It occupies the same rhetorical position as

---

16. For more details, and further reflections on the issues discussed here, see Diamond (1983).

17. I was interested to discover that at least one researcher in AI mistook the rhetorical intent of my new term on first hearing; he took "cognitive wheels" to be an accolade. If one thinks of AI as he does, not as a research method in psychology but as a branch of engineering attempting to extend human cognitive powers, then of course cognitive wheels are breakthroughs. The vast and virtually infallible memories of computers would be prime examples; others would be computers' arithmetical virtuosity and invulnerability to boredom and distraction. See Hofstadter (1982) for an insightful discussion of the relation of boredom to the structure of memory and the conditions for creativity.

the stockbroker's maxim: buy low and sell high. Still, the term is a good theme-fixer for discussion.

Many critics of AI have the conviction that *any* AI system is and must be nothing but a gearbox of cognitive wheels. This could of course turn out to be true, but the usual reason for believing it is based on a misunderstanding of the methodological assumptions of the field. When an AI model of some cognitive phenomenon is proposed, the model is describable at many different levels, from the most global, phenomenological level at which the behavior is described (with some presumptuousness) in ordinary mentalistic terms, down through various levels of implementation all the way to the level of program code—and even further down, to the level of fundamental hardware operations if anyone cares. No one supposes that the model maps onto the processes of psychology and biology *all the way down*. The claim is only that for some high level or levels of description below the phenomenological level (which merely *sets* the problem) there is a mapping of model features onto what is being modeled: the cognitive processes in living creatures, human or otherwise. It is understood that all the implementation details below the level of intended modeling will consist, no doubt, of cognitive wheels—bits of unbiological computer activity mimicking the gross effects of cognitive subcomponents by using methods utterly unlike the methods still to be discovered in the brain. Someone who failed to appreciate that a model composed microscopically of cognitive wheels could still achieve a fruitful isomorphism with biological or psychological processes at a higher level of aggregation would suppose there were good a priori reasons for generalized skepticism about AI.

But allowing for the possibility of valuable intermediate levels of modeling is not ensuring their existence. In a particular instance a model might descend directly from a phenomenologically recognizable level of psychological description to a cognitive wheels implementation without shedding any light at all on how we human beings manage to enjoy that phenomenology. I *suspect* that all current proposals in the field for dealing with the frame problem have that shortcoming. Perhaps one should dismiss the previous sentence as mere autobiography. I find it hard to imagine (for what that is worth) that any of the *procedural details* of the mechanization of McCarthy's circumscriptions, for instance, would have suitable counterparts in the backstage story yet to be told about how human common-sense reasoning is accomplished. If these procedural details lack "psychological reality" then there is nothing left in the proposal that might model psychological processes except the phenomenological-level description in terms of jumping to conclusions, ignoring and the like—and we already know we do that.

There is an alternative defense of such theoretical explorations, however, and I think it is to be taken seriously. One can claim (and I take McCarthy to claim) that while formalizing common-sense reasoning in his fashion would not tell us anything *directly* about psychological processes of reasoning, it would clarify, sharpen, systematize the purely semantic-level characterization of the demands on any such implementation, biological or not. Once one has taken the giant step forward of taking information-processing seriously as a real process in space and time, one can then take a small step back and explore the implications of that advance at a very abstract level. Even at this very formal level, the power of circumscription and the other versions of nonmonotonic reasoning remains an open but eminently explorable question.[18]

Some have thought that the key to a more realistic solution to the frame problem (and indeed, in all likelihood, to any solution at all) must require a complete rethinking of the semantic-level setting, prior to concern with syntactic-level implementation. The more or less standard array of predicates and relations chosen to fill out the predicate-calculus format when representing the "propositions believed" may embody a fundamentally inappropriate parsing of nature for this task. Typically, the interpretation of the formulae in these systems breaks the world down along the familiar lines of objects with properties at times and places. Knowledge of situations and events in the world is represented by what might be called sequences of verbal snapshots. State S, constitutively described by a list of sentences true at time t asserting various n-adic predicates true of various particulars, gives way to state S', a similar list of sentences true at t'. Would it perhaps be better to reconceive of the world of planning in terms of histories and processes?[19] Instead of trying to model the capacity to *keep track of*

---

18. McDermott (1982, "A Temporal Logic for Reasoning about Processes and Plans," Section 6, "A Sketch of an Implementation, ") shows strikingly how many *new* issues are raised once one turns to the question of implementation, and how indirect (but still useful) the purely formal considerations are.

19. Patrick Hayes has been exploring this theme, and a preliminary account can be found in "Naive Physics 1: The Ontology of Liquids" (1978).

things in terms of principles for passing through temporal cross-sections of knowledge expressed in terms of terms (*names* for *things*, in essence) and predicates, perhaps we could model keeping track of things more directly, and let all the cross-sectional information about what is deemed true moment by moment be merely implicit (and hard to extract—as it is for us) from the format. These are tempting suggestions, but so far as I know they are still in the realm of handwaving.[20]

Another, perhaps related, handwaving theme is that the current difficulties with the frame problem stem from the conceptual scheme engendered by the serial-processing von Neumann architecture of the computers used to date in AI. As large, fast parallel processors are developed, they will bring in their wake huge conceptual innovations which are now of course only dimly imaginable. Since brains are surely massive parallel processors, it is tempting to suppose that the concepts engendered by such new hardware will be more readily adaptable for realistic psychological modeling. But who can say? For the time being, most of the optimistic claims about the powers of parallel processing belong in the same camp with the facile observations often encountered in the work of neuroscientists, who postulate marvelous cognitive powers for various portions of the nervous system without a clue of how they are realized.[21]

Filling in the details of the gap between the phenomenological magic show and the well-understood powers of small tracts of brain tissue is the immense research task that lies in the future for theorists of every persuasion. But before the problems can be solved they must be encountered, and to encounter the problems one must step resolutely into the gap and ask how-questions. What philosophers (and everyone else) have always known is that people—and no doubt all intelligent agents—can engage in swift, sensitive, risky-but-valuable ceteris pari-

---

20. Oliver Selfridge's unpublished monograph, *Tracking and Trailing*, promises to push back this frontier, I think, but I have not yet been able to assimilate its messages. [Nor, after many years of cajoling, have I succeeded in persuading Selfridge to publish it. It is still, in 1997, unpublished.] There are also suggestive passages on this topic in Ruth Garrett Millikan's *Language, Thought, and Other Biological Categories*, Cambridge, MA: Bradford Books / The MIT Press, 1984.

21. To balance the "top-down" theorists' foible of postulating cognitive wheels, there is the "bottom-up" theorists' penchant for discovering *wonder tissue*. Wonder tissue appears in many locales. J.J. Gibson's (1979) theory of perception, for instance, seems to treat the whole visual system as a hunk of wonder tissue, resonating with marvelous sensitivity to a host of sophisticated "affordances."

bus reasoning. How do we do it? AI may not yet have a good answer, but at least it has encountered the question.[22]

---

22. One of the few philosophical articles I have uncovered that seem to contribute to the thinking about the frame problem—though not in those terms—is Ronald de Sousa's "The Rationality of Emotions" (de Sousa, 1979). In the section entitled "What are Emotions For?" de Sousa suggests, with compelling considerations, that:

the function of emotion is to fill gaps left by [mere wanting plus] "pure reason" in the determination of action and belief. Consider how Iago proceeds to make Othello jealous. His task is essentially to direct Othello's attention, to suggest questions to ask . . . Once attention is thus directed, inferences which, before on the same evidence, would not even have been thought of, are experienced as compelling.

In de Sousa's understanding, "emotions are determinate patterns of salience among objects of attention, lines of inquiry, and inferential strategies" (p. 50) and they are not "reducible" in any way to "articulated propositions. Suggestive as this is, it does not, of course, offer any concrete proposals for how to endow an inner (emotional) state with these interesting powers. Another suggestive—and overlooked—paper is Howard Darmstadter's "Consistency of Belief" (Darmstadter, 1971, pp. 301–310). Darmstadter's exploration of ceteris paribus clauses and the relations that might exist between beliefs as psychological states and sentences believers may utter (or have uttered about them) contains a number of claims that deserve further scrutiny.

12   Producing Future by Telling Stories[1]

My own contribution to the continuing discussion of the frame problem are some sketchy suggestions about how we might incorporate some of the resources of human culture to build a more adept control structure in our brains. Like "Two Contrasts" (chap. 4 of this volume), it is one of my early explorations of the idea that a human mind is a virtual machine built from cultural resources in a human brain.

Sometimes the way to make progress on a topic is to turn your back on it for a few years. At least I hope so, since I have just returned to the frame problem after several years of concentrating on other topics. It seems to me that I may have picked up a few odds and ends that shed light on the issues.

Perhaps it is true, as Patrick Hayes has claimed (in his remarks in Pensacola), that the frame problem really has nothing directly to do with time pressure. He insists that angels with all the time in the world to get things right would still be beset by the frame problem. I am not convinced; at least I don't see why this would be a *motivated* problem for such lucky beings—unless perhaps Satan offers them a prize for "describing the world in twenty-five words or less."

I still see the frame problem as arising most naturally and inevitably as a problem of finding a *useful,* compact representation of the world—providing actual *anticipations in real time* for purposes of planning and control. From some perspectives it appears utterly remarkable that we get any purchase on nature at all, that our brains are ever able to "produce future" in real time. Some years ago, John McCarthy posed the

Originally appeared in Ford, K., and Pylyshyn, Z., eds., *The Robot's Dilemma Revisited: The Frame Problem in Artificial Intelligence* (Norwood, NJ: Ablex, 1996), pp. 1–7.
1. This paper grew out of my comments on various papers at the conference on the frame problem held at the University of West Florida in Pensacola, Florida in June, 1989.

question of what would be required for an intelligent entity in John Horton Conway's two-dimensional Life world to learn the physics of that world. The physics of the Life world is ideally simple and deterministic, and it is easy for *us*, from our God-like perspective, to discover what it is—especially since nothing at all is hidden from us, thanks to the world's two-dimensionality. It is far from obvious, however, that *any* sequence of "experiences" in that world could lead (logically) to an appreciation of that physics by a two-dimensional proto-scientist living in it. If we assume that nevertheless it must in principle be possible—and I am happy to do so—this is something we must take on faith until McCarthy concocts a proof. Pending such a demonstration, we might ask ourselves a slightly different question: Under what conditions might a being in the Life world *get any predictive advantage at all* from its interactions with other configurations in that world? Even when the physics is deterministic, as in the Life world, it is apt to be computationally intractable for the inhabitant trying to use it to generate better-than-even-money bets about what will happen next. Successful *retro*diction achieved by time-consuming computation might win Nobel Prizes in Flatland, but it won't keep the calculator out of harm's way. Any useful future-producer is bound to be something of a kludge, or else just a lucky hit on a regularity in the world that can be tracked.

Faced with the task of extracting useful future out of our personal pasts, we try to get something for free (or at least for cheap): to find the laws of the world—and if there aren't any, to find approximate laws of the world—anything that will give us an edge. Of course without this luck, there would be no animals, and certainly no engineers, scientists, and philosophers. (There might be plants, which more or less just stand there and take their lumps).

For an animal, then, there is only one Ur-problem: Now what do I do? Here are some solutions:

A. Act at random, and hope for the best.

This is not to be scorned; we all are bound to fall back on this tactic at some level (s) of control (Dennett, 1988b). Alternatives to A are all variations on:

B. Represent the world (in part) and use the representation to guide what you do.

The variations have to do with how much of the world is represented, and how it is represented. At the minimalist extreme we have the creatures who represent as little as possible: just enough to let the world warn them sometimes when they are about to do something bad. Creatures who follow this policy engage in no planning. They plunge ahead benefiting from what we might call *temporally proximal anticipation*. If something starts hurting, they "know enough" to withdraw. They may also be able to duck incoming bricks. That may be because this anticipatory talent was wired in (as it is in our response to "looming" in the visual field [Yonas, 1981]), or because they have wired in the capacity to be conditioned to have such anticipatory talents. In short, such creatures may learn, but they can't learn much. They are blissfully untroubled by the frame problem, since they wait for the world to interrupt them from their courses of action, and when the world fails to sound any alarms, they just take their lumps.

More sophisticated—or just risk-averse—creatures avail themselves of systems of temporally *distal* anticipation: They use their brains to produce more far-ranging versions of the relevant future. So far as I can see, this is really just an extension of letting the world warn you. It attempts to build less direct, more devious sorts of warnings out of masses of individually unthreatening tidbits of information gleaned from the passing show, which it fabricates into internal alarm systems. For instance, watching a conspecific blunder into a trap, such a creature may be capable of adopting the policy that goes with the soliloquy: "Nasty outcome! I must remember never to get that close to one of those things"—actually quite a sophisticated bit of learning, when you think about what it requires. The trick, obviously, is to build the right sorts of filters, and to solve the logistic problem of keeping all one's alarms, signposts and meta-signposts functional at once. The creature that succeeds will have a flexible and subtle appreciation of what happens in the world relevant to its own actions, needs, and plans.

Every organism (or robot) must begin by limiting its sensory sampling of the world and determining how that is to be digested (in the *Reader's Digest* sense of "digested"). Every biological representation system will thus be *narcissistic* from the ground up (Akins, 1988).

This narcissistic strategy gives rise to each creature's *manifest image* (Sellars, 1963). The manifest image is composed of that creature's primitives, the fundamental categories (but not necessarily the primitive *terms* or even *concepts*) with which it confronts the world. The best-studied manifest image is that of (Western, postindustrial) human beings—*our* manifest image. Now it is undeniably tempting to think that:

1. Our manifest image is pretty much identical to our natural language;

2. Thinking is inference is logical deduction using these *terms*;

3. Robots, at least those designed to live in our niche, among us, performing the sorts of actions we do, will largely share our manifest image, or at least an impoverished subset of it.

Those who think that the "expression of our thoughts" in natural language is pretty much a matter of the direct translation or articulation of our cognitive processes find this idea of a language of thought not just plausible. They are inclined to think alternatives are inconceivable. But (1) is beginning to lose its appeal, especially now that we've fossicked around for several decades trying to make it work and failed. Folk wisdom has long ridiculed the worldly powers of "walking encyclopedias" and perhaps this is one time when folk wisdom has the last laugh on the sophisticates. But if (1) looks dubious now, so do (2) and (3), the standard garnishes for this view. What are the alternatives?

Several plausible themes seemed to me to emerge from the remarks of various people at the Pensacola conference, perhaps only because they set off sympathetic vibrations with ideas I have been encountering in other quarters. (In what follows, I will be indiscriminately borrowing ideas from Lars-Erik Janlert, Ron Loui, Yoav Shoham, and others, but I will make few attempts to identify the sources, because I may have gotten them wrong, and there are few fans as embarrassing as the fan who gets you wrong.)

I suppose the *base* for a system that beats the frame problem might be a rather ungainly bag of tricks of the sort just described: roughly Humean habits of *proximal expectation*, derived from experience by conditioning, much as Hume said. For instance, suppose we have hardwired (or as-good-as-hard-wired) expectations about things dropping when we let go of them, things making big crashes when they hit things, liquids making things wet, sharp things penetrating soft things, big huge things (e.g., mountains, houses) staying put, etc. These, let us suppose, are just brute associationist habits, and not *themselves* cognitively penetrable—only suppressible or exploitable. In particular, there is nothing in their basic implementation to preserve consistency, or guarantee them against ludicrous misapplication. (For the development of a similar idea, see Freyd, 1987.) The question, then, is how to exploit this bag of representational habits. And the answer I would propose is: with a batch of meta-tricks. For instance, in any situation you find yourself, *assign* the (initially) salient objects in the situation to these basic Humean habits (which I think of rather like sprites) in more or less a dumb way, and then see what happens when you let them do their thing. If the results "don't look right," reassign some of the salient objects and try again. In this way, we "model x on y," exploiting the various fragments of built-in dynamics in a hit-or-miss way, in something like the way Julian Jaynes (1976) describes when he talks about *metaphiers* and *metaphrands,* or mapping abstract spaces onto behavioral spaces. Note that the habits thus exploited would be only partly analogous to frame axioms. The task of "getting them right" would simply be postponed indefinitely. Instead of "getting them right" the system I am imagining would tolerate getting them wrong and clean up after itself as best it could, according to the ubiquitous biological design principle: oversimplify and self-monitor.

A further trick at this level: we *make* the relevant things in the current situation salient, by whatever makes for salience. These items become marked in the model, as ways in which the modeled world can warn us.

There is no guarantee that this will work well. As Zenon Pylyshyn has often remarked, in criticism of "scale models" made of "mental clay," we would be magically lucky to find an across-the-board match of such hard-wired or otherwise physically caused regularities with the regularities we were hoping to model, but this criticism only bites against the supposition that we are depending on a perfect match. If, on the other hand, we decompose our model into independently working bits, and then try to keep track of the joints, we may be be able to keep errors from propagating wildly through the system. My point is that this strategy of representation management is an instance of *living dangerously.* How dangerously? It depends on the risks as we assess them. I will walk in the dark to the bathroom in my house, counting on my general sense of the layout to be okay, and counting on all the normal persistences (e.g., no chair has been moved while I wasn't looking, etc.). However, all you have to do is put the idea into my head that there is a bomb or a hole or a cliff edge in the offing, and I will not trust my defaults at all.

Another trick is: when it really matters, we *protect* the persistences that matter to us. John McCarthy has drawn our attention to the "potato in the tailpipe problem"—how do we protect ourselves from the myriads of ways a car can't start without representing all kazillion of them? If it really matters to us, we'll keep the car locked in a garage until we're ready to go—or, as the phrase has it, we'll "keep the engine running." It may not work, but it greatly improves our chances. In less stringent contexts, we take our chances and, rarely, our lumps.

So I suppose we exploit a bag of perception- and action-based crutches of imagination, a bunch of probably inconsistent model-bits— little relatively impenetrable engines of change-modeling that we hook up more or less stupidly (we don't want to install too smart a model builder in the middle) and then improve when we can.

Because some of the salient things in the world at any one time may be un-modelable (so far as our stupid model-builders can see), we need some way of including them as important unpredictable elements. Here is where Yoav Shoham's *actions* would come in handy, at least as I understand them. According to Shoham, "actions are the poor man's physics"; faced with horrendous-even-if-determinate transition functions, we put a box around some set of complicated phenomena and call it an agent, and let it "decide" what to do next. Then we add the decision / action, when it happens, to our knowledge base. (Shoham suggests that actions are observer-relative: To a more knowledgeable observer, action is just an agentless change.) If the agent is Mt. Aetna or the weather, that's the best we can do: We just compartmentalize our ignorance into inscrutable "choices" made by "agents" and wait for them to "decide." But if the agent is a person or an animal (or computer, etc.) or even just any more or less regular, nonchaotic entity, we can *regain* some leverage by applying the intentional stance to it (Dennett, 1987). Shoham suggests, then, that even when something isn't what I would call an intentional system (something predictable from the intentional stance), treating it as an agent is not just vestigial animism (though perhaps it is that, too), but a computationally wise strategy—it provides a kludge for doing "poor man's physics." This might then be the "free floating rationale" (Dennett, 1983a, 1987, chap. 8) for the vestigial animism still to be found in folk physics, where water "seeks" its own level and nature "abhors" a vacuum.

Yet another trick, this time one that is almost certainly culture-borne rather than innate (or individually reinvented): Perhaps we do the highest level organization of these anticipatory engines by exploiting a smallish stock of narrative schemata rather like Schank's scripts and plans (Schank and Abelson, 1977), but more tolerant of "metaphor." Here is what I mean, in embarrassingly impressionistic terms: Suppose an agent is supplied with a half a dozen story outlines—or twenty-five or a hundred and three, but not many more—and these are so overlearned that these stories are always "trying to happen." That is, whatever happens to the agent, the stories are crowding around, looking for their particular heroes, heroines, obstacles, opportunities, and circumstances, and very tolerant of mismatches. Suppose these stories happen to encapsulate the major predicaments of mankind (Aristotle's term, *predicament*, rejuvenated in a new use). Suppose, that is, that the difficulties the hero encounters and deals with in each story are typical, and the repertoire of stories is *practically* exhaustive of human problems. Each story, as it "tries" to be reenacted in the agent's own experience, provides the agent with a model of how to behave. It keeps giving the agent hints: Stay on the lookout for dirty tricks of sort A, don't forget to take the key along, perhaps this is an opportunity to try the old "push-the-witch-in-the-oven" trick, wait till the villain falls asleep, perhaps this is a wolf in sheep's clothing, etc. (See Waterhouse, 1990a, 1990b.)

Such stories might at least remind the agent of what sorts of questions to ask about the current situation, and hence provide an entering wedge for intelligent surveillance and updating. Might this not be a "cheap, practical" way of doing without a wise, immune-to-the-frame-problem central planner? An agent equipped with a sufficient stock of stories trying to happen would always be vulnerable to being blindsided by an entirely novel story, but perhaps, after millennia of storytelling, there are no more entirely novel stories. That, at least, is the conclusion despairingly reached by many a blocked novelist and triumphantly reached by many a structuralist anthropologist.

Implicit in this all too impressionistic sketch of an alternative set of mechanisms for eluding (not solving) the frame problem is a criticism of the "logical" school in Artificial Intelligence. My suggestion is that it fosters a phantom ideal, much the way Marr's (1982) theory of vision does. By setting the computational level too pure, by demanding an unreal competence, the problem is miscast when we turn to the lower levels of implementation (Ramachandran, 1985). If instead you start with a "good enough for government work" attitude, different solution areas open up to you.

13

The Logical Geography of Computational Approaches: A View from the East Pole[1]

In 1983–84, Douglas Hofstadter was a visiting professor in the AI Lab at MIT. He gave an amazing seminar, which I regularly attended (along with many students and almost no faculty from any department, aside from Marvin Minsky). He discussed his own work but also the work of others largely ignored or unknown in those precincts: Jerry Feldman, Dana Ballard, Paul Smolensky, Don Norman, Dave Rumelhart, Jay McClelland, Geoff Hinton, Pentti Kanerva, and others. I had discussed connectionism with Feldman at Rochester a few years earlier, so it wasn't all new to me, but Doug's seminar expanded my horizons, and showed me how the pieces might fit together. Clearly something promising was brewing. A few months later, I was invited to give a talk at a conference at MIT on "computational approaches to cognitive science" and at first I declined, suggesting that Doug Hofstadter was clearly the person the organizers should get to give this lecture. They refused to consider my suggestion — that's how insular and dogmatic MIT was at the time: Hofstadter was no cognitive scientist (or philosopher) by their lights. So I relented, but decided to poke some fun at their brittle ideological barriers, exploiting Jerry Fodor's amusing explanation of why MIT was "the East Pole," and dubbing the local orthodoxy "High Church Computationalism." I savor the memory of Ned Block asking me, after my talk, where on earth I'd learned this amazing stuff — it was all news to him. "Mostly in Doug Hofstadter's seminar, right here in your university," I replied. Harry and Betty Stanton attended the conference, and asked me about these new developments. Soon they were conferring with Rumelhart and McClelland about putting together

Originally appeared in Brand, M., and Harnish, M., eds., *The Representation of Knowledge and Belief* (Tucson: University of Arizona Press, 1986), pp. 59–79.

1. This paper was prepared for the Conference on Philosophy and Cognitive Science at MIT, May 17–20, 1984, sponsored by the Sloan Foundation. Written under a deadline for the purpose of providing a glimpse of the state of the art in mid-1984, it will no doubt have a short shelf life. So read it now, or if now is later than 1986, read it as a quaint reflection on how some people thought back in 1984.

the volumes (1986) that became the bibles of connectionism. (In a later essay,
1991c, I returned to these themes and expanded somewhat on them.)

With many different people claiming to be explaining the mind in
"computational" terms, and almost as many denying that this is possible, empirical research and ideological combat are currently proceeding on many fronts, and it's not easy to get one's bearings. But some
themes are emerging from the cacophony, and they tempt me to try
to sketch the logical geography of some of the best-known views, with
an eye to diminishing the disagreements and misrepresentations that
sometimes attend them.

There are still dualists and other mystics in the world who assert
(and hope and pray, apparently) that the mind will forever elude science, but they are off the map for me. A goal that unites all participants
in the conflict area I will explore is the explanation of the aboutness
or intentionality of mental events in terms of systems or organizations
of what in the end must be brain processes. That is, I take it as agreed
by all parties to the discussion that what we want, in the end, is a
materialistic theory of the mind as the brain. Our departure point is
the mind, meaning roughly the set of phenomena characterized in the
everyday terms of "folk psychology" as *thinking about* this and that,
having beliefs about this and that, *perceiving* this and that, and so forth.
Our destination is the brain, meaning roughly the set of cerebral
phenomena characterized in the nonintentional, *non*symbolic, *non*-
information-theoretic terms of neuroanatomy and neurophysiology.
Or we can switch destination with departure and construe the task as
building from what is known of the plumbing and electrochemistry
of the brain toward a theory that can explain—or explain away—the
phenomena celebrated in folk psychology. There has been a surfeit of
debate on the strategic question of which direction of travel is superior,
top-down or bottom-up, but that is now largely behind us and well
understood: obviously both directions can work in principle, both have
peculiar pitfalls and opportunities, and no one with an ounce of sense
would advocate ignoring as a matter of principle the lessons to be
learned from the people moving from the opposite end.

A much more interesting clash concerns what to look for in the way
of interstitial theory. It is here that manifestos about "computation"
vie with each other, and it is this issue I will attempt to clarify. Consider
the extreme positions in their purest forms.

First, there is what I shall call *High Church Computationalism*, which maintains that intervening between folk psychology and brain science will be at least one level of theory quite "close" to the high level of folk psychology that is both "cognitive" and "computational." The defining dogmas of High Church Computationalism (HCC) are a trinity:

1. *Thinking is information processing.* That is, the terms of folk psychology are to be spruced up by the theorist and recast more rigorously: "thinking" will be analyzed into an amalgam of processes ("inference" and "problem solving" and "search" and so forth); "seeing" and "hearing" will be analyzed in terms of "perceptual analysis" which itself will involve inference, hypothesis-testing strategies, and the like.

2. *Information processing is computation (which is symbol manipulation).* The information-processing systems and operations will themselves be analyzed in terms of processes of "computation," and since, as Fodor says, "no computation without representation," a medium of representation is posited, consisting of *symbols* belonging to a *system* which has a *syntax* (formation rules) and *formal rules of symbol manipulation* for deriving new symbolic complexes from old.

3. The semantics of these symbols connects thinking to the external world. For instance, some brain-thingamabob (brain state, brain event, complex property of brain tissue) will be the symbol for MIT, and some other brain-thingamabob will be the symbol for budget. Then we will be able to determine that another, composite brain-thingamabob refers to the MIT budget, since the symbolic structures composable within the representational medium have interpretations that are a systematic function of the semantic interpretations of their elements. In other words, there is a language of thought, and many of the terms of this language (many of the symbols manipulated during computation) can be said to *refer* to things in the world such as Chicago, whales, and the day after tomorrow.

At the other extreme from the High Church Computationalists are those who flatly deny all of its creed: there is no formal, rule-governed, computational level of description intervening between folk psychology and brain science. Thinking is something going on in the brain all right, but is not computation at all; thinking is something holistic and emergent—and organic and fuzzy and warm and cuddly and mysterious. I shall call this extreme version *Zen Holism.*[2]

---

2. Richard Dawkins speaks of those who are "holistier than thou" in *The Extended Phenotype* (1982, p. 113).

In between these extremes are all manner of intermediate compromise positions, most of them still rather dimly envisaged at this inchoate stage of inquiry. It would be handy to have a geographical metaphor for organizing and describing this theory-space, and happily one is at hand, thanks to Fodor.

In a heated discussion at MIT about rival theories of language comprehension, Fodor characterized the views of a well-known theoretician as "West Coast"—a weighty indictment in the corridors of MIT. When reminded that this maligned theoretician resided in Pennsylvania, Fodor was undaunted. He was equally ready, it turned out, to brand people at Brandeis or Sussex as West Coast. He explained that just as when you are at the North Pole, moving away from the Pole in any direction is moving south, so moving away from MIT in any direction is moving West. MIT is the East Pole, and from a vantage point at the East Pole, the inhabitants of Chicago, Pennsylvania, Sussex, and even Brandeis University in Waltham are all distinctly Western in their appearance and manners. Boston has long considered itself the Hub of the Universe; what Fodor has seen is that in cognitive science the true center of the universe is across the Charles, but not so far upriver as the wild and woolly ranchland of Harvard Square. (To a proper East Pole native, my outpost farther afield at Tufts is probably imagined in terms of crashing surf and ukuleles.)

Since MIT is the Vatican of High Church Computationalism, and since the best-known spokesmen of Zen Holism hold forth from various podia in the Bay area, I propose to organize the chaos with an idealized map: Positions about computational models of mental phenomena can be usefully located in a logical space with the East Pole at the center and the West coast as its horizon. (This is not, of course, just what Fodor had in mind when he discovered the East Pole. I am adapting his vision to my own purposes.)

In between the extremes there are many positions that disagree sharply over many matters (they are, as one says, "diametrically opposed"), but can nevertheless all be seen to be more or less Western, depending on which denials or modifications of High Church Computationalism they defend. As in any attempt at cartography, this is just one of many possible projections, claiming no essential rightness but inviting your consideration as a useful organizer.[3]

3. For another attempt at a systematic spatial ordering of views on a closely related issue, see John Haugeland's paper, "The Intentionality All-Stars" (1990), which identifies

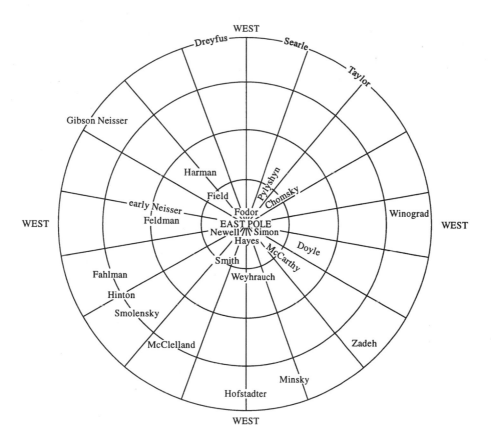

Figure 13.1
A view from the East Pole

These warring doctrines, High Church Computationalism and its many heresies, are not themselves theories; they are ideologies.[4] They are ideologies about what the true theory of the mind will or must be like, when we eventually divine it. Various attempts to create genuine theories—various research programs—*seem* to be committed to various ideologies arrayed in our space, but as we shall see, the bond between research program and ideology is rather loose. In particular, the fact that great progress is (or is not) being made on a research program

---

various positions on intentionality with baseball positions, and in the process creates some striking and illuminating juxtapositions. For instance, Fodor, Kant, and Husserl are all on first; Wittgenstein, Quine, and Ryle are shortstops; Searle is out in right field with Derrida. (Nagel is at the plate, of course, wondering what it's like to be at bat.)
4. Allen Newell (1983) would call them intellectual issues.

might tell us next to nothing about the ultimate soundness of its inspiring ideology.

And vice versa: refutation of an ideology sometimes bodes not very much at all for the research done under its banner. Ideologies are important and even unavoidable; they affect how we imagine the issues, and how we express the questions. A false ideology will typically tempt us to frame the wrong questions and thereby waste time and effort on low-grade research and avoidable artifactual puzzles. But sometimes one can make progress even while asking awkward and misguided questions, and sometimes (quite often, in fact, I think) researchers half-consciously know better than actually to ask the questions their ideology holds to be the right questions. Instead, they ask questions they can see how to answer and hardly notice that these inquiries are rather remotely related to the official questions of their school of thought.

Not surprisingly, it is philosophers who have been the most active formulators and guardians of the ideologies. Jerry Fodor, in *The Language of Thought* (1975) and *RePresentations* (1981), has for some time been the theologian in residence at the East Pole (his more recent heresy in *The Modularity of Mind* (1983) will be discussed in due course). Hubert Dreyfus and John Searle at Berkeley are the gurus of West Coast Zen Holism. Hartry Field (1978) is another East Polar apologist, and so is Gilbert Harman (1973), though he is not entirely Orthodox.

Joining Dreyfus and Searle on the West Coast is Charles Taylor (1983). Other philosophers range in between: Stephen Stich (1983), Robert Cummins (1983), John Haugeland (1978, 1981), and Margaret Boden (1984), to name a few. (For my part, I have always considered myself bicoastal (Dennett, 1982a, 1983b, and chap. 11 of this volume). Philosophers are not the only major participants in this ideological conflict however. Allen Newell (1980), Noam Chomsky (1980a, 1980b), and Zenon Pylyshyn (1978, 1980, 1984), have staunchly represented the East, while Terry Winograd, [5] Lotfi Zadeh, and Douglas Hofstadter are non philosophers in the West who have contributed more than passingly to the formulation of doctrine.[6] And in psychology we have for

---

5. In the 8th edition of Dennett, ed., *The Philosophical Lexicon* (1987), "winograd" (n. sometimes pronounced "wino-grad") is defined as the degree of intoxication occasioned by moving to the West Coast.
6. Hofstadter, on reading an earlier draft of this paper, suggested that Zadeh's fuzzy set theory is actually better seen as an attempt, entirely within the Eastern Orthodoxy, to achieve West Coast ends with East Pole means. I am inclined to agree; this is one of the fine points of interpretation in need of further work.

instance the Apostate Ulric Neisser, whose book, *Cognitive Psychology* (1963), was a founding document of High Church Computationalism, but who, under the influence of J. J. Gibson, renounced the faith in his book, *Cognition and Reality* (1975), and helped to turn Ithaca into something of a West Coast colony.[7]

Real-world geography is obviously only an intermittent clue to logical geography. The San Diego school of Norman, Rumelhart, and McClelland is appropriately Western in its attitude, but now that McClelland is joining the rather Middlewestern group of Hinton and Fahlman at Carnegie Mellon, Pittsburgh (given the Dreyfusian and hence Coastal sympathies of John Haugeland) would begin to look like another Western colony were it not for the counterbalancing Eastern voices of Newell and Simon (and Jon Doyle). Jerry Feldman at Rochester is a founding member of the distinctly Western school of New Connectionists (more on this later), but his colleague Patrick Hayes (who once told me he was quite sure the brain conducts its business in the predicate calculus) is about as East Pole as you can get. John McCarthy at Stanford is also an East Pole missionary, of course, as are Richard Weyhrauch and Brian Smith, in spite of their real-world locations.

All that should ruffle a few feathers. I doubt that the points of agreement between, say, Searle and Hofstadter, or Winograd and Feldman, loom very large in their minds, nor do I suppose Chomsky and Fodor are all that comfortable being lumped with McCarthy and Simon and vice versa. And rightly so, for the defining issues that place these people in the same "latitudes" are less integral to their widely differing research programs and methodological principles than they have acknowledged. So my cartography is indeed in some regards superficial. The dependence of some researchers on the dogmas of High Church Computationalism can be made to loom large at first glance, but I hope to show that it dissolves under scrutiny.

Over the years there has been an intermittent but intense focus on Fodor's and Chomsky's grounds for taking High Church Computationalism seriously in their research programs in linguistics, psycholinguistics, and cognitive psychology, and I consider the issues raised in that focus to be sufficiently well known and analyzed that I need not review them here. Instead I will draw attention to how

---

7. A collaborative effort by psychologist Steven Kosslyn and philosopher Gary Hatfield (1984), "Representation without Symbols, " expresses Western views similar to those developed by Boden and by me in "Styles of Mental Representation."

some other research programs in cognitive science *apparently* broaden the support for—or reveal the breadth of the dependence on— HCC.

Consider John McCarthy's (1980) quest for a *formal representation* of the knowledge an agent requires in order to *prove* that various courses of action are best (or just acceptable) under various circumstances. This is, as McCarthy says, an epistemological question, and the formality constraint McCarthy imposes on the answer *apparently* has the same rationale as Fodor's (1980) formality constraint: The brain, as a mechanism, can respond only to the formal (not semantical) properties of its states.

Or consider Newell and Simon's (1972, 1976) quest for the *rules* of problem-solving strategies adopted by self-conscious, deliberate human problem solvers, and their characterization of the phenomenon of problem solving as a transition between one (formally explicit) representation of the problem and another (formally explicit) representation of the solution. Doesn't their empirical exploration of problem solving cast in these terms presuppose a commitment to the hypothesis that problem solving in human beings is a computational process taking explicit, formal symbol structures into other explicit, formal symbol structures? They often say as much, and when they do, they express what is in any case the common understanding about the whole point of their research program.

In fact, from one vantage point all AI seems unproblematically committed to HCC. If your models are written in LISP and are actually designed to run on computers, how can you take yourself seriously as a theorist or modeler of mental processes without taking yourself to be presupposing the thesis—or at least playing the hunch—that mental processes are analogous to the constituent computer processes of your model at least to the extent of being formal, computational processes of symbol manipulation?

Many cognitivist theorists have been content to avow just such an ideology. After all, what's wrong with it? This is the question that has thrown down the gauntlet to the ideological foes of HCC, who have been so concerned to demonstrate the shortcomings of HCC doctrines *as ideology* that they have seldom cared to ask whether the research programs of the proponents are as deeply committed to the doctrines as the proponents have maintained. (Mightn't the manifestos be more a matter of fancy advertising jingles than enabling assumptions? Your true-blue ideologue doesn't care; all that matters is under what conditions the advertising is defensible.)

Thus a recurrent and powerful line of criticism of High Church Computationalism points out that such computational models as have actually been proposed by workers in AI or cognitive psychology are ludicrously underdetermined by the available data, even when they are quite plausible, as they often are.[8] This criticism usefully reveals how far from being demonstrated the central claims of High Church Computationalism are, but otherwise it strikes a glancing blow, since if there happen to be deep methodological reasons for hoping for a winning computational model, the prospect that early exploratory models will be drastically undetermined by the data should be viewed as a tolerable (and entirely anticipated) phase of the research program.

And Fodor has provided us with a candidate for a deep methodological reason for throwing our lot with HCC: it is the only remotely explicit positive idea anyone has.[9] Fodor's challenge ("What else?") has very effectively embarrassed the opposition for years, since Zen Holism itself is not a positive alternative but only a brute denial. Saying that thinking is holistic and emergent only announces the flavor of your skepticism and gestures in the direction of an alternative.

In the absence of plausible, explicit alternatives and faced with the drastic underdetermination of any HCC theory, ideologues and critics have been lured into a startlingly premature debate on what *would be* good evidence for one brand or another of computational theory. I'm all for thought experiments, but in this instance it seems to me that things have gotten out of hand. While scarcely measurable progress is being made on garnering real evidence for any particular computational theory or model,[10] tremendous effort has been expended on

---

8. See, for instance, Edward Stabler (1983, pp. 391–422), especially the commentaries. See also Chomsky (1980b, and the commentaries).

9. Newell and Simon rely on the same challenge in "Computer Science as Empirical Enquiry: Symbols and Search." See (in Haugeland reprinting) p. 50: "The principal body of evidence for the symbol-system hypothesis that we have not considered is negative evidence: the absence of specific competing hypotheses as to how intelligent activity might be accomplished—whether by man or by machine."

10. Simon has objected (in conversation) that his work with Newell is replete with solid empirical evidence in favor of their "production system" models of human problem solving. But even if I were to grant that *something very like* Newell and Simon's productions have been shown empirically to be involved in—even the basis of—human problem solving, there would still be no empirical evidence as yet showing that the *computational implementation* of production systems in computers realistically models any level of the neural implementation of the production-like processes in human think-

reaching and defending verdicts on imagined future evidential circumstances. (I have played this game as exuberantly as others—I do not exempt myself from these second thoughts.)

But we can ask the challenging question again: What is the alternative? That is, what else ought the troubled skeptic do, faced with an implausible and underdetermined ideology that defends itself with the challenge: what is the alternative? Dreyfus and the other West Coast philosophers have taken the extreme course: They have attempted to find a priori arguments showing that HCC *couldn't possibly* be true—without notable success. They have formulated their arguments but won few converts with them, and the verdict of many onlookers is that the debate conducted in those terms is a standoff at best.

If the a priori gambit has been overdone, there is a more modest Western tactic that has seldom been adopted by philosophers but has been quite influential in some AI circles: trying to explain not why HCC is impossible, but why, even if it is both possible (for all one can tell) and the only articulated possibility to date, it is so unlikely.

High Church Computationalism does seem to me (and to many others) to be highly implausible, for reasons that are hard to express but that hover around the charge that a computational, symbol-manipulating brain seems profoundly unbiological (this volume, chap. 11). This unelaborated suspicion should not be trusted, for one's intuitions about what is biological and what is not are (for most of us, surely) an undisciplined crew. What could seem more unbiological (from one intuitive vantage point) than the clockworky mechanisms of DNA replication, for instance? So if this is to be more than just another way of saying Nay to HCC, we need to say something more explicit about why we think an HCC-style brain would not be Nature's Way.

Douglas Hofstadter (1983b) has recently found a way of expressing this misgiving that strikes me as being on the right track.[11] HCC systems, designed as they are "through a 100% top-down approach" (p. 284), are *too efficient* in their utilization of machinery. As we work our way down through the nested black boxes, "functions calling subfunctions calling subfunctions," decomposing larger homunculi into committees of smaller, dumber homunculi, we provide for no waste

ing. For a related argument see Stabler (1983) and my commentary on Stabler (1983c, pp. 406–407).

11. Hofstadter calls High Church Computationalism the "Boolean Dream."

motion, no nonfunctional or dysfunctional clutter, no featherbedding homunculi or supernumeraries. But that is not Nature's Way; designing systems or organizations with that sort of efficiency requires genuine foresight, a *detailed* anticipation of the problem spaces to be encountered, the tasks the system will be called upon to perform. Another way of saying it is that such systems, by being designed *all the way down,* have too much intelligence implicated in their design at the lower levels.

Nature's Way of providing flexibility and good design involves a different kind of efficiency, the sort of efficiency that can emerge opportunistically out of prodigious amounts of "wasteful" and locally uninterpretable activity—activity that isn't from the outset "for" anything, but is enlisted to play some very modest role (or many roles on many different occasions) in some highly distributed process.

This is a theme to counterbalance the themes of HCC that have so dominated imagination, but is it just a theme? Until very recently, Fodor's challenge stood unanswered: No one had any explicit proposals for how such bottom-up systems could do any recognizable cognitive work. The only suggestions forthcoming from the philosophers (and neuroscientists as well) were metaphorical and mysterious.[12]

But now from out of the West something better is coming. Explicit proposals, and even working, testable models are emerging from a variety of workers clustered around the so-called New Connectionism. (I am still only beginning my attempt to map out the relations between these kindred spirits and no doubt will leave out, misinclude, and misrepresent some people in the course of providing my introductory list, but since this paper cannot wait for a year, I will have to present my half-formed reflections.)

The most compelling *first* impression of the New Connectionists (and the point of their name) is that they are looking closely at neural architecture and trying to model much closer to the brain than the mind. That is, if East Pole AI programs appear to be attempts to *model the mind,* New Connectionist AI programs appear to be attempts to *model the brain.* And some of the purer or more extreme approaches feature explicit commentary on the parallels between neurons or neuron assemblies and the functional units of their models (Feldman and Ballard, 1982). But it is a mistake, I think, to read the movement as "neurophysi-

---

12. In "Cognitive Wheels" (chapter 11), I call this dodge the declaration that "the brain is wonder tissue."

ology carried on by other means."[13] Nor is the distinctive difference simply or mainly a matter of being much more bottom-up than top-down (McClelland, unpublished). For whereas specifically brainish-looking bits and pieces and assemblies do often appear in these new models, what is more important is that at a more abstract level the systems and elements—whether or not they resemble any known brainware—are of recognizable biological types.

The most obvious and familiar abstract feature shared by most of these models is a high degree of parallel processing, either simulated or based on actual parallel hardware (Hillis, 1981; Fahlman, Hinton, and Sejnowski, 1983). Although the point has been brought home to everybody by now that the brain is a massively parallel processor and that this is important in understanding how the mind's work is done by the brain, there is less interest among the New Connectionists in the question of just what kind of parallel processor the brain is than in what the powers of massively parallel processors in general are. Hence some of the parallel processing models are almost willfully "un-realistic" as models of brain organization. For instance, one of the guiding analogies of Hofstadter's Jumbo architecture is the constructing of molecules by enzymes floating freely within the cytoplasm of a cell—but of course Hofstadter doesn't think the cognitive tasks the Jumbo architecture is designed to perform (the example exploited in the exposition and testing of the architecture is solving anagrams) are performed within the cell bodies of people's brain cells! (Hofstadter, 1983)

Another widely and diversely used New Connectionist idea derives from statistical mechanics: "simulated annealing" (Kirkpatrick, Gelatt, and Vecchi, 1983). Computational analogues of alternatively "warming" and "cooling" structures to get them to settle into the best combinations have proven to be powerful new methods in several different domains (Smolensky, 1983).

Although there is a lot of diversity and disagreement among the people in my Western cluster around the New Connectionists, a few characteristics—family resemblances—are worth noting. In these models, typically there is:

---

13. Clark Glymour, in "Android Epistemology, " (1987) declares that AI—and here he is surely referring to East Pole AI—is actually "logical positivism carried on by other means." [The published version of the cited paper, Glymour 1987, does not contain the phrase. In a recent co-authored paper (Glymour, Ford, and Hayes, 1995, p. 3), he says "In fact, AI is philosophy conducted by novel means." The 1995 essay, and the book it appears in, explores the relationship between different philosophical schools and AI in depth.—DCD, 1997]

1. "distributed" memory and processing, in which units play multiple, drastically equivocal roles, and in which disambiguation occurs only "globally." In short, some of these models are what you might call computational holograms. For instance, Pentti Kanerva's (1983) distributed recognition memory has a strictly limited capacity for high-quality memory, but when it is overloaded, the effect is not to create a simple overflow in which no new information can be input. Rather, the input of too much information leads to the partial degradation of information previously stored; the superimposition of the excess information smudges or obscures the information already in memory.[14]

2. no central control but rather a partially anarchic system of rather competitive elements. (See, e.g., the discussion in Feldman and Ballard of "winner take all" or WTA networks. Many of these ideas can be seen to be new versions of much older ideas in AI—e.g., Selfridge's Pandemonium, and of course perceptrons.)

3. no complex message-passing between modules or subsystems. (For instance, no discursive messages "about the outside world." "The fundamental premise of connectionism is that individual neurons *do not transmit large amounts of symbolic information.* Instead they compute by being *appropriately connected* to large numbers of similar units" [Feldman and Ballard 1982, p. 208]).

4. a reliance on statistical properties of ensembles to achieve effects.

5. the relatively mindless and inefficient making and unmaking of many partial pathways or solutions, until the system settles down after a while not on the (predesignated or predesignatable) "right" solution, but only with whatever "solution" or "solutions" "feel right" to the system. This combines the idea of simulated annealing (or a close kin of it) with the idea that in nature not all "problems" have "solutions" and there is a difference between a process stopping and a process being turned off.

The models being explored are still computational, but the level at which the modeling is computational is much closer to neuroscience than to psychology. What is computed is not (for instance) an implication of some predicate-calculus proposition *about Chicago,* or a formal

---

14. John Haugeland, in "The Nature and Plausibility of Cognitivism, " held out bravely for some sort of hologram-like alternative to a computationalist language of thought. Now there are some actual models to examine—and not just the (perhaps visionary but) metaphorical suggestions of Pribram and Arbib.

description *of a grammatical transformation,* but (for instance) the new value of some threshold-like parameter of some element *which all by itself has no univocal external-world semantic role.* At such a low level of description, the semantics of the symbolic medium of computation refers only (at most) to events, processes, states, addresses within the brain—within the computational system itself. In short, on this view the only formal, *computational* "language of thought" is *rather* like a machine language for a computer, and you can't say "it's raining in Chicago" in machine language; all you can express are imperatives about what to do to what contents of what address and the like.

How then do we ever get anything happening in such a system that is properly *about Chicago?* On these views there must indeed be higher levels of description at which we can attribute external-semantical properties to brain-thingamabobs (this brain-thingamabob refers to Chicago, and that one refers to MIT), but at such a level the interactions and relationships between elements will not be computational but (and here we lapse back into metaphor and handwaving) statistical, emergent, holistic. The "virtual machine" that is recognizably psychological in its activity will not be a *machine* in the sense that its behavior is not formally specifiable (using the psychological-level vocabulary) as the computation of some high-level algorithm. Thus in this vision the low, computational level is importantly *un*like a normal machine language in that there is no supposition of a direct translation or implementation relation between the high-level phenomena that do have an external-world semantics and the phenomena at the low level. If there were, the usual methodological precept of computer science would be in order: Ignore the hardware since the idiosyncrasies of its particular style of implementation *add nothing to* the phenomenon, provided the phenomenon is rigorously described at the higher level. (Implementation details do add constraints of time and space, of course, which are critical to the assessment of particular models, but these details are not normally supposed to affect *what information processing is executed,* which is just what makes this Western proposal a break with tradition.)

My favorite metaphor for this proposal is meteorology. (What would you expect from the author of *Brainstorms?* But the analogy is developed in detail in Hofstadter's *Gödel, Escher, Bach,* pp. 302–309.) Think of meteorology and its relation to physics. Clouds go scudding by, rain falls, snow flakes pile up in drifts, rainbows emerge; this is the language of *folk meteorology.* Modern day folk meteorologists—that is, all of us—know perfectly well that *somehow or other* all those individual clouds and rainbows and snowflakes and gusts of wind are just the emergent saliencies (saliencies relative to *our* perceptual apparatus) of vast distributions of physical energy, water droplets, and the like.

There is a gap between folk meteorology and physics but not a very large and mysterious one. Moving back and forth between the two domains takes us on familiar paths, traversed many times a day on the TV news. It is important to note that the meteorologist's instruments are barometers, hygrometers, and thermometers, not cloudometers, rainbometers, and snowflakometers. The regularities of which the science of meteorology is composed concern pressure, temperature, and relative humidity, not the folk-meteorological categories.

There is not, today, any field of computational cloudology. Is this because meteorology is in its infancy, or is such an imagined science as out of place as astrology? Note that there are patterns, regularities, large-scale effects, and, in particular, reactive effects between items in folk-meteorological categories and other things. For instance, many plants and animals are designed to discriminate folk- meteorological categories for one purpose or another. We can grant all this without having to suppose that there is a formal system governing those patterns and regularities, or the reactions to them. Similarly—and this is the moral of the meteorological metaphor—it does not follow from the fact that the folk-psychological level of explanation is the "right" level for many purposes that there must be a computational theory at or near that level. The alternative to HCC is that it is the clouds and rainbows in the brain that have intentionality—that refer to Chicago and grandmother—but that the rigorous computational theory that must account for the passage and transformation of these clouds and rainbows will be at a lower level, where the only semantics is internal and somewhat strained as semantics (in the same way the "semantics" of machine language is a far cry from the semantics of a natural language).

But how are we to move beyond the metaphors and develop these new low-level hunches into explicit theory at the "higher," or more "central," cognitive levels? The bits of theory that are getting explicit in the New Connectionist movement are relatively close to the "hardware" level of description, and the cognitive work they so far can do is often characterized as either relatively peripheral or relatively subordinate. For instance, pattern recognition appears (to many theorists) to be a relatively early or peripheral component in perception, and memory appears (to many theorists) to be a rather subordinate ("merely clerical" one might say) component in the higher intellectual processes of planning or problem solving. To the ideologues of the West, however, these appearances have misled. All thinking, no matter how intellectual or central or (even) rule governed, will turn out to make essential use of fundamentally *perceptual* operations such as versatile pattern recognition; it is no accident that we often say "I see" when we come to understand. And, according to the Western view, the apportionment of responsibility and power between memory and intelligent processing will be unlike the underlying (and ineluctably influential) division of labor in von Neumann machines, in which the memory is inert, and cold storage and all the action happens in the central processing unit; a proper memory will do a great deal of the intelligent work itself.

So far as I know, no one has yet come up with a way of sorting out these competing hunches in a medium of expression that is uniform, clear, and widely understood (even if not formal). What we need is a level of description that is to these bits of theory *roughly* as software talk is to hardware talk in conventional computer science. That is, it should abstract from as many low-level processing details as possible while remaining in the spirit of the new architectures.

The problem is that we do not yet have many clear ideas about what the functions of such systems must be—what they must be able to do. This setting of the problem has been forcefully developed by David Marr (1982) in his methodological reflections on his work on vision. He distinguishes three levels of analysis. The highest level, which he rather misleadingly calls computational, is in fact not at all concerned with computational processes, but strictly (and more abstractly) with the question of what function the system in question is serving—or, more formally, with what function in *the mathematical sense* it must (somehow or other) "compute." Recalling Chomsky's earlier version of the same division of labor, we can say that Marr's computational level is supposed to yield a formal and rigorous specification of a system's *competence*—"*given* an element in the set of x's it yields an element in the set of y's according to the following rules"—while remaining silent or neutral about implementation or *performance*. Marr's second level down is the *algorithmic* level, which does specify the computational processes but remains neutral (as neutral as possible) about the *hardware*, which is described at the bottom level.

Marr's claim is that until we get a clear and precise understanding of the activity of a system at the highest, "computational" level, we cannot properly address detailed questions at the lower levels, or interpret such data as we may already have about processes implementing those lower levels. Moreover, he insists, if you have a seriously mistaken view about what the computational-level description of your system is (as all earlier theorists of vision did, in his view), your attempts to theorize at lower levels will be confounded by spurious artifactual problems. (It is interesting to note that this is also the claim of J. J. Gibson, who viewed all cognitivistic, information-processing models of vision as hopelessly entangled in unnecessarily complex Rube Goldberg mechanisms posited because the theorists had failed to see that a fundamental reparsing of the inputs and outputs was required. Once we get the right way of characterizing what vision receives from the light, he thought, and what it must yield ["affordances"], the theory of vision would be a snap.)

Now Marr claims to have gotten the computational level right for vision, and his claim is not obviously too optimistic. But vision, like any peripheral system, is apparently much more tractable at Marr's computational level than are the central systems of thought, planning, problem solving, and the like that figure so centrally in AI explorations. Fodor argues in *The Modularity of Mind* (1983) that while there has been dramatic progress on the peripheral perceptual "modules" that "present the world to thought," "there is no serious psychology of central cognitive processes."

We have, to put it bluntly, no computational formalisms that show us how to do this, and we have no idea how such formalisms might be developed. . . . If someone—a Dreyfus, for example—were to ask us why we should even suppose that the digital computer is a plausible mechanism for the simulation of global cognitive processes, the answering silence would be deafening. (p. 129)

But what is this? One would have thought that never the twain would meet, but here is Fodor, Archbishop of the East Pole, agreeing with Dreyfus, Guru of the West Coast, that High Church Computationalism has made no progress on "central cognitive processes." If Fodor is right in his pessimism—and I think for the most part he is—what might a reasonable theoretician do?

My proposal: go right on doing the sort of AI that has traditionally been associated with High Church Computationalism but abandon the computationalist ideology altogether and reinterpret the programs of these AI practitioners as *thought experiments*, not *models*.

Here is what I mean. If Marr is right to insist that progress must first be made on the problems at the computational level, then the first task confronting us if we want a theory of "central cognitive processes" is just to say what those processes are supposed to be able to accomplish. What is the nature of those central faculties? Forget for the moment *how* they do what they do. Just what is it that they (are supposed to) do? What is the competence the theorist should try to explain? As Fodor insists, no one has a clear, crisp explicit account of this. But several researchers are trying. Allen Newell (1982), for instance, calls this level of description the Knowledge Level. It is, in effect, Marr's computational level as applied to the central arena. McCarthy (1980) draws a similar level distinction. What these and many other theorists in AI have been doing is not proposing HCC models of human cognition or testing theories with empirical experiments, but casting about, in a *thought*-experimental way, for constraints and relationships that might inform the description (at Marr's "computational" level) of the mysterious "central cognitive processes." And at least this much progress has been made: We have enlarged and refined our vision of what powers human minds actually have. And we now know quite a few ways *not* to try to capture the basic competence—let alone the implementation—of the central cognitive systems. The process of elimination looms large in AI research; virtually every model seriously considered has been eliminated as far too simple for one reason or another. But that is progress. Until the models are seriously considered and eliminated they lurk as serious possibilities to tempt the theorist.

Thus McCarthy's formality constraint is not a commitment to High Church Computationalism (or need not be). It might be nothing more than the demand for enough rigor and precision to set the problem for the next level down, Marr's algorithmic level, except that this would probably not be a good term for the highest level at which the processes (as contrasted with the products) of the New Connectionist sort were described.

And Newell and Simon's search for "rules" of "thinking" need not commit them or their admirers to the HCC doctrine that thinking is rule-*governed* computation. The rules they discover (supposing they succeed) may instead be interpreted as regularities in patterns in the emergent phenomena—the cognitive "clouds" and "rainbows"—but not "mere" regularities. The well-known distinction (in philosophy) between rule-following behavior and rule-described behavior is often illustrated by pointing out that the planets do not compute their orbits, even though *we* can, following rules that describe their motions. The "rules" of planetary motion are law-like regularities, not "followed" rules. This is true, but it ignores a variety of regularity intermediate between the regularities of planets (or ordinary cloud formations) and the regularities of rule-following (that is, rule-*consulting*) systems. These are the regularities that are preserved under selective pressure: the regularities dictated by principles of good design and hence homed in on by self-designing systems. That is, a "rule of thought" may be much more than a mere regularity; it may be a *wise* rule, a rule one would design a system by if one were a system designer, and hence a rule one would expect self-designing systems to "discover" in the course of settling into their patterns of activity. Such rules no more need to be explicitly represented than do the principles of aerodynamics honored in the design of birds' wings.

For example, Marr discovered that the visual system operates with a tacit assumption that moving shapes are articulated in rigid linkages and that sharp light-intensity boundaries indicate physical edges. These assumptions are not "coded" in the visual system; the visual system is designed to work well only in environments where the assumptions are (by and large) true. Such rules and principles should be very precisely formulated at the computational level—not so they can then be "coded" at the algorithmic level but so that the (algorithmic) processes can be designed to honor them (but maybe only with a high degree of regularity).

Are there "rules" of (good) problem solving that must be (and are) tacit in the regularities that emerge in the information processing of mature thinkers? One might discover them by attempting to *codify* such rules in a rule-following system whose behavior exhibited those regularities because those were the regularities it was "told" to follow. Such systems can be put through their paces to test the adequacy of the rules under consideration.[15] It is this testing that has led to the (often informative) elimination of so many tempting models in AI.

In sum, there is no reason I can see for AI or cognitive science to take on the rather unlikely burden of defending HCC. It seems to me

---

15. I think it *may* be helpful to compare this interpretation of AI strategy with the simulations explored by evolutionary theorists such as John Maynard Smith and Richard Dawkins, who ask questions about whether certain behavioral "strategies" are evolutionarily stable by explicitly codifying the strategies in the behavior of imagined organisms, and then pitting them against the alternative (explicit, rule-governed) strategies embodied in rival imaginary organisms, to see which (pure, idealized) strategy would win in Nature under various conditions. See Dawkins (1976, 1982) for good introductory discussions. See also Robert Axelrod (1984) on prisoners' dilemma competitions between simulations for a similarly motivated research effort.

that all the valuable AI research that has been done can be viewed as attempts to sketch competences. (Marr, of course, went far beyond that.) As such it is best viewed as consisting of (preliminary) thought experiments, not as more "mature" genuinely experimental science. But its thought experiments are subject to a modicum of control. One can *test* such a sketch of a competence by test driving an unbiologically produced Rube Goldberg device with that competence (the actual "computational" AI program) to see how it would perform.

This leaves us with an almost embarrassingly ecumenical conclusion. Everyone is right about something. Dreyfus and the Zen Holists are right that we need not commit ourselves to the defining dogmas of High Church Computationalism, but the people engaged in devising computational models of cognitive processes are right that their methodology is probably the best way to make headway on the mysteries of the mind. Everybody agrees that something or other in the brain must be capable of having the semantic property of referring to Chicago and that it is the task of *some* sort of computational theory to explain and ground this power. Residual disagreements are either based on unmotivated allegiances to bits of outworn creed or are substantive disagreements on just which brand of interstitial computational theory is apt to be most promising. There is only one way to settle these latter disagreements: roll up our sleeves and devise and test the theories.[16]

---

16. Douglas Hofstadter has had an even greater role than usual in shaping my thinking on these issues, so if I am all wrong about this, he *is* responsible, and will have to share the blame. But he is not responsible for my failures to understand or do justice to the various efforts I discuss here. Other who have commented on earlier drafts of this paper, including Robert Cummins, Jerry Feldman, John Haugeland, Hilary Putnam, and Herbert Simon, are hereby thanked and absolved in the usual manner.

14

Complexity is halfway between a scholarly journal and a magazine, published by the Santa Fe Institute. My invited review of Douglas Hofstadter's recent book, Fluid Concepts and Creative Analogies, *ran a little longer than the journal's standard, so the editors reshaped it into this somewhat less formal essay, permitting me to fix some flaws in drafts that had circulated rather widely on the Internet among members of the AI community. Here we see the Multiple Drafts Model in action: by reprinting the later version here, I expect to amplify the revisionary effect (don't ask if it is Orwellian or Stalinesque), so that in the long run this will be the more remembered, higher impact version.*

What Douglas Hofstadter is, quite simply, is a phenomenologist, a *practicing* phenomenologist, and he does it better than anybody else. Ever. For years he has been studying the processes of his own consciousness, relentlessly, unflinchingly, imaginatively, but undeludedly. He is not a Phenomenologist with a capital "P"—with few exceptions, Phenomenologists don't actually do phenomenology, they just write about doing it.

In stark contrast to the Husserlian school (s) of Phenomenology, which advocates the *epoché* or "bracketing" that excuses the investigator from all inquiry, speculative or otherwise, into the underlying mechanisms, the Hofstadterian school of phenomenology stresses the need to ask—and answer—the question about how it works. Hofstadter's initial phenomenological observations are laced with questions and suggestions about dynamics and mechanisms; he watches his own mind work the way a stage magician watches another stage magician's show, not in slack-jawed awe at the "magic" of it all, but full of intense and informed curiosity about how on earth the effects might be achieved.

Originally appeared in *Complexity*, 1 (6), 1996, pp. 9–11.

In 1979, Douglas Hofstadter published *Gödel, Escher, Bach: An Eternal Golden Braid*, a brilliant exploration of some of the most difficult and fascinating ideas at the heart of cognitive science: recursion, computation, reduction, holism, meaning, "jootsing" (Jumping Out Of The System), "strange loops," and much, much more. What made the book's expositions so effective were a family of elaborate (and lovingly elaborated) analogies: the mind is like an anthill, a formal system is like a game, theorem and nontheorem are like figure and ground, and Bach's Inventions are like dialogues, to mention a few. The whole analogy-package was wrapped in layers of self-conscious reflection. "Anything you can do I can do meta-" was one of Doug's mottoes, and of course he applied it, recursively, to everything he did.

Then in 1985 came *Metamagical Themas: Questing for the Essence of Mind and Pattern*, its title drawn from the title of his monthly column in *Scientific American*, which was of course an anagram of its predecessor, Martin Gardner's "Mathematical Games." More wordplay, more games, more analogies, more recursion, more self-conscious reflection—all brilliant, but many began to wonder: what, actually, was Hofstadter *doing*? Was there a serious research project here, or just fun and games and self-absorption? His fans were fascinated, but even some of his colleagues and graduate students—even his friend and co-author (of *The Mind's I:* myself)—began to worry a bit about his lengthy odysseys into toy worlds (ambigrams, bizarre fonts, curious doodles on long rolls of paper).

This man wanted to be taken seriously, but where was the focused, rigorous investigation of some phenomena, where was the discipline? It was right in front of our noses—and his. We should have trusted him. He knew what he was doing, and in his new book, *Fluid Concepts and Creative Analogies: Computer Models of the Fundamental Mechanisms of Thought*, he explains and justifies all those curious practices; and shows that while many of the rest of us were rushing off half-cocked on various quests for one cognitive science grail or another, he was patiently, systematically, brilliantly building up an understanding of a foundational area of cognitive science, doing a job that only he could do. And in the end, he and his team test their hunches by building working models that can simulate the particular conscious processes they have been studying (and their semiconscious, subconscious, unconscious penumbra). Can they get realistic performances? If not, back to the drawing board.

Fluid Concepts and Creative Analogies is an anthology of the work of

Hofstadter and his graduate students at FARG, the Fluid Analogies Research Group, which he formed first in Ann Arbor in 1984, and then moved to its current home at Indiana University. His fellow "Fargonauts" are given the role of coauthors, both on the title page, and in the individual chapters, but these are *his* versions, by and large, of their joint projects. It is entirely appropriate for him to produce a volume of his own versions, since it is his idiosyncratic vision of how to do cognitive science that is in need of a full-scale overview and demonstration, which is what this book provides. (His coauthors are very good at grinding their own axes—see their articles listed in Hofstadter's bibliography, and their books: Melanie Mitchell, *Analogy-Making as Perception*, 1993, and Robert French, *The Subtlety of Sameness*, 1995).

Scattered through the book are stunning autobiographical revelations that shed light on his imperviousness to the impatience and doubt that was inconcealable—indeed often vigorously expressed—by his friends and associates. At the outset of one "reenactment of a discovery," he tells us:

I am going to be very faithful to my actual discovery process, not to some idealization thereof. This means that what I will show may seem quite awkward and stupid in spots; but that is the way discoveries are often made. After a discovery has been completed and its ideas well digested, one quite understandably wishes to go back and clean it up, so that it appears elegant and pristine. This is a healthy desire, and doing so certainly makes the new ideas much easier and prettier to present to others. On the other hand, doing so also tends to make one forget, especially as the years pass, how many awkward notations one actually used, and how many futile pathways one tried out. (p. 21)

"Luckily," he goes on to inform us, "having always been fascinated by how the mind works, I have tended to keep careful records of my discovery processes—even back at age sixteen, which is when this particular exploration and discovery took place." Later in the book, he tells of his alphabetic font obsession:

What ensued was a lengthy period of time during which I designed hundreds of new alphabetic styles, relentlessly exploring all sorts of combinations of gracefulness, funkiness, sassiness, sauciness, silliness, softness, pointiness, hollowness, curviness, jaggedness, roundness, smoothness, complexity, austerity, irregularity, angularity, symmetry, asymmetry, minimality, redundancy, ornamentation, and countless other indefinable parameters. . . . I am sure that to somebody who hadn't thought much about alphabets and visual styles and the idea of pushing concepts to their very limits or just beyond, many of my experiments would have looked mysterious and pointless, perhaps even gawky and stupid. But that wouldn't have deterred me, because I had a stable inner compass that was carrying me somewhere, though I couldn't have said exactly where or why. As the years [!] went by . . . (p. 402)

So far so good: by keeping a lifetime of notes, and daring to share them with us, he provides himself, and us, with a wealth of data. But data are only as good as the observer and the phenomena observed warrant. Other phenomenologists and indeed cognitive scientists have scrupulously gathered data on various trains of thought. K. A. Ericsson and H. A. Simon's *Protocol Analysis: Verbal Reports as Data* (1984) comes to mind as a particularly systematic and reflective effort along these lines. But the phenomena they study, like those studied by almost all cognitive scientists and psychologists, are a cramped subset of human thought processes: solving well-defined problems with clear (if hard to find) paths to the correct solution. Hofstadter has always been interested in the more freewheeling, creative, artistic, unpredictable sort of thinking, but as a good scientist he has appreciated that one must simplify one's domain, limiting and controlling it in as many dimensions as possible, so that only a few sources of variation are salient, and hence investigatable, at a time.

Every science needs its toy problems; population genetics has its fruitflies, neuroanatomy has its giant squid axons, developmental biology has its nematode worm, *C. elegans,* GOFAI had its blocks world, Tower of Hanoi puzzle, chess, cryptarithmetic problems, connectionism has its NETTalk domain of uncomprehending pronunciation, and so forth. Hofstadter and his students have been remarkably successful at creating well-behaved toy domains for exploring the shifty, subtle, quirky processes of analogy-making and metaphor appreciation: the anagrams and words of Jumbo, the alphabet-world of Copycat, the concrete and mundane but conventional and limited furnishings of Tabletop, to name a few of the best. This success has been a hard-won evolution, not the result of a saltation of perfect inspiration. The Seek-Whence domain begat the Jumbo domain and the Copycat domain, which then begat the Tabletop domain, and so forth.

One of the simplest but most powerful demonstrations of the superiority of Hofstadter's approach to analogy-finding is to compare his toy problems to the limited domains others have devised to demonstrate their models. Every practical model must oversimplify ruthlessly, but it is quite possible to leave out all the important phenomena and be left with a trivial model, as Hofstadter shows by contrasting the bounty of variegated and even surprising behavior his models can generate with the single-stunt-in-different-costumes behavior of rival models. Hofstadter has numerous important reflections to offer on "the knotty problem of evaluating research," and one of the book's virtues is to draw clearly for us "the vastness of the gulf that can separate different research projects that on the surface seem to belong to the same field. Those people who are interested in *results* will begin with a standard technology, not even questioning it at all, and then build a big system that solves many complex problems and impresses a lot of people" (p. 53). He has taken a different path, and has often had difficulties convincing the grown-ups that it is a good one: "When there's a little kid trying somersaults out for the first time next to a flashy gymnast doing flawless flips on a balance beam, who's going to pay any attention to the kid?" (p. 168) A fair complaint, but part of the problem, now redressed by this book, was that the little kid didn't try to explain (in an efficient format accessible to impatient grown-ups) why his somersaults were so special.

So just what have Hofstadter and the Fargonauts discovered? Hofstadter lists eight themes that have been explored and re-explored in the succession of models, and I cannot improve on his list:

1. perception and high-level cognition are inseparable;

2. high-level perception consists of easily reconfigurable multilevel cognitive representations;

3. there are "subcognitive pressures" that probabilistically influence the building and reforming of these representations;

4. many such pressures commingle, "leading to a nondeterministic parallel architecture in which bottom-up and top-down processing co-exist gracefully";

5. there is a "simultaneous feeling-out of many potential pathways";

6. making analogies is a central component in high-level cognition;

7. cognitive representations have "*deeper and shallower aspects*, with the former remaining relatively immune to contextual pressures, and the latter being more likely to yield under pressure (to 'slip')";

8. a crucial role is played by "the inner structure of concepts and conceptual neighborhoods." (pp. 84–85)

Each of these themes rings a bell, and sometimes a familiar bell, already rung many times by others, but what is exciting about FARG is that they have managed to create models that exhibit *all these themes at once,* and that actually work. I cannot recall any comparable instance in which so many attractive but all too impressionistic ideas have actually been implemented. One of the most impressive features of their architectural ideas, in my view, is the fact that they provide a more fundamental (and much more biologically plausible) platform from which one can implement the more rigid architectural ideas of their predecessors in AI. The parallel terraced scan, for instance, has the nice feature that it can be tuned continuously in several dimensions between rigid and lax. You can screw the system up and get obsessively rigid problem-solving, with stacks and stack-pointers, or relax the parameters and get quite "chaotic" wanderings. You can get temporary structures reminiscent of Schank scripts and Minsky frames to emerge from the interactions between top-down and bottom-up pressures that are variable in the architecture. This is fine, since it was always clear that Schank and Minsky were on to some important ideas, even if the attempts at implementation (and Minsky knew better than to try back then) were implausibly straitjacketed.

There are prices to be paid, of course, for such success. As with all other AI models of toy phenomena, there is the question of whether they will scale up without combinatorial explosion, and the interfaces that would be needed to incorporate these models into whole cognitive systems, whole agents, are currently unimagined. Hofstadter addresses these issues and other criticisms forthrightly, and offers particularly valuable projections of where the Fargonauts and those they inspire should turn next (see especially pp. 314–318).

The models occupy a limbo that is biologically flavored but still quite remote from neuroanatomy; no neuroscientist is going to find any *easy* clues here about how to discover the analogy-making process in the activities of neural networks. There are dynamically connected nodes and spreading activation from node to node, but these are not neurons or simple assemblies thereof. There are broadcast effects that damp or enhance various activities in parallel, but these are not plausibly the discovered roles of neuromodulators diffusing through the interstices of networks. There are functionally defined places where different sorts of things happen, but these are not tied to anatomical locations by any data or even speculations.

The models are thus both mechanical and abstract at the same time. By being mechanical, they amount to a "proof of concept" of sorts: yes, it is possible, by some such mechanism, to get very warm, juicy phenomenology to emerge from the joint activities of lots of very clockworky parts. Good news. We always knew in our hearts it was possible, but it is very reassuring to have models that actually deliver such goods. We can even look at the details of the model for very indirect *hints* about how the phenomena might occur in a whole live brain. Compared to the GOFAI models of yore, Hofstadter's models are much more than halfway to the brain, but there is still a chasm between them and computational neuroscience.

Hofstadter provides useful comparisons along the way with many other projects in the history of AI, from GPS to ACT* and Soar, from Hearsay II and BACON to such current enterprises as Gentner and Forbus's Structure Mapping Engine, and Holyoak and Thagard's ACME. He is devastating with his criticisms, but also generous in his praise—for instance, in his homage to Walter Reitman's Argus. What emerges from these comparisons is, to this reviewer, a tempting but tentative conclusion: Hofstadter may or may not have nailed it, but he has come much closer than any other enterprise in AI to finding the right level at which to conduct further inquiry.

Alan Turing got the idea for the stored-program computer from his own systematic introspection into his mental states when dutifully executing an algorithm, the sort of mental activity that is farthest removed from artistic, creative thought. He saw that the restriction to rigid problem-solving was an inessential feature of the fundamental architecture, and predicted, correctly, the field of AI. We've been loosening the straps, widening the von Neumann bottleneck, ever since. Doug Hofstadter has pioneered the systematic introspection of the other end of the spectrum of mental activities, in a way that could not be done by anyone who lacked his deep understanding of the computational possibilities inherent in Turing's fabulous machine. It is not just that while others have concentrated on problem solving and Scientific Thinking, he has concentrated on daydreaming and Artistic Thinking. He has recognized that even Scientific Thinking is, at its base, analogical. All cognition is analogical. That is where we all must start, with the kid stuff.

15   Foreword to Robert French,
The Subtlety of Sameness

I first met Bob French while he was working on the (French, of course) transla-
tion of Doug Hofstadter's Gödel, Escher, Bach. *He decided to leave his prom-*
ising career as a translator and work for a Ph.D. in computer science with
Doug, meanwhile beginning a long philosophical conversation with me. In
addition to his work in AI, he has published one of the best philosophical papers
on the Turing test, in Mind *(French, 1990).*

If somebody asked me to design a book that would introduce the most
important ideas in Artificial Intelligence (AI) to a wider audience, I
would try to work to the following principles:

1. Go for details. Instead of presenting yet another impressionistic overview of the field, concentrate on the details of a particular AI model, so
that the readers can see for themselves just how and why it works, seeing
its weaknesses and boundaries as well as its showcase triumphs.

2. Model something we all know intimately. Choose a psychological
phenomenon that is familiar to everyone—and intrinsically interesting.
Not everybody plays chess or solves route-minimization problems, and
although we almost all see, unless we are vision scientists, we have scant
direct familiarity with the details of how our visual processes work.

3. Explain exactly how the particular model supports or refutes, sup-
plements or clarifies the other research on the same phenomenon, including work by people in other disciplines.

4. Give concrete illustrations of the important ideas at work. A single
well-developed example of a concept applied is often better than ten
pages of definition.

Originally appeared in French, R., *The Subtlety of Sameness* (Cambridge, MA: Bradford
Books / The MIT Press, 1995), pp. vii–xi.

Bob French's *The Sublety of Sameness*, all about his Tabletop model, fills the bill perfectly, so when I read an early draft of it (I was a member of his Ph.D. dissertation committee), I encouraged him to publish it and offered to write a foreword. From its easily read pages you will come to know the model inside-out, seeing not only *that* it comes up with recognizably human performance, but seeing—really seeing—*how* it comes up with its results. And what does it do? It does something we all do everyday: it appreciates analogies. It creates them, and perceives them, in a manner of speaking. The simple setting of the task is inspired: a game of "Do this!" whose point you will get in an instant, but whose richer possibilities are not only surprising, but quite inexhaustible.

You get to tackle all the problems yourself, and think about them "from the first person point of view." Something goes on in you when you do these problems. What on earth is it? It seems at first the farthest thing from mechanizable—"intuitive," quirky, fluid, aesthetic, quintessentially human—just the sort of phenomenon that the skeptics would be tempted to brandish, saying, "You'll never get a computer to do *this*!" Or, more cautiously, "You'll never get a computer to do this the way *we* do it!" If you are such a skeptic, you are in for a surprise.

Most AI programs model phenomena that are either highly intellectualized thinking exercises in the first place—like playing chess or constructing proofs—or else low-level processes that are quite beneath our ken—like extracting three-dimensional information about the visible world from binocular overlap, texture gradients, and shading. French's program, in contrast, models a phenomenon that is neither difficult nor utterly invisible but rather *just* out of reach to the introspecting reader. We can *almost* analyze our own direct experiences into the steps that French's model exhibits. AI workers love acronyms, and I hereby introduce the term AIGLES—Almost-Introspectible-Grain-Level Events—as the general term for the sort of high-level psychological phenomenon French has modeled. If there *were* a Cartesian Theater in our brains, across whose stage the parade of consciousness marched, his would be a model of something that happens immediately backstage. (Those who join me in renouncing the all-too-popular image of the Cartesian Theater have a nontrivial task of explaining why and how French's model can avoid falling into that forlorn trap, but this is not the time or place for me to discharge that burden. It is left as an exercise for the reader.)

From the particulars, we can appreciate the general. French introduces, exemplifies, and explains some of the most important and ill-understood ideas in current AI. For instance, almost everybody these days speaks dismissively of the bad old days in AI and talks instead about "emergence," while waving hands about self-organizing systems that settle into coherent structures and so forth. (I myself have spoken of Multiple Drafts in competition, out of which transient winners emerge, a tantalizingly metaphorical description of the processes I claim are involved in human consciousness.) French provides a no-nonsense model of just such a system. When posed a problem, the answer it arrives at is "the emergent result of the interaction of many parallel unconscious processes" (p. 20). So here is a fine place to see what all the hoopla is about. You get to see how the currently popular metaphors—a batch of cooling molecules or a system of interconnected resonators coming to vibrate in unison, for instance—apply to an actual nonmetaphorical reality, a system engaged in doing some undeniably mental work.

His model also illustrates a version of "dynamic" memory structures, which deform to fit the current context, and it achieves its results by exploiting a "parallel-terraced scan." It accomplishes "implicit pruning," which must somehow be what we manage to do when we ignore the irrelevancies that always surround us. It does this by building (and rebuilding and rebuilding) the relevant structures on the fly, thereby avoiding at least some of the "combinatorial explosions" that threaten all AI models that have to ignore most of what they *could* attend to without catastrophically ignoring the important points. The central theme of the book is that the processes of producing mental representations and manipulating them are inextricably intertwined. As French puts it, "You *must* take the representation problem into consideration *while* you are doing processing." When you understand this paragraph in detail (and you will when you have read the book), you will have a good grip on some of the central ideas in recent AI.

These ideas are not just French's of course. His work grows out of the family of projects undertaken in recent years by Douglas Hofstadter's group at Indiana University, and, as such, provides a fine demonstration of the powers of that school of thought in AI. Many skeptics and critics of AI from other disciplines have surmised there was something profoundly wrong about the hard-edged, inert (but manipulable) symbols of the "physical-symbol systems" of traditional AI, and hence they have been intrigued by Hofstadter's radical alternative: "active symbols." Active symbols sound great, but what are they, and how on earth could they work? This book takes us a few sure steps toward the answer. French provides a judicious comparison of his own work—which has plenty of its own originality—to that of others who have worked on analogy, in Hofstadter's group, in AI more generally, and in psychology.

If you don't already appreciate it, you will come to appreciate the curious combination of ambition and modesty that marks most work in AI, and the work of Hofstadter and his colleagues in particular. On the one hand, the models are tremendously abstract, not tied at all to brain architecture or to the known details of such processes as "early vision." All the important questions in these research domains are simply sidestepped. That's modesty. On the other hand, the models purport to be getting at something truly fundamental in the underlying structure and rationale of the actual processes that must go on in the brain. That's ambition. Like more traditional AI programs, they often achieve their triumphs by heroic simplification: helping themselves to ruthless—even comical—truncations of the phenomena (more modesty), in order, it is claimed, to provide a feasible working model of the essential underlying process (more ambition). The reader is left, quite properly, with an unanswered question about just which helpings of simplification might be poisoned. Are any of these bold decisions fatal oversimplifications that could not possibly be removed without undoing the ambitious claims? There is something that is both right and deep about this model, I am sure, but saying just what it is and how it will map onto lower-level models of brain function is still beyond me and everybody else at this time, a tantalizing patch of fog.

French's program doesn't learn at all—except what it could be said to learn in the course of tackling a single problem. It has no long-term memory of its activities, and never gets any better. This might seem to be a horrible shortcoming, but it has an unusual bonus: his program never gets bored! You can give it the same problem, over and over and over, and it never rebels, but always takes it in a fresh spirit. This is excellent for "rewinding the tape"—looking, counterfactually, at what *else* a system might do, if put in the same situation again. Heraclitus said that you can never step in the same river twice, and this is particularly true of human beings, thanks to our memories. Aside from a few famous amnesiacs, we normal human beings are never remotely in the same state twice, and this seriously impedes scientific research on human cognitive mechanisms. Is investigating a system with total amnesia, like French's, a worthy substitute for non-doable human experiments, or does the absence of memory and learning vitiate his model? French shows that AI fell in a trap when it opportunistically separated the building of representations from their processing; will some meta-French soon come along to show that he fell in just as bad a trap by setting long-term learning aside for the time being? A good question—which is to say that no one should think that the pessimistic answer is obvious. In the end, at some level, no doubt just about everything is inextricably intertwined with everything else, but if we are to understand the main features of this tangled bank, we must force some temporary separation on them.

A standard conflict in AI is between the hard edges and the fuzzies, a conflict fought on many battlefields, and some of the niftiest features of French's model demonstrate what happens when you slide back and forth between hard edges and fuzzy edges. There are knobs, in effect, that you can turn, thereby setting parameters on the model to give you nice sharp edges or terribly fuzzy edges or something in between. Probability plays a deep role in French's model, something that makes it imperative for him to test his model in action many, many times and gather statistics on its performance—something that would not be at all motivated in most traditional AI. But if you set the model so that some of the probabilities are very close to 1 or 0, you can turn it into what amounts to a deterministic, hard-edged model. Or you can explore the trade-off between depth-first search and breadth-first search by adjusting the "rho" factor, or you can create what French calls a semi-stack, another fuzzy version of a hard-edged idea. This is a particularly attractive set of features, for one of the things we know about ourselves is that the *appearance* of determinism and indeterminism in our mental life is highly variable.

AI is a seductive field. Even a book as scrupulously written as French's may mislead you into ignoring deep problems or deficiencies in the model, or—a very common foible—it may encourage you to overestimate the actual fidelity or power of the model. Here, for the benefit of neophytes, are a few of the tough questions you should keep asking yourself as you read. (You'll get a better sense of the genuine strengths of French's model by making sure you know just what its weaknesses are.)

French claims his domain, the (apparently) concrete world of the Tabletop, is rich enough to "ground" the symbols of his model in a way the symbols of most AI programs are not grounded. Is this really so? We viewers of Tabletop *see* the knives, forks, spoons, cups, bowls, and so forth vividly laid out in space, but what does the model really understand about the shape of these objects? Anything? Does Tabletop know that a spoon, with its concavity, is more like a bowl than a knife is? *We* can see that a spoon is a sort of bowl on a stick, but that is utterly unknown to Tabletop. What other sorts of obvious facts about tableware are left out of Tabletop's semantics, and how could they be added? Perhaps it is here that we see most clearly what the model leaves out when it leaves out learning—in the real world of concrete experience. But what difference, if any, does this make to the groundedness of Tabletop's symbols? Is there some other sense in which Tabletop is clearly superior in "groundedness" to other programs? (I think the answer is yes. Can you see how?)

Tabletop gets its basic perceptual accomplishments for free. It cannot mistake a knife for a fork out of the corner of its eye, or fail to see the second spoon *as* a spoon (if it ever directs its attention to it). Everything placed on the table is, as it were, legibly and correctly labeled according to its type. So what? (Might some of the combinatorial explosions so deftly avoided by Tabletop come back to haunt it if this gift were revoked? Again, so what?)

What would it take to add learning to Tabletop? What would it take to expand the domain to other topics? What would happen if you tried to add episodic memory? Could you readily embed Tabletop in a larger system that could face the decision of whether or not to play the Tabletop game or play it in good faith? (A human player could get fed up and start giving deliberately "bad" answers, to try to drive "Henry" into one amusing state of frustration or another. Is this a feature whose absence from Tabletop could be readily repaired, or would a model builder have to start over from scratch to include it?)

Finally, the granddaddy of all challenging questions for any AI program: Since this model purports to be right about something, how could we tell if it was wrong? What sort of discovery, in particular, would refute it? The boring way of responding to this question is to try to concoct some philosophical argument to show why "in principle" Tabletop couldn't be right. The exciting ways are to be found down the paths leading from the other questions.

My raising of these challenging questions in the foreword is the most unignorable way I can think of to demonstrate my confidence in the strength and value of French's book. Go ahead; give it your best shot.

16

Cognitive Science as Reverse Engineering: Several Meanings of "Top-Down" and "Bottom-Up"

The idea that evolutionary considerations are important in cognitive science has dawned on different people at different times as they confronted different problems. This essay attempts to tie a few of those concerns together, and to get traditional cognitive scientists to relax their grip on antievolutionary prejudices.

The vivid terms "top-down" and "bottom-up" have become popular in several different contexts in cognitive science. My current task is to sort out some different meanings and comment on the relations between them, and their implications for cognitive science.

1 Models and Methodologies

To a first approximation, the terms are used to characterize both research methodologies on the one hand, and models (or features of models) on the other. I shall be primarily concerned with the issues surrounding top-down versus bottom-up methodologies, but we risk confusion with the other meaning if we don't pause first to illustrate it, and thereby isolate it as a topic for another occasion. Let's briefly consider, then, the top-down versus bottom-up polarity in models of a particular cognitive capacity, language comprehension.

When a person perceives (and comprehends) speech, processes occur in the brain which must be partly determined bottom-up, by the input, and partly determined top-down, by effects from on high, such as interpretive dispositions in the perceiver due to the perceiver's particular knowledge and interests. (Much the same contrast, which of

Originally appeared in Prawitz, D., Skyrms, B., and Westerståhl, D., eds., *Logic, Methodology, and Philosophy of Science IX* (Amsterdam: Elsevier Science, BV, 1994), pp. 679–689.

course is redolent of Kantian themes, is made by the terms "data-driven" and "expectation-driven.")

There is no controversy, so far as I know, about the need for this dual source of determination, but only about their relative importance, and when, where, and how the top-down influences are achieved. For instance, speech perception cannot be entirely data-driven because not only are the brains of those who know no Chinese not driven by Chinese speech in the same ways as the brains of those who are native Chinese speakers, but also, those who know Chinese but are ignorant of, or bored by, chess-talk, have brains that will not respond to Chinese chess-talk in the way the brains of Chinese-speaking chess-mavens are. This is true even at the level of perception: what you hear—and not just whether you notice ambiguities, and are susceptible to garden-path parsings, for instance—is in some measure a function of what sorts of expectations you are equipped to have. Two anecdotes will make the issue vivid.

The philosopher, Samuel Alexander, was hard of hearing in his old age, and used an ear trumpet. One day a colleague came up to him in the common room at Manchester University, and attempted to introduce a visiting American philosopher to him. "THIS IS PROFESSOR JONES, FROM AMERICA!" he bellowed into the ear trumpet. "Yes, Yes, Jones, from America," echoed Alexander, smiling. "HE'S A PROFESSOR OF BUSINESS ETHICS!" continued the colleague. "What?" replied Alexander. "BUSINESS ETHICS!" "What? Professor of what?" "PROFESSOR OF BUSINESS ETHICS!" Alexander shook his head and gave up: "Sorry. I can't get it. Sounds just like 'business ethics'!"

Alexander's comprehension machinery was apparently set with too strong a top-down component (though in fact he apparently perceived the stimulus just fine).

An AI speech-understanding system whose development was funded by DARPA (Defense Advanced Research Projects Agency) was being given its debut before the Pentagon brass at Carnegie Mellon University some years ago. To show off the capabilities of the system, it had been attached as the "front end" or "user interface" on a chess-playing program. The general was to play white, and it was explained to him that he should simply tell the computer what move he wanted to make. The general stepped up to the mike and *cleared his throat*—which the computer immediately interpreted as "Pawn to King-4." Again, too much top-down, not enough bottom-up.

In these contexts, the trade-off between top-down and bottom-up is a design parameter of a model that might, in principle, be tuned to fit the circumstances. You might well want the computer to "hear" "Con to Ping-4" as "Pawn to King-4" without even recognizing that it was making an improvement on the input. In these contexts, "top-down" refers to a contribution from "on high"—from the central, topmost information stores—to what is coming "up" from the transducers or sense organs. Enthusiasm for models that have provision for large top-down effects has waxed and waned over the years, from the euphoria of "new look" theories of perception, which emphasized the way perception went "beyond the information given" in Jerry Bruner's oft-quoted phrase, to the dysphoria of Jerry Fodor's (1983) encapsulated modules, which are deemed to be entirely data-driven, utterly "cognitively impenetrable" to downward effects.

David Marr's (1982) theory of vision is a prime example of a model that stresses the power of purely bottom-up processes, which can, Marr stressed, squeeze a lot more out of the data than earlier theorists had supposed. The issue is complicated by the fact that the way in which Marr's model (and subsequent Marr-inspired models) squeeze so much out of the data is in part a matter of fixed or "innate" biases that amount to presuppositions of the machinery—such as the so-called rigidity assumption that permits disambiguation of shape from motion under certain circumstances. Is the rigidity assumption tacitly embodied in the hardware a top-down contribution? If it were an optional hypothesis tendered for the nonce by the individual perceiver, it would be a paradigmatic top-down influence. But since it is a fixed design feature of the machinery, no actual transmission of "descending" effects occurs; the flow of information is all in one inward or upward direction. Leaving the further discussion of these matters for another occasion, we can use the example of Marr to highlight the difference between the two main senses of "top-down." While Marr, as I have just shown, was a champion of the power of bottom-up models of perception (at least in vision), he was also a main spokesperson for the top-down vision of methodology, in his celebrated three-level cascade of the computational, the algorithmic, and the physical level. It is hopeless, Marr argued, to try to build cognitive science models from the bottom-up: by first modeling the action of neurons (or synapses or the molecular chemistry of neurotransmitter production), and then modeling the action of cell assemblies, and then tracts, and then whole systems (the visual cortex, the hippocampal system, the reticular system). You won't be able to see the woods for the trees. First, he insisted, you had to have a clear vision of what the task or function was that the neural machinery was designed to execute. This specification was at what he called, misleadingly, the computational level: It specified "the function" the machinery was supposed to compute and an assay of the inputs available for that computation. With the computational level specification in hand, he claimed, one could then make progress on the next level down, the algorithmic level, by specifying an algorithm (one of the many logically possible algorithms) that actually computed that function. Here the specification is constrained, somewhat, by the molar physical features of the machinery: maximum speed of computation, for instance, would restrict the class of algorithms, and so would macro-architectural features dictating when and under what conditions various subcomponents could interact. Finally, with the algorithmic level more or less under control, one could address the question of actual implementation at the physical level.

Marr's *obiter dicta* on methodology gave compact and influential expression to what were already reigning assumptions in Artificial Intelligence. If AI is considered as primarily an engineering discipline, whose goal is to create intelligent robots or thinking machines, then it is quite obvious that standard engineering principles should guide the research activity: first you try to describe, as generally as possible, the capacities or competences you want to design, and then you try to specify, at an abstract level, how you would implement these capacities, and then, with these design parameters tentatively or defeasibly fixed, you proceed to the nitty-gritty of physical realization.

Certainly a great deal of research in AI—probably the bulk of it— is addressed to issues formulated in this top-down way. The sorts of questions addressed concern, for instance, the computation of three-dimensional structure from two-dimensional frames of input, the extraction of syntactic and semantic structure from symbol strings or acoustic signals, the use of meta-planning in the optimization of plans under various constraints, and so forth. The task to be accomplished is assumed (or carefully developed, and contrasted with alternative tasks or objectives) at the outset, and then constraints and problems in the execution of the task are identified and dealt with.

This methodology is a straightforward application of standard ("forward") engineering to the goal of creating artificial intelligences. This is how one designs and builds a clock, a water pump, or a bicycle, and so it is also how one should design and build a robot. The client or customer, if you like, describes the sought for object, and the client is the boss, who sets in motion a top-down process. This top-down design process is not simply a one-way street, however, with hierarchical delegation of unrevisable orders to subordinate teams of designers. It is understood that as subordinates attempt to solve the design problems they have been given, they are likely to find good reasons for recommending revisions in their own tasks, by uncovering heretofore unrecognized opportunities for savings, novel methods of simplifying or uniting subtasks, and the like. One expects the process to gravitate toward better and better designs, with not even the highest level of specification immune to revision. (The client said he wanted a solar-powered elevator, but has been persuaded, eventually, that a wind-powered escalator better fits his needs.)

Marr's top-down principles are an adaptation, then, of standard AI methodology. Another expression of much the same set of attitudes is my distinction between the intentional stance, the design stance, and the physical stance, and my characterization of the methodology of AI as the gradual elimination of the intentional through a cascade of homunculi. One starts with the ideal specification of an agent (a robot, for instance) in terms of what the agent ought to know or believe, and want, what information-gathering powers it should have, and what capacities for (intentional) action. It then becomes an engineering task to design such an intentional system, typically by breaking it up into organized teams of subagents, smaller, more stupid homunculi, until finally all the homunculi have been discharged—replaced by machines.

A third vision with the same inspiration is Allen Newell's distinction between what he calls the knowledge level and the physical symbol system level. It might seem at first that Newell simply lumps together the algorithmic level and the physical level, the design stance and the physical stance, but in fact he has made the same distinctions, while insisting, wisely, that it is very important for the designer to bear in mind the actual temporal and spatial constraints on architectures when working on the algorithmic level. So far as I can see, there is only a difference in emphasis between Marr, Newell, and me on these matters.[1]

What all three of us have had in common were several things:

1. stress on being able (in principle) to specify the function computed (the knowledge level or intentional level) independently of the other levels;

---

[1]. Newell et al., 1991, make the comparison more explicit, and demonstrate in more detail than I have ever shown, exactly how one descends from the knowledge level to the lower levels of implementation.

2. an optimistic assumption of a specific sort of functionalism: one that presupposes that the concept of the function of a particular cognitive system or subsystem can be specified (it is the function which is to be optimally implemented);

3. A willingness to view psychology or cognitive science as reverse engineering in a rather straightforward way.

Reverse engineering is just what the term implies: the interpretation of an already existing artifact by an analysis of the design considerations that must have governed its creation.

There is a phenomenon analogous to convergent evolution in engineering: entirely independent design teams come up with virtually the same solution to a design problem. This is not surprising, and is even highly predictable: the more constraints there are, the better specified the task is. Ask five different design teams to design a wooden bridge to span a particular gorge and capable of bearing a particular maximum load, and it is to be expected that the independently conceived designs will be very similar: the efficient ways of exploiting the strengths and weaknesses of wood are well known and limited.

But when different engineering teams must design the same sort of thing a more usual tactic is to borrow from each other. When Raytheon wants to make an electronic widget to compete with General Electric's widget, they buy several of GE's widgets, and proceed to analyze them: that's reverse engineering. They run them, benchmark them, x-ray them, take them apart, and subject every part of them to interpretive analysis: Why did GE make these wires so heavy? What are these extra ROM registers for? Is this a double layer of insulation, and if so, why did they bother with it? Notice that the reigning assumption is that all these "why" questions have answers. Everything has a raison d'être; GE did nothing in vain.

Of course if the wisdom of the reverse engineers includes a healthy helping of self-knowledge, they will recognize that this default assumption of optimality is too strong: sometimes engineers put stupid, pointless things in their designs, sometimes they forget to remove things that no longer have a function, sometimes they overlook retrospectively obvious shortcuts. But still, optimality must be the default assumption; if the reverse engineers can't assume that there is a good rationale for the features they observe, they can't even begin their analysis.

What Marr, Newell, and I (along with just about everyone in AI) have long assumed is that this method of reverse engineering was the right way to do cognitive science. Whether you consider AI to be forward engineering (just build me a robot, however you want) or reverse engineering (prove, through building, that you have figured out how the human mechanism works), the same principles apply.

And within limits, the results have been not just satisfactory; they have been virtually definitive of cognitive science. That is, what makes a neuroscientist a cognitive neuroscientist, for instance, is the acceptance, to some degree, of this project of reverse engineering. One benefit of this attitude has been the reversal of a relentlessly stodgy and constructive attitude among some neuroscientists, who advocated abstention from all "speculation" that could not be anchored firmly to what is known about the specific activities in specific neural tracts— with the result that they often had scant idea what they were looking for in the way of functional contribution from their assemblies. (A blatant example would be theories of vision that could, with a certain lack of charity, be described as theories of television—as if the task of the visual system were to produce an inner motion picture somewhere in the brain.)

But as Ramachandran (1985) and others (e.g., Hofstadter—see chap. 13 of this volume) were soon to point out, Marr's top-down vision has its own blind spot: it over-idealizes the design problem, by presupposing first that one could specify the function of vision (or of some other capacity of the brain), and second, that this function was optimally executed by the machinery.

That is not the way Mother Nature designs systems. In the evolutionary processes of natural selection, goal-specifications are not set in advance—problems are not formulated and then proposed, and no selective forces guarantee optimal "solutions" in any case. If in retrospect we can identify a goal that has been optimally or suboptimally achieved by the evolutionary design process, this is something of a misrepresentation of history. This observation, often expressed by Richard Lewontin in his criticism of adaptationism, must be carefully put if it is to be anything but an attack on a straw man. Marr and others (including all but the silliest adaptationists) know perfectly well that the historical design process of evolution doesn't proceed by an exact analogue of the top-down engineering process, and in their interpretations of design they are not committing that simple fallacy of misimputing history. They have presupposed, however—and this is the target of a more interesting and defensible objection—that in spite of the difference in the design processes, reverse engineering is just as applicable a methodology to systems designed by Nature, as to systems designed by engineers. Their presupposition, in other words, has been that even though the *forward* processes have been different, the *products* are of the same sort, so that the *reverse* process of functional analysis should work as well on both sorts of product.

A cautious version of this assumption would be to note that the judicious application of reverse engineering to artifacts already invokes the appreciation of historical accident, suboptimal jury-rigs, and the like, so there is no reason why the same techniques, applied to organisms and their subsystems, shouldn't yield a sound understanding of their design. And literally thousands of examples of successful application of the techniques of reverse engineering to biology could be cited. Some would go so far (I am one of them) as to state that what biology is, is the reverse engineering of natural systems. That is what makes it the special science that it is and distinguishes it from the other physical sciences.

But if this is so, we must still take note of several further problems that make the reverse engineering of *natural* systems substantially more difficult than the reverse engineering of artifacts, unless we supplement it with a signficantly different methodology, which might be called bottom-up reverse engineering—or, as its proponents prefer to call it: *Artificial Life.*

The Artificial Life movement (AL), inaugurated a few years ago with a conference at Los Alamos (Langton, 1989), exhibits the same early enthusiasm (and silly overenthusiasm) that accompanied the birth of AI in the early 1960s, In my opinion, it promises to deliver even more insight than AI. The definitive difference between AI and AL is, I think, the role of bottom-up thinking in the latter. Let me explain.

A typical AL project explores the large-scale and long-range effects of the interaction between many small-scale elements (perhaps all alike, perhaps populations of different types). One *starts* with a specification of the little bits, and tries to move toward a description of the behavior of the larger ensembles. Familiar instances that predate the official Artificial Life title are John Horton Conway's Game of Life and other cellular automata, and, of course, connectionist models of networks, neural and otherwise. It is important to realize that connectionist models are just one family within the larger order of AL models.

One of the virtues of AL modeling strategies is a simple epistemic virtue: it is relatively easy to get interesting or surprising results. The neuroscientist Valentino Braitenberg, in his elegant little book, *Vehicles: Experiments in Synthetic Psychology* (1984), propounded what he called the law of uphill analysis and downhill synthesis, which states, very simply, that it is much easier to deduce the behavioral competence of a system whose internal machinery you have synthesized than to deduce the internal machinery of a black box whose behavioral competence you have observed. But behind this simple epistemological point resides a more fundamental one, first noted, I think, by Langton.

When human engineers design something (forward engineering), they must guard against a notorious problem: unforeseen side effects. When two or more systems, well designed in isolation, are put into a supersystem, this often produces interactions that were not only not part of the intended design, but positively harmful; the activity of one system inadvertently clobbers the activity of the other. By their very nature unforeseeable by those whose gaze is perforce myopically restricted to the subsystem being designed, the only practical way to guard against unforeseen side effects is to design the subsystems to have relatively impenetrable boundaries that coincide with the epistemic boundaries of their creators. In short, you attempt to insulate the subsystems from each other, and insist on an overall design in which each subsystem has a single, well-defined function within the whole. The set of systems having this fundamental abstract architecture is vast and interesting, of course, but—and here is AL's most persuasive theme—it does not include very many of the systems designed by natural selection! The process of evolution is notoriously lacking in all foresight; having no foresight, unforeseen or unforeseeable side effects are nothing to it; it proceeds, unlike human engineers, via the profligate process of creating vast numbers of relatively *un*insulated designs, most of which, of course, are hopelessly flawed because of self-defeating side effects, but a few of which, by dumb luck, are spared that ignominious fate. Moreover, this apparently inefficient design philosophy carries a tremendous bonus that is relatively unavailable to the more efficient, top-down process of human engineers: thanks to its having no bias against unexamined side effects, it can take advantage of the very rare cases where beneficial serendipitous side effects emerge. Sometimes, that is, designs emerge in which systems interact to produce more than was aimed at. In particular (but not exclusively) one gets elements in such systems that have multiple functions.

Elements with multiple functions are not unknown to human engineering, of course, but their relative rarity is signaled by the delight we are apt to feel when we encounter a new one. One of my favorites is to be found in the Diconix portable printer: This optimally tiny printer runs on largish rechargeable batteries, which have to be stored somewhere: inside the platen or roller! On reflection, one can see that such instances of multiple function are epistemically accessible to engineers under various salubrious circumstances, but one can also see that by and large such solutions to design problems must be exceptions against a background of strict isolation of functional elements. In biology, one encounters quite crisp anatomical isolation of functions (the kidney is entirely distinct from the heart, nerves and blood vessels are separate conduits strung through the body), and without this readily discernible isolation, reverse engineering in biology would no doubt be humanly impossible, but one also sees superimposition of functions that apparently goes "all the way down." It is very, very hard to think about entities in which the elements have multiple overlapping roles in superimposed subsystems, and moreover, in which some of the most salient effects observable in the interaction of these elements may not be *functions* at all, but merely by-products of the multiple functions being served.

If we think that biological systems—and cognitive systems in particular—are very likely to be composed of such multiple function, multiple effect elements, we must admit the likelihood that top-down reverse engineering will simply fail to encounter the right designs in its search of design space. Artificial Life, then, promises to improve the epistemic position of researchers by opening up different regions of design space—and these regions include the regions in which successful AI is itself apt to be found!

I will mention one likely instance. A standard feature of models of cognitive systems or thinkers or planners is the separation between a central "workspace" or "working memory" and a long-term memory. Materials are brought to the workspace to be considered, transformed, compared, incorporated into larger elements, etc. This creates what Newell has called the problem of "distal access." How does the central system reach out into the memory and find the right elements at the right time? This is reminiscent of Plato's lovely image of the aviary of knowledge, in which each fact is a bird, and the problem is to get the right bird to come when you call! So powerful is this image that most modelers are unaware of the prospect that there might be alternative images to consider and rule out. But nothing we know in functional neuroanatomy suggests anything like this division into separate workspace and memory. On the contrary, the sort of crude evidence we now have about activity in the cerebral cortex suggests that the very same tissues that are responsible for long-term memory, thanks to relatively permanent adjustments of the connections, are also responsible, thanks to relatively fleeting relationships that are set up, for the transient representations that must be involved in perception and "thought." One possibility, of course, is that the two functions are just neatly superimposed in the same space like the batteries in the platen, but another possibility—at least, an epistemic possibility it would be nice to explore—is that this ubiquitous decomposition of function is itself a major mistake, and that the same *effects* can be achieved by machinery with entirely different joints. This is the sort of issue that can best be explored opportunistically—the same way Mother Nature explores—by bottom-up reverse engineering. To traditional top-down reverse engineering, this question is almost impervious to entry.

There are other issues in cognitive science that appear in a new guise when one considers the differences between top-down and bottom-up approaches to design, but a consideration of them is beyond the scope of this essay.

17   Artificial Life as Philosophy

The first issue of a new journal is an appropriate occasion for manifestos. As a member of the editorial board of Artificial Life, *I was asked to contribute a philosopher's perspective.*

There are two likely paths for philosophers to follow in their encounters with Artificial Life (AL): They can see it as a new way of doing philosophy, or simply as new object worthy of philosophical attention using traditional methods. Is Artificial Life best seen as a new philosophical method or a new phenomenon? There is a case to be made for each alternative, but I urge philosophers to take the leap and consider the first to be the more important and promising.

Philosophers have always trafficked in thought experiments, putatively conclusive arguments about what is possible, necessary, and impossible under various assumptions. The cases that philosophers have been able to make using these methods are notoriously inconclusive. What "stands to reason" or is "obvious" in various complex scenarios is quite often more an artifact of the bias and limitations of the philosopher's imagination than the dictate of genuine logical insight. Artificial Life, like its parent (aunt?) discipline, Artificial Intelligence, can be conceived as a *sort* of philosophy—the creation *and testing* of elaborate thought experiments, kept honest by requirements that could never be imposed on the naked mind of a human thinker acting alone. In short, Artificial Life research is the creation of prosthetically controlled thought experiments of indefinite complexity. This is a great way of confirming or disconfirming many of the intuitions or hunches that otherwise have to pass as data for the sorts of conceptual investigations that define the subject matter of philosophy. Philosophers who see this

Originally appeared in *Artificial Life*, 1, 1994, pp. 291–292.

opportunity will want to leap into the field, at whatever level of abstraction suits their interests, and gird their conceptual loins with the simulational virtuosity of computers.

But perhaps some philosophers won't see the field this way. They will disagree with this assessment of mine, or will worry about some of its presuppositions and implications, and for them, Artificial Life will appear to be just one more controversial object in the world in need of philosophical analysis, criticism, defense, categorization. What are the n defining doctrines of the Artificial Life creed, and what can be said in defense or criticism of them? Already the stirrings of discussion about whether one wants to distinguish "strong AL" from one or another variety of "weak AL" can be heard in the corridors of philosophy. No doubt there is some useful work to be done identifying the popular misconceptions of the field and exposing them, scolding the overambitious partisans on both sides, and clarifying the actual products, as well as the prospects, of work in the field. It would be a shame, however, if this conceptual policeman role were to be the dominant contribution philosophers make to the field.

If we draw the boundaries of AL rather broadly, there are many quite traditional philosophical issues in the philosophy of biology, of science, of mind, and even metaphysics and ethics on which AL explorations have already begun to yield important insights. Even such a relatively simple ancestor as Conway's Life game provides a host of insights into traditional questions about causation, levels of explanation, identity over time, ceteris paribus reasoning, and other topics (see chap. 5 of this volume). Are Hobbesian just-so stories about the possibility of the evolution of cooperation defensible? Certainly Axelrod's pioneering competitions point the way to a rich future of exploration. Under what conditions does (could, would, must, might) communication arise as a feature of interaction between individuals in groups? Can we build a gradualist bridge from simple amoeba-like automata to highly purposive intentional systems, with identifiable goals, beliefs, etc.? These questions of manifest philosophical interest merge seamlessly with the delicious conceptual questions of biology: Why is there sex? Are there fixable scales or measures of complexity or designedness or adaptativeness that we can use to formulate hypotheses about evolutionary trends? Under what conditions does the fate of groups as opposed to individuals play a decisive role in evolution? What *is* an individual? The list goes on and on.

Artificial Life has already provided philosophers with a tidy batch of examples that challenge or illustrate points that have figured prominently in contemporary philosophy. I anticipate that as philosophers acquaint themselves with the field, and actively enter into its explorations, the philosophical progeny of the early work will multiply like fruitflies. After all, the field could hardly be better designed to appeal to a philosopher's habits: You get to *make up* most of the facts! This, as any philosopher knows, is perfectly kosher in a conceptual investigation.

18

When Philosophers Encounter Artificial Intelligence

The American Academy of Arts and Sciences publishes the journal Dædalus, *with each issue designed, like a camel, by a committee. In 1988, an issue was devoted to Artificial Intelligence, and Hilary Putnam and I both served on the planning committee. I had not intended to contribute an essay to the issue, but when Putnam's essay came in, I decided I had to balance it with one of my own. His view of AI was pure contempt: "What's all the fuss about now? Why a whole issue of* Dædalus? *Why don't we wait until AI achieves something and then have an issue?" There are few philosophers of mind from whom I have learned more than Hilary Putnam. Indeed, his classic papers in the field, beginning with "Minds and Machines" in 1961, were a major inspiration for me, as well as a source of guidance. But in one of his characteristic abrupt shifts of outlook, Putnam turned his back on the ideas of functionalism that he had done so much to clarify. He also turned his back on the nonphilosophical literature that began to accumulate, so that his view of Artificial Intelligence in 1988 did not show much sign of current familiarity with the field. I wanted to make that clear, and also to shed some light on how philosophers might think more constructively about both the strengths and weaknesses of AI.*

How is it possible for a physical thing—a person, an animal, a robot— to extract knowledge of the world from perception and then exploit that knowledge in the guidance of successful action? That is a question with which philosophers have grappled for generations, but it could also be taken to be one of the defining questions of Artificial Intelligence. AI is, in large measure, philosophy. It is often directly concerned with instantly recognizable philosophical questions: What is mind? What is meaning? What is reasoning and rationality? What are the nec-

Originally appeared in *Dædalus*, Proceedings of the American Academy of Arts and Sciences, 117 (1), Winter 1988, pp. 283–295. Reprinted with permission.

essary conditions for the recognition of objects in perception? How are decisions made and justified?

Some philosophers have appreciated this aspect of AI, and a few have even cheerfully switched fields, pursuing their philosophical quarries through thickets of LISP.[1] In general, however, philosophers have not welcomed this new style of philosophy with much enthusiasm. One might suppose that this is because they have seen through it. Some philosophers have indeed concluded, after cursory inspection of the field, that in spite of the breathtaking pretension of some of its publicists, Artificial Intelligence has nothing new to offer philosophers beyond the spectacle of ancient, well-drubbed errors replayed in a glitzy new medium. And other philosophers are so sure this must be so that they haven't bothered conducting the cursory inspection. They are sure the field is dismissable on "general principles."

Philosophers have been dreaming about AI for centuries. Hobbes and Leibniz, in very different ways, tried to explore the implications of the idea of breaking down the mind into small, ultimately mechanical, operations. Descartes even anticipated the Turing test (Alan Turing's much-discussed proposal of an audition of sorts for computers, in which the computer's task is to convince the judges that they are conversing with a human being [Turing, 1950]) and did not hesitate to issue a confident prediction of its inevitable result:

It is indeed conceivable that a machine could be made so that it would utter words, and even words appropriate to the presence of physical acts or objects which cause some change in its organs; as, for example, if it was touched in some spot that it would ask what you wanted to say to it; if in another, that it would cry that it was hurt, and so on for similar things. But it could never modify its phrases to reply to the sense of whatever was said in its presence, as even the most stupid men can do. (Descartes, 1637, pp. 41–42)

Descartes's appreciation of the powers of mechanism was colored by his acquaintance with the marvelous clockwork automata of his day. He could see very clearly and distinctly, no doubt, the limitations of that technology. Not even a thousand tiny gears—not even ten thousand—would ever permit an automaton to respond gracefully and rationally! Perhaps Hobbes or Leibniz would have been less confident of this point, but surely none of them would have bothered wondering about the a priori limits on a million tiny gears spinning millions of

---

1. The programming language LISP, created by John McCarthy, is the lingua franca of AI.

times a second. That was simply not a thinkable thought for them. It was unthinkable then, not in the familiar philosophical sense of appearing self-contradictory ("repugnant to reason"), or entirely outside their conceptual scheme (like the concept of a neutrino), but in the more workaday but equally limiting sense of being an idea they would have had no way to take seriously. When philosophers set out to scout large conceptual domains, they are as inhibited in the paths they take by their sense of silliness as by their insights into logical necessity. And there is something about AI that many philosophers find off-putting— if not repugnant to reason, then repugnant to their aesthetic sense.

This clash of vision was memorably displayed in a historic debate at Tufts University in March of 1978, staged, appropriately, by the Society for Philosophy and Psychology. Nominally a panel discussion on the foundations and prospects of Artificial Intelligence, it turned into a tag-team rhetorical wrestling match between four heavyweight ideologues: Noam Chomsky and Jerry Fodor attacking AI, and Roger Schank and Terry Winograd defending. Schank was working at the time on programs for natural language comprehension, and the critics focused on his scheme for representing (in a computer) the higgledy-piggledy collection of trivia we all know and somehow rely on when deciphering ordinary speech acts, allusive and truncated as they are. Chomsky and Fodor heaped scorn on this enterprise, but the grounds of their attack gradually shifted in the course of the match. It began as a straightforward, "first principles" condemnation of conceptual error—Schank was on one fool's errand or another—but it ended with a striking concession from Chomsky: it just might turn out, as Schank thought, that the human capacity to comprehend conversation (and more generally, to think) was to be explained in terms of the interaction of hundreds or thousands of jerry-built gizmos—pseudo-representations, one might call them—but that would be a shame, for then psychology would prove in the end not to be "interesting." There were only two interesting possibilities, in Chomsky's mind: psychology could turn out to be "like physics"—its regularities explainable as the consequences of a few deep, elegant, inexorable laws—or psychology could turn out to be utterly lacking in laws—in which case the only way to study or expound psychology would be the novelist's way (and he much preferred Jane Austen to Roger Schank, if that were the enterprise).

A vigorous debate ensued among the panelists and audience, capped by an observation from Chomsky's Massachusetts Institute of Technology colleague, Marvin Minsky, one of the founding fathers of AI, and founder of MIT's AI Lab: "I think only a humanities professor at MIT could be so oblivious to the third interesting possibility: psychology could turn out to be like engineering."

Minsky had put his finger on it. There is something about the prospect of an engineering approach to the mind that is deeply repugnant to a certain sort of humanist, and it has little or nothing to do with a distaste for materialism or science. Witness Chomsky's physics-worship, an attitude he shares with many philosophers. The days of Berkeleyan idealism and Cartesian dualism are over (to judge from the current materialistic consensus among philosophers and scientists), but in their place there is a widespread acceptance of what we might call Chomsky's fork: there are only two appealing ("interesting") alternatives.

On the one hand, there is the dignity and purity of the Crystalline Mind. Recall Aristotle's prejudice against extending earthly physics to the heavens, which ought, he thought, to be bound by a higher and purer order. This was his one pernicious legacy, but now that the heavens have been stormed, we appreciate the beauty of universal physics, and can hope that the mind will be among its chosen "natural kinds," not a mere gerrymandering of bits and pieces.

On the other hand, there is the dignity of ultimate mystery, the Inexplicable Mind. If our minds can't be Fundamental, then let them be Anomalous. A very influential view among philosophers in recent years has been Donald Davidson's "anomolous monism," the view that while the mind *is* the brain, there are *no* lawlike regularities aligning the mental facts with the physical facts (Davidson, 1970). His Berkeley colleague, John Searle, has made a different sort of mystery of the mind: the brain, thanks to some unspecified feature of its bio-chemistry, has some terribly important—but unspecified—"bottom-up causal powers" that are entirely distinct from the mere "control powers" studied by AI.

One feature shared by these otherwise drastically different forms of mind-body materialism is a resistance to Minsky's tertium quid: in between the Mind as Crystal and the Mind as Chaos lies the Mind as Gadget, an object which one should not expect to be governed by "deep," mathematical laws, but nevertheless a *designed* object, analyzable in functional terms: ends and means, costs and benefits, elegant solutions on the one hand, and on the other, shortcuts, jury-rigs, and cheap ad hoc fixes.

This vision of the mind is resisted by many philosophers despite being a straightforward implication of the current received view among scientists and science-minded humanists of our place in nature: we are biological entities, designed by natural selection, which is a tinker, not an ideal engineer. Computer programmers call an ad hoc fix a "kludge" (it rhymes with Scrooge), and the mixture of disdain and begrudged admiration reserved for kludges parallels the biologists' bemusement with the "panda's thumb" and other fascinating examples of bricolage, to use François Jacob's term (1977). The finest inadvertent spoonerism I ever heard was uttered by the linguist Barbara Partee, in heated criticism of an acknowledged kludge in an AI natural language parser: "That's so *odd hack!*" Nature is full of odd hacks, many of them perversely brilliant. Although this fact is widely appreciated, its implications for the study of the mind are often found repugnant by philosophers, since their traditional aprioristic methods of investigating the mind are relatively powerless to explore phenomena that *may* be contrived of odd hacks. There is really only one way to study such possibilities: with the more empirical mind-set of "reverse engineering."

The resistance is clearly manifested in Hilary Putnam's essay in *Dædalus* (1988), which can serve as a convenient (if not particularly florid) case of the syndrome I wish to discuss. Chomsky's fork, the Mind as Crystal or Chaos, is transformed by Putnam into a pendulum swing he thinks he observes within AI itself. He claims that AI has "wobbled" over the years between looking for the Master Program and accepting the slogan "Artificial Intelligence is one Damned Thing after Another." I have not myself observed any such wobble in the field over the years, but I think I know what he is getting at. Here, then, is a different perspective on the same issue.

Among the many divisions of opinion within AI there is a faction (sometimes called the logicists) whose aspirations suggest to me that they are Putnam's Searchers for the Master Progam. They were more aptly caricatured recently by a researcher in AI as Searchers for "Maxwell's Equations of Thought." Several somewhat incompatible enterprises within the field can be lumped together under this rubric. Roughly, what they have in common is the idea not that there must be a Master Program, but that there must be something more like a master programming language, a single, logically sound system of explicit representation for all the knowledge residing in an agent (natural or artificial). Attached to this library of represented facts (which can be treated as axioms, in effect), and operating upon it computationally, will be one sort or another of "inference engine," capable of deducing the relevant implications of the relevant axioms, and eventually spewing up by this inference process the imperatives or decisions that will forthwith be implemented.

For instance, suppose perception yields the urgent new premise (couched in the master programming language) that the edge of a precipice is fast approaching; this should provoke the inference engine to call up from memory the appropriate stored facts about cliffs, gravity, acceleration, impact, damage, the paramount undesirability of such damage, and the likely effects of putting on the brakes or continuing apace. Forthwith, one hopes, the engine will deduce a theorem to the effect that halting is called for, and straightaway it will halt.

The hard part is designing a system of this sort that will actually work well in real time, even allowing for millions of operations per second in the inference engine. Everyone recognizes this problem of real-time adroitness; what sets the logicists apart is their conviction that the way to solve it is to find a truly perspicuous vocabulary and logical form for the master language. Modern logic has proven to be a powerful means of exploring and representing the stately universe of mathematics; the not unreasonable hope of the logicists is that the same systems of logic can be harnessed to capture the hectic universe of agents making their way in the protean macroscopic world. If you get the axioms and the inference system just right, they believe, the rest should be easy. The problems they encounter have to do with keeping the number of axioms down for the sake of generality (which is a must), while not requiring the system to waste time re-deducing crucial intermediate-level facts every time it sees a cliff.

This idea of the Axiomatization of Everyday Reality is surely a philosophical idea. Spinoza would have loved it, and many contemporary philosophers working in philosophical logic and the semantics of natural language share at least the goal of devising a rigorous logical system in which every statement, every thought, every hunch and wonder, can be unequivocally expressed. The idea wasn't reinvented by AI; it was a gift from the philosophers who created modern mathematical logic: George Boole, Gottlob Frege, Alfred North Whitehead, Bertrand Russell, Alfred Tarski, and Alonzo Church. Douglas Hofstadter calls this theme in AI the Boolean Dream (Hofstadter, 1985, chap. 26, pp. 631–665). It has always had its adherents and critics, with many variations.

Putnam's rendering of this theme as the search for the Master Program is clear enough, but when he describes the opposite pole, he elides our two remaining prospects: the Mind as Gadget and the Mind as Chaos. As he puts it, "If AI is 'One Damned Thing after Another,' the number of 'damned things' the Tinker may have thought of could be astronomical. The upshot is pessimistic indeed: if there is no Master Program, then we may never get very far in terms of simulating human intelligence." Here Putnam elevates a worst-case possibility (the gadget will be totally, "astronomically" ad hoc) as the only likely alternative to the Master Program. Why does he do this? What does he have against exploring the vast space of engineering possibilities in between Crystal and Chaos? Biological wisdom, far from favoring his pessimism, holds out hope that the mix of elegance and Rube Goldberg found elsewhere in Nature (in the biochemistry of reproduction, for instance) will be discernible in mind as well.

There are, in fact, a variety of very different approaches being pursued in AI by those who hope the mind will turn out to be some sort of gadget or collection of partially integrated gadgets. All of these favor austerity, logic, and order in some aspects of their systems, and yet exploit the peculiar utility of profligacy, inconsistency, and disorder in other aspects. It is not that Putnam's two themes don't exist in AI, but that by describing them as exclusive alternatives, he imposes a procrustean taxonomy on the field that makes it hard to discern the interesting issues that actually drive the field.

Most AI projects are explorations of *ways things might be done,* and as such are more like thought experiments than empirical experiments. They differ from philosophical thought experiments not primarily in their content, but in their methodology: they replace some—not all—of the "intuitive," "plausible" hand-waving background assumptions of philosophical thought experiments by constraints dictated by the demand that the model be made to run on the computer. These constraints of time and space, and the exigencies of specification can be traded off against each other in practically limitless ways, so that new "virtual machines" or "virtual architectures" are imposed on the underlying serial architecture of the digital computer. Some choices of trade-off are better motivated, more realistic or plausible than others, of course, but in every case the constraints imposed serve to discipline the imagination —and hence the claims—of the thought-experimenter. There is very little chance that a philosopher will be surprised (and more pointedly, disappointed) by the results of his own thought experiment, but this happens all the time in AI.

A philosopher looking closely at these projects will find abundant grounds for skepticism. Many seem to be based on forlorn hopes, or misbegotten enthusiasm for one architectural or information-handling feature or another, and if we extrapolate from the brief history of the field, we can be sure that most of the skepticism will be vindicated sooner or later. What makes AI an improvement on earlier philosophers' efforts at model sketching, however, is the manner in which skepticism is vindicated: by the demonstrated, concrete failure of the system in question. Like philosophers, researchers in AI greet each new proposal with intuitive judgments about its prospects, backed up by more or less a priori arguments about why a certain feature *has* to be there, or *can't* be made to work. But unlike philosophers, these researchers are not content with their arguments and intuitions; they leave themselves some room to be surprised by the results, a surprise that could only be provoked by the demonstrated, unexpected power of the actually contrived system in action.

Putnam surveys a panoply of problems facing AI: the problems of induction, of discerning relevant similarity, of learning, of modeling background knowledge. These are all widely recognized problems in AI, and the points he makes about them have all been made before by people in AI, who have then gone on to try to address the problems with various relatively concrete proposals. The devilish difficulties he sees facing traditional accounts of the process of induction, for example, are even more trenchantly catalogued by John Holland, Keith Holyoak, Richard Nisbett, and Paul Thagard in their recent book, *Induction* (1986), but their diagnosis of these ills is the preamble for sketches of AI models designed to overcome them. Models addressed to the problems of discerning similarity and mechanisms for learning can be found in abundance. The SOAR project of John Laird, Allen Newell, and Paul Rosenbloom is an estimable example. And the theme of the importance—and difficulty—of modeling background knowledge has been ubiquitous in recent years, with many suggestions for solutions under investigation. Now perhaps they are all hopeless, as Putnam is inclined to believe, but one simply cannot tell without actually building the models and testing them.

That is not strictly true, of course. When an a priori refutation of an idea is sound, the doubting empirical model builder who persists despite the refutation will sooner or later have to face a chorus of "We told you so!" That is one of the poignant occupational hazards of AI. The rub is how to tell the genuine a priori impossibility proofs from the failures of imagination. The philosophers' traditional answer is: more a priori analysis and argument. The AI researchers' answer is: build it and see.

Putnam offers us a striking instance of this difference in his survey of possibilities for tackling the problem of background knowledge. Like Descartes, he manages to imagine a thought-experiment fiction that is now becoming real, and like Descartes, he is prepared to dismiss it in advance. One could, Putnam says,

simply try to program into the machine *all* the information a sophisticated human inductive judge has (including implicit information). At the least this would require generations of researchers to formalize this information (probably it could not be done at all, because of the sheer quantity of information involved); and it is not clear that the result would be more than a gigantic expert system. No one would find this very exciting; and such an "intelligence" would in all likelihood be dreadfully unimaginative . . . (1988, p. 277)

This almost perfectly describes Douglas Lenat's enormous CYC project (Lenat, et al., 1986, pp. 65–85). One might say that Lenat is attempting to create the proverbial walking encyclopedia: a mind-ful of common sense knowledge in the form of a single data base containing *all the facts* expressed—or tacitly presupposed—in an encyclopedia! This will involve handcrafting millions of representations in a single language (which must eventually be unified—no small task), from which the inference engine is expected to be able to deduce whatever it needs as it encounters novelty in its world: for instance, the fact that people in general prefer not to have their feet cut off, or the fact that sunbathers are rare on Cape Cod in February.

Most of the opinion setters in AI share Putnam's jaundiced view of this project: it is not clear, as Putnam says, that it will do anything that teaches us anything about the mind; in all likelihood, as he says, it will be dreadfully unimaginative. And many would go further, and insist that its prospects are so forlorn and its cost so great that it should be abandoned in favor of more promising avenues. (The current estimate is measured in person-*centuries* of work, a figure that Putnam may not have bothered imagining in detail.) But the project is funded, and we shall see.

What we see here is a clash of quite fundamental methodological assumptions. Philosophers are inclined to view AI projects with the patronizing disdain one reserves for those persistent fools who keep trying to square the circle or trisect the angle with compass and straightedge: we have *proved* that it cannot be done, so drop it! But the proofs are not geometric; they are ringed with assumptions about "plausible" boundary conditions and replete with idealizations that may prove as irrelevant here as in the notorious aerodynamicists' proofs that bumblebees cannot fly.

But still one may well inquire, echoing Putnam's challenge, whether AI has taught philosophers anything of importance about the mind *yet*. Putnam thinks it has not, and supports his view with a rhetorically curious indictment: AI has utterly failed, over a quarter century, to solve problems that philosophy has utterly failed to solve over two millennia. He is right, I guess, but I am not impressed.[2] It is as if a philosopher were to conclude a dismissal of contemporary biology by saying that the biologists have not so much as asked the question: What is Life? Indeed they have not; they have asked better questions that ought to dissolve or redirect the philosopher's curiosity.

Moreover, philosophers (of all people) should appreciate that solutions to problems are not the only good gift; tough new problems are just as good! Matching Putnam's rhetorical curiosity, I offer as AI's best contribution to philosophy a deep, new, unsolved epistemological problem ignored by generations of philosophers: the frame problem. Plato almost saw it. In the *Theaetetus*, he briefly explored the implications of a wonderful analogy:

Socrates: Now consider whether knowledge is a thing you can possess in that way without having it about you, like a man who has caught some wild birds—pigeons or what not—and keeps them in an aviary he has made for them at home. In a sense, of course, we might say he "has" them all the time inasmuch as he possesses them, mightn't we?

Theatetus: Yes.

Socrates: But in another sense he "has" none of them, though he has got control of them, now that he has made them captive in an enclosure of his own; he can take and have hold of them whenever he likes by

---

2. In Dennett (1978a, 1979), I have argued that AI has solved what I called "Hume's Problem": the problem of breaking the threatened infinite regress of homunculi consulting (and understanding) internal representations such as Hume's impressions and ideas. I expect Putnam would claim, with some justice, that it was computer science in general, not AI in particular, that showed philosophy the way to break this regress.

catching any bird he chooses, and let them go again; and it is open to him to do that as often as he pleases. (Cornford trans., 1957, 197C–D)

Plato saw that merely possessing knowledge (like birds in an aviary) is not enough; one must be able to command what one possesses. To perform well, one must be able to get the right bit of knowledge to fly to the edge at the right time (in *real time*, as the engineers say). But he underestimated the difficulty of this trick, and hence underestimated the sort of theory one would have to have to give of the organization of knowledge in order to explain our bird-charming talents. Neither Plato nor any subsequent philosopher, so far as I can see, saw this as in itself a deep problem of epistemology, since the demands of *efficiency* and *robustness* paled into invisibility when compared by the philosophical demand for *certainty*, but so it has emerged in the hands of AI.[3]

Just as important to philosophy as new problems and new solutions, however, is new raw material, and this AI has provided in abundance. It has provided a bounty of *objects to think about*—individual systems in all their particularity that are much more vivid and quirky than the systems I (for one) could dream up in a thought experiment. This is not a trivial harvest. Compare philosophy of mind (the analytic study of the limits, opportunities, and implications of possible theories of the mind) with the literary theory of the novel (the analytic study of the limits, opportunities, and implications of possible novels). One could in principle write excellent literary theory in the absence of novels as exemplars. Aristotle, for instance, could in principle have written a treatise on the anticipated strengths and weaknesses, powers and problems, of different possible types of novels. Today's literary theorist is not *required* to examine the existing exemplars, but they are, to say the least, a useful crutch. They extend the imaginative range, and surefootedness, of even the most brilliant theoretician and provide bracing checks on enthusiastic generalizations and conclusions. The minitheories, sketches, and models of AI may not be great novels, but they are the best we have to date, and just as mediocre novels are often a boon to literary theorists—they wear their deficiencies on their sleeves—so bad theories, failed models, hopelessly confused hunches in AI are a boon to philosophers of mind. But you have to read them to get the benefit.

Perhaps the best example of this currently is the wave of enthusiasm for connectionist models. For years philosophers of mind have been

---

3. I present an introduction to the Frame Problem, explaining why it is an epistemological problem, and why philosophers didn't notice it, in chapter 11 of this volume.

vaguely and hopefully waving their hands in the direction of these models—utterly unable to conceive them in detail but sure in their bones that some such thing had to be possible. (My own first book, *Content and Consciousness* [1969] is a good example of such vague theorizing.) Other philosophers have been just as sure that all such approaches were doomed (Jerry Fodor is a good example). Now, at last, we will be able to examine a host of objects in this anticipated class, and find out whose hunches were correct. In principle, no doubt, it could be worked out without the crutches, but in practice, such disagreements between philosophers tend to degenerate into hardened positions defended by increasingly strained arguments, redefinitions of terms, and tendentious morals drawn from other quarters.

Putnam suggests that since AI is first and foremost a subbranch of engineering, it cannot be philosophy. He is especially insistent that we should dismiss its claims of being epistemology. I find this suggestion curious. Surely Hobbes and Leibniz and Descartes were doing philosophy, even epistemology, when they waved their hands and spoke very abstractly about the limits of mechanism. So was Kant, when he claimed to be investigating the conditions under which experience was possible. Philosophers have traditionally tried to figure out the combinatorial powers and inherent limitations of *impressions* and *ideas*, of *petites perceptions, intuitions,* and *schemata.* Researchers in AI have asked similar questions about various sorts of *data structures,* and *procedural representations* and *frames* and *links* and, yes, *schemata,* now rather more rigorously defined. So far as I can see, these are fundamentally the same investigations, but in AI, they are conducted under additional (and generally well-motivated) constraints and with the aid of a host of more specific concepts.

Putnam sees engineering and epistemology as incompatible. I see at most a trade-off: to the extent that a speculative exploration in AI is more abstract, more idealized, less mechanistically constrained, it is "more philosophical"—but that does not mean it is thereby necessarily of more interest or value to a philosopher! On the contrary, it is probably because philosophers have been *too* philosophical—too abstract, idealized, and unconstrained by empirically plausible mechanistic assumptions—that they have failed for so long to make much sense of the mind. AI has not yet solved any of our ancient riddles about the mind, but it has provided us with new ways of disciplining and extending philosophical imagination, which we have only begun to exploit.

19

Review of Allen Newell, *Unified Theories of Cognition*

Allen Newell was another member of the committee that produced the Dæda-*lus issue on Artificial Intelligence, and on the committee he played the role of both Chief Spokesperson and Enforcer of AI, a role he often played in the field itself. I attended his wonderful William James lectures at Harvard, which became the book under review, finished shortly before his untimely death. I think Allen enjoyed being one of my tutors, and he certainly taught me a great deal, but we also had sharp disagreements about the value of various ideas and approaches in both AI and philosophy, and I like to think I changed his mind about a few things. He had planned to write a reply to this review, but he had more important things to do in his last days.*

The time for unification in cognitive science has arrived, but who should lead the charge? The immunologist-turned-neuroscientist Gerald Edelman (1989, 1992) thinks that neuroscientists should lead—or more precisely that he should (he seems to have a low opinion of everyone else in cognitive science). Someone might think that I had made a symmetrically opposite claim in *Consciousness Explained* (Dennett, 1991a): philosophers (or more precisely, those that agree with me!) are in the best position to see how to tie all the loose ends together. But in fact I acknowledged that unifying efforts such as mine are proto-theories, explorations that are too metaphorical and impressionistic to serve as the model for a unified theory. Perhaps Newell had me in mind when he wrote in his introduction (p. 16) that a unified theory "can't be just a pastiche, in which disparate formulations are strung together with some sort of conceptual bailing wire," but in any case the shoe more or less fits, with some pinching. Such a "pastiche" theory can be a good staging ground, however, and a place to stand while

Originally appeared in *Artificial Intelligence*, 59 (1–2), Feb. 1993, pp. 285–294.

considering the strengths and weaknesses of better built theories. So I agree with him.

It is not just philosophers' theories that need to be made honest by modeling at this level; neuroscientists' theories are in the same boat. For instance, Gerald Edelman's (1989) elaborate theory of "re-entrant" circuits in the brain makes many claims about how such re-entrants can accomplish the discriminations, build the memory structures, coordinate the sequential steps of problem solving, and in general execute the activities of a human mind, but in spite of a wealth of neuroanatomical detail, and enthusiastic and often plausible assertions from Edelman, we won't know what his re-entrants can do—we won't know that re-entrants are the *right* way to conceive of the functional neuroanatomy—until they are fashioned into a whole cognitive architecture at the grain-level of ACT* or Soar and put through their paces. (Dennett, 1991a, p. 268)

So I begin with a ringing affirmation of the central claim of Newell's book. Let's hear it for models like Soar. Exploring whole cognitive systems at roughly that grain-level is the main highway to unification. I agree, moreover, with the reasons he offers for his proposal. But in my book I also alluded to two reservations I have with Newell's program without spelling out or defending either of them. This is obviously the time to make good on those promissory notes or recant them. "My own hunch," I said, "is that, for various reasons that need not concern us here, the underlying medium of production systems is *still* too idealized and oversimplified in its constraints" (1991a, p. 267). And a little further along I expressed my discomfort with Newell's support for the traditional division between working memory and long-term memory, and the accompanying notion of *distal access* via symbols, since it encourages a vision of "movable symbols" being transported here and there in the nervous system—an image that slides almost irresistibly into the incoherent image of the Cartesian Theater, the place in the brain where "it all comes together" for consciousness.

Preparing for this review, I reread *Unified Theories of Cognition*, and read several old and recent Newell papers, and I'm no longer confident that my reservations weren't based on misunderstandings. The examples that Newell gives of *apparently* alternative visions that can readily enough be accommodated within Soar make me wonder—semantic and episodic memory within the single, unified LTM; Koler's proceduralism; Johnson-Laird's mental models, for instance—make me wonder. It's not that Soar can be all things to all people (that would make it vacuous) but that it is easy to lose sight of the fact that Soar's level is a *low* or foundational architectural level, upon which quasi-architectural or firmware levels can be established, at which to render the features and distinctions that at first Soar seems to deny. But let's put my reservations on the table and see what we make of them.

On the first charge, that Soar (and production systems in general) are still too idealized and oversimplified, Newell might simply agree, noting that we must begin with oversimplifications and use our experience with them to uncover the complications that matter. Is Soar *the* way to organize cognitive science, or is it "just" a valiant attempt to impose order (via a decomposition) on an incredibly heterogeneous and hard-to-analyze tangle? There's a whole messy world of individualized and unrepeatable mental phenomena out there, and the right question to ask is not: "Does Soar idealize away from these?"—because the answer is obvious: "Yes—so what?" The right question is: "Can the *important* complications be reintroduced gracefully as elaborations of Soar?" And the answer to that question depends on figuring out which complications are really important and why. Experience has taught me that nothing short of considerable mucking about with an actual implementation of Soar, something I still have not done, would really tell me what I should think about it, so I won't issue any verdicts here at all, just questions.

First, to put it crudely, what about pleasure and pain? I'm not just thinking of high-urgency interrupts (which are easy enough to add, presumably), but a more subtle and encompassing focusing role. Newell recognizes the problem of focusing, and even points out—correctly, in my view—that the fact that this can be a problem for Soar is a positive mark of verisimilitude. "Thus the issue for the standard computer is how to be interrupted, whereas the issue for Soar and Act* (and presumably for human cognition) is how to keep focused" (Newell, Rosenbloom, and Laird, 1989). But the Soar we are shown in the book is presented as hyperfunctional.

Soar's mechanisms are dictated by the functions required of a general cognitive agent. We have not posited detailed technological limitations to Soar mechanisms. There is nothing inappropriate or wrong with such constraints. They may well exist, and if they do, they must show up in any valid theory. (p. 354)

Doesn't this extreme functionalism lead to a seriously distorted foundational architecture? Newell provides an alphabetized list (see his figure 8.1, 1990, p. 434) of some mental phenomena Soar has not yet tackled, and among these are daydreaming, emotion and affect, imagery, and play. Soar is all business. Soar is either working or sound asleep, always learning-by-chunking, always solving problems, never idling. There are no profligate expenditures on dubious digressions, no along-for-the-ride productions cluttering up the problem spaces, and Soar is never too tired and cranky to take on yet another impasse. Or so it seems. Perhaps if we put just the right new menagerie of operators on stage, or the right items of supplementary knowledge in memory, a sprinkling of suboptimal goals, etc., a lazy, mathophobic, lust-obsessed Soar could stand forth for all to see. That is what I mean about how easy it is to misplace the level of Soar; perhaps all this brisk, efficient problem-solving should be viewed as the biological (rather than psychological) activities of elements too small to be visible to the naked eye of the folk-psychological observer.

But if so, then there is a large element of misdirection in Newell's advertising about his functionalism. "How very functional your teeth are, Grandma!" said Red Riding Hood. "The better to model dysfunctionality when the time comes, my dear!" replied the wolf. Moreover, even when Soar deals with "intendedly rational behavior" of the sort we engage in when we are good experimental subjects—comfortable, well paid, and highly motivated—I am skeptical about the realism of the model. Newell acknowledges that it leaves out the "feelings and considerations" that "float around the periphery" (p. 369), but isn't there also lots of *non*peripheral waste motion in human cognition? (There certainly seems to me to be a lot of it when I think hard—but maybe Newell's own mental life is as brisk and no-nonsense as his book!)

Besides, the hyperfunctionality is *biologically* implausible (as I argue in my book). Newell grants that Soar *did* not arise through evolution (see his figure 8.1), but I am suggesting that perhaps it *could* not. The Spock-like rationality of Soar is a very fundamental feature of the architecture; there is no room *at the architectural level* for some thoughts to be harder to think *because they hurt*, to put it crudely. But isn't that a fact just as secure as any discovered in the psychological laboratory? Shouldn't it be a primary constraint? Ever since Hume got associationism underway with his quasi-mechanical metaphors of combination and attraction between ideas (1739, Book I), we have had the task of describing the dynamics of thought: what makes the next thought follow on the heels of the current thought? Newell has provided us, in Soar, with a wonderfully deep and articulated answer—the best ever—but it is an answer that leaves out what I would have thought was a massive factor in the dynamics of thought: pain and pleasure. Solving some problems is a joy; solving others is a bore and a headache, and there are still others that you would go mad trying to solve, so painful would it be to contemplate the problem space. Now it *may just be* that these facts are emergent properties at a higher level, to be discerned in special instances of Soar chugging along imperturbably, but that seems rather unlikely to me. Alternatively, it may be that the *Sturm und Drang* of affect can be piped in as a later low-level embellishment without substantially modifying the basic architecture, but that seems just as unlikely.

David Joslin has pointed out to me that the business-like efficiency we see in the book is largely due to the fact that the various implementations of Soar that we are shown are all special-purpose, truncated versions, with tailor-made sets of operators and productions. In a fully general-purpose Soar, with a vastly enlarged set of productions, we would probably see more hapless wandering than we would want, and have to cast about for ways to focus Soar's energies. And it is here, plausibly, that an affective dimension might be just what is needed, and it has been suggested by various people (Sloman and Croucher, 1981; de Sousa, 1987) that it cannot be packaged within the contents of further knowledge, but must make a contribution orthogonal to the contribution of knowledge.

That was what I had in mind in my first reservation, and as one can see, I'm not sure how sharply it cuts. As I said in my book, we've come a long way from the original von Neumann architecture, and the path taken so far can be extrapolated to still brainier and more biological architectures. The way to find out how much idealization we can afford is not to engage in philosophical debates.

My second reservation, about symbols and distal access, opens some different cans of worms. First, there is a communication problem I want to warn other philosophers about, because it has bedeviled me up to the time of revising the draft of this review. I think I now understand Newell's line on symbols and semantics, and will try to explain it. (If I still don't get it, no harm done—other readers will set me straight.) When he introduces symbols he seems almost to go out of his way to commit what we philosophers call use-mention errors. He gives examples of symbol tokens in figure 2.9 (p. 73). He begins with words in sentences (and that's fine), but goes on to *numbers* in equations. We philosophers would say that the symbols were *numerals*—names for numbers. Numbers aren't symbols. He goes on: atoms in formulas. No. Atom-symbols in formulas; formulas are composed of symbols, not atoms; molecules are composed of atoms. Then he lists objects in pictures. No. Object-depictions in pictures. I am sure Newell knows exactly what philosophers mean by a use-mention error, so what is his message supposed to be? Is he saying: "For the purposes of AI it doesn't matter"? Or "We AI-types never get confused about such an obvious distinction, so we can go on speaking loosely"? If that is what he is saying, I don't believe it. There is a sort of willful *semantic descent* (the opposite of Quine's semantic ascent, in which we decide to talk about talk about things) that flavors many AI discussions. It arises, I think, largely because in computer science the expressions up for semantic evaluation do in fact refer very often to things inside the computer—to subroutines that can be called, to memory addresses, to data structures, etc. Moreover, because of the centrality of the domain of arithmetic in computers, the topic of "discussion" is often numbers, and arithmetical expressions for them. So it is easy to lose sight of the fact that when you ask the computer to "evaluate" an expression, and it outputs "3," it isn't *giving* you a number; it's *telling* you a number. But that's all right, since all we ever want from numbers is to have them identified—you can't eat 'em or ride 'em. (Compare "Gimme all your money!" "OK. $42.60, including the change in my pocket.") Can it be that this confusion of numbers with symbols is also abetted by a misappreciation of the fact that, for instance, the binary ASCII code for the *numeral* "9" is not the binary expression of the number 9?

Whatever its causes—or even its justifications—this way of speaking creates the impression that, for people in AI, semantics is something entirely internal to the system. This impression is presumably what led Jerry Fodor into such paroxysms in "Tom Swift and his Procedural Grandmother" (1978). It is too bad he didn't know how to put his misgivings constructively. I tried once:

We get the idea [from Newell, 1986] that a symbol designates if it gives access to a certain object or if it can affect a certain object. And this almost looks all right as long as what we're talking about is internal states. . . . But of course the real problem is that that isn't what reference is all about. If that were what reference was all about, then what would we say about what you might call my Julie Christie problem? I have a very good physically instantiated symbol for Julie Christie. I know it refers to her, I know it really designates her, but it doesn't seem to have either of the conditions that Professor Newell describes, alas. (Dennett, 1986a, p. 53; see also Smith, 1986)

Newell's answer:

The criticisms seemed to me to be a little odd because to say that one has access to something does not mean that one has access to *all* of that thing; having some information about Julie Christie certainly doesn't give one complete access to Julie Christie. That is what polite society is all about. . . . The first stage is that

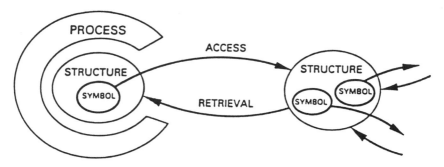

Figure 19.1
Symbols provide distal access. (From *Unified Theories of Cognition* by Allen Newell. © 1990 by the President and Fellows of Harvard College. Reprinted by permission of Harvard University Press.)

there are symbols *which lead to internal structures.* I don't think this is obscure, and it is important in understanding where the aboutness comes from. . . . [T]he data structures *contain knowledge about things in the outside world.* So you then build up further symbols which access things that you can think of as knowledge about something—knowledge about Julie Christie for instance. If you want to ask why a certain symbol says something about Julie Christie, you have to ask why the symbolic expression that contains the symbol says something about Julie Christie. And the answer may be . . . because of processes that put it together which themselves have knowledge about Julie Christie. . . . Ultimately it may turn out to depend upon history, it may depend on some point in the history of the system when it came in contact with something in the world which provided it with that knowledge. (1986, p. 171, emphasis mine)

What we have here, I finally realize, is simply a two-stage (or *n*-stage) functional role semantics: *in the end* the semantics of symbols is anchored to the world via the knowledge that can be attributed to the whole system *at the knowledge level* in virtue of its capacity, exercised or not, for perspicuous behavior vis-à-vis the items in the world its knowledge is about. And that's my view, too. What makes a data structure about Julie Christie is that it's the part of the system the presence of which explains my capacity to pick her out of a crowd, answer questions about her in quiz shows, etc., etc. That's all there is to it. But it is certainly misleading to say that the symbol gives one *any* "access" (partial access, in polite society!) to the object itself. (It turns out that Julie Christie and I have a mutual friend, who sent her an offprint of Dennett 1986a. And what do you know, she . . . sent me a Christmas card. "Getting closer," I thought. "Maybe Newell's right after all! You just have to be patient. Porsche, Porsche, Porsche.")

Newell's diagram in his figure 2.10 (p. 75) makes it all clear (in retrospect) as long as you realize that it is not just that he concentrates (in his book and in his earlier writing) on the semantic link-arrows in the middle of the diagram—the access links tying symbols to their distal knowledge-stores—but that he simply *assumes* there is a solution to any problems that might arise about the interpretation of the arrows on the right hand side of the diagram: Those arrows, as I understand him now, lead one *either* to more data structures or eventually to something in the external world—but he is close to silent about this final, anchoring step. This is fine by me, but then I'm one of the few philosophers who thinks Twin Earth and narrow content are artifactual philosophical conundrums of no importance to cognitive science (Dennett, 1982a; 1987). Make no mistake, though: serious or not, Newell sweeps them under the rug right here.[1]

What concerns him is rather the interesting question of Plato's aviary: How does an intelligent agent with more knowledge than it can "contemplate" all at once get the right birds to come when it calls? (Dennett, 1991a, pp. 222–225) And how do you do this without relying on a dubious *transportation* metaphor, which would require shipping symbol-tokens here and there in the system? I'm not sure I understand his answer entirely, but the crucial elements are given on page 355:

Functionally, working memory must be a short-term memory. It is used to hold the coded knowledge that is to be processed for the current task. It is necessary to replace that knowledge when the task changes. That replacement can be achieved in many ways, by moving the data [bad idea!—DCD], by moving the processes [better!—DCD], or by changing the access path [best!—DCD]. . . . Working memory for cognition has no continued functional existence outside these limits, however, since elements that are no longer linked to the goal stack become unavailable. Furthermore, problem spaces themselves have no existence independent of the impasses they are created to resolve.

---

1. In a more recent paper, he goes a bit further in defense of this interpretation: "The agent's knowledge is embodied in the knowledge of the four problem space components. However, this latter knowledge is about the problem space, states, and operators; hence it cannot of itself be the knowledge of the agent, which is about the goal, actions, and environment. It becomes the agent's knowledge by means of the relationships just described. That is, states are about the external world because of KL [knowledge level] perception; operators are about the external world because of KL actions; the desired states are about the goal of the KL agent because of formulate-task; and the means-ends knowledge of select-operator is about performing tasks in the environment because it links environment-referring operators on environment-referring states to descriptions of environment-referring desired states." (Newell et al., 1992, p. 23)

I find these ideas some of the most difficult to understand in cognitive science, for they require setting aside, for once, what we might call the concrete crutch: the lazy picture of places (with boxes around them) and things moving to and fro. *That* vision, for all its utility at the symbol level, is a dangerous companion when we turn to the question of mapping computational processes onto brain processes. When Newell says "Search leads to the view that an intelligent agent is always operating within a *problem space*" (p. 98) we should recognize that this is really being presented as an a priori constraint on how we shall interpret intelligent agents. Show me an intelligent agent, and whatever it does, I'll show you a way of interpreting it as setting up a problem space. Since the key term "distal" is defined relative to *that* space—that logical space—we should be cautious of interpreting it too concretely (cf. Fodor and Pylyshyn, 1988).

So my second reservation is blunted as well. Two strikes, or maybe foul balls. There is one more issue I want to take a swing at as long as I'm up at bat. Newell's silence on the issue of natural language as a symbolic medium of cognition in human beings is uncanny. We know that Soar can (in principle) learn from taking *advice* (e.g., p. 312), and Newell sketches out the way Soar would or might handle language acquisition and comprehension (pp. 440–449; see especially his discussion of redundant encoding, p. 453), but I cannot figure out from these brief passages what Newell thinks happens to the overall shape of the competence of a cognitive system when it acquires a natural language, and I think his reticence on this score hides major issues. Early on he gives an eloquent survey of what he calls the "efflorescence of adaptation" by the human (and only the human) species (pp. 114–115), but does this paean to productive versatility proclaim that the symbols *of an internalized natural language* are necessary, or is it rather that one needs a prelinguistic language of thought—in which case we may wonder why the human language of thought gives us such an edge over the other species, if it does not get most of its power from the external language we learn to speak. For instance, Newell's discussion of annotated models (pp. 393ff) is a fine perspective on the mental models debates, but I am left wondering: can a nonhuman intelligent agent—a dog or dolphin or ape, for instance—avail itself of an annotated model, or is that level of cognitive sophistication reserved for language-users? This is just one instance of a sort of empirical question that is left curiously burked by Newell's reticence.

This gap is all the more frustrating since in other regards I find Newell's treatment in chapters 1 and 2 of the standard debating topics in the philosophy of cognitive science a refreshing challenge. These chapters are simply required reading henceforth for any philosophers of cognitive science.[2] Newell doesn't waste time surveying the wreckage; he gets down to business. He says, in effect: "Sit down and listen; I'll show you how to think about these topics." He simply *makes moves* in all the games we play, and largely leaves it to us to object or play along. This should be a model for all nonphilosopher scientists who aspire (correctly!) to philosophical probity. Don't try to play the philosophers' games. Just make your moves, clearly and explicitly, and see if you can get away with them.

I very largely agree with his moves, and it will be a pity if philosophers who disagree with him don't rise to the bait. They may not, alas. At times Newell underestimates how ingrown his jargon is. I have pushed portions of his text on some very smart philosophers and neuroscientists, and they are often completely at sea. (These issues are awfully hard to communicate about, and I am well aware that the alternative expository tactics I have tried in my own writing run their own risks of massive misconstrual.)

It might seem odd, finally, for me not to comment at all on Newell's deliberate postponement of consideration of consciousness, which gets just a brief apology on page 434. Is this not unconscionable? Not at all. Newell's project is highly compatible with mine in *Consciousness Explained.* For instance, I endorse without reservation his list of multiple constraints on mind (in his figure 1.7, p. 19). How can he achieve this divorce of consciousness? Just look! The enabling insight, for Newell and for me, is that handsome is as handsome does; you don't need any *extra witnesses* in order to explain cognition. Newell modestly denies that he has yet touched on consciousness; I disagree. He's made a big dent.

---

2. Philosophers will find important material throughout the book, not just in the foundational chapters at the beginning. For instance, the discussion of the discovery of the data-chunking problem in Soar and its handling (pp. 326–345) can be interpreted as a sort of inverse version of Meno's paradox of inquiry. The problem is not how can I search for something if I don't already know what it is, but how can I set myself up so that when I confront a real Meno-problem, there will be a way I can solve it? (Alternatively, if Soar couldn't solve the data-chunking problem, Meno's claim would not be paradoxical when applied to Soar, but simply true.) I think the memory-management search control strategies that are adopted can be read as part of an explicit answer—much more explicit than any philosopher's answer—to Meno's challenge.

III

Ethology, Animal Mind

20

Out of the Armchair and into the Field

The Dahlem Conference on Animal Mind/Human Mind held in Berlin in 1981 (Griffin, 1982) was a turning point for me. I had speculated about animals as higher-order intentional systems in "Conditions of Personhood" (1976), and began talking with David Premack about the theoretical importance of deceptive behavior and false beliefs at a conference around that time. My (1978d) commentary on Premack and Woodruff's important paper about a chimpanzee's "theory of mind" in Behavioral and Brain Sciences *brought my ideas to the attention of psychologists and ethologists, and this led to my being invited to the Dahlem conference, where I had my first intensive introduction to thinking about animal cognition, and met many of the key participants in cognitive ethology. This led to my own target article in* Behavioral and Brain Sciences, *"Intentional Systems in Cognitive Ethology: The 'Panglossian Paradigm' Defended" (1983), which set in motion two long-running themes in my work: cooperation on the one hand — theoretical discussions about, and occasional participation in, actual fieldwork in cognitive ethology, with Robert Seyfarth and Dorothy Cheney, Carolyn Ristau, and others — and confrontation on the other hand, with Stephen Jay Gould and Richard Lewontin about the scope and power of adaptationism in evolutionary theory. On the cooperation front, my introduction to ethological field work with Seyfarth and Cheney had a large salutary effect in widening and deepening my powers of imagination when it came to thinking about animal minds. I originally wrote this piece for* Psychology Today, *a commission that financed my trip to Kenya, but while I was in Africa, the magazine changed hands and the new editors unceremoniously canceled all unfinished projects — but not the commissions, thank goodness. My essay, minus all the photographs I had taken, soon found a home in* Poetics Today *(of all places), in a special issue on Interpretation.*

Originally appeared in *Poetics Today*, 9, 1988, pp. 205–221.

As a philosopher of mind, I have often imagined myself in exotic surroundings, engaged in one fantastic thought experiment or another—stranded on Mars or living as a brain in a vat or attempting to decipher the alien tongue of apparently intelligent creatures—but in June 1983 I had an opportunity to set aside thought experiments in favor of real experiments designed to explore the minds—and "language"—of some real alien creatures: vervet monkeys, living not in lab cages or enclosures but fending for themselves against a daunting array of predators in the beautiful, dangerous world of the East African savannah.

What makes vervet monkeys particularly interesting to a philosopher—or to anyone interested in the origins of human language and consciousness—is that they have the *rudiments* of a language, which serves them well in circumstances that must be quite similar to the world our ancestors faced at the dawn of human language and culture. Vervets have a variety of different vocalizations—calls and grunts—which seem to have clearly definable meanings. The most obvious (to an alien observer) are the alarm calls: one for snakes, another for eagles, a third for leopards, and each call evokes its own distinct and appropriate sort of behavior—for instance, scanning the sky and heading for cover in response to the eagle alarm. These might have been nothing more than instinctual cries, of course, no more like real, versatile human language than the famous dance of the honeybee, or the alarm calls of birds, but there is some tantalizing evidence suggesting that something more is going on with these monkeys. Unlike the birds and the bees, vervets *seem* to be engaged in a practice that could involve learning, insincerity, trustworthiness, deception, divided loyalty. While it would be wildly romantic to suppose that a vervet could *tell a joke,* it is not so clear that there isn't room in their way of life for one to *tell a lie.*

For instance, two bands or groups of vervets were once observed in a territorial skirmish; one group was losing ground and one of the losing-side monkeys, temporarily out of the fray, seemed to get a bright idea: it suddenly issued a leopard-alarm (in the absence of any leopards), leading all the vervets to head for the trees—creating a truce and regaining the ground his side has been losing. Does this anecdote reveal real cleverness and versatility among the speakers of Vervetese or was it just a coincidence or a bit of dumb luck for the losing-side monkeys—or a case of overeager interpretation on the part of the observers? Could further observation—or better experiments—shed light on these questions? This is what I had come to Kenya to investigate.

Several years ago, at the Dahlem Conference on animal intelligence in Berlin, I had been delighted to discover that some of my "purely philosophical" ideas about how to interpret creatures as having minds—having beliefs and desires and intentions—had struck a chord in some of the animal behavior experts. It might just be, they thought, that my philosophical theory provided a theoretical framework in which to describe their investigations and perhaps some of my philosophical suggestions could be harnessed to good effect in field research. Among those I met at the conference was Robert Seyfarth, who, with his wife Dorothy Cheney, has spent years studying the social organization and communication system of bands of vervets living in Amboseli National Park, in Kenya. In the aftermath of the conference, I continued discussing these prospects with Seyfarth and others in the field and even wrote a scholarly article on the subject (1983a). But reading, writing, and discussing were still just armchair work. I would never be able to tell whether my suggestions were capable of doing real work until I had had some field experience and seen firsthand the sort of difficulties that researchers face. Philosophical thought experiments, unlike real ones, have the happy property of never running into snags—the weather is always perfect, there is always film in your camera and no distracting circumstances intrude on the scenario. Proposals that make sense in such idealized situations are often hopeless in the real world.

So I was delighted when Seyfarth invited me to visit their research camp and spend some time actually observing and experimenting on the monkeys. Before my visit, I had devoted considerable armchair time to pondering the presuppositions and implications of everything I had learned about vervet monkeys but, as one would expect, reality outstripped all my anticipatory imaginings.

Vervets are monkeys, not apes, so they are millions of years less closely related to us than chimps, for instance. You can actually see—and feel—the difference quite directly; their faces and facial expressions are nowhere near as human and evocative as the mugging of chimps and gorillas and, in many other ways, they are strangely—often disappointingly—alien. For instance, while they exhibit terror and sometimes prolonged grief when one of the group is killed, a monkey won't bring food to a starving or injured member of the group, even though they cooperate in other ways and spend a great deal of time in mutual grooming. But in one important regard they seem to be more like our ancestors than are the larger apes and monkeys: their lives are more harrowing, more fraught with danger. While baboons, for instance, are nonchalant, swaggering bullies, able to defend them-selves, the much smaller vervets are fearful, defenseless and hence su-percautious. (Occasionally a wild vervet will die under circumstances that permit an autopsy; most are found to suffer from gastric ulcers.) Perhaps the reason vervets have such a surprisingly advanced "lan-guage" is that they are more desperately in need of communicating with each other than many other species.

How does one go about learning the language of these monkeys? This is a case of what the philosopher W. V. O. Quine calls "radical translation"—since there are no bilingual interpreters to help the in-vestigator compile the Vervetese-English manual. Here is where phi-losophy might come in handy, for this is not just a question of another language; it is the traditional philosophical problem of Other Minds.

My proposal, in simplest terms, was this. First, observe their behav-ior for a while and make a tentative catalogue of their needs—their immediate biological needs as well as their derivative, *informational* needs—what they *need to know* about the world they live in. Then adopt what I call the *intentional stance:* treat the monkeys as if they were—as they may well turn out to be—rational agents with the "right" be-liefs and desires. Frame hypotheses about what they believe and desire by figuring out what they *ought* to believe and desire, given their cir-cumstances, and then test these hypotheses by assuming that they are rational enough to do what they ought to do, given those beliefs and desires. The method yields predictions of behavior under various con-ditions; if the predictions are falsified, something has to give in the set of tentative hypotheses and further tests will sift out what should give.

There is nothing particularly novel or "scientific" about the method: it is, I claim, the method we all habitually use to interpret each other, after all. But if it is done self-consciously and carefully, it can become a powerful and reliable strategy of discovery. In particular, the tactic of *assuming* some particular beliefs and desires in the monkeys and then asking what ought to follow from those assumptions can lead to the design of particularly telling experiments—setting up situations where the monkeys will "betray" their beliefs by doing otherwise un-likely things. I call this the "Sherlock Holmes method"—since it is the attempt to play the sort of tricks in the real world that catch the culprits in thousands of mystery stories. (Only someone who *believed there was a corpse in the closet* would go to such lengths to prevent Sherlock from opening the closet door—that sort of trick.) But would the sort of stunt that works so deliciously in fiction—and philosophers' thought experi-ments—be at all practical in the field?

After breakfast the first day, we drove the 10 kilometers from the camp to the vervets' home ranges. Robert and Dorothy always drive as close as possible to the place they expect the monkeys to be and Dorothy explained that this is not just to save walking in the hot sun. We must be careful never to get more than about a hundred yards from the jeep and must keep an eye on the intervening ground for interlopers. We were unarmed—no firearms are permitted in Amboseli—and if a lion or elephant or buffalo should suddenly appear, we would retreat as swiftly and noiselessly as possible to the safety of the enclosed vehicle. Since keeping an eye out for lions and elephants is not part of my normal routine, I found all this very romantic and not a little frightening but for Robert and Dorothy, such precautions are as routine as the precautions I take when crossing a busy street.

Seyfarth and Cheney study three adjacent groups of vervets intensively and several other neighboring groups quite comprehensively. The first task of the day is simply to find the group of monkeys in whose territory we have decided to begin. While the home ranges of groups are small—less than a kilometer across in any direction—finding the monkeys (more than a dozen in a group, usually)—can be a time-consuming process. The task was made slightly more difficult by my presence. I was a novel and hence suspect creature; the monkeys could be expected to take some time to "habituate" to me. Robert and Dorothy, after more than six years of observing these monkeys at close range, are utterly familiar—and uninteresting—to the monkeys and can stand within a few feet of them, apparently without disturbing their behavior at all. Since I was accompanied by these familiar beings, the monkeys habituated to me after only fifteen or twenty minutes and I too could then walk in their midst so long as I didn't make prolonged eye contact.

At first it bothered me that the three of us could stand around in the open, talking quietly, taking photos and moving equipment around, without provoking any apparent reaction in the monkeys. Were they so stupid, so oblivious, so incurious that these noisy, looming bipeds-with-clothes made no difference to them? "But remember," Robert reminded me, "that you *would* provoke their curiosity and fear if you came here by yourself. It is only because they are habituated to us that you can come in under our protective mantle."

"How can you get the animals to habituate to you in the first instance?"

"It takes weeks of patient waiting," Robert replied. "Bring along a few good books and just sit down as close to them as you can get. Gradually they lose their fear of you and you can move closer."

The rule to follow is best expressed from the intentional stance: never act in such a way as to *give a vervet reason* to pay attention to you in the future. That is the general rule, of which these are a few instances: never provide food or show the monkeys that you have food (we were careful to eat our box lunches some distance away from the monkeys); never warn the monkeys of danger or help them out of a difficulty; never interact with them by responding to threats. Make sure, in other words, that *paying attention* to you is an investment that never pays the monkeys a dividend; then you can count on the rational, self-interested vervets to ignore that unattractive investment opportunity. If you follow the general rule scrupulously, you soon disappear, for the vervets, into the background—which after all contains a lot of other large, moving, things that are irrelevant to vervet concerns: wildebeests and warthogs—and elephants. The ideal is to be as boring to a vervet as any wildebeest; that puts you almost in the observer's dream position: the proverbial fly on the wall, who sees and hears all but is perfectly unobtrusive.

Whatever further doubts I had about the extent of the vervets' habituation to me were erased as we rode home in the jeep that evening and I suddenly realized that we had just continued an animated conversation without the tiniest hitch or reaction while half a dozen zebras had galloped across the road in front of us. After only three or four days of driving through Kenya's fabulous game parks, I had become so habituated to zebras—zebras!—that I paid no more attention to their crossing in front of us than I would to a pedestrian in Boston. A few days later in camp, the point was brought home to me again when an elephant briefly interrupted our breakfast conversation by emerging from the thicket and grazing on the tall grass next to the clothesline. After taking note of the elephant, we went on with our conversation, while the elephant continued to graze, more or less ignored, for about a half an hour. Advice to eavesdroppers: if you want to listen in unobtrusively on Seyfarth and Cheney in the dining tent, why not try dressing up as an elephant and standing in broad daylight about thirty feet in front of them.

Once we had found the monkeys, the daily census began. Each monkey has been given a name and each of more than seventy monkeys in the studied groups is readily identifiable by Robert and Dorothy. There is a system: each season's new babies get names with a common theme. There are the London underground stations: Picadilly, Charing Cross, and Holborn; the prisons: Sing Sing, Wormwood Scrubs, Attica;

the dictators: Amin, Marcos, Pinochet, Somoza, and Duvalier; and the cooks: Escoffier, Claiborne, Brillat-Savarin, and "Julian" Child. The infants are named before their gender can be determined; Julia turned out to be Julian but you just have to get used to the fact that Amin, Newton (from the cosmologist cohort), Burgess, McLean, and Philby are all females.

I was frankly skeptical, at first, witnessing Robert and Dorothy glancing at distant monkeys scampering though trees or facing away or in silhouette and tallying up: "There's Runnymede, and Tycho. Have you seen Jenkin's Ear?" "Yes, she's in the top of the tortilis tree." (I could barely make her out to be a monkey with my binoculars.) But I gradually had to grant that they were not playing a trick on me; they really could identify these monkeys, with complete reliability. To me, the monkeys looked as indistinguishable as any identical twins—but that of course is the point. After a while it is uncannily easy to tell identical twins apart—often without being able to say just how you do it.

It is not enough to just keep track of the monkeys as individuals. You have to know how they are related, what their rank in the group is and their recent history of alliances and confrontations. When I asked Robert if there was any background reading that would particularly prepare me for participating in the experience, he had suggested—only partly in jest—that I refresh my acquaintance with the novels of Jane Austen. In fact, my first day or so of monkey-watching with Robert and Dorothy was full of the sort of confusion I often suffer when reading the opening chapters of a complicated novel of manners. "Look," Dorothy would say, "that's Wormwood trying to supplant Tycho, who's grooming Amin; but here comes Holborn, who will no doubt side with Tycho—they're sisters, after all—but Picadilly outranks them both, and . . . " —I would flip back through my notes, utterly confused, muttering "Isn't Picadilly Wormwood's aunt? I thought Wormwood and Sing Sing were sisters. No, wait, Marcos is Wormwood's mother and she's from a low-ranking family . . . " I wanted to go back to chapter one and get a reminder of who all the characters were.

Without a good fix on all these relationships, the significance of much of the communication and interaction is completely inscrutable. (Imagine trying to make sense of knowing glances and frowns—to say nothing of the words—in a foreign film without having any idea of how the characters were related to each other.) In one experiment, for instance, Robert played tape recordings of the screams of juveniles where their mothers (and other adults) could hear them. Not only did the mother—and only the mother—drop everything to go to the aid of her child but as soon as the other mothers heard the cries, they looked at the mother of the juvenile. They not only know which cry belongs to which juvenile, they know which offspring belong to which mother. (It seems unlikely that they have much knowledge, if any, of paternity but experiments soon to be conducted may shed light on this.) Those telltale glances betray their knowledge just as surely as the guilty glances in many a mystery story, but interpreting those glances requires a mountain of reliable background information.

Only after witnessing the births in a group over several seasons can one reliably sort a group into its families, siblings, cousins, and more distant relatives. It takes years to gather this information—something a philosopher is apt to forget when concentrating on what the "observable evidence" is; you can't observe *directly* that Nut is the granddaughter of Marcos but it's an empirical fact with plenty of implications in experiments. That is why it is so important to take a census of the monkeys in the watched groups every day. Only thus can accurate records of deaths, births, and shifting social relationships be maintained. Every now and then, for one reason or another, a daily census must be missed but it is the first order of business on a normal day and it can be frustrating, especially if a group of monkeys has moved deep into the swamp where they cannot be followed.

After the census of a group, which includes taking notes on any noteworthy behavior, changes of appearance, and the like, Robert and Dorothy can think about trying to run an experiment or two. Most of their voluminous data on a wide variety of ecological factors have been gathered by patient observations, not experiment, and this information is an invaluable asset when it comes to designing and interpreting experiments. Robert and Dorothy can already confidently answer many of the questions that come up. When a male matures and leaves his natal group for another, are the relations between those two groups more cordial than between groups where there has been no recent male interchange? Yes. Are higher-ranking animals more likely to fall to predations than to illness or starvation? Yes, much more so. Do low-ranking monkeys scan the habitat with the same frequency as high-ranking monkeys? Yes, but they issue fewer alarm calls. *Aha!* Are they perhaps keeping mum in hopes of seeing a higher-ranking competitor knocked off? This would seem to make evolutionary sense. (Robert and Dorothy, working with a group of captive vervets back in the States, have shown that under controlled conditions, if an adult male sees a predator and he's in the presence of a higher-ranking male, he doesn't alarm-call at all; but if the same male sees a predator when in the presence of a female, he gives alarm calls.)

Most of their experiments have involved playing recordings of vocalizations and other sounds from a hidden speaker and filming and recording the monkey's reactions. This means figuring out opportunistically where to hide the speaker for a more or less definite experiment, from a long menu of experiments-to-be-done. All experiments are one-shot and nonrepeatable. No practice runs and no allowance for technical foul-up. For instance, if all the juveniles in a group are to be tested to see whether they react in a certain way to a particular sound, each juvenile gets just one exposure to the test and care must be taken to ensure that, when the test runs, the subject is generally facing the right direction (not in the direction of the hidden speaker) and not running out of camera range and not being harassed by a higher ranking monkey and so forth. Some experiments are designed to answer questions that have much more particular conditions: will a monkey who has been recently groomed (within a half hour) by another be more ready to respond to a request for alliance from that monkey (whose call will be played on the speaker) than one who has not been so groomed?

How do you run a single trial of this experiment? First observe the grooming of a monkey who has yet to be tested; then try to predict where that target monkey is apt to be during the next half hour. Then hide the speaker in an appropriate place, locate the groomer's call for assistance on the tape and get it ready to roll and wait for the groomer to move out of sight in the right general direction (to be consistent with a call for help from that area). Then make sure that no other monkey (e.g., the groomer's mother) is in a position to interfere. If all is well, turn on the movie camera, start the countdown to playback and cross your fingers hoping that no sudden change in conditions will ruin your "take."

Sometimes, after the speaker is set out, the "right" monkey or monkeys will wander out of range but others will move in who can be subjected to another experiment, with no more bother than advancing the tape on the playback machine. But that is a rare and lucky break. Patience, patience, patience. Most often, when the speaker is set out and everything is made ready for an experiment, something happens to call off the test. But this is actually an important generality, however frustrating it is on the occasion. The monkeys have seen Robert walking around a bush with a speaker in his hand and returning empty-handed hundreds of times and it is important that they not be able to associate this with a subsequent interesting noise from the bush. *Usually,* such hiding episodes are followed by . . . nothing memorable at all. So the monkeys are not interested in the speaker; it has never been associated with any interesting regularities at all in their experience. If they acquired an interest in it and began to investigate it, no further experimentation using speakers would be possible.

One of the most puzzling facts about vervets is that they are apparently so smart about some things—social relationships among their conspecifics, in particular—and so stupid about other things one would think were at least equally important to them and no more difficult. As Dorothy puts it, they seem to have "laser beam" intelligence: brilliant, narrowly specialized cognitive talents, with almost no carry-over of skill to other topics. They *seem* to be able to reason by analogy and recognize one thing as a sign or symptom of another, for instance, *so long as the topic is social relations* but then they appear unable to draw the same sort of conclusions about other matters. What are the boundaries of their competence? This is where the intentional stance and the Sherlock Holmes method ought to yield the results we want—by showing us just where knowledge or belief shades off into ignorance. Thought experiments suggest just which circumstances would be particularly telling but designing actual experiments to rig these circumstances is a frustrating business.

A big difference between real experiments and thought experiments is that, whereas thought experiments are usually taken to wear their meanings on their sleeves—or worse, their intended interpretation is simply stipulated—when you try to design a real experiment, you often notice to your initial dismay that any result you get is open to multiple interpretations. This is a concern in any science, of course, but when you adopt the intentional stance and use it to chart the (likely) beliefs and desires of some (possibly) rational agents, any *single* experiment suggests a profusion of serious hypotheses, ranging from romantic to killjoy and only a large family of related experiments taken together can narrow the field. There are no short cuts.

This was brought home vividly to me one evening. Earlier in the year, Robert had made a recording of a leopard "sawing"—marking its territorial boundary by stopping and scratching the ground and growling in a peculiar, loud, rhythmic, rasping way. To any knowledgeable human naturalist, the sound is unmistakable evidence of a nearby leopard. Can the monkeys also draw this conclusion? They almost certainly have heard the sound and probably witnessed leopards making it; but can they recognize its import in isolation? One evening after supper, in an exploratory mood, Robert and Dorothy and I drove out of camp in the jeep and parked quietly under the nearby sleeping tree of a group of vervets—not a habituated group but one that had often seen the jeep. After waiting a bit, I held the loudspeaker out the window and Robert played the leopard-sawing tape. Silence from the tree. We tried it again. Again silence. A third playing also yielded nothing. No audible reaction at all—even though during the day, if the monkeys spot a leopard they leap from branch to branch, warning each other and making a great hullabaloo.

How is this silence to be interpreted? Maybe the monkeys just don't recognize the sound. Perhaps this is one of those topics that are outside the monkey's narrow competence. That is what Robert and Dorothy think and they may be right. But what other candidate explanations offer themselves? The monkeys are heavy sleepers? Almost certainly not. The monkeys are on to the playback tricks? Again, almost certainly not—this was an unhabituated group that had never been experimented upon. But perhaps the monkeys are confused by the simultaneous presence of a jeep, and a leopard? Would *silence* be the expected sign of such a confusion, though? And in any case, there is nothing particularly odd about a jeep and a leopard in close proximity; after all, the leopard sawing Robert had recorded had been right at the edge of their camp. Perhaps, though, the monkeys realize that a sawing leopard is not a (stealthy) hunting leopard and hence is temporarily no threat. Perhaps, but there is no obvious reason why a sawing leopard would refrain from taking advantage of any easy predation that came his way. Sawing would not seem to be a high-priority behavior.

Then how about this: at night the risk-benefit payoff of giving an alarm changes dramatically; if you make a noise at night you give away your presence—which may be entirely unsuspected—and for what? If *you* heard the leopard sawing, presumably any vervet who could hear your alarm also heard the sawing. *Seeing* a leopard is apt to create a radical *information-gradient:* the sharp-eyed one is *alone* in having the information about the leopard. *Hearing* a leopard, on the other hand, is apt to be an occasion of group or mutual knowledge; everyone gets the bad news at once. But then if vervets did disturb the night with a chorus of alarms on hearing the leopard sawing, this would seem less intelligent than the discrimination they (apparently) make. (Not, by the way, that this wily calculation of risks and benefits might not "run through each vervet's head" and yet *still* be the rationale that actually explains why the vervets are silent; it would be what I call a "free-floating" rationale—a rationale that explains the evolutionary development of this instinctual policy—if it is merely instinctual.)

Passive observation, no matter how patient and careful, is not likely to settle the issue between these hypotheses, since every particular telling observation raises the question "But would they have done the same thing if the circumstance were altered in this way or that?" And the likelihood of all the right variations on the theme showing up without the experimenter's connivance is minuscule. Only a series of carefully designed experiments can put enough pressure on the hypotheses to sort them out. It could turn out that much of the puzzling "stupidity" of the vervets is actually disguised cleverness (or "cleverly designed" instincts). Or it could turn out that vervets are caught in the evolutionary trap of specialization: they developed special-purpose cognitive mechanisms that served them well enough to make the development of general-purpose problem-solving or reasoning mechanisms (like ours) too costly. (After all, researchers in *Artificial* Intelligence are finding that it is much, much easier to design weirdly narrow-minded "expert systems" than it is to design a general-purpose common-sense reasoner, and natural selection may have discovered a similar way to get some of the benefits of intelligence via a cheap substitute.)

The vervets' different alarm calls were identified (or, one might say, translated) by Robert and Dorothy several years ago and these translations have stood up well and been further sharpened and confirmed during their subsequent efforts to decipher the other vocalizations. (One day around noon we heard the eagle alarm of a superb starling, which the monkeys immediately heeded. Amin, the dominant female in the group, looked up, found the eagle in a treetop about a hundred and fifty meters away and gave a vervet eagle alarm. The others followed her gaze, *but didn't take up the alarm.* They saw, as she did on second glance, that it was not a martial eagle, which preys on vervets, but a snake eagle—just about the same size and with very similar markings but no threat to vervets. Only through binoculars could I observe the minor differences in the eagle's crest and coloration that had put the monkeys' minds at ease.)

Among the other vocalizations that have been identified are "grunt to a dominant" and "grunt to a subordinate" and a chatter that could be translated "I spy vervets from another group." A vocalization that

Robert and Dorothy are currently studying has been dubbed the Moving Into the Open (or MIO) grunt. Shortly before a monkey in a bush moves out into the open, it often gives a MIO grunt. Other monkeys in the bush will often repeat it—spectrographic analysis has not (yet) revealed a clear mark of difference between the initial grunt and this response. If no such echo is made, the original grunter will often stay in the bush for five or ten minutes and then repeat the MIO. Often, when the MIO is echoed by one or more other monkeys, the original grunter will thereupon move cautiously into the open.

But what does the MIO grunt mean? I suggested to Robert and Dorothy that we sit down and make a list of possible translations and see which we could eliminate or support on the basis of evidence already at hand. I started with what seemed to be the most straightforward and obvious possibility:

"I'm going."

"I read you. You're going."

But what would be the use of saying this? Vervets are in fact a taciturn lot, who keep silent most of the time, and are not given to anything that looks like passing the time of day by making obvious remarks. Like E. F. Hutton, when a vervet talks, others listen. "Well, then," I asked, "could it be a request for permission to leave?"

"May I go, please?"

"Yes, you have my permission to go."

This hypothesis could be knocked out if higher ranking vervets ever originated the MIO in the presence of their subordinates. In fact, higher-ranking vervets do tend to move into the open first, so it doesn't seem that MIO is a request for permission. Could it be a command, then?

"Follow me!"

"Aye, aye, Cap'n."

Not very plausible, Dorothy thought. "Why waste words with such an order when it would seem to *go without saying* in vervet society that low-ranking animals follow the lead of their superiors? For instance, you would think that there would be a vocalization meaning 'May I?' to be said by a monkey when approaching a dominant in hopes of grooming it. And you'd expect there to be two responses: 'You may' and 'You may not' but there is no sign of any such vocalization. Apparently such interchanges would not be useful enough to be worth the effort. There are gestures and facial expressions which may serve this purpose, but no audible signals."

Perhaps, Dorothy thought, the MIO grunt served simply to acknowledge and share the fear:

"I'm really scared."

"Yes. Me too."

Another interesting possibility was that the grunt helped with coordination of the group's movements:

"Ready for me to go?"

"Ready whenever you are."

A monkey that gives the echo is apt to be the next to leave. Or perhaps even better:

"Coast clear?"

"Coast is clear. We're covering you."

The behavior so far observed is compatible with this reading, which would give the MIO grunt a robust purpose, orienting the monkeys to a task of cooperative vigilance. The responding monkeys do watch the leave-taker and look in the right directions to be keeping an eye out.

"Suppose then, that this is our best candidate hypothesis," I said. "Can we think of anything to look for that would particularly shed light on it?" Among males, competition overshadows cooperation more than among females. Would a male bother giving the MIO if its only company in a bush was another male? Robert had a better idea: suppose a male originated the MIO grunt; would a rival male be devious enough to give a dangerously misleading MIO response when he saw that the originator was about to step into trouble? The likelihood of ever getting any good evidence of this is minuscule, for you would have to observe a case in which Originator didn't see and Responder did see a nearby predator *and* Responder saw that Originator didn't see the predator. (Otherwise Responder would just waste his credibility and incur the wrath and mistrust of Originator for no gain.) Such a coincidence of conditions must be extremely rare.

"But perhaps we could contrive it," Robert went on. "Perhaps we could do it with something like a stuffed python that we could very slyly and surreptitiously reveal to just one of two males who seemed about to venture out of a bush." The technical problems would clearly be nasty and at best it would be a long shot but with luck we might just manage to lure a liar into our trap.

But on further reflection, the technical problems looked virtually insurmountable. How would we establish that the "liar" had actually seen (and been taken in by) the "predator," and wasn't just innocently and sincerely reporting that the coast was clear? I found myself tempted (as often before in our discussions) to indulge in a fantasy: "If only I were small enough to dress up in a vervet suit, or if only we could introduce a trained vervet, or a robot or puppet vervet who could . . ." and slowly it dawned on me that this recurring escape from reality had a point: there is really no substitute, in the radical translation business, for going in and *talking with the natives.* You can test more hypotheses in half an hour of attempted chitchat than you can in a month of observation and unobtrusive manipulation. But to take advantage of this you have to become obtrusive; you—or your puppet—have to enter into communicative encounters with the natives, if only in order to go around pointing to things and asking "Gavagai?" in an attempt to figure out what "Gavagai" means. Similarly, in your typical mystery story caper, some crucial part of the setting up of the "Sherlock Holmes method" trap is—*must be*—accomplished by imparting some (mis)information verbally. Maneuvering your subjects into the right frame of mind—and knowing you've succeeded—without the luxurious efficiency of words can prove to be arduous at best, and often next to impossible.

In particular, it is often next to impossible in the field to establish that particular monkeys have been shielded from a particular bit of information. And since many of the theoretically most interesting hypotheses depend on just such circumstances, it is often very tempting to think of moving the monkeys into a lab, where a monkey can be physically *removed* from the group and given opportunities to acquire information that the others don't have *and that the test monkey knows they don't have.* Just such experiments are being done, by Robert and Dorothy with a group of captive vervets in California, and by other researchers with chimpanzees. The early results are tantalizing but equivocal (of course) and *perhaps* the lab environment, with its isolation booths, will be just the tool we need to open up the monkeys' minds, but my hunch is that being isolated in that way is such an unusual predicament for vervet monkeys that they will prove to be unprepared by evolution to take advantage of it.

The most important thing I think I learned from actually watching the vervets is that they live in a world in which secrets are virtually impossible. Unlike orangutans, who are solitary and get together only to mate and when mothers are rearing offspring, and unlike chimps, who have a fluid social organization in which individuals come and go, seeing each other fairly often but also venturing out on their own a large proportion of the time, vervets live in the open in close proximity to the other members of their groups and have no solitary projects of any scope. So it is a rare occasion indeed when one vervet is in a position to learn something that it alone knows *and knows that it alone knows*. (The knowledge of the others' ignorance, and of the possibility of maintaining it, is critical. Even when one monkey is the first to see a predator or a rival group, and knows it, it is almost never in a position to be sure the others won't very soon make the same discovery.) But without such occasions in abundance, there is little to impart to others. Moreover, without frequent opportunities to *recognize* that one knows something that the others don't know, devious reasons for or against imparting information cannot even exist—let alone be recognized and acted upon. People who live in glass houses have no stones to throw— or hoard—and hence have no use for a sophisticated delivery system with lots of options and decision points.

In sum, the vervets couldn't really make use of most of the features of a human language, for their world—or you might even say their lifestyle—is too simple. Their communicative needs are few but intense, and their communicative opportunities are limited. Like honeymooners who have not been out of each other's sight for days, they find themselves with not much to say to each other (or to decide to withhold). But if they couldn't make use of a fancy, human-like language, we can be quite sure that evolution hasn't provided them with one. Of course *if* evolution provided them with an elaborate language in which to communicate, the language itself would radically change their world, and permit them to create and pass secrets as profusely as we do. And then they could go on to use their language, as we use ours, in hundreds of diverting and marginally "useful" ways. But without the original information-gradients needed to prime the evolutionary pump, such a language couldn't get established.

So we can be quite sure that the MIO grunt, for instance, is not crisply and properly translated by *any* familiar human interchange. It can't be a (pure, perfect) command or request or question or exclamation because it isn't part of a system that is elaborate enough to make room for such sophisticated distinctions. When you say "Wanna go for a walk?" to your dog and he jumps up with a lively bark and expectant wag of the tail, this is not really a question and answer. There are only a few ways of "replying" that are available to the dog. It can't do anything tantamount to saying "I'd rather wait till sundown," or "Not if you're going to cross the highway," or even "No thanks." Your utterance is a question *in English* but a sort of melted-together mixture of question, command, exclamation, and mere *harbinger* (you've made some of those going-out-noises again) to your dog. The vervets' MIO grunt is no doubt a similar mixture, but while that means we shouldn't get our hopes too high about learning Vervetese and finding out all about monkey life by having conversations with the vervets, it doesn't at all rule out the utility of these somewhat fanciful translation hypotheses as ways of interpreting—and uncovering—the actual informational roles or functions of these vocalizations. When you think of the MIO as "Coast clear?" your attention is directed to a variety of testable hypotheses about further relationships and dependencies that ought to be discoverable if that is what MIO means—or even just "sort of" means.

Alas, some of the most interesting hypotheses are testable "in principle" (as a philosopher would say) but not really testable in practice. Sometimes this is due to the sort of technical difficulties that would make our MIO liar-trap so hard to set up. But it was brought home to me that there are other obstacles I hadn't counted on as well. Overexperimentation is a constant temptation but must be resisted. These monkeys have been scrupulously and unobtrusively studied for years and enough is now known about them—as individuals—to make them gloriously valuable subjects in these subtle probes into their beliefs. They could easily be spoiled for further research, however, by being subjected to experiments that drew their attention to their human observers or to the equipment, or that disrupted their lives in other ways.

For instance, a good way to try to *refute* the "Coast clear?" hypothesis about MIO—and such an attempt should of course be made—would be to originate MIO from a speaker hidden in the same bush with some monkeys. If they respond *without being able to see just where the originator is*, it is very unlikely that their response means "I'm covering you." But if your hypothesis turns out to be correct, the monkeys should be motivated to *find the originator* before responding and this would lead them to the hidden speaker in a state of heightened curiosity. The experiment threatens to blow the cover of the hidden speakers.

Robert and Dorothy have an informal list of experiments like this, what you might call last-one-out-the-door experiments, which they may someday run. If they ever learned, for instance, that changes in Kenya's political or social circumstances were about to make further experimentation impossible, then on the eve of their departure and knowing that no one else would be in a position to continue studying their groups, they might run through these experiments, roughly ranked in order of the damage they might do, as best they could.

Other experiments which at first glance seem tempting would involve getting the monkeys into a certain frame of mind by repeatedly presenting them with certain evidence, but nothing that smacks of *training* must enter their lives. They are well situated to be studied for what they know now or can pick up easily with a normal investment of normally motivated attention, not for what can be dinned into them under extraordinary conditions. (You can train a bear to ride a bicycle—an astonishing fact of elusive theoretical significance.) But without resorting to intensive training and without the luxury of a rich language with which you can simply *tell* your subjects the information that gets them into the "right" state for the experiment, it is often just impossible to assure yourself that your subjects have the one or two critical (and typically false) beliefs that can make a Sherlock Holmes trap so devastatingly revealing.

So this is what I learned. I learned that my methods, which work so well on people (especially in thought experiments and other fictional settings!), are strictly limited in application to animals who cannot be prepared as subjects with the help of language. But (looking on the bright side) the attempt to apply the methods helps uncover the very features of the monkeys' predicament that make them poor customers for a language that would give more power to the methods. Wittgenstein once said "If a lion could speak, we could not understand him." I disagree. If a monkey could speak—really speak a language—we could understand him just fine because, if a monkey could speak, his way of life would have to be very much more like ours than it is.

21

Cognitive Ethology:
Hunting for Bargains
or a Wild Goose Chase[1]

The discussion of the vervet monkeys' MIO (Moving Into the Open) grunt in the previous essay is repeated intact in this essay, where it is placed in a somewhat broader context of theory and controversy. The collaboration envisaged here between ethologists and researchers in Artificial Intelligence is now a thriving movement, with a slogan ("From Animals to Animats"), an excellent journal, Adaptive Behavior, *international congresses, summer schools, and workshops. This essay grew out of seminars in Oxford with David McFarland and others. The next chapter was presented at an earlier gathering, and my most recent contribution to this interdisciplinary enterprise, "Cog as a Thought Experiment," will soon appear in a special issue of* Robotics and Autonomous Systems, *the proceedings of the Monte Verità workshop of 1995.*

I Strategies of Simplification

The field of Artificial Intelligence has produced so many new concepts—or at least vivid and more structured versions of old concepts—that it would be surprising if none of them turned out to be of value to students of animal behavior. Which will be most valuable? I will resist the temptation to engage in either prophecy or salesmanship; instead of attempting to answer the question: "How might Artificial Intelligence inform the study of animal behavior?" I will concentrate on the converse: "How might the study of animal behavior inform research in Artificial Intelligence?"

Originally appeared in Montefiore, A., and Noble, D., eds., *Goals, No-Goals, and Own Goals: A debate on goal-directed and intentional behaviour* (London: Unwin Hyman, 1989), pp. 101–116.
1. I am grateful to K. Akins and C. M. Heyes for helpful suggestions on my handling of the topics in this chapter.

I take it we all agree that in the end we want to be able to describe and explain the design and operation of animal nervous systems at many different levels, from the neurochemical to the psychological and even the phenomenological (where appropriate!), and we want to understand how and why these designs have evolved, and how and why they are modulated in the individual organisms. AI research, like all other varieties of research on this huge topic, must make drastic over-simplifications in order to make even apparent progress. There are many strategies of simplification, of which these five, while ubiquitous in all areas of mind/brain research, are particularly popular in AI:

1. Ignore both learning and development; attempt to model the "mature competence" first, postponing questions about how it could arise.

2. Isolate a particular subcomponent or sub-subcomponent, ignoring almost all problems about how it might be attached to the larger system.

3. Limit the domain of operation of the modeled system or subsystem to a tiny corner of the real domain—try to solve a "toy problem," hoping that subsequent scaling-up will be a straightforward extrapolation.

4. Bridge various gaps in one's model with frankly unrealistic or even deliberately "miraculous" stopgaps—"oracles," or what I have called "cognitive wheels" (see chap. 11 of this volume). (In the neurosciences, one posits what I have called "wonder tissue" to bridge these gaps.)

5. Avoid the complexities of real-time, real-world coordination by ignoring robotics and specializing in what I call "bedridden" systems: systems that address the sorts of problems that can be presented via a narrow "verbal" channel, and whose solutions can be similarly narrowly conveyed to the world (Dennett, 1980).

Many of the best-known achievements of AI have availed themselves of all five of these strategies of simplification: chess-playing programs, and natural language parsers and speech recognition systems, for instance. Some critics are hostile to any efforts in cognitive science enabled by these strategies, but there is no point in attempting to "refute" them a priori. Since they are strategies, not doctrines or laws or principles, their tribunal is "handsome is as handsome does." The results to date are an inconclusive mixture. One theorist's deep but narrow insight is another's falsely lit detour; just which points of verisimilitude between model and modeled should count as telling partial confirmation and which as tricked up and misleading is often a matter of free-form dispute.

Instead of spending yet more time debating the wisdom of these strategies of simplification, one might just adopt some rival strategy or strategies, and let posterity decide which are the most fruitful. An obvious candidate, especially on this occasion, is to turn from the simulation of human cognition to the simulation of animal cognition. If human minds (or brains) are too complex, why not start with simpler minds—insect minds or bird brains?

Why not try to do a whole starfish, for instance? It has no eyes or ears, only rudimentary pattern-discrimination capacities, few modes of action, few needs or intellectual accomplishments. That could be a warm-up exercise for something a bit more challenging: a turtle, perhaps, or a mole. A turtle must organize its world knowledge, such as it is, so that it can keep life and limb together by making real-time decisions based on that knowledge, so while a turtle-simulation would not need a natural language parser, for instance, it would need just the sorts of efficient organization and flexibility of control distribution you have to provide in the representation of world knowledge behind a natural language parsing system of a simulated human agent such as SHRDLU (Winograd, 1972). (Dennett, 1978c)

So one reasonable motive for attempting AI modeling of animals is that it permits simplicity without unnatural truncation of systems— and you can get as much simplicity as you want by just descending the phylogenetic scale. If starfish are too hard, try *paramecia*. A simplifying *side* step in this descent is to opt for the modeling of *imaginary* simple animals, living in simulated simple environments. Such thought experiments can be brought to half-life, so to speak, and halfway put to the test, thanks to the computer's capacity to keep track of, and resolutely follow up the implications of, the loose ends among one's assumptions. The three-wheeled Martian iguana I fantasized in 1978 has not, to my knowledge, been born in any computer, but several of its brethren have been created. Braitenberg (1984), coming from the neuroscientific end of the spectrum, has described a considerable menagerie of ever more complex "vehicles" exhibiting increasingly "psychological" competences, and coming from the opposite, AI corner, we have Rod Brooks's artificial insects, real robots that perform uncannily biological-seeming feats with extremely simple control circuits (Brooks, 1991).

Of course the farther you get from human beings the less likely your successes are to shed light on the puzzles of *our* cognitive economies, but by training our attention on the differences that emerge, as well as the invariances that persist, as one moves along the actual phylogenetic scale, we may harvest insights about fundamental design principles of nervous systems, and about the traditions and precedents of design that are the raw materials of subsequent design innovations.

There is nothing new about this strategy, except for the relative ease with which very intricate models can now be "built" and "flight-tested," thanks to computer modeling. Some will object that much of the best computer modeling of simple nervous systems has had nothing in common with AI—and is indeed often the work of people quite hostile to the methods, assumptions, and pretensions of the ideologues of AI. That is true, but I think it is a fact of diminishing interest. The gulf between neuroscientists trying to build realistic models of simple neural systems from the bottom up (e.g., Hawkins and Kandel, 1984) and "pure" AI modelers who frankly ignore all biological constraints (e.g., Doyle, 1979) is being filled in with just about every intermediate variety of modeler. The antagonisms that remain say more about the economics and sociology of science than about the issues.

One reason people in AI have been dissuaded from simulating animal cognition is that they would have to give up one of their favorite sources of inspiration: introspection and reflection about how *they* perform the cognitive operations they choose to model. I say "inspiration" and not "data" since only under the most structured and well-studied conditions do people in AI count a match between model and "introspection" as corroboration of their model (Ericsson and Simon, 1984) But without the luxury of such self-modeling, or even the wealth of everyday lore we all accrue about human habits of thought, AI modelers are short on materials for the task of modeling animal cognition. It is here, of course, where the study of animal behavior might come to the rescue.

II   The Intentional Stance as a Designer's Strategy

All the AI efforts to simulate cognition, variously enriched by data from experimental studies of real creatures (and people) and by casual observation and introspection, are essentially *engineering* projects: attempts to design "machinery" with particular "psychological" talents. As engineering projects, their success depends heavily on the imaginative and organizational powers of the designers, who must juggle an ever increasing number of somewhat vague, somewhat conflicting "specs"—specifications—of the phenomena being modeled.

One way of imposing order—at least a temporary, tentative, order—on the interdependent tasks of *clarifying (and revising) the specs* and *de-*

signing a system that meets the specs is to adopt the intentional stance. One adopts a strategy of treating the systems in question as *intentional systems*, approximations of rational agents, to whom one attributes beliefs, desires, and enough rationality to choose the actions that are likely to fulfill their desires given the truth of their beliefs. We all adopt the intentional stance toward our friends and relatives and other human beings, but one can also get results by adopting the stance when designing or diagnosing certain artifacts—typically computer systems—and when studying the behavior of nonhuman animals.

My analysis and defense of adopting the intentional stance in the study of animal behavior (Dennett, 1983a) has been greeted by workers in the field with about equal measures of enthusiasm, dismissal, utter disinterest, and skeptical curiosity. A particularly insightful curious skeptic is C. M. Heyes (1987), who slyly wonders whether I have managed to drum up the enthusiasm by merely "providing a concert party for the troops"—making ethologists feel better about their lonely and ill-understood campaigns in the bush—while failing utterly to make good on my promise to show how "disciplined application of the intentional stance in cognitive ethology will yield descriptions of animal behavior that are especially useful to the information processing theorist."

This would seem to be the ideal forum for me to respond to Heyes's challenge, for while I am always willing to entertain, I do aspire to something more. Heyes quotes my central claim:

The intentional stance, however, provides just the right interface between specialties: a "black box" characterization of behavioral and cognitive competences observable in the field, but couched in language that (ideally) heavily constrains the design of machinery to put in the black box. (Dennett, 1983a, p. 350)

and then goes on to ask "but *how* might intentional accounts 'constrain' information processing theories?" In particular, since the ultimate destination of theory on my view is an utterly mechanistic account of the brain's activities, and since I insist that the most the intentional stance yields is an idealized and instrumentalistic account, it seems to Heyes that the intentional stance is at best a digression and distraction from the task at hand. How can a frankly idealizing model—which unrealistically describes (or prescribes) presumably optimal performance—actually constrain the development (from what I call the design stance) of a mechanistic and realistic model? To put it even more bluntly, how could instrumentalistic fictions help us figure out the mechanistic facts?

One can view the intentional stance as a limiting case of the design stance: one predicts by taking on just one assumption about the design of the system in question; whatever the design is, it is optimal. This assumption can be seen at work whenever, in the midst of the design stance proper, a designer or design investigator inserts a frank homunculus (an intentional system as subsystem) in order to bridge a gap of ignorance. The theorist says, in effect, "I don't know how to design this subsystem yet, but I know what it's supposed to do, so let's just pretend there is a demon there who wants nothing more than to do that task and knows just how to do it." One can then go on to design the surrounding system with the simplifying assumption that this component is "perfect." One asks oneself how the rest of the system must work, given that this component will not let down the side.

Occasionally such a design effort in AI proceeds by *literally* installing a human module pro tempore in order to explore design alternatives in the rest of the system. When the HWIM speech recognition system was being developed at Bolt, Baranek, and Newman (Woods and Makhoul, 1974), the role of the phonological analysis module, which was supposed to generate hypotheses about the likely phonemic analysis of segments of the acoustic input, was temporarily played by human phonologists looking at segments of spectrograms of utterances. Another human being, playing the role of the control module, could communicate with the phonology demon and the rest of the system, asking questions, and posing hypotheses for evaluation.

Once it was determined what the rest of the system had to "know" in order to give the phonologist module the help it needed, that part of the system was designed (discharging, inter alia, the control demon) and then the phonologists themselves could be replaced by a machine: a subsystem that used the same input (spectrograms—but not visually encoded, of course) to generate the same sorts of queries and hypotheses. During the design testing phase the phonologists tried hard not to use all the extra knowledge they had—about likely words, grammatical constraints, etc.—since they were mimicking *stupid* homunculi, specialists who only knew and cared about acoustics and phonemes.

Until such time as an effort is made to replace the phonologist subsystem with a machine, one is committed to virtually none of the sorts of design assumptions *about the working of that subsystem* that are genuinely explanatory. But in the meantime one may make great progress on the design of the other subsystems it must interact with, and the design of the supersystem composed of all the subsystems.

The first purported chess-playing automaton was a late eighteenth century hoax: Baron Wolfgang von Kempelen's wooden mannikin which did indeed pick up and move the chess pieces, thereby playing a decent game. It was years before the secret of its operation was revealed: a human chess master was hidden in the clockwork under the chess table, and could see the moves through the translucent squares— a literal homunculus (Raphael, 1976). Notice that the success or failure of the intentional stance as a predictor is so neutral with regard to design that it does not distinguish von Kempelen's homunculus-in-the-works design from, say, Berliner's Hitech, a current chess program of considerable power (Berliner and Ebeling, 1986). Both work; both work well; both must have a design that is a fair approximation of optimality, so long as what we mean by optimality at this point focuses narrowly on the task of playing chess and ignores all other design considerations (e.g., the care and feeding of the midget versus the cost of electricity— but try to find a usable electrical outlet in the eighteenth century!). Whatever their internal differences, both systems are intentional systems in good standing, though one of them has a subsystem, a homunculus, that is itself as unproblematic an intentional system as one could find. Intentional system theory is almost literally a black box theory— but that hardly makes it behavioristic in Skinner's sense (see Dennett, 1981a).

On the contrary, intentional system theory is an attempt to provide what Chomsky, no behaviorist, calls a competence model, in contrast to a performance model. Before we ask ourselves how mechanisms are designed, we must get clear about what the mechanisms are supposed to (be able to) do. This strategic vision has been developed further by Marr (1982) in his methodological reflections on his work on vision. He distinguishes three levels of analysis. The highest level, which he misleadingly calls *computational*, is in fact not at all concerned with computational processes, but strictly (and more abstractly) with the question of what function the system in question is serving—or, more formally, with what function *in the mathematical sense* it must (somehow or other) "compute." At this computational level one attempts to specify formally and rigorously the system's proper competence (Millikan, 1984, would call it the system's proper function). For instance, one fills in the details in the formula:

given an element in the set of x's as input, it yields an element in the set of y's as output according to the following formal rules . . .

—while remaining silent or neutral about the implementation or performance details of whatever resides in the competent black box. Marr's second level down is the *algorithmic* level, which does specify the computational processes but remains as neutral as possible about the *hardware*, which is described at the bottom level.

Marr claims that until we get a clear and precise understanding of the activity of a system at its highest, "computational" level, we cannot properly address detailed questions at the lower levels, or interpret such data as we may already have about processes implementing those lower levels. This echoes Chomsky's long insistence that the diachronic process of language-learning cannot be insightfully investigated until one is clear about the end-state mature competence toward which it is moving. Like Chomsky's point, it is better viewed as a strategic maxim than as an epistemological principle. After all, it is not impossible to stumble upon an insight into a larger picture while attempting to ask yourself what turn out to be subsidiary and somewhat myopically posed questions.

Marr's more telling strategic point is that if you have a seriously mistaken view about what the computational-level description of your system is (as all earlier theories of vision did, in his view), your attempts to theorize at lower levels will be confounded by spurious artifactual puzzles. What Marr underestimates, however, is the extent to which computational-level (or intentional stance) descriptions can also mislead the theorist who forgets just how idealized they are (Ramachandran, 1985).

The intentional stance *postpones consideration of* several types of cost. It assumes that in the black box are *whatever cognitive resources are required* to perform the task or subtask intentionally described, without regard (for the time being) of how much these resources might cost, either in terms of current space, material, and energy allocations, or in terms of "research and development"—the costs to Mother Nature of getting to such a design from a pre-existing design. And so long as cost is no object, there is no reason not to overdesign the system, endowing it with a richer intentional competence than it usually needs, or can afford.

But it is precisely these costs that loom large in biology, and that justify the strategic recommendation that we should be bargain hunters when trying to uncover the design rationales of living systems: always look for a system that provides a mere approximation of the competence described from the intentional stance, a cheap substitute that works well enough most of the time.

When great tits do a surprisingly good job of approximating the optimal foraging strategy in Krebs's "two-armed bandit" apparatus (Krebs, Kacelnik, and Taylor, 1978), we do not make the mistake of installing a mathematician-homunculus in their brains to work out the strategy via a dynamic programming algorithm. As Krebs notes, we cast about for cheaper, more realistic machinery that would obtain similar results. When the honey bees' oleic acid trigger was uncovered, this deposed the public-health-officer-homunculus whose task it was to recognize bee corpses as health hazards and order the right measures.

But if such intentional systems are always destined to be replaced by cheap substitutes, what constraining power do the interim intentional stance descriptions actually have? Only this: they describe the ideal against which to recognize the bargain. They remind the theorist of the point of the bargain device, and why it may be such a good deal. For instance, the vertical symmetry detectors that are ubiquitous machinery in animal vision are baffling until we consider them, as Braitenberg (1984) recommends, as quick-and-dirty discriminators of the ecologically important datum that *some other organism is looking at me*. The intentional stance provides a tentative background against which the researcher can contrast the observed behavior *as a competence*—in this case the competence to detect something in the environment *as* another organism facing head on, about which one might want to ask certain questions, such as: What is the prowess and cost-effectiveness of this machinery?—a question that cannot even be posed until one makes an assumption about what the machinery is for. If you consider it merely as a symmetry detector, you miss the rationale for its speedy triggering of orientation and flight-preparation subsystems, for instance. It is the intentional characterization that can vividly capture the larger role of the machinery in the whole system.

To return to Heyes's question, with which we began, in what way does the intentional stance *constrain* the development of design hypotheses in information processing theories? It constrains in the same way arithmetic constrains the design of hand calculators. Arithmetic can also be viewed as an abstract, ideal, normative system (how one *ought* to add, subtract, multiply, and divide), and then we can see that although individual hand calculators all "strive" to meet this ideal, they all fall short in ways that can be explained by citing cost-effectiveness considerations. For instance, arithemtic tells us that 10 divided by 3 multiplied by 3 is 10, but hand calculators will tell you that it is 9.9999999, owing to round-off or truncation error, a shortcoming the designers have decided to live with, even though such errors are extremely destructive under many conditions in larger systems that do not have the benefit of human observer / users (or very smart homunculi!) to notice and correct them.

Just as there are many different designs for hand calculators, all of which implement—with various different approximations and shortcomings—the arithmetical system, so many different designs of the neural hardware might implement any particular intentional system—with different attendant fallings short. So an intentional stance characterization does constrain design, but only partially. It is one constraint among others, but a particularly fruitful and central one: the one that reminds the designer or design-interpreter of *what the system is supposed to do.*

III   Why Vervet Monkeys Don't Perform Speech Acts

Another way of looking at the intentional stance as a tactic to adopt in the field is to consider the likely fruits of *taking it as seriously as possible.* One says to oneself, in effect: "Now if these animals *really* believed such-and-such and *really* desired such-and-such, they would have to believe (desire, intend, expect, fear) such-and-such as well. Do they?" It is the intentional stance's rationality assumption that generates ("a priori" as it were) the consequent to be tested. Such an excercise can help uncover particular aspects of falling-short, particular hidden cheap shortcuts in the design, and help explain otherwise baffling anomalies in an animal's behavior. One uses the intentional stance to ask the question: What is it about the world in which this animal lives that makes *this* cheap substitute a good bargain? I will sketch an example of this drawn from my own very limited experience as an amateur ethologist (see chap. 20 of this volume).

In June of 1983, I had a brief introduction to ethological field work, observing Seyfarth and Cheney observing the vervet monkeys in Kenya. In Dennett 1983a I had discussed the vervets and their fascinating proto-language, and had speculated on the likely fruits of using the intentional stance to get a better fix on the "translation" of their utterance-types. In particular, I had proposed attempting to use what I called the Sherlock Holmes method: setting cognitive ruses and traps for the vervets, to get them to betray their knowledge and understanding in one-shot experiments.

Once I got in the field and saw firsthand the obstacles to performing such experiments, I found some good news and some bad news. The bad news was that the Sherlock Holmes method, in its classical guise, has very limited applicability to the vervet monkeys—and by extrapolation, to other "lower" animals. The good news was that by adopting the intentional stance one can generate some plausible and indirectly testable hypotheses about why this should be so, and about the otherwise perplexing limitations of the cheap substitutes discovered in the vervets.

A vocalization that Seyfarth and Cheney were studying during my visit had been dubbed the Moving Into the Open (or MIO) grunt. Shortly before a monkey in a bush moves out into the open, it often gives a MIO grunt. Other monkeys in the bush will often repeat it—spectrographic analysis has not (yet) revealed a clear mark of difference between the initial grunt and this response. If no such echo is made, the original grunter will often stay in the bush for five or ten minutes and then repeat the MIO. Often, when the MIO is echoed by one or more other monkeys, the original grunter will thereupon move cautiously into the open.

But what does the MIO grunt mean? We listed the possible translations to see which we could eliminate or support on the basis of evidence already at hand. I started with what seemed to be the most straightforward and obvious possibility:

"I'm going."

"I read you. You're going."

But what would be the use of saying this? Vervets are in fact a taciturn lot, who keep silent most of the time, and are not given to anything that looks like passing the time of day by making obvious remarks. Then could it be a request for permission to leave?

"May I go, please?"

"Yes, you have my permission to go."

This hypothesis could be knocked out if higher ranking vervets ever originated the MIO in the presence of their subordinates. In fact, higher ranking vervets do tend to move into the open first, so it doesn't seem that MIO is a request for permission. Could it be a command, then?

"Follow me!"

"Aye, aye, Cap'n."

Not very plausible, Cheney thought. "Why waste words with such an order when it would seem to *go without saying* in vervet society that low-ranking animals follow the lead of their superiors? For instance, you would think that there would be a vocalization meaning 'May I?' to be said by a monkey when approaching a dominant in hopes of grooming it. And you'd expect there to be two responses: 'You may' and 'You may not,' but there is no sign of any such vocalization. Apparently such interchanges would not be useful enough to be worth the effort. There are gestures and facial expressions which may serve this purpose, but no audible signals." Perhaps, Cheney mused, the MIO grunt served simply to acknowledge and share the fear:

"I'm really scared."

"Yes. Me too."

Another interesting possibility was that the grunt helped with coordination of the group's movements:

"Ready for me to go?"

"Ready whenever you are."

A monkey that gives the echo is apt to be the next to leave. Or perhaps even better:

"Coast clear?"

"Coast is clear. We're covering you."

The behavior so far observed is compatible with this reading, which would give the MIO grunt a robust purpose, orienting the monkeys to a task of cooperative vigilance. The responding monkeys do watch the leave-taker and look in the right directions to be keeping an eye out. "Suppose then, that this is our best candidate hypothesis," I said. "Can we think of anything to look for that would particularly shed light on it?" Among males, competition overshadows cooperation more than among females. Would a male bother giving the MIO if its only company in a bush was another male? Seyfarth had a better idea: suppose a male originated the MIO grunt; would a rival male be devious enough to give a dangerously misleading MIO response when he saw that the originator was about to step into trouble? The likelihood of ever getting any good evidence of this is minuscule, for you would have to observe a case in which Originator didn't see and Responder did see a nearby predator *and* Responder saw that Originator didn't see the predator. (Otherwise Responder would just waste his credibility and incur the wrath and mistrust of Originator for no gain.) Such a coincidence of conditions must be extremely rare. This was an ideal opportunity, it seemed, for a Sherlock Holmes ploy.

Seyfarth suggested that perhaps we could spring a trap with something like a stuffed python that we could very slyly and surreptitiously reveal to just one of two males who seemed about to venture out of a bush. The technical problems would clearly be nasty, and at best it would be a long shot, but with luck we might just manage to lure a liar into our trap. But on further reflection, the technical problems looked virtually insurmountable. How would we establish that the "liar" had actually seen (and been taken in by) the "predator," and wasn't just innocently and sincerely reporting that the coast was clear? I found myself tempted (as often before in our discussions) to indulge in a fantasy: "If only I were small enough to dress up in a vervet suit, or if only we could introduce a trained vervet, or a robot or puppet vervet who could . . ." and slowly it dawned on me that this recurring escape from reality had a point: there is really no substitute, in the radical translation business, for going in and *talking with the natives*. You can test more hypotheses in half an hour of attempted chitchat than you can in a month of observation and unobtrusive manipulation. But to take advantage of this you have to become obtrusive; you—or your puppet—have to enter into communicative encounters with the natives, if only in order to go around pointing to things and asking "Gavagai?" in an attempt to figure out what "Gavagai" means. Similarly, in your typical mystery story caper, some crucial part of the setting up of the "Sherlock Holmes method" trap is—*must be*—accomplished by imparting some (mis)information verbally. Maneuvering your subjects into the right frame of mind—and knowing you've succeeded—without the luxurious efficiency of words can prove to be arduous at best, and often next to impossible.

In particular, it is often next to impossible in the field to establish that particular monkeys have been shielded from a particular bit of information. And since many of the theoretically most interesting hypotheses depend on just such circumstances, it is often very tempting to think of moving the monkeys into a lab, where a monkey can be physically *removed* from the group and given opportunities to acquire information that the others don't have *and that the test monkey knows they don't have*. Just such experiments are being done, by Seyfarth and

Cheney with a group of captive vervets in California, and by other researchers with chimpanzees. The early results are tantalizing but equivocal (of course), and *perhaps* the lab environment, with its isolation booths, will be just the tool we need to open up the monkeys' minds, but my hunch is that being isolated in that way is such an unusual predicament for vervet monkeys that they will prove to be unprepared by evolution to take advantage of it.

The most important thing I think I learned from actually watching the vervets is that they live in a world in which secrets are virtually impossible. Unlike orangutans, who are solitary and get together only to mate and when mothers are rearing offspring, and unlike chimps, who have a fluid social organization in which individuals come and go, seeing each other fairly often but also venturing out on their own a large proportion of the time, vervets live in the open in close proximity to the other members of their groups, and have no solitary projects of any scope. So it is a rare occasion indeed when one vervet is in a position to learn something that it alone knows *and knows that it alone knows.* (The knowledge of the others' ignorance, and of the possibility of maintaining it, is critical. Even when one monkey is the first to see a predator or a rival group, and knows it, it is almost never in a position to be sure the others won't very soon make the same discovery.) But without such occasions in abundance, there is little to impart to others. Moreover, without frequent opportunities to *recognize* that one knows something that the others don't know, devious reasons for or against imparting information cannot even exist—let alone be recognized and acted upon. I can think of no way of describing this critical simplicity in the *Umwelt* of the vervets, this missing ingredient, that does not avail itself explicitly or implicitly of higher-order intentional idioms.

In sum, the vervets couldn't really make use of most of the features of a human language, for their world—or you might even say their lifestyle—is too simple. Their communicative needs are few but intense, and their communicative opportunities are limited. Like honeymooners who have not been out of each other's sight for days, they find themselves with not much to say to each other (or to decide to withhold). But if they couldn't make use of a fancy, human-like language, we can be quite sure that evolution hasn't provided them with one. Of course *if* evolution provided them with an elaborate language in which to communicate, the language itself would radically change their world, and permit them to create and pass secrets as profusely as we do. And then they could go on to use their language, as we use ours, in hundreds of diverting and marginally "useful" ways. But without the original information-gradients needed to prime the evolutionary pump, such a language couldn't get established.

So we can be quite sure that the MIO grunt, for instance, is not crisply and properly translated by *any* familiar human interchange. It can't be a (pure, perfect) command or request or question or exclamation because it isn't part of a system that is elaborate enough to make room for such sophisticated distinctions. When you say "Wanna go for a walk?" to your dog and he jumps up with a lively bark and expectant wag of the tail, this is not really a question and answer. There are only a few ways of "replying" that are available to the dog. It can't do anything tantamount to saying "I'd rather wait till sundown," or "Not if you're going to cross the highway," or even "No thanks." Your utterance is a question *in English* but a sort of melted-together mixture of question, command, exclamation, and mere *harbinger* (you've made some of those going-out-noises again) to your dog (Bennett, 1976; 1983). The vervets' MIO grunt is no doubt a similar mixture, but while that means we shouldn't get our hopes too high about learning Vervetese and finding out all about monkey life by having conversations with the vervets, it doesn't at all rule out the utility of these somewhat fanciful translation hypotheses as ways of interpreting—and uncovering—the actual informational roles or functions of these vocalizations. When you think of the MIO as "Coast clear?" your attention is directed to a variety of testable hypotheses about further relationships and dependencies that ought to be discoverable if that is what MIO means—or even just "sort of" means.

But is that all there is? Perhaps *this* is the "concert party for the troops" Heyes supposes I am offering: I seem to end up saying that vervet monkeys don't *really* mean anything at all by their vocalizations. Am I also saying that vervet monkeys don't *really* believe anything? What *literally* can the intentional stance show us about animal belief—about what is going on in the minds of the animals being studied?

That question, I am saying, is misguided. The intentional stance attributions of belief, for all their caveats, are as literal as any attributions of belief—including self-attributions—can ever get. There are no deeper facts about the beliefs of animals—or about our own.[2] If you

---

2. In disagreement with Griffin (1981, 1984), I think the more particular hope that cognitive ethology will shed light on animal *consciousness* is a red herring. The only concepts of consciousness that yield genuinely explanatory attributions are applicable only to creatures with a full-fledged natural language—human beings.

want to know the deep, objective *truth* about the contents of animal minds, then either you are curious about the actual design of their brains (at many levels of analysis), and the rationale of that design, or you just want to know the most predictive intentional stance characterization of the animal, with all its idealizations. If you think there is another, deeper sort of fact about animal minds, then the intentional stance won't help you find it—but then nothing will, since if that is your curiosity, you are no longer doing the cognitive science of wild animals; you are on a wild goose chase.

An international summer school was held at the École d'Art d'Aix-en-Provence in 1992, "a meeting that brought together scientists and artists interested in animals and robots," in the words of the editors of the volume in which this essay originally appeared. Scientists and artists, and the odd philosopher or two—it was a strange and potent mix. Though the levels of mutual incomprehension and even occasional mutual disrespect were high, they were no higher than I have seen at conferences attempting to bring together, say, computer scientists and neuroscientists, or linguists and psychologists, and the artists provided an exhilarating atmosphere of exploratory boldness. It worked. The added opportunity to rethink the issues in French (and in Robot) brought home to me some of the parochiality of the standard discussions of these issues among Anglo-American philosophers.

According to one more or less standard mythology, behaviorism, the ideology and methodology that reigned in experimental psychology for most of the century, has been overthrown by a new ideology and methodology: cognitivism. Behaviorists, one is told, didn't take the mind seriously. They ignored—or even denied the existence of—mental states such as beliefs and desires, and mental processes such as imagination and reasoning; behaviorists concentrated exclusively on external, publicly observable behavior, and the (external, publicly observable) conditions under which such behavior was elicited. Cognitivists, in contrast, take the mind seriously, and develop theories, models, and explanations, that invoke, as real items, these internal, mental goings-on. People (and at least some other animals) have minds after all; they are *rational agents*.

Originally appeared in Roitblat, H., and Meyer, J.-A., eds., *Comparative Approaches to Cognitive Science* (Cambridge, MA: Bradford Books/The MIT Press, 1995), pp. 111–118.

Like behaviorists, cognitivists believe that the purely physical brain controls all behavior, without any help from poltergeists or egos or souls, so what does this supposedly big difference come to? When you ask a behaviorist what the mind is, the behaviorist retorts: "What mind?" When you ask a cognitivist, the reply is: "The mind is the brain." Since both agree that it is the brain that does all the work, their disagreement looks at the outset to be merely terminological. When, if ever, is it right, or just perspicuous, to describe an animal's brain processes as thinking, deciding, remembering, imagining? This question suggests to some that the behaviorists may have been right about lower animals—perhaps about pigeons and rats, and certainly about frogs and snails; these simple brains are capable of nothing that should be dignified as properly "cognitive." Well then, where do we "draw the line" and why?

Do animals have beliefs? One of the problems with this question, which has provoked a lot of controversy among animal researchers and the ideologues of cognitive science, is that there is scant agreement on the meaning of the term "belief" as it appears in the question. "Belief" has come to have a special, non-ordinary, sense in the English of many (but not all) of these combatants: it is supposed by them to be the *generic*, least-marked term for a *cognitive* state. Thus, if you look out the window and *see* that a cow is in the garden, you ipso facto have a belief that a cow is in the garden. If you are not ignorant of arithmetic, you believe the proposition that $2 + 2 = 4$ (and an infinity of its kin). If you *expect* (on whatever grounds) that the door you are about to open will yield easily to your tug, then you have a belief to that effect, and so on. It would be more natural, surely, to say of such a person "He thinks the door is unlocked" or "He's under the impression that the door is open" or even less positively, "He doesn't know the door is locked." "Belief" is ordinarily reserved for more dignified contents, such as religious belief, political belief, or—sliding back to more quotidian issues—specific conjectures or hypotheses considered. But for Anglophone philosophers of mind in particular, and other theoreticians in cognitive science, the verb "believe" and the noun "belief" have been adopted to cover all such cases; whatever information guides an agent's actions is counted under the rubric of belief.

This particularly causes confusion, I have learned, among non-native speakers of English; the French term *"croyance,"* for instance, stands even further in the direction of "creed" or "tenet," so that the vision my title question tends to conjure up for Francophones is an almost comical surmise about the religious and theoretical convictions of animals—not, as it is meant to be understood, as a relatively bland question about the nature of the cognitive states that suffice to account for the perceptuo-locomotory prowess of animals. But even those Anglophones most comfortable with the artificially enlarged meaning of the term in their debates suffer, I think, from the same confusion. There is much less agreement than these theorists imagine about just what one would be asserting in claiming, for instance, that dogs have beliefs.

Consider the diversity of opinion. Do animals have beliefs? I have said yes, supporting my claim by pointing to the undeniable fact that animals' behavior can often be predicted (and explained and manipulated) using what I call the intentional stance (Dennett, 1971, 1987)—the strategy of treating them as "rational agents" whose actions are those they deem most likely to further their "desires" given their "beliefs." One can often predict or explain what an animal will do by simply noticing what it notices and figuring out what it wants. The raccoon wants the food in the box-trap, but knows better than to walk into a potential trap where it can't see its way out. That's why you have to put two open doors on the trap—so that the animal will dare to enter the first, planning to leave by the second if there's any trouble. You'll have a hard time getting a raccoon to enter a trap that doesn't have an apparent "emergency exit" that closes along with the entrance.

I take it that this style of explanation and prediction is uncontroversially valuable: it works, and it works *because* raccoons (for instance) are that smart. That fact *suffices*, given what I mean by "belief," to show that raccoons have beliefs—and desires, of course. One might call the latter items preferences or goals or wants or values, but whatever you call them, their specification involves the use of intentional (mentalistic) idioms. That guarantees that translating between "desire" talk and "preference" or "goal" talk is trivial, so I view the connotational differences between these terms as theoretically irrelevant. The same thing holds for beliefs, of course: you might as well call the state of the raccoon a belief, since if you call it a "registration" or a "data-structure" in the "environmental information store" or some other technical term, the logic you use to draw inferences about the animal's behavior, given its internal states, will be the standard, "intentionalistic" logic of belief. (For more on the logic of intentionality, see Dennett, 1969; 1971; 1983a; 1987, or the article on intentionality in *Oxford Companion to the Mind* [Gregory, 1987].)

When called upon to defend this indifference to terminological nice-ties, I like to point out that when economists, for example, consider the class of *purchases* and note the defining condition that the purchaser believes he is exchanging his money for something belonging to the seller, and desires that item more than the money he exchanges for it, the economist is not requiring that the purchaser engage in any particu-larly salient act of *creed-endorsing* (let alone suffer any spasms of *desire*). A purchaser can meet the defining "belief-desire" conditions while daydreaming, while concentrating on some other topic, while treating the seller *almost* as if he / she / it were a post stuck in the ground. All that has to be the case is that the purchaser has somehow or other come into a cognitive state that identifies a seller, a price, and an opportunity to exchange and has tipped the balance in favor of completing the transaction. This is not nothing; it would be a decidedly nontrivial task to design a robot that could distinguish an apple seller from an apple tree, while not becoming a money-pump when confronted by eager salesmen. But if you succeeded in making a successful purchaser-robot, you would ipso facto have made a robot believer, a robot desirer, be-cause belief and desire, in this maximally bland (but maximally useful!) sense is a logical requirement of purchasing behavior.

Others do not approve of this way with words. Donald Davidson (1975), for instance, has claimed that only creatures with the concepts of truth and falsehood can properly be said to have beliefs, and since these are meta-linguistic concepts (I am simplifying his argument somewhat), only language-using animals such as human beings can have beliefs. And then there are those who have some other criterion for belief, according to which some animals do have beliefs and others don't. This criterion must be an empirical question for them, presum-ably, but *which* empirical question it is—which facts would settle it one way or the other—is something about which there is little agreement. David Premack (1988) has claimed that chimpanzees—and perhaps only chimpanzees—demonstrate belief, while Jerry Fodor (1990) has suggested that frogs—but not paramecia—have beliefs. Janet Halperin (at the conference in Aix-en-Provence, July 2–22, 1992) expressed mixed feelings about the hypothesis that her Siamese fighting fish have beliefs; on the one hand, they do seem richly amenable (in some re-gards) to intentional interpretation, while on the other hand she has a neural-net-like model of their control systems that seems to lack any components with the features beliefs are often supposed to have.

The various assumptions tacitly made about how to use these words infect other controversies as well. Does it follow from the hypothesis that there is something it is like to be a bat (Nagel, 1974) that bats have beliefs? Well, could it be the case that there was indeed something it was like to be a bat, but no bat knows what it is like? But could the bat know what it is like without having any beliefs about what it is like? If knowledge entails belief, as philosophical tradition declares, then a bat must have beliefs about what it is like to be it—if it is like anything at all to be a bat. But philosophers have different intuitions about how to answer all these questions, so of course they also have clashing opinions on whether robots could have beliefs.

The maximal leniency of the position I have recommended on this score is notoriously illustrated by my avowal that even lowly thermostats have beliefs. John McCarthy (1979) has joined me in this provocative stance, and proposes just the right analogy in defense, I think. Is zero a number? Some people were outraged when the recommendation was first made that zero be considered a number in good standing. What kind of a number is zero? It stands for no quantity at all! But the number system you get if you include zero is vastly more perspicuous and elegant than the number system you get if you exclude zero. A thermostat, McCarthy and I claim, is one of the simplest, most rudimentary, least interesting systems that should be included in the class of believers—the class of intentional systems, to use my term. Why? Because it has a rudimentary goal or desire (which is set, dictatorially, by the thermostat's owner, of course), which it acts on appropriately whenever it believes (thanks to a sensor of one sort or another) that its desire is unfulfilled. Of course you don't *have* to describe a thermostat in these terms. You can describe it in mechanical terms, or even molecular terms. But what is *theoretically interesting* is that if you want to describe the set of all thermostats (cf. the set of all purchasers) you have to rise to this intentional level. Any particular purchaser can also be described at the molecular level, but what purchasers—or thermostats—all have in common is a systemic property that is captured *only* at a level that invokes belief talk and desire talk (or their less colorful but equally intentional alternatives—semantic information talk and goal registration talk, for instance).

It is an open empirical question which other things, natural and artificial, fall into this class. Do trees? The case can be made—and in fact was made (or at least discussed, in the appropriate terms) by Colin Allen in the conference. One can see why various opponents of this view have branded it as "instrumentalism" or "behaviorism" or "eliminative materialism." But before accepting any of these dismissive labels, we should look at the suggested alternative, which is generally called *realism*, because it takes seriously the questions: Which animals *really* have beliefs, and (of those that do) what do they *really* believe? Jerry Fodor (1990), John Searle (1992), and Thomas Nagel (1986) are three prominent philosophical realists. The idea that it makes sense to ask these questions (and expect that in principle, they have answers), depends on a profound difference of vision or imagination between these thinkers and those who see things my way. The difference is clearest in the case of Fodor, as we can see by contrasting two pairs of propositions:

1. Fodor: *Beliefs are like sentences.* Beliefs have structure, are composed of parts, take up room in some spatial or temporal medium. Any finite system can contain only a finite number of beliefs. When one claims that Jones believes *that the man in the blue suit is the murderer,* this is true if and only if the belief in Jones's head really is composed of parts that mean just what the words in the italicized phrase mean, organized in a structure that has the same syntactic—and semantic—analysis as that string of words.

1A. Dennett: *Beliefs are like dollars.* Dollars are abstract (unlike dollar bills, which are concrete). The system of dollars is just one of many possible systems for keeping track of economic value. Its units do not line up "naturally" with any salient differences in the economic value of goods and services in the world, nor are all questions of intersystemic translation guaranteed to be well founded. How many US dollars (as of July 4, 1992) did a live goat cost in Beijing on that date? One has to operationalize a few loose ends to make the question meaningful: Do you take the exchange rate from the black market or use the official rate, for instance? Which *should* you use, and why? Once these loose ends are acknowledged and tied off, this question about the dollar value of goats in Beijing has a relatively satisfactory answer. That is, the various answers that might be reasonably defended tend to cluster in a smallish area about which disagreement might well be dismissed as trivial. How many dollars (as of July 4, 1992) was a live goat worth in ancient Athens? Here *any* answer you might give would have to be surrounded by layers of defense and explanation.

Now, no one doubts that a live goat really had value in ancient Athens, and no one doubts that dollars are a perfectly general, systematic system for measuring economic value, but I don't suppose anyone would ask, after listening to two inconclusive rival proposals about how to fix the amount in dollars, "Yes, but how many dollars did it *really* cost back then?" There may be good grounds for preferring one rival set of auxiliary assumptions to another (intuitively, one that pegs ancient dollars to the price per ounce of gold then and now is of less interest than one that pegs ancient dollars to assumptions about "standard of living," the cost-per-year to feed and clothe a family of four, etc.), but that does not imply that there must be some one translation scheme that "discovers the truth." Similarly, when one proposes and defends a particular scheme for expressing the contents of some agent's beliefs via a set of English sentences, the question of whether these sentences—supposing their meaning is fixed somehow—describe what the agent *really* believes betrays a certain naiveté about what a belief might be.

2. Fodor: *Beliefs are independent, salient states.*

2A. Dennett: *There are independent, salient states which belief talk "measures" to a first approximation.*

What's the difference between these two propositions? We both agree that a brain filled with sawdust or jello couldn't sustain beliefs. There has to be structure; there have to be elements of plasticity that can go into different states and thereby secure one revision or another of the contents of the agent's beliefs. Moreover these plastic elements have to be to some considerable extent *independently* adjustable to account for the productivity (or less grandly, the versatility) of beliefs in any believer of any interest (of greater interest than the thermostat).

The difference is that Fodor stipulates that the ascribing language (the sentences of English or French, for instance) must have much the same degrees of freedom, the same planes of revision, the same joints, as the system the sentences describe. I disagree. Consider the information contained in a map, drawn on some plane surface according to some mapping rules, and utilizing some finite set of labeling conventions. Imagine a robot that located itself by such a system, moving a symbol for itself on its own map as it moved through the world. At any moment, its system would contain lots of information (or misinformation) about its circumstances—for example, *that* it was nearer to A than to B, *that* it was within the boundary of C, *that* it was between F and G, *that* it was fast approaching D, who was on the same path but moving slower, etc. (Notice that I capture this limited selection of information in a series of "that" clauses expressed in English.) Some of this information would be utilizable by the robot, we may suppose, and some not. Whatever it can use, it believes (I would say); whatever it cannot use, it does not believe, since although the information is *in* the system, it is not *for* the system: it cannot be harnessed by the system to modulate behavior in ways that are appropriate to the system. Perhaps the fact *that* J, K, and L all lie on a straight line would be a fact that *we* could see from looking at the robot's map, but that the robot would be unable to extract from its map, using all the map-reading apparatus at its disposal.

There is a temptation here to think of this map-reading or extraction as a process having the map as its "input" and some sentence expressing one or more of these propositions or "that" clauses as its "output." But no such sentence formation is required (although it may be possible, in a talking robot). The information extraction may just as well consist of the generation of locomotory control signals sufficient for taking some action appropriate to the state of affairs alluded to by the "that" clause. (Appropriate, that is, given some assumptions about the agent's current "desires.") That locomotory recipe might not be executed; it might be evaluated and discarded in favor of some option deemed better under the circumstances. But since its generation as a candidate was dependent on the map's containing the information that-p, we can attribute the belief that-p to the system. All this is trivial if you think about the beliefs a chess-playing computer has about the location and value of the pieces on the chess board, and the various ways it might utilize that information in generating and evaluating move candidates. Belief talk can do an acceptable job of describing the information storage and information revision contained in a *map* system.

Are map systems as versatile as "propositional" systems? Under what conditions does each flourish and fail? Are there other data structures or formats even better for various tasks? These are good empirical questions, but if we are going to raise them without confusing ourselves, we will need a way of speaking—a level of discourse—that can neutrally describe what is in common between different robot implementations of the same cognitive competence. I propose the intentional stance (and hence belief talk) as that level. Going along with that proposal means abjuring the inferences that depend on treating belief talk as implying a *language* of thought.

Alternatively, one could reserve belief talk for these more particular hypotheses, and insist on some other idiom for describing what information processing systems have in common whether or not they utilize beliefs (now understood as sentences in the head). I am not undivorcibly wed to the former way of speaking, though I have made out the case for its naturalness. The main thing is not to let misinterpretations cloud the already difficult arena of theoretical controversy.

There are important and interesting reasons, for example, for attempting to draw distinctions between different *ways* in which information may be utilized by a system (or organism). Consider the information that is "interwoven" into connectionist nets (as in Janet Halperin's example). As Andy Clark and Annette Karmiloff-Smith (1993) say, "it is knowledge *in* the system, but it is not yet knowledge *to* the system." What must be added, they ask, (or what must be different) for information to be knowledge *to* the system? (See also Dennett, 1993b.) This is one of the good questions we are on the brink of answering, and there is no reason why we can't get clear about preferred nomenclature at the outset. Then we will have some hope of going on to consider the empirical issues without talking past each other. That would be progress.

Do animals have beliefs, then? It all depends on how you understand the term "belief." I have defended a maximally permissive understanding of the term, having essentially no specific implications about the format or structure of the information structures in the animals' brains, but simply presupposing that whatever the structure is, it is sufficient to permit the sort of intelligent choice of behavior that is well predicted from the intentional stance. So yes, animals have beliefs. Even amoebas—like thermostats—have beliefs. Now we can ask the next question: What structural and processing differences make different animals capable of having more sophisticated beliefs? We find that there are many, many differences, almost all of them theoretically interesting, but none of them, in my opinion, marking a well-motivated chasm between the mere mindless behavers and the genuine rational agents.

23

Why Creative Intelligence Is Hard to Find: Commentary on Whiten and Byrne

The ethologists Andrew Whiten and Richard Byrne published a fascinating and influential anthology of work on tactical deception by animals, Machiavellian Intelligence *(1988a). They also published a target article on the same topic in* Behavioral and Brain Sciences *(1988b). This commentary shows why a systematic perspectival effect makes creative intelligence so hard to catch in the act — whether in an individual mind or in the design of the biosphere. It also fends off a persistent misconstrual of my own position by ethologists who mistook me to be advocating anecdote-gathering as an alternative to experimentation.*

The concluding question and answer of Whiten and Byrne's (W&B's) (1988b) valuable survey is worth repeating, if only to save W&B from a likely misreading: "But can anecdotes ever be more than a jumping off point for more systematic work? We propose that the answer must be 'no.' . . ." I have been dismayed to learn that my own limited defense (Dennett, 1983a) of the tactic of provoking "anecdotes"—generating single instances of otherwise highly improbable behaviors under controlled circumstances—has been misinterpreted by some enthusiasts as giving them license to replace tedious experimentation with the gathering of anecdotes. But as W&B stress, anecdotes are a prelude, not a substitute, for systematic observation and controlled experiments.

They describe in outline the further courses of experimental work that would shed light on the phenomena of tactical deception, and suggest that the postponed question of whether these behaviors arise as a result of "creative intelligence" may be settled by the outcome of such research. This research should certainly be pursued, and if properly conducted its results are bound to shed light on these issues, but it is

Originally appeared in *Behavioral and Brain Sciences*, 11 (2), 1988, p. 253.

worth noting in advance that no matter how clean the data are, and indeed no matter how *uniform* they are, there is a systematic instability in the phenomenon of creatively intelligent tactical deception (if it exists!) that will tend to frustrate efforts of interpretation.

To see this, consider the range of possibilities available in the generic case, stripped to its essentials. Suppose AGENT intelligently creates a deceptive tactic that is devastatingly effective on a first trial against TARGET. Will it tend to be repeated in similar circumstances? Yes; ex hypothesi it was intelligently created rather than a result of blind luck or sheer coincidence, so AGENT can be supposed to recognize and appreciate the effect achieved. But then there are two possible outcomes to such repetition: Either it will provoke countermeasures from TARGET (who is no dummy, and can be fooled once or twice, but will eventually catch on), or it won't (TARGET is not so smart after all). If it doesn't, then the exploitative behavior will become (and be seen to be) stereotyped, and ipso facto will be interpretable not as a sign of creative intelligence but as a useful habit whose very cleverness is diminished by our lower regard for the creative intelligence of the TARGET. If, on the other hand, TARGET attempts countermeasures, then either they will work or they won't. If they don't work, TARGET will be seen once again to be an unworthy opponent, and the deceptive behavior a mere good habit. If the countermeasures tend to work, then either AGENT notices that they do, and thereupon revises his schemes, or not. If not, then AGENT's intelligence will be put into question, whereas if AGENT does come up with a suitable revision then he will tend *not* to repeat the behavior with which we began, but rather some relatively novel successor behavior.

In other words, if both AGENT and TARGET are capable of creative intelligence, then what must ensue is either an escalating arms race of ploy and counterploy or a semistable equilibrium in which the frequency of deceptive tactics is close to "chance" (a tactic will work against a wily TARGET only if infrequently used, something a wily AGENT will understand). Escalations, however, are bound to be short-lived phenomena, punctuating relatively static periods. (If AGENTS and TARGETS are so smart, one might ask, why haven't they already discovered—and exhausted—the opportunities for escalation?) So the conditions one would predict in any community in which there is genuine creative intelligence are conditions systematically difficult to distinguish from "mere chance" fluctuations from a norm of trustworthiness. Any regularly repeated exploitative behaviors are in themselves grounds for diminishing our esteem for the creative intelligence of either AGENT or TARGET or both.

Our estimation of AGENT's cleverness is in part a function of our estimation of TARGET's cleverness. The more stupid TARGET appears, the less we will be impressed by AGENT's success. The smarter TARGET is with countermeasures, the less success AGENT will have. If AGENT persists in spite of failure, AGENT's intelligence is rendered suspect, while if AGENT largely abandons the tactic, we will not have any clear way of determining whether AGENT's initial success was dumb luck, unrecognized by AGENT, or a tactic wisely perceived by AGENT to have outlived its usefulness.

This can be made to appear paradoxical—a proof that there couldn't be any such thing as genuine creative intelligence. Once or twice is dumb luck; many times is boring habit; in between there is no stable rate that counts clearly and unequivocally as creative intelligence. If we set the threshold in this fashion we can guarantee that nothing could count as genuine creative intelligence. Using just the same move, evolutionists could prove that no history of natural selection could count as an unproblematic instance of adaptation; the first innovation counts as luck, while its mere preservation unenhanced counts as uncreative.

Clearly, we must adjust our presuppositions if we want to make use of such concepts as creative intelligence or adaptation. The stripped-down paradigmatic case exposes the evidential problem by leaving out all the idiosyncratic but telling details that are apt to convince us (one way or the other) in particular cases. If we see AGENT adjusting his ploys to the particularities of TARGET's counterploys, or even just reserving his ploys for those occasions in which he can detect evidence that TARGET can be caught off guard, our conviction that AGENT's infrequent attempts at deception are intelligently guided will be enhanced. But this seeing is itself a product of interpretation, and can only be supported by longitudinal observation of variegated, not repeated, behavior. There could be no surefire signs of creative intelligence observable in isolated, individual bits of behavior.

What we will always have to rely on to persuade us of the intelligence of the members of a species is the *continued* variation, enhancement, and adjustment of ploys in the face of counterploys. So it is not repeated behaviors but changing behaviors that are the sign of creative intelligence, and this can be observed only in the long term. Moreover, the long-term history of any genuinely intelligent agent will show this proclivity to make novel and appropriate advances mixed with a smattering of false starts, unlucky breaks, and "bad ideas." So we should set aside the illusory hope of finding "conclusive" empirical evidence of creative intelligence, evidence that can withstand all skeptical attempts at a "demoting" reinterpretation. When we recognize that the concept of intelligence is not a neutral or entirely objective one, but rather an evaluative one, this should not surprise us.

24

Animal Consciousness:
What Matters and Why

Thomas Nagel's famous essay, "What Is It Like to Be a Bat?" has had the curious effect of discouraging subsequent researchers from asking (and attempting to answer) such questions. The effect is easy to understand: Nagel said that it was impossible to answer such questions and many readers believed him. Nagel didn't so much argue for this conclusion as assume it and then discuss its implications, however, so one might well reopen the question. A conference entitled In the Company of Animals, *at the New School for Social Research, was a good forum in which to try to undo some of the defeatism engendered by Nagel and other philosophers.*

Are animals conscious? The way we are? Which species, and why? *What is it like* to be a bat, a rat, a vulture, a whale?

But perhaps we really don't want to know the answers to these questions. We should not despise the desire to be kept in ignorance—aren't there many facts about yourself and your loved ones that you would wisely choose not to know? Speaking for myself, I am sure that I would go to some lengths to prevent myself from learning all the secrets of those around me—whom they found disgusting, whom they secretly adored, what crimes and follies they had committed, or thought I had committed! Learning all these facts would destroy my composure, cripple my attitude toward those around me. Perhaps learning too much about our animal cousins would have a similarly poisonous effect on our relations with them. But if so, then let's make a frank declaration to that effect and drop the topic, instead of pursuing any further the pathetic course upon which many are now embarked.

For current thinking about animal consciousness is a mess. Hidden and not so hidden agendas distort discussion and impede research. A

Originally appeared in *Social Research*, 62 (3), Fall 1995, pp. 691–710.

kind of comic relief can be found—if you go in for bitter irony—by turning to the "history of the history" of the controversies. I am not known for my spirited defenses of René Descartes, but I find I have to sympathize with an honest scientist who was apparently the first victim of the wild misrepresentations of the lunatic fringe of the animal rights movement. Animal rights activists such as Peter Singer and Mary Midgley have recently helped spread the myth that Descartes was a callous vivisector, completely indifferent to animal suffering *because of* his view that animals (unlike people) were mere automata. As Justin Leiber (1988) has pointed out, in an astringent re-examination of the supposed evidence for this, "There is simply not a line in Descartes to suggest that he thought we are free to smash animals at will or free to do so *because* their behavior can be explained mechanically." Moreover, the favorite authority of Descartes's accusers, Montaigne, on whom both Singer and Midgley also uncritically rely, was a gullible romantic of breathtaking ignorance, eager to take the most fanciful folktales of animal mentality at face value, and not at all interested in *finding out,* as Descartes himself was, how animals actually work!

Much the same attitude is common today. There is a curious tolerance of patent inconsistency and obscurantism, and a bizarre one-sidedness in the treatment of evidence regarding animal minds. Elizabeth Marshall Thomas writes a book, *The Hidden Life of Dogs* (1993), which mixes acute observation and imaginative hypothesis-formulation with sheer fantasy, and in the generally favorable welcome the book receives, few if any point out that it is irresponsible, that she has polluted her potentially valuable evidence with well-meant romantic declarations that she could not have any defensible grounds for believing. If you want to *believe* in the consciousness of dogs, her poetry is just the ticket. If you want to *know* about the consciousness of dogs, you have to admit that although she raises many good questions, her answers are not to be trusted. That is not to say that she is wrong in all her claims, but that they *just won't do* as answers to the questions, not if we really want to know the answers.

A forlorn hope, some say. Certain questions, it is said, are quite beyond science at this point (and perhaps forever). The cloaks of mystery fall conveniently over the very issues that promise (or threaten) to shed light on the *grounds* for our moral attitudes toward different animals. Again, a curious asymmetry can be observed. We don't require absolute, Cartesian certainty that our fellow human beings are conscious—what we require is what is aptly called *moral* certainty. Can we not have the same moral certainty about the experiences of animals? I have not yet seen an argument by a philosopher to the effect that we cannot, with the aid of science, establish facts about animal minds with the same degree of moral certainty that satisfies us in the case of our own species. So whether or not a case has been made for the "in principle" mystery of consciousness (I myself am utterly unpersuaded by the arguments offered to date), it's a red herring. We can learn enough about animal consciousness to settle the questions we have about our responsibilities. The moral agenda about animals is important, and for that very reason it must not be permitted to continue to deflect the research, both empirical and conceptual, on which an informed ethics could be based.

A striking example of one-sided use of evidence is Thomas Nagel's famous paper "What Is It Like to Be a Bat?" (1974). One of the rhetorical peculiarities of Nagel's paper is that he chose bats, and went to the trouble to relate a *few* of the fascinating facts about bats and their echolocation, because, presumably, those hard-won, third-person-perspective scientific facts tell us *something* about bat consciousness. What? First and least, they support our conviction that bats *are* conscious. (He didn't write a paper called "What Is It Like to Be a Brick?") Second, and more important, they support his contention that bat consciousness is very unlike ours. The rhetorical peculiarity—if not outright inconsistency—of his treatment of the issue can be captured by an obvious question: if a few such facts can establish *something* about bat consciousness, wouldn't more such facts establish more? He has already relied on "objective, third-person" scientific investigation to establish (or at least render rationally credible) the hypothesis that bats are conscious, but not in just the way we are. Why wouldn't further such facts be able to tell us in exactly what ways bats' consciousness isn't like ours, thereby telling us what it *is* like to be a bat? What kind of fact is it that only works for one side of an empirical question?

The fact is that we all do rely, without hesitation, on "third-person" behavioral evidence to support or reject hypotheses about the consciousness of animals. What else, after all, could be the source of our "pretheoretical intuitions"? But these intuitions in themselves are an untrustworthy lot, much in need of reflective evaluation. For instance, do you see "sentience" or "mere discriminatory reactivity" in the Venus' flytrap, or in the amoeba, or in the jellyfish? What more than mere discriminatory reactivity—the sort of competence many robots exhibit—are you *seeing* when you *see* sentience in a creature? It is in fact ridiculously easy to induce powerful intuitions of not just sentience but full-blown consciousness (ripe with malevolence or curiosity or friendship) by exposing people to quite simple robots *made to move in familiar mammalian ways at mammalian speeds.*

Cog, a delightfully humanoid robot being built at MIT, has eyes, hands, and arms that move the way yours do—swiftly, relaxedly, compliantly (Dennett, 1994c). Even those of us working on the project, knowing full well that we haven't even *begun* to program the high level processes that might arguably endow Cog with consciousness, get an almost overwhelming sense of being in the presence of another conscious observer when Cog's eyes still quite blindly and stupidly follow one's hand gestures. Once again, I plead for symmetry: when you acknowledge the power of such elegant, lifelike motions to charm you into an illusion, note that it ought to be an open question, still, whether you are also being charmed by your beloved dog or cat, or the noble elephant. Feelings are too easy to provoke for them to count for much here.

If behavior, casually observed by the gullible or generous-hearted, is a treacherous benchmark, might composition—material and structure—provide some important leverage? History offers a useful perspective on this question. It was not so long ago—Descartes's day—when the hypothesis that a material brain by itself could sustain consciousness was deemed preposterous. Only immaterial souls could *conceivably* be conscious. What was inconceivable then is readily conceivable now. Today we can readily conceive that a brain, without benefit of immaterial accompanists, can be a sufficient seat of consciousness, even if we wonder just how this could be. This is surely a *possibility* in almost everybody's eyes, and many of us think the evidence for its truth mounts close to certainty. For instance, few if any today would think that the "discovery" that, say, lefthanders don't have immaterial minds, but just brains, would show unmistakably that they are just zombies.

Unimpressed by this retreat, some people today baulk at the *very idea* of silicon consciousness or artifactual consciousness, but the reasons offered for these general claims are unimpressive to say the least. It looks more and more as if we will simply have to look at what entities—animals in this case, but also robots and other things made of nonstandard materials—*actually can do*, and use that as our best guide to whether animals are conscious, and if so, why, and of what.

I once watched with fascination and, I must admit, disgust while hundreds of vultures feasted on a rotting elephant carcass in the hot sun of a June day in Kenya. I found the stench so overpowering that I had to hold my nose, and breathe through a kerchief to keep from gagging, all the time keeping my distance, but there were the vultures eagerly shouldering each other aside and clambering inside the carcass for the tastiest morsels. (I will spare you the most mind-boggling details.) Now I am quite confident, and I expect you agree with me, that I was thereby given very good evidence that those vultures do not share my olfactory quality space. In fact, as I have subsequently learned, these Old World vultures, unlike their rather distant New World cousins, don't rely on olfaction at all; they use their keen eyesight to spot carrion. The peculiar, nauseating odors of rotting carrion, carried by such well-named amines as *cadaverine* and *putrescine*, are attractants to the New World turkey vultures (*Cathartes aura*), however, and the presumed explanation is that in the New World these birds evolved in an ecology in which they hunted for food hidden under a canopy of trees, which diminished the utility of vision, and heightened the utility of olfaction. David Houston (1986), has conducted experiments using fresh, ripe, and very-ripe chicken carcasses, hidden from sight in the forests of a Panamanian island, to titrate the olfactory talents of turkey vultures. So we're making progress; we now know—to a moral certainty—something about the difference between what it is like to be an African vulture and what it is like to be a Central American turkey vulture.

So let's go on. What does a rotting chicken carcass smell like to a turkey vulture? At first blush it may seem obvious that we can confidently set aside the philosophers' problem of other minds in this instance, and assume, uncontroversially, that these vultures rather go in for the smell of carrion. Or does anybody present suppose that vultures might be heroic martyrs of the scavenger world, bravely fighting back their nausea while they performed their appointed duties?

Here, it seems, we correct one extrapolation from our own case by another: we dismiss our imputation to them of our own revulsion by noting their apparent *eagerness*—as revealed by their behavior. When *we* exhibit such eagerness, it is because we *like* something, so they must like what they are doing and feeling. Similarly, we do not worry about the poor seal pups on their ice floe, chilling their little flippers. We would be in agony, lying naked on the ice with the wind blowing over us, but they are designed for the cold. They are not shivering or whimpering, and indeed they exhibit the demeanor of beasts who could not be more content with their current circumstances—home sweet home.

"But wait!" says the philosopher. "You are being awfully sloppy in these everyday attributions. Let's consider what is *possible in principle.* Vulture revulsion is possible in principle, is it not? You would not make their observed behavior *criterial* of pleasure, would you? Are you some benighted *behaviorist?* The suggestion that it makes no sense for vultures to be disgusted by their designated diet is nothing but Panglossian optimism. Perhaps vultures have been misdesigned by evolution; perhaps vulture ancestors found themselves in a sort of evolutionary cul-de-sac, hating the taste and smell of the only food available in their niche, but having no choice but to overcome their distaste and gag it down; perhaps they have since developed a sort of stoic demeanor, and what you have interpreted as gusto is actually desperation!"

Fair enough, I reply. My rush to judgment was perhaps a bit rash, so let's explore further to see whether any supporting evidence can be found for your alternative hypothesis. Here is a relevant fact: Turkey vultures are attracted by the smell of one-day-old or two-day-old carcasses, but they ignore older, still more pungent fare. It is conjectured that the toxin level in such flyblown remains eventually is too great even for the toxin-tolerant vultures, who leave them for the maggots. Insects, it is believed, use the onset of these later products of decomposition as their cue that a carcass is sufficiently decomposed to be a suitable site for egg-laying, and hence maggot formation. This still leaves unanswered the residual question of whether turkey vultures actually *like* the smell of middle-aged carrion. At this point, my knowledge of actual or contemplated vulture research gives out, so I'll have to consider some invented possibilities, for the time being. It would be fascinating to discover something along the lines of an incompletely suppressed gag-reflex as part of the normal vulture feeding behavior, or perhaps some traces of approach-avoidance opponent systems tugging away at each other in their brains, a sort of activity not to be found, we might imagine, in the brains of birds with more savory diets. Such discoveries would indeed add real support to your surprising hypothesis, but of course they would be just more "behavioral" or "functional" evidence. Once again, a superficially plausible but retrospectively naive or oversimple interpretation would be overthrown by more sophisticated use of behavioral considerations. And you can hardly accept the support of this imagined evidence without agreeing that *not* discovering it would count *against* your alternative and in *favor* of my initial interpretation.

This might be—indeed ought to be—just the beginning of a long and intricate examination of the possible functional interpretations of events in the vultures' nervous systems, but let us cut to the chase, for I imagine our dissenting philosopher to insist, in the end, after one or another hypothesis regarding complexities of vulture *reactivity* to carrion had been effectively confirmed, that still, no amount of such merely third-personal investigation could ever ("in principle") tell us what carrion *actually smelled like* to a vulture. This would be asserted not on the basis of any further argument, mind you, but just because eventually this is the "intuitive" card that is standardly played.

What I find insupportable in this familiar impasse is the coupling of blithe assertion of consciousness with the equally untroubled *lack of curiosity* about what this assertion might amount to, and how it might be investigated. Leiber (1988) provides a handy scorecard:

Montaigne is ecumenical in this respect, claiming consciousness for spiders and ants, and even writing of our duties to trees and plants. Singer and Clarke agree in denying consciousness to sponges. Singer locates the distinction somewhere between the shrimp and the oyster. He, with rather considerable convenience for one who is thundering hard accusations at others, slides by the case of insects and spiders and bacteria; they, *pace* Montaigne, apparently and rather conveniently do not feel pain. The intrepid Midgley, on the other hand, seems willing to speculate about the subjective experience of tapeworms. . . . Nagel . . . appears to draw the line at flounders and wasps, though more recently he speaks of the inner life of cockroaches.

The list could be extended. In a recent paper, Michael Lockwood (1993) supposes, as so many do, that Nagel's "what it is like to be" formula *fixes a sense* of consciousness. He then says: "Consciousness in this sense is presumably to be found in all mammals, and probably in all birds, reptiles and amphibians as well." It is the "presumably" and "probably" that I want us to attend to. Lockwood gives no hint as to how he would set out to replace these terms with something more definite. I'm not asking for certainty. Birds aren't just *probably* warm blooded, and amphibians aren't just *presumably* air-breathing. Nagel confessed at the outset not to know—or to have any recipe for discovering—where to draw the line as we descend the scale of complexity (or is it the cuddliness scale?). This embarrassment is standardly waved aside by those who find it just obvious that there is something it is like to be a bat or a dog, equally obvious that there is *not* something it is like to be a brick, and unhelpful *at this time* to dispute whether it is like anything to be a fish or a spider. What does it mean to say that it is or it isn't?

It has passed for good philosophical form to invoke mutual agreement here that we know what we're talking about even if we can't explain it yet. I want to challenge this. I claim that this standard methodological assumption has no *clear* pretheoretical meaning—in spite of its undeniable "intuitive" appeal—and that since this is so, it is ideally suited to play the deadly role of the "shared" intuition that conceals the solution from us. *Maybe* there really is a huge difference between us and all other species in this regard; *maybe* we should consider "radical" hypotheses. Lockwood says "probably" all birds are conscious, but *maybe* some of them—or even all of them—are rather like sleepwalkers! Or what about the idea that there could be unconscious pains (and that animal pain, though real, and—yes—morally important, was unconscious pain)? *Maybe* there is a certain amount of generous-minded delusion (which I once called the Beatrix Potter syndrome) in our bland mutual assurance that, as Lockwood puts it, "*Pace* Descartes, consciousness, thus construed, isn't remotely, on this planet, the monopoly of human beings."

How, though, could we ever explore these "maybes"? We could do so in a constructive, anchored way by first devising a theory that concentrated exclusively on *human* consciousness—the one variety about which we will brook no "maybes" or "probablys"—and then *look and see* which features of that account apply to which animals, and why. There is plenty of work to do, which I will illustrate with a few examples—just warm-up exercises for the tasks to come.

In *Moby-Dick*, Herman Melville asks some wonderful questions about what it is like to be a sperm whale. The whale's eyes are located on opposite sides of a huge bulk: "the front of the Sperm Whale's head," Melville memorably tells us, "is a dead, blind wall, without a single organ or tender prominence of any sort whatever" (chap. 76). As Melville notes: "The whale, therefore, must see one distinct picture on this side, and another distinct picture on that side; while all between must be profound darkness and nothingness to him" (chap. 74).

Nevertheless, any one's experience will teach him, that though he can take in an indiscriminating sweep of things at one glance, it is quite impossible for him, attentively, and completely, to examine any two things—however large or however small—at one and the same instant of time; never mind if they lie side by side and touch each other. But if you now come to separate these two objects, and surround each by a circle of profound darkness; then, in order to see one of them, in such a manner as to bring your mind to bear on it, the other will be utterly excluded from your contemporary consciousness. How is it, then, with the whale? . . . is his brain so much more comprehensive, combining, and subtle than man's, that he can at the same moment of time attentively examine two distinct prospects, one on one side of him, and the other in an exactly opposite direction?

Melville goes on to suggest that the "extraordinary vacillations of movement" exhibited by sperm whales when they are "beset by three or four boats" may proceed "from the helpless perplexity of volition, in which their divided and diametrically opposite powers of vision must involve them" (chap. 74).

Might these "extraordinary vacillations" rather be the whale's attempt to keep visual track of the wheeling boats? Many birds, who also "suffer" from eyes on opposite sides of their heads, achieve a measure of "binocular" depth perception by bobbing their heads back and forth, giving their brains two slightly different views, permitting the relative motion of parallax to give them approximately the same depth information we get all at once from our two eyes with their overlapping fields.

Melville assumes that whatever it is like to be a whale, it is similar to human consciousness in one regard: there is a single boss in charge, an "I" or "ego" that either superhumanly distributes its gaze over disparate scenarios, or humanly flicks back and forth between two rivals. But might there be even more radical discoveries in store? Whales are not the only animals whose eyes have visual fields with little or no overlap; rabbits are another. In rabbits there is no interocular transfer of learning! That is, if you train a rabbit that a particular shape is a source of danger by demonstrations carefully restricted to its *left* eye, the rabbit will exhibit no "knowledge" about that shape, no fear or flight behavior, when the menacing shape is presented to its *right* eye. When we ask what it is like to be that rabbit, it appears that at the very least we must put a subscript, *dexter* or *sinister*, on our question in order to make it well-formed.

Now let's leap the huge chasm that separates our cousins, the whale and the rabbit, from a much more distant relative, the snake. In an elegant paper, "Cued and detached representations in animal cognition," Peter Gärdenfors (1996) points out "why a snake can't think of a mouse."

It seems that a snake does not have a central representation of a mouse but relies solely on transduced information. The snake exploits three different sensory systems in relation to prey, like a mouse. To strike the mouse, the snake uses its *visual* system (or thermal sensors). When struck, the mouse normally does not die immediately, but runs away for some distance. To locate the mouse, once the prey has been struck, the snake uses its sense of *smell*. The search behavior is exclusively wired to this modality. Even if the mouse happens to die right in front of the eyes of the snake, it will still follow the smell trace of the mouse in order to find it. This unimodality is

particularly evident in snakes like boas and pythons, where the prey often is held fast in the coils of the snake's body, when it e.g. hangs from a branch. Despite the fact that the snake must have ample proprioceptory information about the location of the prey it holds, it searches stochastically for it, all around, only with the help of the olfactory sense organs. (Sjölander, 1993, p. 3)

Finally, after the mouse has been located, the snake must find its head in order to swallow it. This could obviously be done with the aid of smell or sight, but in snakes this process uses only *tactile* information. Thus the snake uses three separate modalities to catch and eat a mouse.

Can we talk about what the snake *itself* "has access" to, or just about what its various parts have access to? Is any of that obviously sufficient for consciousness? The underlying presumption that Nagel's "what is it like" question makes sense at all, when applied to a snake, is challenged by such possibilities.

I have argued at length, in *Consciousness Explained* (1991a), that the sort of informational unification that is the most important prerequisite for *our* kind of consciousness is not anything we are born with, not part of our innate "hard-wiring" but in surprisingly large measure an artifact of our immersion in human culture. What that early education produces in us is a sort of benign "user-illusion"—I call it the Cartesian Theater: the illusion that there is a place in our brains where the show goes on, toward which all perceptual "input" streams, and whence flow all "conscious intentions" to act and speak. I claim that other species—and human beings when they are newborn—simply *aren't beset by* the illusion of the Cartesian Theater. Until the organization is formed, there is simply no user in there to be fooled. This is undoubtedly a radical suggestion, hard for many thinkers to take seriously, hard for them even to *entertain*. Let me repeat it, since many critics have ignored the possibility that I mean it—a misfiring of their generous allegiance to the principle of charity.

In order to be conscious—in order to be the sort of thing it is like something to be—it is necessary to have a certain sort of informational organization that endows that thing with a wide set of cognitive powers (such as the powers of reflection, and re-representation). This sort of internal organization does not come automatically with so-called sentience. It is not the birthright of mammals, or warm-blooded creatures, or vertebrates; it is not even the birthright of human beings. It is an organization that is swiftly achieved in one species, ours, and in no other. Other species no doubt achieve *somewhat similar* organizations, but the differences are so great that most of the speculative translations of imagination from our case to theirs *make no sense.*

My claim is not that other species lack our kind of *self*-consciousness, as Nagel (1991) and others have supposed. I am claiming that what must be added to mere responsivity, mere discrimination, to count as consciousness *at all* is an organization that is not ubiquitous among sentient organisms. This idea has been dismissed out of hand by most thinkers.[1] Nagel, for instance, finds it to be a "bizarre claim" that "implausibly implies that babies can't have conscious sensations before they learn to form judgments about themselves." Lockwood is equally emphatic: "Forget culture, forget language. The mystery begins with the lowliest organism which, when you stick a pin in it, say, doesn't merely react, but actually *feels* something."

Indeed, that is where the *mystery* begins if you insist on starting *there*, with the assumption that you know what you mean by the contrast between merely reacting and actually feeling. And the mystery will never stop, apparently, if that is where you start.

In an insightful essay on bats (and whether it is like anything to be a bat), Kathleen Akins (1993) pursues the sort of detailed investigation into functional neuroscience that Nagel eschews, and she shows that

---

1. Two rare—and widely misunderstood—exceptions to this tradition are Julian Jaynes (1976) and Howard Margolis (1987), whose cautious observations survey the field of investigation I am proposing to open up:

A creature with a very large brain, capable of storing large numbers of complex patterns, and capable of carrying through elaborate sequences of internal representations, with this capability refined and elaborated to a very high degree, would be a creature like you and me. Somehow, as I have stressed, consciousness conspicuously enters the scheme at this point of highly elaborate dynamic internal representations. Correctly or not, most of us find it hard to imagine that an insect is conscious, at least conscious in anything approximating the sense in which humans are conscious. But it is hard to imagine that a dog is not conscious in at least something like the way an infant is conscious (Margolis, 1987, p. 55)

Nagel is at best ill advised in simply *assuming* that a bat *must* have a point of view. Akins sketches a few of the many different stories that can be told from the vantage point of the various subsystems that go to making up a bat's nervous system. It is tempting, on learning these details, to ask ourselves "and where in the brain does the bat *itself* reside?" but this is an even more dubious question in the case of the bat than it is in our own case. There are many parallel stories that could be told about what goes on in you and me. What gives one of those stories about *us* pride of place at any one time is *just this:* it is the story you or I will tell if asked (to put a complicated matter crudely).

When we consider a creature that isn't a teller—has no language—what happens to the supposition that one of *its* stories is privileged? The hypothesis that there is one such story that would tell us (if we could understand it) what it is actually like to be that creature dangles with no evident foundation or source of motivation—except dubious tradition. Bats, like us, have plenty of relatively peripheral neural machinery devoted to "low level processing" of the sorts that are routinely supposed to be entirely unconscious in us. And bats have no machinery analogous to our machinery for issuing public protocols regarding their current subjective circumstances, of course. Do they then have some *other* "high level" or "central" system that plays a privileged role? Perhaps they do and perhaps they don't. Perhaps there is no role for such a level to play, no room for any system to perform the dimly imagined task of elevating merely unconscious neural processes to consciousness. After all, Peter Singer has no difficulty supposing that an insect might keep its act together without the help of such a central system. It is an open empirical question, or rather, a currently unimagined and complex set of open empirical questions, what sorts of "high levels" are to be found in which species under which conditions.

Here, for instance, is one possibility to consider: the bat lacks the brain-equipment for *expressing* judgments (in language), but the bat may nevertheless have to *form* judgments (of some inarticulate sort), in order to organize and modulate its language-free activities. Wherever these inarticulate judgment-like things happen is where we should look for the bat's privileged vantage point. But this would involve just the sort of postulation about sophisticated judgments that Nagel found so implausible to attribute to a baby. If the distinction between conscious and unconscious has nothing to do with anything sophisticated like judgment, what else could it involve?

Let us return to our vultures. Consider the hypothesis that for all I could ever know, rotting chicken carcass smells to a turkey vulture exactly the way roast turkey smells to me. Can science shed any light, pro or con, on this hypothesis? Yes, it can almost effortlessly refute it: since *how roast turkey smells to me* is composed (and exhausted) by the huge set of reactive dispositions, memory effects, etc., etc., that are detectable in principle in my brain and behavior, and since many of these are utterly beyond the machinery of any vulture's brain, it is flat impossible that anything could smell to a vulture the way roast turkey smells to me.

Well, then, what *does* rotting chicken smell like to a turkey vulture? (Exactly?) How patient and inquisitive are you prepared to be? We can uncover the corresponding family of reactive dispositions in the vulture by the same methods that work for me, and as we do, we will learn more and more about the no doubt highly idiosyncratic relations a vulture can form to a set of olfactory stimuli. But we already know a lot that we *won't* learn. We will never find a vulture being provoked by those stimuli to wonder, as a human being might, whether the chicken isn't just slightly *off* tonight. And we won't find any amusement, or elaborate patterns of association, or Proustian reminiscence. Am I out in front of the investigations here? A little bit, but note what kind of investigations they are. It turns out that we end up where we began: analyzing patterns of behavior (external and internal—but not "private"), and attempting to interpret them in the light of evolutionary hypotheses regarding their past or current functions.

The very idea of there being a dividing line between those creatures "it is like something to be" and those that are mere "automata" begins to look like an artifact of our traditional presumptions. I have offered (Dennett, 1991a) a variety of reasons for concluding that in the case of adult human consciousness there is no principled way of distinguishing when or if the mythic light bulb of consciousness is turned on (and shone on this or that item). Consciousness, I claim, even in the case we understand best—our own—is not an all-or-nothing, on-or-off phenomenon. If this is right, then consciousness is not the sort of phenomenon it is assumed to be by most of the participants in the debates over animal consciousness. Wondering whether it is "probable" that all mammals have *it* thus begins to look like wondering whether or not any birds are *wise* or reptiles have *gumption:* a case of overworking a term from folk psychology that has lost its utility along with its hard edges.

Some thinkers are unmoved by this prospect. They are still unshaka-
bly sure that consciousness—"phenomenal" consciousness, in the
terms of Ned Block (1992; 1993; 1994; 1995)—*is* a phenomenon that is
either present or absent, rather as if some events in the brain glowed
in the dark and the rest did not.[2] Of course if you simply will not contemplate the hypothesis that consciousness might turn out *not* to be a
property that thus sunders the universe in twain, you will be sure that
I must have overlooked consciousness altogether. But then you should
also recognize that you maintain the mystery of consciousness by simply refusing to consider the evidence for one of the most promising
theories of it.

---

2. John Searle also holds fast to this myth. See, e.g, Searle, 1992, and my review, 1993e.

Postscript: Pain, Suffering, and Morality

In the discussion following my presentation at the conference at the New School, attention was focused on a question about animal consciousness that is not explicitly addressed above: According to my model, how would one tell which animals were capable of pain or suffering (or both)? Drawing on the presentations and discussions later in the conference, I offer here an oversimplified sketch of the direction my theory recommends for answering this question.[3]

The phenomenon of pain is neither homogeneous across species, nor simple. We can see this in ourselves, by noting how unobvious the answers are to some simple questions. Are the "pains" that usefully prevent us from allowing our limbs to assume awkward, joint-damaging positions while we sleep experiences that require a "subject" (McGinn, 1995) or might they be properly called unconscious pains? Do they have moral significance in any case? Such body-protecting states of the nervous system might be called "sentient" states without thereby implying that they were the experiences of any self, any ego, any subject. For such states to matter—whether or not we call them pains, or conscious states, or experiences—there must be an enduring, *complex* subject *to whom* they matter because they are a source of suffering. Snakes (or parts of snakes!) may feel pain—depending on how we choose to define that term—but the evidence mounts that snakes lack the sort of overarching, long-term organization that leaves room for significant suffering. That doesn't mean that we ought to treat snakes the way we treat worn out tires, but just that concern for their suffering should be tempered by an appreciation of how modest their capacities for suffering are.

---

3. For a more detailed discussion, see "Minding and Mattering, " pp. 448–454 in Dennett, 1991a.

While the distinction between pain and suffering is, like most everyday, nonscientific distinctions, somewhat blurred at the edges, it is nevertheless a valuable and intuitively satisfying mark or measure of moral importance. When I step on your toe, causing a brief but definite (and definitely conscious) pain, I do you scant harm—typically none at all. The pain, though intense, is too brief to matter, and I have done no long-term damage to your foot. The idea that you "suffer" for a second or two is a risible misapplication of that important notion, and even when we grant that my causing you a few seconds pain may irritate you a few more seconds or even minutes—especially if you think I did it deliberately—the pain itself, as a brief, negatively signed experience, is of vanishing moral significance. (If in stepping on your toe I have interrupted your singing of the aria, thereby ruining your operatic career, that is quite another matter.)

Many discussions seem to assume tacitly: (1) that suffering and pain are the same thing, on a different scale; (2) that all pain is "experienced pain"; and (3) that "amount of suffering" is to be calculated ("in principle") by just adding up all the pains (the awfulness of each of which is determined by duration-times-intensity). These assumptions, looked at dispassionately in the cold light of day—a difficult feat for some partisans—are ludicrous. A little exercise may help: would you exchange the sum total of the suffering you will experience during the next year for one five-minute blast of no doubt excruciating agony that summed up to the "same amount" of total pain-and-suffering? I certainly would. In fact, I'd gladly take the bargain even if you "doubled" or "quadrupled" the total annual amount—just so long as it would be all over in five minutes. (We're assuming, of course, that this horrible episode does not kill me, or render me insane—after the pain is over—or have other long-term effects that amount to or cause me further suffering; the deal was to pack all the suffering into one jolt.) I expect anybody would be happy to make such a deal. But it doesn't really make sense. It implies that the benefactor who provided such a service gratis to all would, ex hypothesi, be doubling or quadrupling the world's suffering—and the world would love him for it.

It seems obvious to me that something is radically wrong with the assumptions that permit us to sum and compare suffering in any such straightforward way. But some people think otherwise; one person's reductio ad absurdum is another's counterintuitive discovery. We ought to be able to sort out these differences, calmly, even if the best resolution we can reasonably hope for is a recognition that some choices of perspective are cognitively impenetrable.

IV

Standing Back

25   Self-Portrait

This essay "provoked" Bo Dahlbom to write a "more unorthodox kind of intro-duction" to my work in his volume Dennett and His Critics *(1993). As usual, two perspectives are better than one, and his is particularly insightful.*

In my opinion, the two main topics in the philosophy of mind are con-tent and consciousness. As the title of my first book, *Content and Con-sciousness* (1969) suggested, that is the order in which they must be addressed: first, a theory of content or intentionality—a phenomenon more fundamental than consciousness—and then, building on that foundation, a theory of consciousness. Over the years I have found myself recapitulating this basic structure twice, partly in order to re-spond to various philosophical objections, but more importantly, be-cause my research on foundational issues in cognitive science led me into different aspects of the problems. The articles in the first half of *Brainstorms* (1978a) composed, in effect, a more detailed theory of con-tent, and the articles in the second half were concerned with specific problems of consciousness. The second recapitulation has just been completed, with a separate volume devoted to each half: *The Intentional Stance* (1987) is all and only about content; *Consciousness Explained* (1991a) presupposes the theory of content in that volume and builds an expanded theory of consciousness.

1 Beginnings and Sources

Although quite a few philosophers agree that content and conscious-ness are the two main issues confronting the philosophy of mind,

---

Originally appeared in Guttenplan, S., ed., *A Companion to the Philosophy of Mind* (Oxford: Blackwell, 1994), pp. 236–244.

many—perhaps most—follow tradition in favoring the opposite order: consciousness, they think, is the fundamental phenomenon, upon which all intentionality ultimately depends. This difference of perspective is fundamental, infecting the intuitions with which all theorizing must begin, and it is thus the source of some of the deepest and most persistent disagreements in the field. It is clear to me how I came by my renegade vision of the order of dependence: as a graduate student at Oxford, I developed a deep distrust of the methods I saw other philosophers employing, and decided that before I could trust any of my intuitions about the mind, I had to figure out how the brain could possibly accomplish the mind's work. I knew next to nothing about the relevant science, but I had always been fascinated with how things worked—clocks, engines, magic tricks. (In fact, had I not been raised in a dyed-in-the-wool "arts and humanities" academic family, I probably would have become an engineer, but this option would never have occurred to anyone in our family.) So I began educating myself, always with an eye to the curious question of how the mechanical responses of "stupid" neurons could be knit into a fabric of activity that actually discriminated meanings. Somehow it had to be possible, I assumed, since it was obvious to me that dualism was a last resort, to be postponed indefinitely.

So from the outset I worked from the "third-person point of view" of science, and took my task to be building—or rather sketching the outlines of—a physical structure that could be seen to accomplish the puzzling legerdemain of the mind. At the time—the mid-1960s—no one else in philosophy was attempting to build that structure, so it was a rather lonely enterprise, and most of the illumination and encouragement I could find came from the work of a few visionaries in science and engineering: Warren McCulloch, Donald MacKay, Donald Hebb, Ross Ashby, Allen Newell, Herbert Simon, and J. Z. Young come to mind. Miller, Galanter and Pribram's 1960 classic, *Plans and the Structure of Behavior*, was a dimly understood but much appreciated beacon, and Michael Arbib's 1964 primer, *Brains, Machines and Mathematics*, was very helpful in clearing away some of the fog.

Given my lack of formal training in any science, this was a dubious enterprise, but I was usually forgiven my naïveté by those who helped me into their disciplines, and although at the time I considered myself driven by (indeed defined by) my disagreements with my philosophical mentors, Quine and Ryle, in retrospect it is clear that my deep agreement with both of them about the nature of philosophy—so deep as to be utterly unexamined and tacit—was the primary source of such intellectual security as I had.

The first stable conclusion I reached, after I discovered that my speculative forays always wandered to the same place, was that the only thing brains could do was to *approximate* the responsivity to meanings that we *presuppose* in our everyday mentalistic discourse. When mechanical push came to shove, a brain was always going to do what it was caused to do by current, local, mechanical circumstances, whatever it *ought* to do, whatever a God's-eye view might reveal about the actual meanings of its current states. But over the long haul, brains could be designed—by evolutionary processes—to do the right thing (from the point of view of meaning) with high reliability. This found its first published expression in *Content and Consciousness* (1969, sec. 9, "Function and Content") and it remains the foundation of everything I have done since then. As I put it in *Brainstorms* (1978a), brains are *syntactic engines* that can mimic the competence of *semantic engines*. (See also the thought experiment—a forerunner of Searle's Chinese Room—about being locked in the control room of a giant robot, in 1978b.) Note how this point forces the order of dependence of consciousness on intentionality. The appreciation of meanings—their discrimination and delectation—is central to our vision of consciousness, but this conviction that *I*, on the inside, deal directly with meanings turns out to be something rather like a benign "user-illusion." What Descartes thought was most certain—his immediate introspective grasp of the items of consciousness—turns out to be not even quite true, but rather a metaphorical by-product of the way our brains do their approximating work. This vision tied in beautifully with a doctrine of Quine's that I had actually vehemently resisted as an undergraduate: the indeterminacy of radical translation. I could now see why, as Quine famously insisted, indeterminacy was "of a piece with" Brentano's thesis of the irreducibility of the intentional, and why those irreducible intentional contexts were unavoidably a "dramatic idiom" rather than an expression of unvarnished truth. I could also see how to reinterpret the two philosophical works on intentionality that had had the most influence on me, Anscombe's *Intention* (1957) and Taylor's *The Explanation of Behaviour* (1964).

If your initial allegiance is to the physical sciences and the third-person point of view, this disposition of the issues can seem not just intuitively acceptable, but inevitable, satisfying, natural. If on the other hand your starting point is the traditional philosophical allegiance to the mind and the deliverances of introspection, this vision can seem outrageous. Perhaps the clearest view of this watershed of intuitions can be obtained from an evolutionary perspective. There was a time, before life on earth, when there was neither intentionality nor consciousness, but eventually replication got under way and simple organisms emerged. Suppose we ask of them: Were they conscious? Did their states exhibit intentionality? It all depends on what these key terms are taken to mean, of course, but underneath the strategic decisions one might make about pre-emptive definition of terms lies a fundamental difference of outlook. One family of intuitions is comfortable declaring that while these earliest ancestors were unconscious automata, not metaphysically different from thermostats or simple robotic toys, some of their states were nevertheless semantically evaluable. These organisms were, in my terms, rudimentary intentional systems, and somewhere in the intervening ascent of complexity, a special subset of intentional systems has emerged: the subset of conscious beings. According to this vision, then, the intentionality of our unconscious ancestors was as real as intentionality ever gets; it was just rudimentary. It is on this foundation of unconscious intentionality that the higher-order complexities developed that have culminated in what we call consciousness. The other family of intuitions declares that *if* these early organisms were mere unconscious automata, then their so-called intentionality was not the real thing. Some philosophers of this persuasion are tempted to insist that the earliest living organisms were conscious—they were alive, after all—and hence their rudimentary intentionality was genuine, while others suppose that somewhere higher on the scale of complexity, real consciousness, and hence real intentionality, emerges. There is widespread agreement in this camp, in any case, that although a robot might be what I have called an intentional system, and even a higher-order intentional system, it could not be conscious, *and so* it could have no genuine intentionality at all.

In my first book, I attempted to cut through this difference in intuitions by proposing a division of the concept of consciousness into awareness$_1$, the fancy sort of consciousness that we human beings enjoy, and awareness$_2$, the mere capacity for appropriate responsivity to stimuli, a capacity enjoyed by honeybees and thermostats alike. The tactic did not work for many thinkers, who continued to harbor the hunch that I was leaving something out; there was, they thought, a special sort of sensitivity—we might call it animal consciousness—that no thermostat or fancy robot could enjoy, but that all mammals and birds (and perhaps all fish, reptiles, insects, mollusks, . . .) shared. Since robotic devices of considerably greater behavioral and perceptual complexity than the simplest of these organisms are deemed unconscious by this school of thought, it amounts to some sort of latter-day vitalism. The more one learns about how simple organisms actually work, the more dubious this hunch about a special, organic sort of sensation becomes, but to those who refuse to look at the science, it is a traditional idea that is about as comfortable today as it was in the seventeenth century, when many were horrified by Descartes's claims about the mechanicity of (nonhuman) animals. In any event, definitional gambits are ineffective against it, so in later work I dropped the tactic and the nomenclature of "aware$_1$" and "aware$_2$"—but not the underlying intuitions.

My accounts of content and consciousness have subsequently been revised in rather minor ways and elaborated in rather major ways. Some themes that figured heavily in *Content and Consciousness* lay dormant in my work through the 1970s and early 1980s, but were never abandoned, and are now re-emerging, in particular the theme of learning as evolution in the brain and the theme of content being anchored in distributed patterns of individually ambiguous nodes in networks of neurons. The truth is that while I can fairly claim to have seen the beauty, and indeed the inevitability, of these ideas in *Content and Consciousness* (see also Dennett, 1974), and to have sketched out their philosophical implications quite accurately, I simply couldn't see how to push them further in the scientific domain, and had to wait for others— not philosophers—to discover these ideas for themselves and push them in the new directions that have so properly captured recent philosophical attention. My own recent discussions of these two themes are to be found in chapters 4, 13, and 16 of this volume; and Dennett, 1987, chap. 8; 1991a; and 1991c.

2   Content: Patterns Visible from the Intentional Stance

My theory of content is functionalist: all attributions of content are founded on an appreciation of the *functional roles* of the items in question in the biological economy of the organism (or the engineering economy of the robot). This is a specifically "teleological" notion of function (not the notion of a mathematical function or of a mere "causal role," as suggested by David Lewis and others). It is the concept of function that is ubiquitous in engineering, in the design of artifacts, but also in biology. (It is only slowly dawning on philosophers of science that biology is not a science like physics, in which one should strive to find "laws of nature," but a species of engineering: the analysis, by "reverse engineering," of the found artifacts of nature—which are composed of thousands of deliciously complicated gadgets, yoked together opportunistically but elegantly into robust, self-protective systems.) These themes were all present in *Content and Consciousness,* but they were clarified in "Intentional Systems" (1971) when I introduced the idea that an intentional system was, by definition, anything that was amenable to analysis by a certain tactic, which I called the intentional stance. This is the tactic of interpreting an entity by adopting the presupposition that it is an approximation of the ideal of an optimally designed (i.e., rational) self-regarding agent. No attempt is made to confirm or disconfirm this presupposition, nor is it necessary to try to specify, in advance of specific analyses, wherein consists rationality. Rather, the presupposition provides leverage for generating specific predictions of behavior, via defeasible hypotheses about the content of the control states of the entity.

My initial analysis of the intentional stance and its relation to the design stance and physical stance was addressed to a traditional philosophical issue—the problem of free will and the task of reconciling mechanism and responsibility (1973). The details, however, grew out of my reflections on practices and attitudes I observed to be ubiquitous in Artificial Intelligence. Both Allen Newell (1982) and David Marr (1982) arrived at essentially the same breakdown of stances in their own reflections on the foundations of cognitive science. The concept of intentional systems (and particularly, higher-order intentional systems) has been successfully exploited in clinical and developmental psychology, ethology, and other domains of cognitive science, but philosophers have been reluctant to endorse the main metaphysical implications of the theory.

In particular, I have held that since *any* attributions of function necessarily invoke optimality or rationality assumptions, the attributions of intentionality that depend on them are *interpretations* of the phenomena—a "heuristic overlay" (1969), describing an inescapably idealized "real pattern" (see chap. 5 of this volume). Like such *abstracta* as centers of gravity and parallelograms of force, the beliefs and desires posited by the highest stance have no independent and concrete existence, and since this is the case, there would be no deeper facts that could settle the issue if—most improbably—rival intentional interpretations arose that did equally well at rationalizing the history of behavior of an entity. Quine's thesis of the indeterminacy of radical translation carries all the way in, as the thesis of the indeterminacy of radical interpretation of mental states and processes.

The fact that cases of radical indeterminacy, though possible in principle, are vanishingly unlikely ever to confront us is small solace, apparently. This idea is deeply counterintuitive to many philosophers, who have hankered for more "realistic" doctrines. There are two different strands of "realism" that I have tried to undermine:

1. realism about the entities purportedly described by our everyday mentalistic discourse—what I dubbed folk psychology (1981)—such as beliefs, desires, pains, the self;

2. realism about content itself—the idea that there have to be events or entities that *really* have intentionality (as opposed to the events and entities that only behave *as if* they had intentionality).

Against (1), I have wielded various arguments, analogies, parables. Consider what we should tell the benighted community of people who speak of "having fatigues" where we speak of being tired, exhausted, etc. (1978a) They want us to tell them what fatigues *are*, what bodily states or events they are identical with, and so forth. This is a confusion that calls for diplomacy, not philosophical discovery; the choice between an "eliminative materialism" and an "identity theory" of fatigues is not a matter of which "ism" is right, but of which way of speaking is most apt to wean these people of a misbegotten feature of their conceptual scheme.

Against (2), my attack has been more indirect. I view the philosophers' demand for content realism as an instance of a common philosophical mistake. Philosophers often maneuver themselves into a position from which they can see only two alternatives: infinite regress versus some sort of "intrinsic" foundation—a prime mover of one sort or another. For instance, it has seemed obvious that for some things to be valuable as means, other things must be intrinsically valuable—ends in themselves—otherwise we'd be stuck with a vicious regress (or circle) of things valuable only as means. It has seemed similarly obvious that although some intentionality is "derived" (the aboutness of the pencil-marks composing a shopping list is derived from the intentions of the person whose list it is), unless some intentionality is *original* and underived, there could be no derived intentionality.

There is always another alternative, which naturalistic philosophers should look on with favor: a *finite* regress that peters out without marked foundations or thresholds or essences. Here is an easily avoided paradox: every mammal has a mammal for a mother—but this implies an infinite genealogy of mammals, which cannot be the case. The solution is not to search for an essence of mammalhood that would permit us in principle to identify the Prime Mammal, but rather to tolerate a finite regress that connects mammals to their nonmammalian ancestors by a sequence that can only be partitioned arbitrarily. The reality of today's mammals is secure without foundations.

The best-known instance of this theme in my work is the idea that the way to explain the miraculous-seeming powers of an intelligent intentional system is to decompose it into hierarchically structured teams of ever more stupid intentional systems, ultimately discharging all intelligence-debts in a fabric of stupid mechanisms (1971; 1974; 1978a; 1991a). Lycan (1981) has called this view homuncular functionalism. One may be tempted to ask: Are the subpersonal components *real* intentional systems? At what point in the diminution of prowess as we descend to simple neurons does *real* intentionality disappear? Don't ask. The reasons for regarding an individual neuron (or a thermostat) as an intentional system are unimpressive, but not zero, and the security of our intentional attributions at the highest levels does not depend on our identifying a lowest level of real intentionality. Another exploitation of the same idea is found in *Elbow Room* (1984d): At what point in evolutionary history did real reason-appreciators, real selves, make their appearance? Don't ask—for the same reason. Here is yet another, more fundamental, version: At what point in the early days of evolution can we speak of *genuine* function, genuine *selection-for* and not mere fortuitous preservation of entities that happen to have some self-replicative capacity? Don't ask. Many of the most interesting and important features of our world have emerged, gradually, from a world that initially lacked them—function, intentionality, consciousness, morality, value—and it is a fool's errand to try to identify a first or most simple instance of the "real" thing. It is for the same reason a mistake to suppose that real differences in the world must exist to answer all the questions our systems of content attribution permit us to ask. Tom says he has an older brother living in Cleveland *and* that he is an only child (1975b). What does he *really* believe? Could he really believe that he had a brother if he also believed he was an only child? What is the *real* content of his mental state? There is no reason to suppose there is a principled answer.

The most sweeping conclusion I have drawn from this theory of content is that the large and well-regarded literature on propositional attitudes (especially the debates over wide versus narrow content, *"de re versus de dicto"* attributions, and what Pierre believes about London) is largely a disciplinary artifact of no long-term importance whatever, except perhaps as history's most slowly unwinding unintended reductio ad absurdum. By and large the disagreements explored in that literature cannot even be given an initial expression unless one takes on the assumptions I have argued are fundamentally unsound (see especially 1975b; 1978a; 1982a; 1987, chap. 8; and chap. 5 of this volume): strong realism about content, and its constant companion, the idea of a language of thought, a system of mental *representation* that is decomposable into elements rather like terms, and larger elements rather like sentences. The illusion that this is inevitable, or even plausible, is particularly fostered by the philosophers' normal tactic of working from examples of "believing-that-*p*" that focus attention on mental states that are directly or indirectly language-infected, such as believing that the shortest spy is a spy, or believing that snow is white. (Do polar bears believe that snow is white? In the way we do?) There are such states—in language-using human beings—but they are not exemplary or foundational states of belief; needing a term for them, I call them *opinions* ("How to Change your Mind," in 1978a; see also chap. 4 of this volume). Opinions play a large, perhaps even decisive, role in our concept of a person, but they are not paradigms of the sort of cognitive element to which one can assign content in the first instance. If one starts, as one should, with the cognitive states and events occurring in nonhuman animals, and uses these as the foundation on which to build theories of human cognition, the language-infected states are more readily seen to be derived, less directly implicated in the explanation of behavior, and the chief but illicit source of plausibility of the doctrine of a language of thought. Postulating a language of thought is in any event a postponement of the central problems of content ascription, not a necessary first step. (Although a few philosophers—especially Ruth Garrett Millikan, Robert Stalnaker, Stephen White—have agreed with me about large parts of this sweeping criticism, they have sought less radical accommodations with the prevailing literature.)

3   Consciousness as a Virtual Machine

My theory of consciousness has undergone more revisions over the years than my theory of content. In *Content and Consciousness*, the theory concentrated on the role of language in constituting the peculiar but definitive characteristics of human consciousness, and while I continue to argue for a crucial role of natural language in generating the central features of consciousness (our kind), my first version overstated the case in several regards. For instance, I went slightly too far in my dismissal of mental imagery (see the corrections in 1978a; 1991a), and I went slightly too fast—but not too far!—in my treatment of color vision, which was unconvincing at the time, even though it made all the right moves, as recent philosophical work on color has confirmed, in my opinion. But my biggest mistake in *Content and Consciousness* was positing a watershed somewhere in the brain, the "awareness line," with the following property: revisions of content that occurred prior to crossing the awareness line *changed the content* of consciousness; later revisions (or errors) counted as postexperiential tamperings; all adjustments of content, veridical or not, could be located, in principle, on one side or the other of this postulated line. The first breach of this intuitive but ultimately indefensible doctrine occurred in "Are Dreams Experiences?" (1975a), in which I argued that the distinction between proper and improper entry into memory (and thence into introspective report, for instance) could not be sustained in close quarters. Related arguments appeared in "Two Approaches to Mental Imagery" (in 1978a) and "Quining Qualia" (1988e), but only in *Consciousness Explained* (1991a) and "Time and the Observer" (Dennett and Kinsbourne, 1992b) was an alternative positive model of consciousness sketched in any detail, the Multiple Drafts model.

The best way to understand this model is in contrast to the traditional model, which I call the Cartesian Theater. The fundamental work done by any observer can be characterized as confronting something "given" and *taking* it—responding to it with one interpretive judgment or another. This corner must be turned somehow and somewhere in any model of consciousness. On the traditional view, all the taking is deferred until the raw given, the raw materials of stimulation, have been processed in various ways and sent to central headquarters. Once each bit is "finished" it can enter consciousness and be appreciated for the first time. As C. S. Sherrington (1934) put it:

The mental action lies buried in the brain, and in that part most deeply recessed from the outside world that is furthest from input and output.

In the Multiple Drafts model, this single unified taking is broken up in cerebral space and real time; the judgmental tasks are fragmented into many distributed moments of micro-taking (Dennett and Kins-bourne, 1992b). Since there is no place where "it all comes together," no line the crossing of which is definitive of the end of preconscious processing and the beginning of conscious appreciation, many of the familiar philosophical assumptions about the denizens of human phenomenology turn out to be simply wrong, in spite of their traditional obviousness.

For instance, from the perspective provided by this model one can see more clearly the incoherence of the absolutist assumptions that make *qualia* seem like a good theoretical idea. It follows from the Multiple Drafts model that "inverted spectrum" and "absent qualia" thought experiments, like the thought experiments encountered in the propositional attitude literature (Twin Earth, what Pierre believes, beliefs about the shortest spy), are fundamentally misbegotten, and for a similar reason: the "common-sense" assumption of "realism" with regard to the mental items in question—beliefs, in the first instance, qualia, in the second—is too strong.

4   Overview

The intermediate ontological position I recommend—I call it "mild realism"—might be viewed as my attempt at a friendly amendment to Ryle's (1949) tantalizing but unpersuasive claims about category mistakes and different senses of "exist" (see especially 1969, chap. 1; and chap. 5 of this volume). What do you get when you cross a Quine with a Ryle? A Dennett, apparently. But there is a novel texture to my work, and an attitude, which grows primarily, I think, from my paying attention to the actual details of the sciences of the mind—and asking philosophical questions about those details. This base camp in the sciences has permitted me to launch a host of differently posed arguments, drawing on overlooked considerations. These arguments do not simply add another round to the cycle of debate, but have some hope of dislodging the traditional intuitions with which philosophers previously had to start. For instance, from this vantage point one can see the importance of evolutionary models (1969; 1974; 1978a; 1983a; 1984d; 1990a; 1990b) and, concomitantly, the perspective of cognitive science as reverse engineering (1989; 1991a; and chap. 16 of this volume), which goes a long way to overcoming the conservative mindset of pure philosophy. The idea that a mind could be a contraption composed of hundreds or thousands of gadgets takes us a big step away from the overly familiar mind presupposed by essentially all philosophers from Descartes to the present.

Something else of mine that owes a debt to Quine and Ryle is my philosophical style. No sentence from Quine or Ryle is ever dull, and their work always exhibits the importance of *addressing* an audience of nonphilosophers, even when they know that philosophers will be perhaps 95% of their actual and sought-for audience. They also both embody a healthy skepticism about the traditional methods and presuppositions of our so-called discipline, an attitude to which I have always resonated. I have amplified these points, attempting to follow their example in my own writing. But I have also been self-conscious about philosophical methods and their fruits, and presented my reflections in various meta-level digressions, in particular about the role of intuition pumps in philosophy (1980; 1984d; 1991a), and about the besetting foible of philosophers: mistaking failures of imagination for insights into necessity.

My insistence on the need for philosophers to stoke up on the relevant science before holding forth, and my refusal to conduct my investigations by the traditional method of definition and formal argument, have made me a distinctly impure philosopher of mind. Moreover, on both main topics, content and consciousness, I maintain a "radical" position, which in rather lonely and implausible fashion declares that much of the work at the presumed cutting edge is beyond salvage. I thus cut myself off from some of the controversies that capture the imaginations of others in the field, but the philosophical problems that arise directly in nonphilosophical research in cognitive science strike me as much more interesting, challenging, and substantive. So I concentrate on them: the frame problem (chaps. 11 and 12 of this volume), problems about mental imagery and "filling in" (1992a), the binding problem and the problem of temporal anomalies (1991a; Dennett and Kinsbourne, 1992b). I take these to be the real, as opposed to artifactual, problems of mental representation, and I encourage philosophers of mind to contribute to their solution.

26

Information, Technology and the Virtues of Ignorance

If there is one thing philosophers agree upon in ethics, it is that "ought" implies "can"; what is beyond your powers is beyond your obligations. Computers, then, are a mixed blessing, since they vastly increase our powers, and hence threaten — yes, threaten — to increase our obligations, making it harder, not easier, to live a decent life. In the mid-1980s, I began devoting a much larger share of my time and energy to computers — to learning and teaching about them, to creating educational software at Tufts's Curricular Software Studio, and to thinking and talking about the impact computer technology was going to have on human culture. Computers could ruin our lives, I realized. I began to worry about how to write The Moral First Aid Manual, *an imaginary vade mecum to consult until the Doctor of Philosophy arrives. It is an unfinished project to which I am now returning, having learned how much more complicated the issues are than I surmised in this opening gambit.*

When I was about ten years old, I read *Robinson Crusoe* for the first time and could scarcely contain my delight with the ingenious and resourceful ways Crusoe transformed his island world, bending its inventory to his own purposes, surrounding himself with contrivances of his own design and manufacture for enhancing his powers, and providing for his safety, nourishment, and pleasure. I discovered right then that that I was in love with technology, as no doubt many of you are. We should recognize—we technophiles—that our love affair with technology, like all good love affairs, is not entirely rational, try as we might to rationalize our devotions. Crusoe the technocrat—it is one of the great fantasy themes, right up there with sexual adventure, athletic triumph, being able to fly, being invisible. It rivals them all in its capti-

Originally appeared in *Dædalus*, Journal of the American Academy of Arts and Sciences, "Art and Science, " 115 (3), Summer 1986, pp. 135–153. Reprinted with permission.

vation, in the luxuriousness of its details in our minds' eyes. It is far more satisfying than magic, precisely because it is *not* magic; it is something *we create*, and hence are presumably responsible for; it is something we *understand*, presumably, and hence, presumably, control.

We live today in a wonderful world in which the fantasy of unlimited technological enhancement seems to be coming true. This is convenient for us technophiles, for we can point to the many blessings our loved one has provided for us all—even the ingrates. Which technophobe would choose to live the harrowing and desperate life of the medieval peasant or the Stone Age hunter? Yet, like Crusoe, we pay some price for whatever we gain, requiring some minor revision in our habits, some curtailing of our options, some petty irritations that crop up as side effects with the adoption of each new marvel. Some find it easy to push these slightly nagging debits into the background; they say "Yes, there are costs of course, but it's not worth our while trying to sum them—whatever they come to, they are a small price to pay for the gains." Others find their uneasiness harder to quell; they wonder if, when we total costs of some of the more indirect effects of our new technology are rendered, we may not find that we have moved imperceptibly into a world we do not know how to inhabit and cannot leave.

I propose to focus attention on certain troubling aspects of the relationship between technology and morality.[1] I wish to consider the possibility that information technology, which has been a great boon in the past, is today poised to *ruin our lives*—unless we are able to think up some fairly radical departures from the traditions that have so far sustained us.

We all want to lead good lives—in at least two senses. We want to lead lives that are interesting, exciting, fulfilling, and happy, and we want to lead lives that are morally good as well: we would like to be useful, and to make a difference—a difference in the right direction, whatever direction that is. There is no doubt that technology in the past has facilitated both these aspirations, freeing us from drudgery and misery, making it possible for many of us to improve the lives of others. But unless we can find solutions to certain problems, the curve

---

1. These reflections have grown out of discussions in the Norbert Wiener Forum, a policy workshop at Tufts, funded by the CSK corporation of Japan, and under the co-directorship, currently, of Professors Tadatoshi Akiba and David Isles. Earlier versions of parts of this paper were presented at the joint meeting of the Norbert Wiener Forum with its counterpart forum at Tokai University in Japan, July, 1985, and in lectures at the MIT Laboratory for Computer Science, and the Yale Humanities Center in Spring 1986.

will turn. We have reached a point where the advance of technology makes the *joint realization* of these two goals less likely—we may have to make an unpalatable choice between lives that are morally good, and lives that are interesting.

Since my message is one that many may find unpalatable, it may be useful for me to start with a very specific instance of the trend that concerns me, before drawing on it for wider implications. As technology imposes new sources of knowledge, it renders obsolete the standards that guided our actions in the past. Consider the rural doctor. Today, there are doctors who have chosen, commendably, to forsake lucrative urban or suburban practices for more valuable and meaningful lives as doctors in small rural communities. Their virtues have often been sung (most recently and convincingly by McPhee, 1985), so I need not dwell on them. These doctors know their patients well; their personal, intricate, involved knowledge stands them in good stead when they come to diagnose, treat and advise the members of their communities.

Such doctors are, for better or for worse, an endangered species. Technology is on the verge of rendering their style of medical treatment not just obsolete, but—because of its obsolescence—morally indefensible. As expert systems for medical diagnosis become available, such doctors will have to decide whether or not to avail themselves of the new technology. Let us suppose, for the sake of argument, that the systems will work as well as their supporters claim; they really will provide swift, reliable, accurate diagnoses of ailments across with as wide a spectrum of cases as the average physician is apt to encounter.

If so, the doctors, in good conscience, will have no choice: they will have to avail themselves of expert systems. To choose not to equip themselves with the best available means of securing accurate diagnosis would be a gross dereliction of duty, just as if—for some romantic whim—they chose to deny themselves use of a telephone, or insisted on making their rounds on horseback, or refused to consult x-rays before operating. Quaintness is fine when matters of life and death are not at stake, but few would be charmed by a doctor who insisted on relying on old-fashioned methods, particularly if it meant a serious and avoidable risk of misdiagnosis or mistreatment.

Doctors have always been obliged to keep up-to-date about their medicine, and, typically, have responded to this obligation with fairly serious efforts to stay abreast of medical journals, to take refresher courses, and so forth. The situation has been getting out of hand; until

now, rural doctors have been somewhat excused from knowing everything their urban counterparts are held responsible for—there are limits to what people can be expected to carry around in their heads.

But now the technology is promised that will render those limits
obsolete. All you will have to do is install a modem and a cellular
telephone in your four-wheel drive van and have, at your fingertips,
a credible approximation of the finest corps of specialist consultants,
available twenty four hours a day. It would be a curious sort of moral
stand that one would have to take to resist becoming reliant on such
a system. How dare you turn your back on such a fine source of information, when lives—lives entrusted in your care—depend on your
giving the best informed diagnoses of which you are capable?

The standards of excusable ignorance for even the most isolated of
rural doctors will shift, and the doctors will be required to alter their
practices to meet wholly new standards. All doctors will be expected
to avail themselves of the new technology, just as all doctors now are
required to maintain standards of antiseptic practice. We may suppose
that expert systems will enable doctors to practice much better medicine, but in order to use expert systems they will have to relinquish
something they may well have prized in their earlier modus operandi.

At present, rural doctors can take a rather varied and informal approach to gathering facts about their patients. If old Sam looks OK,
and sounds just about the way he always sounds at this time of year,
and doesn't complain about anything new, the doctor can leave well
enough alone. Besides, if there really is anything new wrong with old
Sam, it is too esoteric, or too obscure at this stage, for the rural doctor
to be expected to be able to diagnose. After all, rural medicine is not
the Massachusetts General Hospital. But expert systems will change
this. Doctors will be obliged to ask all their patients a battery of questions they were never obliged to ask before—for what, in good conscience, could they have done with the answers?

They will also be obliged to perform a variety of generally simple
tests they were never obliged to perform before. They will be obliged
to do so because, ex hypothesi, the feeding of expert systems with such
data will have proven to be a practice that bears valuable results—
leading to a much higher rate of early diagnosis of treatable cancer,
for instance. Gathering information by these two methods—asking
questions and performing simple tests—will be made as easy, straightforward, unequivocal as possible. It will be made *as routine as possible,*
for the more routine it is, the more uniform the feeding of the expert

systems will be, and hence the less likelihood there will be of misinforming them.

In this way, the "art" of diagnosis, and the "art" of "taking a patient's history" will be reduced, as far as ingenuity can manage, to something in which there is no "art" but only the capacity to follow directions. I am not claiming that such systems would place a positive value on the deliberate suppression of imaginative, "artful" investigation and diagnosis, but just that whatever room remained for such activities would be the room left over *after* the doctors had done their duty and asked all the *obligatory* questions and performed all the *obligatory* tests.

Since the direction of "progress" in medicine (and technology generally) proceeds by replacing art with obligatory practices whenever and wherever the principles governing the "art" become well enough understood and justified to be codified, we can expect that insofar as the technology of medical diagnosis succeeds, insofar as it becomes so demonstrably reliable that doctors will be obliged to use it, it will do this by diminishing the regular, daily contribution of the practitioners who use it. Once in a while, one can presume, the artful doctor will find a moment in which to exercise his or her art, and even save a life now and then by filling a gap in the technology, but these will become rarer opportunities as the technology improves.

And so, a subspecies of doctor will become extinct, succeeded by a new species that delegates more and more diagnostic responsibility to expert systems, not because of the doctors' indolence or stupidity, but simply because they will not be able to defend the claim that they can do as well or better without the systems.

Should we mourn the passing of this species of doctor? We can see why, from the doctors' own point of view, they might well regret this development: it will makes their own lives less exciting, less indispensable; they will begin to slide down the slippery slope toward being mere go-betweens, mere living interfaces between patient and system, consolidating their direct observations into machine-readable symptomatology, and executing the therapeutic directives of the system.

It may help to conceive of their predicament if we imagine their secret yearnings: they will occasionally be tempted to "live dangerously," to "fly by the seat of their pants," to take risks with their patients' lives just to prove to themselves that they still have the "right stuff"—that they can do barehanded diagnosis as well as the best of the old-time doctors, the swashbuckling specialists of the 1970s and

1980s. The more adventurous (or self-indulgent) of them may seek out those few exotic environments where they can practice medicine released from the obligation to use the boring technology—much the way people like to "rough it" by going camping or sailing small boats across the ocean. But thanks to communication satellites, even Robinson Crusoe's island will provide no asylum for the physician who seeks refuge from expert systems. Being a doctor won't be anywhere near as much fun in the future.

This extinction of social roles is a familiar process in history. There was a time when artists, calligraphers, potters, and tailors were much more essential to their communities than they are now. Although there is still a role for such artists, it is a luxury role; some people are willing to pay extra for that special, personal, artistic touch—but the realm in which the handmade is superior to the machine-made has shrunk to an almost purely ceremonial, even mystical remnant of its former status.

Fortunately for potters, there are still enough people who prize handmade pottery so that one can sustain a career as a potter, but the social position of the potter has been ineluctably damaged; potters aren't as needed as they once were. Hence while being a potter is still a pretty good life compared with most others—it has more than its share of satisfactions and delights—it is not as good a life as it once was, since any reflective potter must recognize that he or she survives by satisfying the desires of a rather rarified subset of the population. Doctors won't even be that lucky, for who in his right mind would acquire a taste for funky, handmade medical care—just like Grandma used to get?

No doubt the rich and foolish would recognize a certain *cachet* in keeping a personal—and personable—physician in their entourage. Compare this doctor of the future with the apartment doorman. This descendant of the concierge, who had a relatively challenging and varied life work, has an almost purely ceremonial function today. One can telephone for a taxi with greater ease than your obliging doorman can lure one to the door, and the security he provides is typically almost redundant, given the twenty-four-hour surveillance and alarm system. But it looks nice to have a doorman. It adds a personal touch—of sorts. It's posh to live somewhere that is so well-heeled that it can afford to pay a grown human being to stand around in a uniform smiling all day. The doorman's life is not pleasant to contemplate; it is a travesty of human service, however well reimbursed.

Every doctor must begin to worry that he or she is heading toward becoming a sort of health-care doorman. Can it be that in another generation, all that will be left of today's doctor will be minimal "computer literacy" and a bedside manner?

The advocates of expert systems in medicine will be aching to intervene here by pointing out that far from diminishing the life of the physician, expert systems will enhance it! The physician will have *more* time to spend dealing personally with patients, and can care effectively with *more* patients, because the drudgery and galling uncertainty or poring through textbooks and journals for snatches of half-remembered wisdom will be eliminated. Yes, and today's apartment doorman can "deal personally" with ten times as many inhabitants as the old-fashioned concierge could, since all the drudgery has been removed from his life as well. The doorman has certainly been relieved of drudgery, but also of responsibility, variety of challenge, and autonomy. Like the Cheshire cat, all that is left is the smile. As the responsibility for diagnosis and treatment shifts imperceptibly away from the physician—the "field operative"—and lodges in the expert system (or system of expert systems), doctors will suffer a similar—if less drastic—diminution of role.

Notice that I am not saying that today's rural doctors are heroes, and that their sad fate is the result of evil, rapacious technocrats seducing them out of their noble lives. Greed and evil intentions do not come into the equation at all—though of course they are not in short supply. It is precisely because doctors want to practice the best medicine they can that they will find it incumbent on them to make these choices; for they will see that they will actually be able to save lives more reliably and efficiently by availing themselves of the technology. The interesting and risky life they had been leading will no longer be morally defensible, so, wanting to be responsible and do good, they will have to settle for a less exciting service role. We may suppose equally pure and altruistic motives on the part of those who design, develop, and promote the technology. They do not *intend* to spoil career opportunities; it is simply one of the foreseeable side-effects of their effort to do a better job of saving lives through technology. What I am talking about is not a cheap melodrama with a convenient villain at which I can shake my finger, but more in the nature of a tragedy.

In a tragedy, according to the theorists, the hero's ultimate fate must be seen to be inevitable, and that is one reason why I shrink from calling this a tragedy. If I thought that this unhappy dénouement were strictly inevitable, I would perhaps have decided to keep the grim news to myself. How, then, might some other future await the physicians?

First, of course, the technology of expert systems may not turn out to work all that well. We may discover that expert systems are so limited and unreliable, taken by themselves, that doctors will still have to be very self-reliant, very individually knowledgeable, very artful in the use they make of the technology. Perhaps they will not even be obliged to use it, so untrustworthy will it prove to be. (In several conversations with advocates of such technology I have been amused to be assured, most solemnly, that I have vastly overestimated the actual powers of expert systems. These spokespeople for expert systems have failed to see the irony in their protestations: "Don't worry!" they say: "These expert systems aren't going to be *reliable!*—they aren't going to be *foolproof!* Why, in the hands of an unskilled practitioner they would be positively dangerous!" I am strongly inclined to agree, but if I had told them that, they would have dismissed me as a technology-hating humanist.)

So that is one hopeful route: this particular technology *won't work* after all, and hence won't be obligatory, and hence won't spread to destroy this enviable and admirable variety of human life. If one thought that the technology *might* work, and thought that preserving the way of life of today's physician was of prime importance, one could take steps to avert this future: either by the Luddite tactic of destroying expert systems as they appeared; or by attempting to prohibit or prevent the development and improvement of the technology in the first place. But Luddism has never worked well in the past. It tends to postpone crises and aggravate situations, and is in any event not likely to inspire those who would have to support the policy today.

Alternatively, it may turn out that I have overestimated the physicians' commitment to practicing the best medicine they can. According to several observers, many doctors have given the new expert systems a lukewarm reception largely because they are more interested in "talking shop" with consultants, and in spreading liability, than in obtaining diagnostic assistance. If such resistance is widespread, it may prevent the public from perceiving the value of expert systems, and thereby keep the obligation to use them at bay.

Finally, of course, one could decide that saving the role of *midtwentieth century physician* was, in the end, no more defensible a goal than saving the role of the linotype operator in the production of newspapers. These roles must pass, perhaps, and as long as we ease the plight of the current holders of these positions, and prevent the recruitment of a new generation, little harm will be done to specific individuals. People in the future will just have other, no doubt, better occupations.

While that sentiment has a certain plausibility when the displaced workers are miners, linotype operators or secretaries, it is far from clear what exalted work will remain for displaced physicians. And if a social role as obviously valuable and impressive as that of the physician is in jeopardy, what will happen to the rest of us?[2]

Let us review the situation: if expert systems in medicine live up to their advertised promise, then the tradition and the current trajectory of development suggest that they will probably ruin one of the most exciting and fulfilling career opportunities in modern life. They won't destroy it, but they will diminish it greatly; people who want to live a good life and not just do good in life will want to think twice before entering this part of the service sector. Perhaps the role of physician is not worth preserving. Or, perhaps expert systems won't be all that powerful, so that physicians will not be obliged to cede their responsibility to them. Or, hoping that expert systems will fail to establish themselves, we might even take steps, violent or legislative, to forestall their deployment.

I see two further possibilities. First and most likely is that we will get the worst of both worlds: expert systems will not work anywhere near well enough for physicians to be *obliged* to rely on them, but the physicians will come to depend on them anyway, succumbing to the pressure of overoptimistic public opinion, lack of self-confidence, and even laziness, greed, and fear of malpractice suits. Second and somewhat utopian, but certainly worth striving for: perhaps we can design computer systems that support only the wily and self-reliant physician. We should look for design principles that would lead to the creation of systems that preserve or (better yet) enhance the contribution of the individual physician, while not sacrificing diagnostic power. I do not think that designing such systems is impossible, but it will not be easy, and it will require thinking about the design task in a different way.

Compare expert systems to musical instruments: today's expert systems are rather like autoharps, designed so that anyone can learn to

2. "Even physicians, formerly a culture's very symbol of power, are powerless as they increasingly become mere conduits between their patients and the major drug manufacturers." (Weizenbaum, 1976, p. 259).

play them, and with an easily reached plateau of skill. We should aim instead to develop systems more like violins and pianos—instruments that indefinitely extend and challenge the powers of the individual.

Do I have any proposals about how to do this? In fact, I do have some tentative ideas on this score, growing out of my work with my colleague George Smith at Tufts's Curricular Software Studio (Dennett, 1982c; Smith, 1986). We are creating several different kinds of "concept pianos" for the exploration of complex phenomena—such as population genetics and the computer's own internal architecture. If our ideas survive their current testing, we shall subsequently present them as steps toward a new design philosophy for expert systems, but in the meanwhile there is still plenty of philosophical work to be done on these issues, to which I will devote my remaining remarks.

Why should doctors find themselves riding this obligation-train to tedium? To understand this particular phenomenon, we must step back and take a more general view of the relations between information technology and our ethical lives as decision-making agents.

Our ancestors were, relative to us, epistemically impoverished: there were few means of finding out much about nonlocal, nonimmediate effects and problems, so they could plan and act with a clear conscience on the basis of a more or less manageable stock of local knowledge. They were thus *capable* of living lives of virtue—of a virtue that *depended on* unavoidable ignorance. Modern technology has robbed us of the sorts of virtue that depend on such ignorance. Ignorance is all too avoidable today. Information technology has multiplied our *opportunities to know*, and our traditional ethical doctrines overwhelm us by turning these opportunities into newfound *obligations to know*.

We have always had "principles of excusable ignorance." According to tradition, we are responsible for knowing whatever is "common knowledge," plus whatever is the received wisdom of those who occupy our specialized social role—such as the role of physician—plus whatever is obviously and directly relevant to our particular circumstances of the moment. We are all responsible for knowing the standardly understood relationships between smoke and fire, rainstorms and slippery roads, voting and democracy. Plumbers—but only plumbers—have been responsible for knowing the particular effects, opportunities, and hazards of the plumbing trade, and everyone is responsible for knowing whether anyone is standing behind one's car before backing out of a parking place.

The rough-hewn boundaries of these classes of knowledge were fixed by default by the limitations of human capacity. One could not be expected to carry around vast quantities of information in one's head, nor to calculate, in the time available, any of the longer-range effects of action. We have just seen in some detail how technology interacts with the obligation to know in a specialized field, but its effects on "common knowledge" are even more severe and imponderable.

"Common knowledge" is no longer the relatively stable, inertial mass it once was. We *can* acquire knowledge almost effortlessly on almost any topic; when knowledge is "at your fingertips," how can you not be responsible for acquiring it? The obligation to know—a burden of guilt that weighs excruciatingly on every academic, but that in milder forms is ubiquitous today—creates the situation where, if we read everything we "ought" to read, we would do nothing else. Thanks to science and mass communication, we *all* now know that we don't just have to worry about someone standing behind our car when we back up; we also have to wonder about the effects of our personal auto-driving (and auto-buying) activities on air pollution, acid rain, the local and global economy, and so forth.[3]

The well-known glut of information has inspired a host of responses from those who must cope with it, or wish to exploit it. Since everyone knows that no one can possibly keep abreast of all this information, meta-techniques and meta-strategies and meta-meta-structures and meta-meta-meta-tactics have arisen. The "common knowledge" we are now held responsible for knowing is not the whole of what is in fact almost instantaneously *available* to just about everyone, but rather a small, shifting core of what might be called "temporarily famous" common knowledge. (Recall Andy Warhol's prediction of the future time when each person will be famous for fifteen minutes.) Getting items of information into the spotlight of temporary fame has become a major enterprise. Whether your problem is the eradication of Third World hunger, the deposition of an evil dictator, stopping the Star Wars lunacy, or selling cornflakes, your solution is going to have to start with

---

3. "Now I used to think that I was cool
Runnin' around on fossil fuel
Until I saw what I was doin'
Was drivin' down the road to ruin"
—James Taylor, "Damn This Traffic Jam"

"advertising": attracting the fleeting attention of the well-intentioned, and *imposing* your item of information on their good intentions.

So much information is available that mere accessibility is no better than invisibility. Most books that are published are not read, and even being read does not guarantee their influence. This depends on higher-order effects: a book must not only be reviewed, but (thanks to the reviews) included on some influential list of books to be read, etc. If it achieves sufficient visibility in the higher-order structures, it need not even be read to have vast influence. This profusion of information filters, duplicators and amplifiers is the product of helter-skelter competition, and there is little reason to suppose this process is anything like optimal. On the contrary, there is good reason to suppose that there is scant direct relationship between the content and value of information and its capacity to exploit the structures in the publicity environment and reproduce itself across the society.

Richard Dawkins's excellent book, *The Selfish Gene* (1976) introduces the idea of what he calls *memes*—a "new kind of replicator" living in "the soup of human culture." Memes are, to a first approximation, ideas in particular forms—the sort of thing one might be able to copyright:

Examples of memes are tunes, ideas, catch-phrases, clothes fashions, ways of making pots or of building arches. Just as genes propagate themselves in the gene pool by leaping from body to body via sperm or eggs, so memes propagate themselves in the meme pool by leaping from brain to brain via a process which, in the broad sense, can be called imitation. (Dawkins, 1976, p. 206)

The analogy between memes and genes runs deep, as Dawkins shows. Recasting my argument in his terms, my claim is that, thanks to *some* technological memes, we have entered a population explosion of memes—parasites which are overwhelming their hosts. Unless we can find some new ideas, some antibodies for these new antigens, we are in for a hard time. The new memes we need will be *conceptual* innovations, not just new technology.

It is technology that has created this embarrassment of riches. To see this, consider our obligations to those in misery on other planets. It is quite possible that there is life elsewhere in the universe, and if there is life, there is almost certainly misery as well. Fortunately for us, the most shocking and gruesome calamities on other planets—plagues, obscene dictatorships, nuclear holocausts—are nothing to us, because even if we knew about them (which, fortunately for our peace of mind, we don't), there would be absolutely nothing we could do about them. Perhaps we should be wary about proceeding with the project Carl Sagan champions of trying to communicate with the civilizations on other planets; after all, we might succeed, and find that their first message to us was a heart-rending plea for help—together with detailed information on just how we could be of assistance![4]

Not so long ago, on the astronomical or even biological time scale, the Western Hemisphere was as remote from the Eastern as any planet is from us now. Even well into the nineteenth century, few people had the knowledge and power to have any clear obligations to anyone or anything beyond their local communities. The average person then could not reasonably expect to have much effect on the lives of those in distant lands, and hence was absolved from worrying about it. The question just did not arise—any more than the question of what to do about starvation in other solar systems arises for us.

A few people of enhanced power and knowledge found, however, that they could not hide behind their powerlessness. Their attitude was captured in the slogan *noblesse oblige:* those of noble birth had special obligations.[5] While the slogan originally applied only to the titled few, the idea was subsequently extended to all those who had power, inherited or otherwise acquired. The price they paid for their "noblesse," in this extended sense of their not having to devote their waking hours to providing daily bread and shelter, was an enlarged social purpose. In the nineteenth century, every well-read person could ask whether he or she shouldn't become fully committed to ending slavery, for instance, and many decided they should. And they did, in fact, just about eradicate slavery.

Others took on other causes, with varying degrees of success. It is often noted how curiously and sometimes eccentrically focused the moral sensitivities of such people can be, both then and now. Some antislavery crusaders were amazingly oblivious of the suffering of their own poor, the degradation of their own servants, the exploitation of the workers in their factories. And today there are single-minded zealots for the cause of environmentalism or animal rights who are apparently unmoved by the outrages committed against their own species by various dictators—at least they devote none of their energies to tak-

---

4. There are suggestive observations on the role of technology in expanding our moral universe in Peter Singer (1981) and in Derek Parfit (1984, part I).
5. Duc de Lévis, (1764–1830) *Maxims, Préceptes et Réflexions,* is the first use I have uncovered so far in my casual inquiries.

ing any action on these fronts. And there are nuclear disarmers who cannot be bothered to reform the sexism out of their own language and practices, or who routinely discard unopened all mail beseeching them to enlist in the cause of Amnesty International or Oxfam.

There can be little doubt how these exotic specimens of do-gooder come into existence. We are *all* of the noblesse these days. We all have the daunting luxury of the time, energy, knowledge, and power to undertake a broader purpose than merely staying alive and keeping our immediate kin in the same condition. Technology has created innumerable opportunities for us to know, and to act. We don't want to react to this bounty irresponsibly, but *we don't know how* to deal responsibly with the wealth of opportunities. When we turn to the question of which priority should engage our best efforts, we drown in the available information, and can make no truly principled decisions. The result is a sort of Rorschach magnification of whatever minor personal proclivities emerge from the noise of competing and imponderable alternatives. The results, as we have seen, may often be eccentric, but they are arguably better than the course chosen by those who sit on their hands and ignore all appeals, on the grounds that they cannot figure out—have no time to figure out—which appeal is the worthiest.

One would think that if there were any solution to this practical dilemma, it would come from philosophy, and more narrowly from ethics. But much as I would relish telling you that the humanists either have the answer or at least have undertaken the research program that ought to yield the answer, I must report that almost no direct attention has yet been paid to this ubiquitous and troubling moral problem by professional philosophers.

The reason is not hard to find. Ethics, like any theoretical enterprise in science, has always been conducted with the aid of idealizations. Reality, in all its messy particularity, is too complicated to theorize about, taken straight. A favorite idealization in ethics has been the useful myth of the moral agent with unlimited knowledge and time for ethical decision-making. For instance, consequentialist theories, such as the various brands of utilitarianism, declare that what ought to be done is always whatever course of action will have the best expected consequences *all things considered*. Consequentialists know perfectly well that no one can ever truly consider all things—even all relevant things—but have still chosen to couch their theories in terms of what the ideally reflective and conscientious decision-maker would have made of all the available facts. This presumably gives one a standard of conduct at which to aim, if never in fact to hit. *In practice,* we tend to overlook important considerations and bias our thinking in a hundred idiosyncratic ways, but *in principle* what we should do is what this ideal calculator of consequences decides will most probably maximize utility (or whatever we call the good consequences).

The brute fact that we are all finite and forgetful and have to rush to judgment is standardly regarded, not implausibly, as a real but irrelevant bit of friction in the machinery whose blueprint we are describing. It is as if there might be two disciplines—ethics proper, which undertakes the task of calculating the principles of what one ought to do under all circumstances—and then the less interesting, "merely practical" discipline of *Moral First Aid,* or *What to Do Until the Doctor of Philosophy Arrives,* which tells you, in rough-and-ready terms, how to make decisions under time pressure.

My suspicion is that traditional theories of ethics all either *depend on* or *founder on* the very sorts of friction that are ignored by the standard idealization. Information technology, by removing the friction, helps expose the emptiness of much that has passed for sound in ethics. For instance, a bench test that most ethical theories pass with flying colors is the problem: what should you do if you are walking along, minding your own business, and you hear a cry for help from a drowning man? But almost no one faces predicaments with that logical form any more; instead we hear, every day, while desperately trying to mind our own business, a thousand cries of help, complete with volumes of information on how we might oblige.[6] On this ubiquitous problem, traditional ethical systems are essentially reduced to silence or the most transparent handwaving.

This is too large a claim to support here, but I can at least sketch the problem as I currently see it. How could we write the *Moral First Aid Manual?* Or, might we replace the manual with something fancier: an Expert System for Moral Advice-Giving in Real Time?

The fantasy of just such an expert system often lurks in the shadows of ethical theory. "If what I ought to do is whatever has the highest

---

6. John Stuart Mill, in *Utilitarianism,* 1863, thought he could defend his utilitarianism thus: ". . . the occasions on which any person (except one in a thousand) has it in his power to . . . be a public benefactor . . . are but exceptional; and on these occasions alone is he called on to consider public utility; in every other case, private utility, the interest or happinesss of some few persons, is all he has to attend to." I doubt that this was an entirely convincing claim in 1863; it is transparently unrealistic today.

expected utility, how on earth shall I calculate it in the time available?" This question has been familiar for over a hundred years, and the standard response from the moral philosopher is John Stuart Mill's, who borrowed a technological metaphor from his own day:

> Nobody argues that the art of navigation is not founded on astronomy because sailors cannot wait to calculate the Nautical Almanac. Being rational creatures, they go to sea with it ready calculated; and all rational creatures go out upon the sea of life with their minds made up on the common questions of right and wrong. . . . (Mill, 1863, p. 31)

This is a fine idea today as it was in Mill's time, but what the comparison conceals is that the future position of the heavenly bodies could *actually* be calculated in advance, using the technology of the day. Where is the Moral Almanac that would guide the moral chooser through the stormy seas of life? We're still debugging it. Jeremy Bentham, Mill's contemporary, set out to create a "hedonic calculus," and while no one takes it seriously today, the descendants of this quaint museum piece are still being produced, elaborated, and, most of all, advertised, not just by philosophers, but by "cost-benefit analysts," computer modelers, and other futurologists.

What should be evident to computer scientists, if still fairly easy for philosophers to overlook, is that the idea of actually producing a reliable or authoritative consequentialist almanac of any generality is sheer fantasy, now and forever. Compare the demanding specifications for such a system with the now well-known limitations on far simpler forecasting and problem-solving tools. *Short*-range real-time weather forecasting, for instance, has reached useful levels of reliability by restricting itself severely to a handful of measures, coarse-grained data-grids, and relatively simple equations, and then exhausting the powers of the world's fastest super-computers. Reliable, long-range forecasting of the weather months into the future is probably computationally intractable under any circumstances.[7] If it proves not to be intractable, it will be only because microclimatic effects will be shown not to propagate chaotically after all. But we already know, from a thousand everyday experiences, that "microsocial" effects—for example, some unknown individual's dislike of Tylenol—wildly interfere with the best-laid human plans and social trends.

---

7. Very short-range forecasting of local disturbances such as thunderstorms and tornados is proving extremely difficult, but is currently receiving considerable attention from NASA and the expert systems community, among others.

Even supposing the prediction problem could somehow be tamed, the evaluation problem would remain. In chess-playing programs, the problem of when to terminate look-ahead and evaluate the resulting position has led to the framing of the *principle of quiescence:* Always look several moves beyond any flurry of exchanges and postpone final evaluation until a relatively quiescent board position obtains. This satisfactory, though not foolproof, strategy of chess design is systematically inapplicable to the design of our moral advice giver, because of what we might call the Three Mile Island Effect. It has now been several relatively quiescent years since the meltdown at Three Mile Island, but can we yet say, with confidence better than a coin flip, whether that was one of the good things that have happened, or one of the bad? If our imagined system were to generate a future path of probability p with Three Mile Island as its terminus, should it assign a high or low utility to the event? The trouble is, of course, that in life there is no checkmate, no fixed point finitely in the future at which we get one definitive result or another, from which we might calculate, by retrograde analysis, the actual values of the alternatives that lie along the paths followed and not followed. So there is no way, and *could be* no way, to tune the parameters of any prototype expert system we designed—except by the invocation, as usual, of ideology and hand-waving.

The suspicion that consequentialist theories are systematically infeasible in this way is nothing new. It has fueled support for the so-called Kantian or duty-based ethical alternative for over a century.[8] As the Pirate King says to Frederick, the self-styled "slave of duty" in *Pirates of Penzance*, "Always follow the dictates of your conscience, me boy— and chance the consequences!" The trouble is, of course, that such duty-based theories, while not always leading to results as comical or pathetic as Frederick's myopic posings and blunderings in *Pirates of Penzance*, have hardly coalesced into a stable and compelling system of recipes for real action. Kant's own *categorical imperative*, which he quite consciously conceived as the one and only rule that needed to

---

8. The Kantian philosopher, Onora O'Neill (1980), offers a convincing analysis of the fundamental embarrassment of utilitarianism: two competent and well-informed utilitarians, Garrett Hardin and Peter Singer, addressing the same issue (what if anything to do about famine relief), holding the same ethical theory, and having access to the same empirical information, arrive at opposing counsels: one thinks the case is compelling for dramatic forms of aid; to the other it is equally "obvious" that all such aid should be withheld (see also O'Neill, 1986).

be printed in the *Moral First Aid Manual,* appears today about as naive and impractical a guide as Bentham's hedonic calculus.

Still, it is a step in the right direction, and what *is* new is the opportunity to reconceive of these alternatives to consequentialism through the lens of Artificial Intelligence as responses to the inescapable demands of real-time heuristic decision-making. When viewed from this perspective, for instance, what would count as a justification or defense of an ethical principle shifts significantly. This opens up a promising research program in philosophy, in my opinion, and I think it will gain more than just jargon from its engineering perspective.

The first, general result is appealing: we can already see that since *any* "system" for ethical decision-making must be bounded arbitrarily by limitations that are far from content-neutral, no technological black-box oracle can give you a principled, objective, reliable answer to your ethical problems, no matter what anyone advertises. When the choice is between "flying by the seat of your own pants" on the one hand and paying to fly by the seat of somebody else's pants on the other, you are entitled to keep both the responsibility and the excitement to yourself.

Bibliography

Akins, K. A., 1988, "Information and Organisms: or Why Nature Doesn't Build Epistemic Engines," unpublished doctoral dissertation, Ann Arbor: University of Michigan.

———, 1993, "What Is It Like to Be Boring and Myopic?" in Dahlbom, B., ed., *Dennett and His Critics*, Oxford: Blackwell.

Albini, T. K., 1988, "The Unfolding of the Psychotherapeutic Process in a Four Year Old Patient with Incipient Multiple Personality Disorder" in Braun, B. (1988), p. 37.

American Psychiatric Association, 1980, *Diagnostic and Statistical Manual III*, Washington, DC: American Psychiatric Association.

Anscombe, G. E. M., 1957, *Intention*, Oxford: Blackwell.

Arbib, M., 1964, *Brains, Machines and Mathematics*, New York: McGraw Hill.

Axelrod, R., 1984, *The Evolution of Cooperation*, New York: Basic Books.

Bennett, J., 1976, *Linguistic Behaviour*, Cambridge: Cambridge University Press.

———, 1983, "Cognitive Ethology: Theory or Poetry?" (commentary on Dennett, 1983a), *Behavioral and Brain Sciences*, 6, pp. 356–358.

Berliner, H., and Ebeling, C., 1986, "The SUPREM Architecture: A New Intelligent Paradigm," *Artificial Intelligence*, 28, pp. 3–8.

Block, N., 1981, review of Jaynes, *Cognition and Brain Theory*, 4, pp. 81–83.

———, 1982, "Psychologism and Behaviorism," *Philosophical Review*, 90, pp. 5–43.

———, 1992, "Begging the question against phenomenal consciousness," (commentary on Dennett and Kinsbourne), *Behavioral and Brain Sciences*, 15, pp. 205–206.

———, 1993, review of Dennett, 1991, *Journal of Philosophy*, 90, pp. 181–193.

———, 1994, "What Is Dennett's Theory a Theory of?" *Philosophical Topics*, 22 (1 & 2) (Spring & Fall), pp. 23–40.

———, 1995, "On a Confusion about a Function of Consciousness," *Behavioral and Brain Sciences*, 18, pp. 227–247.

Boden, M., 1984, "What Is Computational Psychology?" *Proceedings of the Aristotelian Society*, 58 (Suppl.), pp. 17–53.

Braitenberg, V., 1984, *Vehicles: Experiments in Synthetic Psychology*, Cambridge, MA: Bradford Books / The MIT Press.

Braun, B. G., ed., 1984, *Psychiatric Clinics of North America*, 7 (March) [special issue of MPD].

———, 1988, *Dissociative Disorders: 1988*, Dissociative Disorders Program, Department of Psychiatry, Rush University, 1720 West Polk Street, Chicago, IL 60612.

Brooks, R., 1991, "Intelligence Without Representation," *Artificial Intelligence* 47, pp. 139–159.

Chaitin, G., 1975, "Randomness and Mathematical Proof," *Scientific American*, 232.

Chalmers, D., 1995, "Absent Qualia, Fading Qualia, Dancing Qualia," in Thomas Metzinger, ed., *Conscious Experience*, Schöningh: Imprint Academic, pp. 309–328.

Charniak, E., 1974, "Toward a Model of Children's Story Comprehension," unpublished doctoral dissertation, MIT, and MIT AI Lab Report 266.

Cheney, D., and Seyfarth, R., 1990, *How Monkeys See the World*, Chicago: University of Chicago Press.

Cherniak, C., 1983, "Rationality and the Structure of Memory," *Synthèse*, 57 (2), pp. 163–186.

Chomsky, N., 1957, *Syntactic Structures*, The Hague: Mouton.

———, 1980a, *Rules and Representations*, New York: Columbia University Press.

———, 1980b, "Rules and Representations," *Behavioral and Brain Sciences*, 3, pp. 1–61.

———, 1988, *Language and Problems of Knowledge*, Cambridge, MA: The MIT Press.

Churchland, P., 1979, *Scientific Realism and the Plasticity of Mind*, Cambridge: Cambridge University Press.

———, 1981, "Eliminative Materialism and the Propositional Attitudes," *Journal of Philosophy*, 78 (2) (Feb.).

———, 1991, "Folk Psychology and the Explanation of Human Behavior," in Greenwood, J., ed., *The Future of Folk Psychology: Intentionality and Cognitive Science*, Cambridge: Cambridge University Press, chapter 2.

Clark, A., 1993, *Associative Engines: Connectionism, Concepts, and Representational Change*, Cambridge, MA: The MIT Press.

———, 1997, *Being There*, Cambridge, MA: The MIT Press.

———, forthcoming (1998), "Magic Words: How Language Augments Human Computation," in P. Carruthers, ed., *Language and Thought: Interdisciplinary Themes*, Cambridge University Press.

Clark, A., and Karmiloff-Smith, A., 1993, "The Cognizer's Innards: A Psychological and Philosophical Perspective on the Development of Thought, " *Mind and Language*, 8, pp. 487–519.

Colby, K. M., 1981, "Modeling a Paranoid Mind," *Behavioral and Brain Sciences* 4 (4).

Coons, P., 1986, "Treatment Progress in 20 Patients with Multiple Personality Disorder," *Journal of Nervous and Mental Disease, 174.*

Cornford, F. M., trans., 1957, *Plato's Theaetetus,* New York: Macmillan.

Cummins, R., 1983, *The Nature of Psychological Explanation,* Cambridge, MA: Bradford Books / The MIT Press.

Dahlbom, B., 1993, *Dennett and his Critics,* Oxford: Blackwell.

Damasio, A., 1989, "The brain binds entities and events by multiregional activation from convergence zones," *Neural Computation,* 1, pp. 123–132.

————, 1994, *Descartes' Error: Emotion, Reason, and the Human Brain,* New York: G. P. Putnam.

Damgaard, J., Van Benschoten, S., and Fagan, J., 1985, "An updated bibliography of literature pertaining to multiple personality," *Psychological Reports,* 57.

Darmstadter, H., 1971, "Consistency of Belief," *Journal of Philosophy,* 68, pp. 301–310.

Davidson, D., 1970, "Mental Events," in Foster, L., and Swanson J. W., eds., *Experience and Theory,* Amherst: University of Massachusetts Press, pp. 79–101.

————, 1975, "Thought and Talk" in *Mind and Language: Wolfson College Lectures, 1974,* Oxford: Clarendon Press, pp. 7–23.

————, 1991, "What Is Present to the Mind?" in Villaneuva, E., ed., *Consciousness,* Atascadero, CA: Ridgeview Publishing, pp. 197–313.

Dawkins, R., 1976, *The Selfish Gene,* Oxford: Oxford University Press.

————, 1982, *The Extended Phenotype,* Oxford: Oxford University Press.

————, 1984, *The Selfish Gene,* (New Edition) Oxford: Oxford University Press.

de Groot, A. D., 1965, *Thought and Choice in Chess,* The Hague: Mouton.

de Sousa, R., 1979, "The Rationality of Emotions," *Dialogue,* 18, pp. 41–63.

————, 1987, *The Rationality of Emotion,* Cambridge, MA: The MIT Press.

Dennett, D. C., 1969, *Content and Consciousness,* London: Routledge & Kegan Paul.

————, 1971, "Intentional Systems," *Journal of Philosophy,* 68, pp. 87–106.

————, 1973, "Mechanism and Responsibility" in Honderich, T., ed., *Essays on Freedom of Action,* London: Routledge & Kegan Paul. Republished in Dennett (1978a).

————, 1974, "Why the Law of Effect Will Not Go Away," *Journal of the Theory of Social Behaviour,* 5, pp. 169–187.

————, 1975a, "Are Dreams Experiences?" *Philosophical Review,* 73, pp. 151–171.

————, 1975b, "Brain Writing and Mind Reading," in Gunderson, K., ed., *Language, Mind, and Meaning,* Minnesota Studes in Philosophy of Science, 7, Minneapolis: University of Minnesota Press.

————, 1976, "Conditions of Personhood," in A. Rorty, (ed.), *The Identities of Persons,* University of California Press.

——, 1978a, *Brainstorms: Philosophical Essays on Mind and Psychology*, Cambridge, MA: Bradford Books / The MIT Press.

——, 1978b, "Current Issues in the Philosophy of Mind," *American Philosophical Quarterly*, 15, pp. 249–261.

——, 1978c, "Why not the whole iguana?" (commentary on Pylyshyn), *Behavioral and Brain Sciences*, 1 (1), pp. 103–104.

——, 1978d, "Beliefs about Beliefs," (commentary on Premack and Woodruff), *Behavioral and Brain Sciences*, 1, 568–570.

——, 1979, "Artificial Intelligence as Philosophy and as Psychology," in Ringle, M., ed., *Philosophical Perspectives in Artificial Intelligence*, Atlantic Highlands, NJ: Humanities Press International.

——, 1980, "The Milk of Human Intentionality," (commentary on Searle, "Minds, Brains, and Programs,") *Behavioral and Brain Sciences*, 3, pp. 428–430.

——, 1981, "Three Kinds of Intentional Psychology," in Healey, R., ed., *Reduction, Time, and Reality*, Cambridge: Cambridge University Press.

——, 1982a, "Beyond Belief," in Woodfield, A., ed., *Thought and Object*, Oxford: Clarendon Press), reprinted as chapter 5 of *The Intentional Stance*.

——, 1982b, "How to Study Consciousness Empirically: or Nothing Comes to Mind," *Synthèse*, 53, pp. 159–180.

——, 1982c, "Notes on Prosthetic Imagination," *Boston Review* 7 (3) (June), pp. 3–7.

——, 1982d, "Why do we think what we do about why we think what we do?" *Cognition*, 12, pp. 219–227.

——, 1983a, "Intentional Systems in Cognitive Ethology: the 'Panglossian Paradigm' Defended," *Behavioral and Brain Sciences*, 6, pp. 343–390.

——, 1983b, "Styles of Mental Representation," *Proceedings of the Aristotelian Society*, 83, pp. 213–226.

——, 1983c, "When do Representations Explain?" *Behavioral and Brain Sciences*, 6, pp. 406–407.

——, 1984a, "Carving the Mind at Its Joints," *Contemporary Psychology* 29, pp. 285–286.

——, 1984b, "Cognitive Wheels: the Frame Problem of AI," in Hookway, C., ed., *Minds, Machines, and Evolution*, Cambridge: Cambridge University Press, pp. 129–151.

——, 1984c, "Computer Models and the Mind—A View from the East Pole," *Times Literary Supplement* (Dec. 14).

——, 1984d, *Elbow Room: The Varieties of Free Will Worth Wanting*, Cambridge, MA: Bradford Books / The MIT Press.

——, 1986a, "Is There an Autonomous 'Knowledge Level'?" in Pylyshyn, Z., and Demopoulos, W., eds., *Meaning and Cognitive Structure*, Norwood, NJ: Ablex, pp. 51–54.

——, 1986b, "The Logical Geography of Computational Approaches: a View from the East Pole," in Harnish, M., and Brand, M., eds., *The Representation of Knowledge and Belief*, Tucson: University of Arizona Press.

———, 1987, *The Intentional Stance*, Cambridge, MA: Bradford Books / The MIT Press.

———, ed., 1987, *The Philosophical Lexicon* (8th Edition). Available from the American Philosophical Association.

———, 1988a, "Eliminate the Middletoad!" (commentary on Ewert's "Prey-Catching in Toads"), *Behavioral and Brain Sciences*, 10 (3), pp. 372–374.

———, 1988b, "The Moral First Aid Manual," in McMurrin, S., ed., *The Tanner Lectures on Human Values*, Vol 7, Salt Lake City: University of Utah Press, pp. 119–148.

———, 1988c, "Out of the Armchair and into the Field," *Poetics Today*, 9 (1), pp. 205–221.

———, 1988d, "Précis of *The Intentional Stance*," *Behavioral and Brain Sciences*, 11, pp. 493–544 (including response to Goldman, p. 541).

———, 1988e, "Quining Qualia," in Marcel, A., and Bisiach, E., eds., *Consciousness in Contemporary Science*, Oxford: Oxford University Press.

———, 1989, "The Autocerebroscope," lecture given at a symposium in memory of Heinz Pagels, The Reality Club, Alliance Française, New York City, February 1, 1989.

———, 1990a, "The Interpretation of Texts, People, and Other Artifacts," *Philosophy and Phenomenological Research*, 50, pp. 177–194

———, 1990b, "Ways of Establishing Harmony" in McLaughlin, B., ed., *Dretske and His Critics*, Oxford: Blackwell. Reprinted (slightly revised), in Villanueva, E., ed., *Information, Semantics, and Epistemology* (Oxford: Blackwell, 1990).

———, 1991a, *Consciousness Explained*, Boston: Little, Brown.

———, 1991b, "Lovely and Suspect Qualities," (commentary on Rosenthal, "The Independence of Consciousness and Sensory Quality"), in Villanueva, E., ed., *Consciousness*, Atascadero, CA: Ridgeview.

———, 1991c, "Mother Nature versus the Walking Encyclopedia," in Ramsey, W., Stich, S., and Rumelhart, D., eds., *Philosophy and Connectionist Theory*, Hillsdale, NJ: Erlbaum.

———, 1991d, "Real Patterns," *Journal of Philosophy*, 87 (1), pp. 27–51.

———, 1991e, "Two Contrasts: Folk Craft versus Folk Science and Belief versus Opinion," in Greenwood, J., ed., *The Future of Folk Psychology: Intentionality and Cognitive Science*, Cambridge: Cambridge University Press.

———, 1992a, "Filling In versus Finding Out: a Ubiquitous Confusion in Cognitive Science," in Pick, H., Van den Broek, P., and Knill, D., eds, *Cognition: Conceptual and Methodological Issues*, Washington, DC: American Psychological Association.

———, 1992b, "Temporal Anomalies of Consciousness: Implications of the Uncentered Brain," in Christen et al., eds., *Neurophilosophy amd Alzheimer's Disease*, Berlin / Heidelberg: Springer-Verlag.

———, 1993a, "Caveat Emptor," *Consciousness and Cognition*, 2, pp. 48–57.

———, 1993b, "Learning and Labeling" (Comments on Clark and Karmiloff-Smith), *Mind and Language*, 8, pp. 540–548.

———, 1993c, "Living on the Edge," *Inquiry*, 36, pp. 135–159.

————, 1993d, "The Message Is: There Is no Medium," *Philosophy and Phenomenological Research*, 53 (4) (Dec. 1993), pp. 889–931.

————, 1993e, review of John Searle, *The Rediscovery of the Mind*, in *Journal of Philosophy*, 90, pp. 193–205.

————, 1993f, "Back from the Drawing Board" (reply to critics) in *Dennett and His Critics: Demystifying Mind*, Bo Dahlbom, ed., Oxford: Blackwell.

————, 1994a, "Cognitive Science as Reverse Engineering: Several Meanings of 'Top-Down' and 'Bottom-Up,' " in Prawitz, D., Skyrms, B., and Westerståhl, D., eds., *Logic, Methodology and Philosophy of Science IX*, Amsterdam: Elsevier Science, BV, pp. 679–689.

————, 1994b, "Get Real," *Philosophical Topics*, 22 (1 & 2), pp. 505–568.

————, 1994c, "The practical requirements for making a conscious robot," *Philosophical Transactions of the Royal Society of London A* 349, pp. 133–146.

————, 1995a, "Is Perception the 'Leading Edge' of Memory?" in Spadafora, A., ed., *Iride: Luoghi della memoria e dell'oblio*, anno. VIII (14) (April 1995), pp. 59–78.

————, 1995b, Interview with Michael Gazzaniga, *Journal of Cognitive Neuroscience*, 7, pp. 408–414.

————, 1996a, *Kinds of Minds*, New York: Basic Books.

————, 1996b, "Producing Future by Telling Stories," in Ford K., and Pylyshyn, Z., eds., *The Robot's Dilemma Revisited: the Frame Problem in Artificial Intelligence*, Norwood, NJ: Ablex, pp. 1–7.

Dennett, D. C., and Kinsbourne, M., 1992a, "Escape from the Cartesian Theater," (response to commentators), *Behavioral and Brain Sciences*, 15, pp. 183–200.

————, 1992b, "Time and the Observer: the Where and When of Consciousness in the Brain," *Behavioral and Brain Sciences*, 15, pp. 183–247.

————, 1994, "Counting Consciousnesses: None, one, two, or none of the above?" (continuing commentary on "Time and the Observer"), *Behavioral and Brain Studies*, 17, (1), 178–180.

Descartes, R., 1637, *Discourse on Method*, LaFleur, Lawrence, trans., New York: Bobbs Merrill, 1960.

Diamond, J., 1983, "The Biology of the Wheel," *Nature*, 302, pp. 572–573.

Doyle, J., 1979, "A Truth Maintenance System," *Artificial Intelligence*, 12, pp. 231–272.

Dretske, F., 1981, *Knowledge and the Flow of Information*, Cambridge, MA: Bradford Books / The MIT Press.

————, 1985, "Machines and the Mental," *Proceedings and Addresses of the American Philosophical Association*, 59 (1), pp. 23–33.

————, 1986, "Misrepresentation," in Bogdan, R., ed., *Belief*, Oxford: Oxford University Press.

————, 1988, "The Stance Stance," commentary on *The Intentional Stance*, in *Behavioral and Brain Sciences*, 11, pp. 511–512.

————, 1990, "Does Meaning Matter?" in Villanueva, E., ed., *Information, Semantics, and Epistemology*, Oxford: Blackwell, pp. 5–17. Originally delivered as "The Causal Role of

Content," at a conference on Information, Semantics and Epistemology, SOFIA, Tepozstlan, Mexico, August 7, 1988.

Dreyfus, H. L., 1972, *What Computers Can't Do,* New York: Harper & Row.

Dreyfus, H., and Dreyfus, S., 1986, *Mind Over Machine,* New York: Macmillan.

Edelman, G. M., 1987, *Neural Darwinism: the Theory of Neuronal Group Selection,* New York: Basic Books.

————, 1989, *The Remembered Present: A Biological Theory of Consciousness,* New York: Basic Books.

————, 1992, *Bright Air, Brilliant Fire: On the Matter of the Mind,* New York: Basic Books.

Ericsson, K. A., and Simon, H. A., 1984, *Protocol Analysis: Verbal Reports as Data,* Cambridge, MA: The MIT Press.

Fahlman, S., Hinton, G., and Sejnowski, T., 1983, "Massively Parallel Architectures for AI: NETL, Thistle, and Boltzmann Machines," *Proceedings of the American Association of Artificial Intelligence,* 83, pp. 109–113.

Fahy, T. A., 1988, "The Diagnosis of Multiple Personality Disorder: a Critical Review," *British Journal of Psychiatry,* 153.

Feldman, J., and Ballard, D., 1982, "Connectionist Models and Their Properties," *Cognitive Science,* 6, pp. 205–254.

Field, H., 1978, "Mental Representation," *Erkenntnis,* 13, pp. 9–61.

Fikes, R., and Nilsson, N., 1971, "STRIPS: a New Approach to the Application of Theorem Proving to Problem Solving," *Artificial Intelligence,* 2, pp. 189–208.

Fine, A., 1986, *The Shaky Game: Einstein Realism, and the Quantum Theory,* Chicago: Chicago Unviersity Press.

Flanagan, O., 1992, *Consciousness Reconsidered,* Cambridge, MA: The MIT Press.

Flanagan, O., and Polger, T., 1995, "Zombies and the Function of Consciousness," *Journal of Consciousness Studies,* 2 (4), pp. 313–321.

Fodor, J., 1975, *The Language of Thought,* New York: Crowell.

————, 1978, "Tom Swift and his Procedural Grandmother," *Cognition,* Vol 6, reprinted in Fodor, 1981, *RePresentations,* Cambridge, MA: Bradford Books / The MIT Press.

————, 1980, "Methodological Solipsism Considered as a Research Strategy," *Behavioral and Brain Sciences,* 3, pp. 63–110.

————, 1983, *The Modularity of Mind,* Cambridge, MA: Bradford Books / The MIT Press.

————, 1987, *Psychosemantics,* Cambridge, MA: Bradford Books / The MIT Press.

————, 1990, *A Theory of Content,* Cambridge, MA: Bradford Books / The MIT Press.

Fodor, J., and Pylyshyn, Z., 1988, "Connectionism and Cognitive Architecture: a Critical Analysis," *Cognition,* 28 (1–2), pp. 3–71.

Ford, K., and Hayes, P., 1991, *Reasoning Agents in a Dynamic World: The Frame Problem,* Greenwich, CT: JAI Press.

Ford, K., and Pylyshyn, Z., eds., 1996, *The Robot's Dilemma Revisited*, Norwood, NJ: Ablex.

Fraser, S., 1988, *My Father's House*, New York: Ticknor and Fields.

French, R., 1990, "Subcognition and the Turing Test," *Mind*, 99, pp. 53–65.

———, 1995, *The Subtlety of Sameness*, Cambridge, MA: Bradford Books / The MIT Press.

Freyd, J. J., 1987, "Dynamic Mental Representations," *Psychological Review*, 94, pp. 427–438.

Gärdenfors, P., 1996, "Cued and detached representations in animal cognition," *Behavioural Processes*, 35 (1–3), p. 263.

Gibson, J. J., 1975, *Cognition and Reality*, San Francisco: Freeman.

———, 1979, *The Ecological Approach to Visual Perception*, Boston: Houghton Mifflin.

Glymour, C., 1987, "Android Epistemology and the Frame Problem: Comments on Dennett's 'Cognitive Wheels'," in Pylyshyn, 1987, pp. 63–75.

Glymour, C., Ford, K. M., and Hayes, P., 1995, "The Prehistory of Android Epistemology," in Ford, Glymour, and Hayes, eds., *Android Epistemology*, Cambridge, MA: The MIT Press.

Goodman, N., 1965, *Fact, Fiction, and Forecast*, 2nd ed., Indianapolis: Bobbs-Merrill.

———, 1982, "Thoughts without Words," *Cognition*, 12, pp. 211–217.

Gould, S. J., and Lewontin, R., 1979, "The Spandrels of San Marco and the Panglossian Paradigm: A Critique of the Adaptationist Program," *Proceedings of the Royal Society*, B205, pp. 581–598.

Gregory, R., ed., 1987, *The Oxford Companion to the Mind*, Oxford: Oxford University Press.

Griffin, D., 1981, *The Question of Animal Awareness* (Revised and Enlarged Edition), New York: The Rockefeller University Press.

———, 1982, *Animal Mind — Human Mind*, Berlin: Spring Verlag.

———, 1984, *Animal Thinking*, Cambridge, MA: Harvard University Press.

Guttenplan, S., ed., 1994, *A Companion to the Philosophy of Mind*, Oxford: Blackwell.

Hacking, I., 1986, "Making Up People," in Heller, Sosna, and Wellbery, eds., *Reconstructing Individualism*, Stanford, CA: Stanford University Press.

Harman, G., 1973, *Thought*, Princeton, NJ: Princeton University Press.

Harnad, S., 1990, "The Symbol Grounding Problem," *Physica*, D42, pp. 335–346.

Haugeland, J., 1978, "The Nature and Plausibility of Cognitivism," *Behavioral and Brain Sciences*, 1, pp. 215–260. Also published in Haugeland (1981, pp. 243–281).

———, ed., 1981, *Mind Design: Philosophy, Psychology, Artificial Intelligence*, Cambridge, MA: Bradford Books / The MIT Press.

———, 1985, *Artificial Intelligence: the Very Idea*, Cambridge, MA: Bradford Books / The MIT Press.

————, 1990, "The Intentionality All-Stars," in *Action theory and philosophy of mind, 1990* (Philosophical perspectives series, no. 4), Atascadero, CA: Ridgeview, pp. 383–427.

Hawkins, R. D., and Kandel, E., 1984, "Steps toward a cell-biological alphabet for elementary forms of learning," in Lynch, G., McGaugh, J. L., and Weinberger, N. M., eds., *Neurobiology of Learning and Memory*, New York: Guilford, pp. 385–404.

Hayes, P., 1978, "Naive Physics 1: The Ontology of Liquids," Working Paper 35, *Institut pour les Etudes Semantiques et Cognitives, Université de Génevè.*

————, 1980, "The Naive Physics Manifesto," in Michie, D., ed., *Expert Systems in the Microelectronic Age*, Edinburgh: Machine Intelligence Research Unit, University of Edinburgh.

Heiser, J. F., Colby, K. M., Faught, W. S., and Parkinson, R. C., 1980, "Can Psychiatrists Distinguish a Computer Simulation of Paranoia from the Real Thing? The Limitations of Turing-Like Tests as Measures of the Adequacy of Simulations," *Journal of Psychiatric Research* 15 (3).

Heyes, C. M., 1987, "Cognisance of Consciousness in the Study of Animal Knowledge," in Callebaut, W., and Pinxten, R., eds., *Evolutionary Epistemology: a Multiparadigm Approach*, Dordrecht / Boston: Reidel.

Hilgard, E. R., 1970, *Personality and Hypnosis: A Study of Imaginative Involvement*, Chicago: University of Chicago Press.

Hillis, D., 1981, "The Connection Machine (Computer Architecture for the New Wave)," *MIT AI Memo 646*, (Sept.).

Hobbes, T., 1651, *Leviathan* (London: Crooke).

Hofstadter, D., 1979, *Gödel, Escher, Bach: An Eternal Golden Braid*, New York: Basic Books.

————, 1982, "Can Inspiration be Mechanized?" *Scientific American*, 247, pp. 18–34.

————, 1983, "The Architecture of JUMBO," in *Proceedings of the Second International Machine Learning Workshop*, Urbana: University of Illinois, pp. 161–170.

————, 1983b, "Artificial Intelligence: Subcognition as Computation," in F. Machlup and U. Mansfield, eds., *The Study of Information: Interdisciplinary Messages*, New York: Wiley, pp. 263–285.

————, 1985, *Metamagical Themas: Questing for the Essence of Mind and Pattern*, New York: Basic Books.

Hofstadter, D., and Dennett, D. C., 1981, *The Mind's I*, New York: Basic Books.

Hofstadter, D., and the Fluid Analogies Research Group, 1995, *Fluid Concepts and Creative Analogies: Computer Models of the Fundamental Mechanisms of Thought*, New York: Basic Books.

Holland, J., Holyoak, K., Nisbett, R., and Thagard, P., 1986, *Induction*, Cambridge, MA: Bradford Books / The MIT Press.

Houston, D. C., 1986, "Scavenging Efficiency of Turkey Vultures in Tropical Forest," *The Condor*, 88, pp. 318–323. Cooper Ornithological Society.

Hume, D., 1739, *A Treatise of Human Nature*, London: Noon.

———, 1748, *Inquiry Concerning Human Understanding* [1973], New York: Bobbs Merrill.

Humphrey, N., 1983, *Consciousness Regained,* Oxford: Oxford University Press.

———, 1986, *The Inner Eye,* London: Faber & Faber.

———, 1992, *A History of the Mind,* London: Vintage Books.

Jackendoff, R., 1993, *Patterns in the Mind: Language and Human Nature,* New York: Basic Books).

Jacob, F., 1977, "Evolution and Tinkering," *Science,* 196, pp. 1161–1166.

Janlert, L.-E., 1987, "Modeling Change—The Frame Problem," in Pylyshyn, 1987, pp. 1–40.

Jaynes, J., 1976, *The Origin of Consciousness in the Breakdown of the Bicameral Mind,* Boston: Houghton Mifflin.

Kanerva, P., 1983, "Self-Propagating Search: A Unified Theory of Memory," *Technical Report,* Palo Alto: Center for the Study of Language and Information.

Kinsbourne, M., in preparation,"The distributed brain basis of consciousness."

———, 1988, "Integrated field theory of consciousness," in A. Marcel and E. Bisiach, eds., *Consciousness in Contemporary Science,* Oxford: Oxford University Press.

Kirkpatrick, S., Gelatt, C., Jr., and Vecchi, M., 1983, "Optimization by simulated annealing," *Science* (13 May), pp. 671–680.

Kluft, R., 1988, "The Dissociative Disorders," in Talbott, J. A., Hales, R. E., and Yudofsky, S. C., eds., *The American Psychiatric Press Textbook of Psychiatry,* Washington, DC: American Psychiatric Press.

Kohut, H., 1985, "On Courage," reprinted in *Self Psychology and the Humanities,* Charles B. Strozier, ed., New York: W. W. Norton.

Kolodner, J. L., 1983a, "Retrieval and Organization Strategies in Conceptual Memory: A Computer Model" (Ph.D. diss.), Research Report #187, Dept. of Computer Science, Yale University.

———, 1983b, "Maintaining Organization in a Dynamic Long-term Memory," *Cognitive Science 7.*

———, 1983c, "Reconstructive Memory: A Computer Model," *Cognitive Science 7.*

Kosslyn, S., and Hatfield, G., 1984, "Representation without Symbols," *Social Research,* 51 (4), pp. 1019–1045.

Krebs, J. R., Kacelnik, A., and Taylor, P., 1978, "Test of optimal sampling by foraging great tits," *Nature,* 275, pp. 127–131.

Laird, J., Newell, A., and. Rosenbloom, P., 1987, "SOAR: An Architecture for General Intelligence" *Artificial Intelligence,* 33 (Sept.), pp. 1–64.

Langton, C. G., ed., 1989, *Artificial Life,* New York: Addison Wesley.

Leiber, J., 1988, "'Cartesian Linguistics'?" *Philosophia,* 118, pp. 309–346.

Lenat, D. B., and Guha, R. V., 1990, *Building Large Knowledge-Based Systems: Representation and Inference in the CYC Project,* Reading, MA: Addison-Wesley.

Lenat, D., Prakash, M., and Shepherd, M., 1986, "CYC: using common-sense knowledge to overcome brittleness and knowledge acquisition bottlenecks," *AI Magazine* 6 (4) pp. 65–85.

LePore, E., and Loewer, B., 1987, "Mind Matters," *Journal of Philosophy*, 84, pp. 630–642.

Leslie, A., 1994, "TOMM, ToBy, and Agency: Core architecture and domain specificity," in Hirschfeld, L., and Gelman, S., eds., *Mapping the Mind: Domain Specificity in Cognition and Culture*, Cambridge: Cambridge University Press.

Levesque, H., 1984, "Foundations of a Functional Approach to Knowledge Representation," *Artificial Intelligence*, 23, pp. 155–212.

Levine, J., 1994, "Out of the Closet: a Qualophile Confronts Qualophobia," *Philosophical Topics*, 22 (1 & 2), pp. 107–126.

Lifton, R. J., 1979, *The Broken Connection*, New York: Simon & Schuster.

———, 1986, *The Nazi Doctors*, New York: Basic Books.

Locke, J., 1685, *Essay Concerning Human Understanding*, Amherst, NY: Prometheus Books, 1982.

Lockwood, M., 1993, "Dennett's Mind," *Inquiry*, 36, pp. 59–72.

Lord, A., 1960, *The Singer of Tales*, Cambridge, MA: Harvard University Press.

Lucas, J. R., 1994, "A View of One's Own," *Philosophical Transactions of the Royal Society*, A349, p. 147.

Lycan, W. G., 1981, "Form, Function, and Feel," *Journal of Philosophy*, 78, pp. 24–49.

Mangan, B., 1993, "Dennett, Consciousness, and the Sorrows of Functionalism," *Consciousness and Cognition*, 2, pp. 1–17.

Mann, D., and Goodwin, J., 1988, "Obstacles to Recognizing Dissociative Disorders in Child and Adolescent Males" in Braun, B. (1988), p. 35.

Marais, E. N., 1937, *The Soul of the White Ant*, London: Methuen.

Margolis, H., 1987, *Patterns, Thinking, and Cognition*, Chicago: University of Chicago Press.

Marr, D., 1982, *Vision*, Cambridge, MA: The MIT Press.

Mayr, E., 1983, "How to Carry out the Adaptationist Program," *American Naturalist*, 121, pp. 324–334.

McCarthy, J., 1960, "Programs with Common Sense," *Proceedings of the Teddington Conference on the Mechanization of Thought Processes*, London: Her Majesty's Stationers.

———, 1962, "Programs with Common Sense," International Conference on Machine Translation of Languages and Applied Language Analysis (1961: Teddington), *Proceedings of the conference held at the National Physical Laboratory, Teddington, Middlesex, on 5th, 6th, 7th and 8th September*, London: H. M. S. O. A version is reprinted in Minsky, M., ed., *Semantic Information Processing* (Cambridge: The MIT Press, 1968).

———, 1979, "Ascribing Mental Qualities to Machines," in Ringle, M., ed., *Philosophical Perspectives in Artificial Intelligence*, Atlantic Highlands, NJ: Humanities Press.

———, 1980, "Circumspection—A Form of Non-Monotonic Reasoning," *Artificial Intelligence,* 13, pp. 27–39.

McCarthy, J., and Hayes, P., 1969, "Some Philosophical Problems from the Standpoint of Artificial Intelligence," in Meltzer, B., and Michie, D., eds., *Machine Intelligence 4,* Edinburgh: Edinburgh University Press, pp. 463–502.

McClelland, J., unpublished, "Models of Perception and Memory Based on Principles of Natural Organization," University of California, San Diego, preprint.

McDermott, D., 1982, "A Temporal Logic for Reasoning about Processes and Plans," *Cognitive Science,* 6, pp. 101–155.

McDermott, D., and Doyle, J., 1980, "Non-Monotonic Logic," *Artificial Intelligence,* 13, pp. 41–72.

McGinn, C., 1995, "Animal Minds, Animal Morality," *Social Research,* 62, pp. 731–747.

McPhee, J., 1985, "Heirs of General Practice," in *Table of Contents,* New York: Farrar, Straus, Giroux.

Mill, J. S., 1863, *Utilitarianism,* Indianapolis, IN: Hackett.

Miller, S. D., 1988, "The Psychophysiological Investigation of Multiple Personality Disorder: Review and Update," in Braun, B. (1988), p. 113.

Miller, G., Galanter, E., and Pribram, K., 1960, *Plans and the Structure of Behavior,* New York: Holt, Rinehart and Winston.

Millikan, R. G., 1984, *Language, Thought, and Other Biological Categories,* Cambridge, MA: The MIT Press.

Minsky, M., 1981, "A Framework for Representing Knowledge," originally published as Memo 3306, AI Lab, MIT. Quotation drawn from excerpts reprinted in Haugeland, J., ed., *Mind Design,* Cambridge, MA: The MIT Press, 1981.

———, 1985, *The Society of Mind,* New York: Simon & Schuster.

Mitchell, M., 1993, *Analogy-Making as Perception,* Cambridge, MA: The MIT Press.

Moody, T. C., 1994, "Conversations with Zombies," *Journal of Consciousness Studies,* 1 (2), pp. 196–200.

Mulhauser, G., unpublished, "Building a Zombie."

Nagel, T., 1974, "What Is It Like to Be a Bat?" *Philosophical Review,* 83, pp. 435–450.

———, 1986, *The View from Nowhere,* Oxford: Oxford University Press.

———, 1991, "What we have in mind when we say we're thinking," review of *Consciousness Explained, Wall Street Journal,* 11/7/91.

———, 1995, *Other Minds: Critical Essays, 1969–1994,* Oxford: Oxford University Press.

Neisser, U., 1963, *Cognitive Psychology,* New York: Appleton-Century-Crofts.

———, 1975, *Cognition and Reality,* San Francisco: Freeman.

Nelkin, N., 1994, "Patterns," *Mind & Language,* 9 (1) (Mar.).

Newell, A., 1980, "Physical Symbol Systems," *Cognitive Science*, 4, pp. 135–183.

———, 1982, "The Knowledge Level," *Artificial Intelligence*, 18, pp. 87–127.

———, 1983, "Intellectual Issues in the History of Artificial Intelligence," in Machlup, F., and Mansfield, U., eds., *The Study of Information: Interdisciplinary Messages*, New York: Wiley, pp. 187–227.

———, 1986, "The Symbol Level and the Knowledge Level," in Pylyshyn, Z., and Demopoulos, W., eds., *Meaning and Cognitive Structure*, Norwood, NJ: Ablex, pp. 31–39 & 169–193.

———, 1990, *Unified Theories of Cognition*, Cambridge, MA: Harvard University Press.

Newell, A., and Simon, H., 1972, *Human Problem Solving*, Englewood Cliffs, NJ: Prentice-Hall.

———, 1976, "Computer Science as Empirical Inquiry: Symbols and Search," *Communications of the Association for Computing Machinery*, 19, pp. 113–126. Also published in Haugeland (1981), pp. 35–66.

Newell, A., Rosenbloom, P. S., and Laird, J. E., 1989, "Symbolic Architectures for Cognition," in Posner, M., ed., *Foundations of Cognitive Science*, Cambridge, MA: The MIT Press.

Newell, A., Yost, G., Laird, J. E., Rosenbloom, P. S., and Altmann, E., 1992, "Formulating the Problem Space Computational Model," in Rashid, R., ed., *CMU computer science: a 25th anniversary commemorative*, New York and Reading, MA: ACM Press/Addison-Wesley.

Nietzsche, F., 1954, *Thus Spake Zarathustra*, Kauffman, tr., New York: Modern Library.

Nissen, M. J., Ross, J. L., Willingham, D. B., MacKenzie, T. B., Schachter, D. L., 1988, "Memory and Awareness in a Patient with Multiple Personality Disorder," *Brain and Cognition*, 8 (1), pp. 117–134.

———, 1994, "Evaluating Amnesia in Multiple Personality Disorder," in Klein, R. M., and Doane, B. K. eds., *Psychological Concepts and Dissociative Disorders*, Hillsdale, NJ: Erlbaum.

Ornstein, R., and Thompson, R. F., 1984, *The Amazing Brain*, Boston: Houghton Mifflin.

O'Neill, O., 1980, "The Perplexities of Famine Relief," in Regan, T., ed., 1980, *Matters of Life and Death*, New York: Random House.

———, 1986, *Faces of Hunger*, Boston, MA: Allen and Unwin.

Parfit, D., 1984, *Reasons and Persons*, Oxford: Oxford University Press.

Peirce, C. S., 1905, "What Pragmatism Is," *The Monist*, reprinted as "The Essentials of Pragmatism," in Buchler, J., ed., *Philosophical Writings of Peirce*, New York: Dover, 1955), p. 258.

Pinker, S., 1993, *The Langage Instinct: How the Mind Creates Language*, New York: William Morrow.

Poundstone, W., 1985, *The Recursive Universe: Cosmic Complexity and the Limits of Scientific Knowledge*, New York: Wm. Morrow.

Premack, D., 1986, *Gavagai! Or the Future History of the Animal Language Controversy*, Cambridge, MA: Bradford Books / The MIT Press.

————, 1988, "Intentionality: How to Tell Mae West from a Crocodile," *Behavioral and Brain Sciences*, 11, pp. 522–523.

Putnam, F. W., 1984, "The Psychophysiologic Investigation of Multiple Personality Disorder," *Psychiatric Clinics of North America*, 7 (March).

Putnam, F. W., et al., 1986, "The clinical phenomenology of multiple personality disorder: Review of 100 recent cases," *Journal of Clinical Psychiatry*, 47.

Putnam, H., 1961, "Minds and Machines," in Sidney Hook, ed., *Dimensions of Mind*, New York: NYU Press, pp. 148–179.

————, 1988, "Much Ado About Not Very Much," *Dædalus*, 117, pp. 269–282 (reprinted in S. Graubard, ed., 1988, *The Artificial Intelligence Debate: False Starts, Real Foundations*, The MIT Press).

Pylyshyn, Z., 1978, "Computational Models and Empirical Constraints," *Behavioral and Brain Sciences*, 1, pp. 93–127.

————, 1980, "Computation and Cognition: Issues in the Foundations of Cognitive Science," *Behavioral and Brain Sciences*, 3, pp. 111–169.

————, 1984, *Computation and Cognition: Toward a Foundation for Cognitive Science*, Cambridge, MA: Bradford Books / The MIT Press.

————, ed., 1987, *The Robot's Dilemma: The Frame Problem in Artificial Intelligence*, Norwood, NJ: Ablex.

Quine, W. V. O., 1960, *Word and Object*, Cambridge, MA: The MIT Press.

Ramachandran, V., 1985, Editorial, *Perception*, 14, pp. 97–103.

Ramsey, W., Stich, S., and Garon, J., 1991, "Connectionism, Eliminativism and the Future of Folk Psychology," in Greenwood, J., ed., *The Future of Folk Psychology: Intentionality and Cognitive Science*, Cambridge: Cambridge University Press), chapter 4.

Raphael, B., 1976, *The Thinking Computer: Mind Inside Matter*, San Francisco: Freeman.

Reiter, R., 1980, "A Logic for Default Reasoning," *Artificial Intelligence*, 13, 81–132.

Ristau, C., 1991, "Aspects of the Cognitive Ethology of an Injury-Feigning Bird, the Piping Plover," in Ristau, C., ed., *Cognitive Ethology*, Hillsdale, NJ: Erlbaum, pp. 91–126.

Rosenshein, S., and Kaelbling, L. P., 1986, "The Synthesis of Digital Machines with Provable Epistemic Properties," in Halpern, J., ed., *Proceedings of the 1986 Conference*, AAAI, Monterey, Calif. March, 1986., Los Altos: Morgan Kaufmann.

Rosenthal, D., 1991a, "The Independence of Consciousness and Sensory Quality," in Villanueva, E., ed., *Consciousness*, Atascadero, CA: Ridgeview, pp. 15–36.

————, 1991b, *The Nature of Mind*, New York: Oxford University Press.

Rumelhart, D., and McClelland, J., and the PDP Research Group, 1986, *Parallel Distributed Processing: Explorations in the Microstructure of Cognition*, Vols. I and II, Cambridge, MA: The MIT Press.

Ryle, G., 1949, *The Concept of Mind*, London: Hutchinson's.

Schank, R., and Abelson, R., 1977, *Scripts, Plans, Goals, and Understanding: an Inquiry into Human Knowledge*, Hillsdale, NJ: Erlbaum.

Schiffer, S., 1987, *Remnants of Meaning*, MIT Press / A Bradford Book.

Searle, J., 1980, "Mind, Brains, and Programs," *Behavioral and Brain Sciences*, 3, pp. 417–458.

———, 1992, *The Rediscovery of the Mind*, Cambridge, MA: The MIT Press.

Selfridge, O., unpublished, *Tracking and Trailing*.

Sellars, W., 1954, "Some Reflections on Language Games," *Philosophy of Science*, 21.

———, 1963, *Science, Perception, and Reality*, London: Routledge & Kegan Paul.

Sharpe, R. A., 1989, "Dennett's Journey Towards Panpsychism," *Inquiry*, 32.

Sherrington, C. S., 1934, *The Brain and its Mechanism*, Cambridge: Cambridge Univ. Press.

Singer, P., 1981, *The Expanding Circle*, Oxford: Oxford University Press.

Sjölander, S., 1993, "Some cognitive breakthroughs in the evolution of cognition and consciousness, and their impact on the biology of language," *Evolution and Cognition*, 3, pp. 1–10.

Sloman, A., and Croucher, M., 1981, "Why Robots Will Have Emotions," in *Proceedings IJCAI-81*, Vancouver, BC: American Association for Artificial Intelligence.

Smith, B. C., 1986, "The Link from Symbol to Knowledge," in Pylyshyn, Z., and Demopoulos, W., eds., *Meaning and Cognitive Structure*, Norwood, NJ: Ablex, pp. 40–50.

Smith, G. E., 1986, "The Dangers of CAD," *Mechanical Engineering* 108 (2) (Feb.), pp. 58–64.

Smith, P., 1988, "Wit and Chutzpah," review of *The Intentional Stance* and Fodor's *Psychosemantics*, *Times Higher Education Supplement* (August 7).

Smolensky, P., 1983, "Harmony Theory: A Mathematical Framework for Learning and Parallel Computation," *Proceedings of the American Association of Artificial Intelligence*, 83, pp. 114–132.

———, 1988, "On the Proper Treatment of Connectionism," *Behavioral and Brain Sciences*, 11, pp. 1–74.

Snowden, C., 1988, "Where Are all the Childhood Multiples? Identifying Incipient Multiple Personality in Children," in Braun, B. (1988), p. 36.

Snyder, D., 1988, "On the Time of a Conscious Peripheral Sensation," *Journal of Theoretical Biology*, 130, pp. 253–254.

Stabler, E., 1983, "How are Grammars Represented?" *Behavioral and Brain Sciences*, 6, pp. 391–422.

Stich, S., 1983, *From Folk Psychology to Cognitive Science*, Cambridge, MA: Bradford Books / The MIT Press.

Taylor, C., 1964, *The Explanation of Behaviour*, London: Routledge & Kegan Paul.

————, 1983, "The Significance of Significance: The Case of Cognitive Psychology," in Mitchell, S., and Rosen, M., eds., *The Need for Interpretation*, London: Athlone, pp. 141–169.

Taylor, W. S., and Martin, M. F., 1944, "Multiple personality," *Journal of Abnormal and Social Psychology*, 39, pp. 281–300.

Thomas, E. M., 1993, *The Hidden Life of Dogs*, Boston: Houghton Mifflin.

Turing, A., 1950, "Computing Machinery and Intelligence," *Mind*, 59 (236), pp. 433–460. Reprinted in Hofstadter, D., and Dennett, D. C., eds., *The Mind's I* (New York: Basic Books, 1981), pp. 54–67.

Turkle, S., 1984, *The Second Self*, New York: Simon & Schuster.

van Gulick, R., 1988, "Consciousness, Intrinsic Intentionality, and Self-Understanding Machines," in Marcel, A., and Bisiach, E., eds., *Consciousness in Contemporary Science*, Oxford: Oxford University Press.

Waltz, D., 1988, "The Prospects for Building Truly Intelligent Machines," *Dædalus*, 117, pp. 191–222.

Waterhouse, L., 1990a, "Myth and Memory: the Empowering Constraint of Narrative," lecture delivered at Princeton University Colloquium, Psychology Department, Princeton N.J., February 21, 1990.

————, 1990b, "Narrative form as a cultural constraint on imagination," lecture delivered in Palma, Mallorca, July 19, 1990.

Weizenbaum, J., 1974, letter to the editor, *Communications of the Association for Computing Machinery*, 17 (9) (September).

————, 1976, *Computer Power and Human Reason*, San Francisco: Freeman.

Whiten, A., and Byrne, R. W., eds., 1988a, *Machiavellian Intelligence*, Oxford: Clarendon Press.

————, 1988b, "Tactical Deception in Primates," *Behavioral and Brain Sciences*, 11 (2), pp. 233–244.

Wimsatt, W., 1980, "Randomness and Perceived Randomness in Evolutionary Biology," *Synthese*, 43.

Winograd, T., 1972, *Understanding Natural Language*, New York: Academic Press.

Wittgenstein, L., 1958, *Philosophical Investigations*, Oxford: Blackwell.

Woods, W., and Makhoul, J., 1974, "Mechanical Inference Problems in Continuous Speech Understanding," *Artificial Intelligence*, 5, pp. 73–91.

Wooldridge, D., 1963, *The Machinery of the Brain*, New York: McGraw-Hill.

Yonas, A., 1981, "Infants' responses to optical information for collision," in Aslin, R., Alberts, J., and Peterson, M., eds., *Development of Perception: Psychobiological Perspectives, Vol 2: The Visual System*, New York: Academic Press, pp. 110–142.

Zabludowski, A., 1989, "On Quine's Indeterminacy Doctrine," *Philosophical Review*, 98.

Index

Abduction, alien, 55
Abelson, R., 198, 212, 401
Aboutness, 216, 228, 283–284, 361. *See also* Intentionality
Absolutism, 365
Abstracta, 85, 96–97, 360
Abuse, child, 34, 36, 54–55, 58
Access, conscious, 195
  as distal, 258, 278, 281–283, 285
  to meaning, 76
  of a snake, 346
Achromatopsia, cerebral, 152
ACME, 241
ACT*, 241, 278
Actions, as poor man's physics, 212
Actors, abuse victims among, 55
Acupuncture, 38
Adam, as an adult knower, 189
Adaptation, 335
  consciousness as, 175
  efflorescence of, 285
  minimal conditions for, 75
Adaptationism, 124–125, 255, 289
Adaptive Behavior, 307
Adaptiveness, 262
Ad hoc, and "odd hack," 269
Advertising, 378
Affect, 281
Affordance, 204n, 231
Agency, 62, 212
"Aha" feeling, 60, 79
AI (Artificial Intelligence), 6,7, 39, 40n, 65, 71, 74, 86, 91–93, 129, 158, 166–167, 169, 181–205, 215–249, 275, 300, 307–310, 312, 360
  strong, 168
AIGLES, 244

AI Lab, MIT, 153, 160, 215, 268, 340
Akiba, T., 368n
Akins, K., 59n, 95n, 209, 307n, 348, 397
Alarm call, 290, 296–298
Albini, T. K., 50n, 387
Alexander, S., 250
Algorithm, 91, 228, 241, 315
  compression, 101n, 103
Allen, C., 327
Ambigram, 236
Ambiguity, 7
American Academy of Arts and Sciences, 265
America's Cup, 155
Amnesia, 246
  selective, 43, 49
Amoeba, 331
Analogy, 236–241, 244–248
Analysis by synthesis, 249–250
Anecdote, 290
  role of, 333–336
Anglo-American philosophy, 323–325
Animal behavior, 307–333
Animal rights movement, 338
Animat, 307
Animism, vestigial, 212
Anomalous monism, 268
Anscombe, G. E. M., 111, 116, 357, 387
Anteaters, 104n
Anthropocentrism, 13
Anthropology, 82–3
Anthropomorphism, 164
Anticipation, temporally proximal and distal, 209
Aprioristic thinking, 125, 269, 272–273
Arab-Israeli conflict, 8
Arbib, M., 227n, 356, 387

Archeology, 130
Aristotle, 65, 111, 112n, 213, 268, 275
Arms race, of deception and detection, 334
Artifact hermeneutics, 73
Artifacts, consciousness in, 156–157
Artificial Intelligence. *See* AI
Artificial Life (AL), 166, 256–259, 261–263
Artists, 323
Ashby, R., 356
"As if," 64
Associationism, 185, 210, 280
Astrology, 53, 119
Attention, 294, 306, 378
Attribution, to one's self, 321
Audition, for orchestra, 5
Austen, Jane, 267, 295
Author, 75
of design, 71
Authorship, 62
Autism, simulation of, 14
Automata, 262. *See also* Robots
cellular, 108, 256
conscious, 129
unconscious, 349, 358
Aviary, knowledge as, 258, 274–275, 284
Awareness$_1$ and awareness$_2$, 358–359
Awareness line, 364
Axelrod, R., 233n, 262
Axiomatization of everyday reality, 270

Baboon, 291–292
Bach, Johann Sebastian, 236
Background, 272
BACON, 241
Ballard, D., 215, 225, 227, 393
Bar-code, 102–104, 113
Bargain hunting, 314
Baseball, 128
Basic English, 12
Bats, 327, 337, 339, 347–348
Beatrix Potter syndrome, 344
Bedridden, AI programs as, 21–22, 308
Bee dance, 290
Behavior, 361
animal, 307–322
dispositions, 174, 186
interpretation of, 349
prediction of, 360
Behavioral and Brain Sciences, 289, 333

Behaviorism, 172, 177, 313, 323–324, 327, 342–343
Belief, 60, 70, 88–89, 95, 116–118, 216, 262, 291–292, 311, 323–333
and desire, 360
false, 289
fixation, 71–72, 194
vs. knowledge, 194
real, 321
as restricted, to dignified topics, 324
as structures, individuatable, 88
Belief-desire psychology, 65, 68
Beneficiary, of understanding, 75
Bennett, J., 321, 387
Bentham, Jeremy, 382, 384
Berkeley, George, 268
Berliner, H., 313, 387
Beta-manifold of beliefs, 174
Bicameral minds, 126
Bieri, P., 21
Bilgrami, A., 95n
Biological constraints, 310
Biological level, vs. psychological level, 280
Biology, 202, 224, 240, 269, 271, 314, 360
as reverse engineering, 256
molecular, 154
Bit map, 100–101
Black box, 224, 257, 311, 313–314
oracle, 384
Blindness, of evolution, 67
Block, N., 12, 127, 171, 215, 350, 387
Blocks world, 238
Boden, M., 220, 221n, 387
Boole, G., 270
Boolean Dream, 224n, 270
Bottom-up, vs. top-down, 239–240
and causal powers, 268
Boxology, 285
Boyle, R., 142, 146
Bracketing, 235
Brain
as large computer, 13
human, 153–154
task of, 73
in a vat, 290
writing, 75n
Brainstorms, 355, 357, 390
Braitenberg, V., 257, 309, 315, 388
Brand, M., 215n
Brandeis University, 218
Braun, B., 32n, 34n, 388

Brentano, F., 357
Bricolage, 269
British crown jewels, 8
British Empire, 135–136
Broca's area, 114
Brooks, R., 153, 160, 164, 167, 309
Building on the fly, 245
Business ethics, 250
Byrne, R., 77, 333

Cadaverine, 341
Calculator, hand, design of, 315–316
Cartesian. *See also* Descartes, René
  bottleneck, 132
  materialism, 62n
  Theater, 132–133, 137, 139, 244, 255, 278,
    346, 364
Categorical imperative, 383
Category mistake, 365
Causality, 188
Causal powers, 63–67, 112n, 122
Causal role, 70, 77–78, 85
  of content, 70
Causation and meaning, 65–67
C. elegans, 238
Cells, as what we are composed of, 158–
  159
Center of gravity, 85, 95–97, 99, 360
Center of narrative gravity, 39
Center of population, 96–97
Central
  cognitive processes, 231–232
  processing, 72
  workshop of understanding, 62
Central processing unit (CPU), 124, 230
Cerebral celebrity, consciousness as, 137,
  138n
Certainty, Cartesian vs. moral, 338–389
Ceteris paribus, 98–100, 184n, 204–205,
  262
Cézanne, Paul, 156
Chaitin, G., 101, 388
Chalmers, D., 141, 176, 388
Chance, 334. *See also* Random
Chaos, 240, 268–269
Charcot, J. M., 50–51
Charisma, 55
Charity, principle of, 347
Charniak, E., 86, 388
Chauvinism, species, 13
Cheney, D. 289, 291–306, 316–322, 388
Cherniak, C., 185n, 388

Cherokee, 156
Chess, 98n, 109–110, 238, 243–244, 250–
  251
  patterns in, 102
  world championship, 8, 20
Chess-playing automaton (von Kem-
  pelen), 313
Chess-playing computer, 124, 308, 313,
  330, 383
Chimpanzees, 89, 289, 303–304, 320, 326
Chinese Room thought experiment, 357
Chomsky, N., 163, 220–221, 223n, 230,
  267–268, 313–314, 388
Christie, Julie, 282–283
Church, A., 270
Churchland, P., 82, 90, 99, 111n, 113,
  119–120, 388
Circumscription, 200, 203
Clark, A., 81, 331, 388
Clarke, S., 343
Classical cognitive science, 81, 88, 91. *See
  also* East Pole; High Church Computa-
  tionalism; Physical symbol system
Cog, 153–170, 307, 340
Cognitive
  ethology, 307–322
  level, 91
  psychology, 73
  science, 42–43, 191n, 201, 215, 222–223,
    236, 238, 254–255, 259, 277, 279, 284–
    286, 308, 322, 324, 355, 360, 365–366
  philosophy of, 286
  wheel, 200–201, 204n, 308
Cognitivism, 323–324
Coincidence, cosmic, 64, 74–75
Colby, K., 13–15, 388
Collins, A., 87
Color, 142–143, 145–152, 364
  vision, of Cog, 160
Combinatorial explosion, 12–13, 22, 240,
  245, 248
Common cold, folk theory of, 85
Common sense, illusions of, 24
  reasoning, 202, 300 (*see also* Ceteris
    paribus)
Communication, 295, 320
Competence, 315
  mature, 308
  model, 313–314
  and performance, 330, 232
Competition, 173, 245
  and consciousness, 138

Competitive systems of control, 168. *See also* Pandemonium
Complexity
and consciousness, 159
measure of, 262
Computation, as symbol manipulation, 217
Computational
model, 227, 246
processes, 222
Computer, 73, 122, 125, 367. *See also* Automaton
as bearer of concepts, 129
Computer animation, 157–158
Computer Museum, Boston, 27–29
Computer science, 282
Concept, 127–128
preconscious, 128, 130
and "schmoncept," 128
Concept piano, 376
Conditioning, 68–69, 71
Connectionism, 81, 85, 90–93, 215, 225–227, 229, 232, 238, 256, 275–276, 331
new, 225
Conscious design, 70
Consciousness, 122–139, 171–177, 235–236, 244, 278, 286, 355–359, 363–364, 366
animal, 321n, 337–352
concept of, 127–128
definition of, 122
phenomenal, 350
robot, 153–170, 340
of self (self-consciousness), 23–24, 222, 236
stream of, 133–134
Consciousness Explained, 346, 355, 364, 391
Consequentialism, 383–384
Constraints
biological, 310
of intentional stance, 311, 315–316
Content, 62, 68, 328–329, 355–356, 359, 366. *See also* Meaning; Intentionality
ascription of, 60, 64
of consciousness, 364
narrow and wide, 363
real, 361–363
responsivity to, 78
Content and Consciousness, 276, 357, 359–360, 363–364, 389
Control, 208
exerted by a demon, 312

central, lack of, 227
of behavior, 65, 68, 78
powers of, 268
processes of, 74–75
states of, 360
Convergent evolution, 254
Conway, J. H., 105, 208, 256, 262
Coons, P., 34n
Cooperation, evolution of, 262
Copycat, 238
Cortex, cerebral, 134–135
Cosmic coincidence, 66–67, 74–75
Cost-benefit analysis, 315, 382–383
Counterfactuals, 78, 191
Counterintuitiveness, 83
Craft, vs. theory, 82–84
Creativity, 201n, 238
Crick, F., 138n
Criteria, behavioral, 342–343
Croucher, M., 281
Croyance, as French for "belief," 324–325
Crusoe, Robinson, 184n
Cryptarithmetic, 238
Cryptography, 110
Cuckoo, 76
Cultural evolution, 126
Culture, 207, 378
role of in consciousness, 346–347
Cummins, R., 220, 234n, 389
Curiosity, 293
in Cog, 164
lack of, 343
Curricular Software Studio, 367, 376
CYC, 74, 166, 273, 74
CYRUS, 16–18

Daedalus, 265, 277, 367n
Dahlbom, B., 182n, 355, 389
Dahlem Conference, 289–291
Damasio, A., 133, 389
Damgaard, J., 34n, 389
Darmstadter, H., 205, 389
DARPA, 250
Darwinism, neural, 67
Data structures, 276, 282–284, 325, 330
Davidson, D., 88, 91, 95n, 114, 118–120, 268, 326, 389
Dawkins, R., 217n, 233n, 378, 389
Deception, 289
in animals, 333–336
Decision, 212
Decision making, 266

Deduction, 210
Deeper facts of the matter, 118, 322, 360
Definitions, 122
de Groot, A. D., 102, 389
Dennett test (of great cityhood), 9–10, 19
Depth perception, in birds, 345
De re vs. *de dicto*, 64, 363
Derrida, Jacques, 219n
Descartes, René, 5–6, 43, 58, 62n, 65, 84,
    132, 266, 268, 273, 276, 338, 340, 357,
    359, 366, 392
Design, 79, 104, 316, 333
  as "all the way down," 225
  of brains, 322
  as evolved, 308
  good, 233
  of ideas, 186
  and the mind, as a designed object, 268
  and misdesign, by evolution, 342
  and over-design, 314
  partial, 61
  principles of, 211, 309–310
  problems of, 254–256
  process of, 67, 69, 71
    top-down, 252–254
  and redesign, 199
  and self-design, 77–79, 112, 233
    by Cog, 166
  of space, 258
  stance, 120n, 312, 360
Desire, 70, 88–89, 116–118, 164, 291–292,
    311, 325–333. *See also* Belief-desire psy-
    chology; Intentional stance
de Sousa, R., 205n, 281, 389
Determinism, of Life, 208
Deterministic models, 247
Deus ex machina, 67
Diagnostic and Statistical Manual, III
    (DSM-III), 33
Diagnostic fad, MPD as, 54
Diamond, J., 201n, 392
Diconix printer, 258
Discrimination, 347
Disney, Walt, 29, 157–158
Disposition, reactive, 349
Dispositional
  powers, 142–143
  properties, 146–147
Distal access, 258, 278, 281–283, 285
Distribution
  of control, 309
  of memory, in Cog, 165

of processing, 227
of work
  of consciousness, 365
  of understanding, 62
DNA, 224
Doctors, plight of, 369–365
Dog, as marijuana detector, 62, 64
Dollars, beliefs as similar to, 328–329
Dominant activity, in cortex, 134–135
Dopamine, 43
Doyle, J., 200, 221, 310, 392
Dretske, F., 59–80, 96–97, 392–393
Dreyfus, H., 166, 184, 193n, 196n, 220–
    221, 224, 231, 234, 393
Dreyfus, S., 166, 393
*DSM-III. See Diagnostic and Statistical
    Manual, III*
Dualism, 65, 84, 154–155, 184, 216, 268
  as last resort, 356
Dynamics, 235
  of thought, 280

East Pole, 215, 218–220, 231
Ebeling, C., 313, 387
Economics, 326
Economic value, 328–329
Economists, 166
Edelman, G., 67, 277–278, 393
Ego, 324, 345
Einstein, Albert, 105
Elbow Room, 362, 390
Electrons, reality of, 99
Elephant bush, 115–116
Elephant seal, 144
Eliminative materialism, 85, 95, 327
Elizabeth I, Queen of England, 55
Ella, the elephant bush, 115–116
Embodiment, 166
Emergence, 217, 223, 228, 240, 245
  of design, 257
Emotion, 98, 205n, 279, 281
Encyclopedia, walking, 190, 194–195, 210
Endogenous opiates, 38
Engineering, 66–70, 73–74, 77–78, 91,
    108, 155, 208, 275–276, 310, 356, 359–
    360, 384
  AI as, 252–253
  psychology as, 268
  reverse, 254–259, 269, 360, 365
Engineers, 166
Epiphenomena, 78, 112n
Epiphenomenal gremlins, 177

Epiphenomenalism, 63, 65
Episodic memoy, 248
Epistemological problem, vs. heuristic
    problem, 189n
Epistemology, 181, 222, 265, 276
    android, 226n
    problem of, 274–275
    vs. strategic maxim, 314
Epoché, 235
Equilibrium, semi-stable, 334
Ericsson, K., 238, 310, 393
Essence, 362
Essentialism, 22
    origin, 156
Ethology, 360
    cognitive, 289–322, 333–336
Eugenics, 126
Evaluation, 282
Evolution, 66–68, 75, 112, 163, 249, 255,
    257, 262–263, 280, 289, 295, 304, 321,
    335, 349, 357–358, 362, 365
    convergent, 254
    cultural, 104 126, 378
    vs. genetic, 104
    intracerebral, 68
    by natural selection, 233, 269
Evolutionarily stable strategy, 233n
Evolutionary explanation, 173–175
Evolutionary trap, 300
Excluded middle, law of, 188
Expectation, 185, 193
    how generated, 82–83
Experientially sensitive, 173, 175
Experiments, with monkeys, 295–306
Expert system, 15–16, 18–19, 300, 381–
    382
    in medicine, 369–375
Explanation, 111–112
    of behavior, 65–66, 74–76
Explanatory bite, 64, 67–69, 77

Fahlman, S., 221, 226. 393
Fahy, T. A., 34n, 393
Fame, 137–139, 377
    Hall of, 137–138
Famometer, 138
Fantasy, Philosopher's, 66
FARG, 237–240, 245–246
Fatigues, as real entities, 361
Feedback, 73
Feeling of understanding, 77n
Feldman, J., 215, 221, 225, 227, 393

Fiction, 96–97, 292
    explanatory, 38, 40–41
    theorist's, 311
Field, H., 220, 393
Fikes, R., 196, 393
Filters of information, 378
Final cause, 112n
Fine, A., 99, 118, 393
Firmware, 279
First-person
    authority, in Cog, 170
    point of view, 244
Fisette, D., 59n
Flanagan, O., 138n, 141, 171, 173–176
Focusing, 279
Fodor, J., 63–65, 71–72, 84–90, 92–94, 98,
    111, 113, 117, 120, 182, 215, 218, 219n,
    220–223, 225, 231–232, 267, 276, 282,
    285, 326, 328–329
Folk physics, 82–83, 212
Folk psychology, 65n, 81–94, 97–98, 216–
    217
Fonts, 236–237
Forbus, K., 241
Ford, K., 181, 207n, 226n, 393–394
Formalist's Motto, 65
Formality Constraint, 63, 72, 222
Form and matter, 65
Forster, E. M., 43
Forty-hertz oscillation, 138n
Foveas
    of Cog, 160, 165
    of eagles, 160
Frame axioms, 195, 211
Frame problem, 181–205, 207–213, 275n,
    366
Frames, Minsky, 99–100, 199, 240, 276
Fraser, S., 34n
Free-floating rationale, 212, 300
Free will, 360
Frege, Gottlob, 270
French, R, 237, 243–248, 394
Freyd, J., 210, 394
Front End Processor, 165
FRUMP, 16
Function, 65, 69, 159, 254–255
    attribution of, 360
    birth of, 362
    mathematical, 359
    multiple, 257–258
    past or current, 349
    proper, 313

specification of, 252–253
Functional
  analysis, 256
  evidence, 342–343
  role, 70, 359–360
Functionalism, 254–255, 268, 279
  homuncular, 362
Future, producing, 208
Fuzzy, vs. hard-edge, 247

Gadget, mind as, 365
Gag-reflex, 342
Galanter, E., 356, 398
Gärdenfors, P., 346, 394
Garden path sentences, 250
Gardner, M., 105n, 236
Garon, J., 85–87, 90–91, 400
Gavagai, 303
Geisteswissenschaft, 184n
Gelatt, C., 226, 294
Generate and test, 67, 78
Genes, 105
Genetics, 23
Genotype vs. phenotype, 68
Gentner, D., 241
Geography, logical, 216
Ghandi, Indira, 17
Ghost in the machine, 72
Gibson, J., 98, 204n, 221, 231
Given, taking the, 133, 364
Glymour, C., 226n, 394
God, 66–67
GOFAI (Good Old Fashioned AI), 65, 81,
    90–92, 165, 169, 238, 241
Goldberg, Rube, 231, 234, 271
Good and evil, origin of, 126–128
Goodman, N., 194, 186n, 394
Goodwin, J., 50n
Gould, S. J., 124–5, 289
GPS, 241
Gravity, 127, 171, 189, 228
  center of, 85, 95–97, 99, 360
  center of narrative, 39
Great Falls, Montana, 10, 19
Great tits, 315
Greenwood, J., 81n
Gregory, R., 325, 394
Griffin, D. 289, 321n, 394
Group selection, 262
Guha, R. V., 166
Gumption, animal, 350
Guttenplan, S., 355n, 394

Habit
  of attention, 199
  good, 334
  of thought, 185, 192
Habituation, 293
Hacking, I., 50n, 394
Hallucinations, 126
Hallucinatory control, 125
Halperin, J., 326, 331, 394
Hannan, B., 95n
Hardin, G., 196, 383n
Harman, G., 220, 394
Harmony, pre-established, 65–67, 73, 78
Harnad, S., 168, 394
Harnish, M., 215n
Hatfield, G., 221n
Haugeland, J., 12, 65, 90, 114, 165, 169,
    182n, 218n, 220–221, 223n, 227n, 234n,
    394–395
Hawkins, R. D., 310, 395
Hayes, P., 82–83, 181, 183, 187n, 189n,
    196n, 203n, 221, 226n, 395
Health, 175–177
Hearing, in Cog, 163
Hearsay II, 241
Hebb, D., 356
Hedonic calculus, 382, 384
Hegemony of the artificer, 170
Heil, J., 85, 87, 89
Heiser, J. F., 15n, 395
Henry VIII, King of England, 55
Heraclitus, 246
Herodotus, 128
Hetero-phenomenology, 188, 191–192
Heuristic, 189n
  overlay, 360
  intentional terms as, 63
Heyes, C. M., 307n, 311, 315, 321, 395
Hidden hand, 111–112
High Church Computationalism, 65,
    215–225, 229, 231–232, 234
Higher-order
  intentional idioms, 320
  reflection, 175
Hilgard, E. R., 51n, 395
Hillis, D., 226, 395
Hinton, G., 91, 215, 221, 226, 393
Historical processes and rights, 156–157
History, 128
  importance of, 21
  role of, 64, 71, 78
Hitech, 313

Hobbes, Thomas, 126–127, 262, 266, 276
Hofstadter, D., 40n, 41n, 95n, 192n, 201n,
    215, 220–221, 224, 226, 228, 234n,
    235–241, 243, 245–246, 255, 270
Holism, 228, 236
  of belief attribution, 89
  and Zen, 217–218, 220, 223, 234
Holland, J., 272, 395
Hologram, 227n
Holyoak, K., 241, 272, 395
Homunculi, 39, 60, 70, 224–225, 253,
    312–313, 315–316, 362
  regress of, 274n
Honey bee, 315, 358
Hookway, C., 181n
Horserace, as model of consciousness, 132
Houston, D., 341, 395
Hume, David, 38, 185, 194, 210–211,
    274n, 280
Hume's Problem, 274n
Humor, in Cog, 164
Humphrey, N., 31, 41n, 396
Husserl, Edmund, 219n, 235
HWIM, 312
Hyperfunctional, Soar, 279–280
Hypnosis, 51n, 55
Hypothesis-testing, 217
Hysteria, 51

"I," 43, 60, 345, 357
Iatrogenesis, in MPD, 49–52
IBM, 32, 149
Idealism, 268
Idealization, 117
  of intentional stance, 322
  of model, 105, 311, 314
  semantic engine as, 63
Ideas, combined, 280
Identity
  over time, 262
  theory of, 361
Ideology, 82–84, 223
  vs. theory, 219–220
Ignorance, excusable, 370, 376–377
Ignoring, 197, 203
  catastrophically, 245
Iguana, whole Martian, 309
Illusion, of direct response to meaning,
    70
Imagery, 364, 366
Imagination, 190–191
  failure of, 28, 366

poverty of, 172
prosthesis for, 3, 212
Impenetrability, cognitive, 352
Implication, 182
Impotence, of meaning, 63
Impressions and ideas, 276
Incompressibility, 101
Inconceivability, inconstancy of, 340
Indeterminacy, 138n
  of translation, 114, 116, 118n, 120, 357,
    361
Indiana University, 237
Indiscernibility, 100
Induction, 194, 272
Ineffability, 142–143
Inert historical fact, 63
Inessentialism, health, 175–176
Infancy, artificial, 161
Inference, 72, 216
  engine, 270
Inflation, of interpretations, 69
Information, 61, 64–65, 72–73, 100–103,
    189, 192, 209, 329–331
  processing, 203, 228, 231
    thinking as, 216
  semantic, 69
  sensitivity to, 173, 175
  theory, 216
  transformation, 60
Information-gradient, 299, 304, 321
Innate, 212
  biases, 251
  correspondence, 70
  features of Cog, 162–163
  knowledge, 187–189
"In principle," 343. See also Possibility in
  principle
Insects, 174
Instinct, 300
Instrumentalism, 120, 177, 311, 327
Intelligence, 184
  creative, 333–336
  "laser-beam," of vervets, 298
  and speed, 190
Intentional
  action, 109
  higher-order, 289, 358, 360
  idioms, higher order, 320
  interpretation, 326
  realism, Fodor's, 84–85, 90
  stance, 63, 70–71, 82, 85, 96, 99, 105,
    110–111, 117, 119n, 120, 212, 292, 294,

298, 310–312, 316, 321–322, 325, 330–
331, 355, 359
system, 60, 63, 212, 253, 262, 311, 313,
315–316, 327, 358, 360, 362
Intentionality, 216, 229, 283–284, 325,
355–358. *See also* Content; Meaning
original and derived, 73, 361
Intentional Stance, The, 355
Intentions, 111, 116–118
conscious, 346
of designer, 70
good, 378
Interpretation, 60, 98, 117–118, 133, 289,
291–292, 360–361
by the brain, 73
in the central workshop, 72
demoting, 336
functional, 343
inflation of, 69
of neural structures, 63
radical, 98, 115
romantic vs. killjoy, 298
over time, 335
Intrinsic, 146–147, 361
power, 78
properties, 141–143,
and historical processes, 156
Introspection, 62, 76, 79, 123, 188, 190–
191, 244, 310, 357–358, 364
Intuition, 76, 83, 146, 276, 343–344, 356,
358–359, 365
bogus, 157
pretheoretical, 339–340
pump, 24, 152, 366
role of, 272
Inverted spectrum, 365
Irishman joke, 8
Isles, D., 368n

Jacob, F., 269, 396
Janlert, L.-E., 183n, 210, 396
Jaynes, J., 121–130, 211, 347n, 396
Jewish names, 52
Joan of Arc, 55
Johannsen, G., 189n
Johnson-Laird, P., 278
Jootsing, 236
Joslin, D., 281
Judgment, 134, 348–349
unconscious, 133
Jumbo architecture, 226, 238
Just-so stories, 124–127, 262

Kacelnik, A., 315, 394
Kamppinen, M., 131n, 141n
Kandel, E., 310
Kanerva, P., 215, 227, 396
Kant, Immanuel, 219n, 250, 276, 383
Karmiloff-Smith, A., 81, 331, 388
King, Rodney, 137
Kinsbourne, 131, 133, 135, 364–366, 396
Kipling, Rudyard, 125
Kirkpatrick, S., 226, 396
Kludge, 269
Kluft, R., 34n, 396
Knobs, turn the, 247
Knowledge, 188, 284
background, 272
and belief, 194, 327
common, 377
of ignorance, 320
level, 189, 232, 253, 283, 284n
mutual, 299
representation of, 269–270
to the system, 331
Koch, C., 138n
Kohut, H., 44, 396
Koler, P., 278
Kolodner, J., 16, 18, 396
Kosslyn, S., 221n, 396
Krebs, J., 315, 394, 396
Kuipers, B., 18

Labeling, of buttons and lights in the control room, 73
Laird, J., 272, 279, 396
Lamarckianism, 163
Langton, C. 256–257, 396
Language
and belief, 90, 326
in Cog, 163–164
and consciousness, 348, 363–364
evolution of, 321
human, 320–321
machine, 228
of monkeys, 290–306
natural, 210, 229, 285, 304, 364
theories of, 218
of thought, 64–65, 190, 210, 227n, 228,
285, 330–331, 363
Language Acquisition Device, 163
Language-learning, 314
Laws, of physics, 112
Learning, 66–68, 71, 75, 78, 185–186, 209,
246, 272

Learning (cont.)
  and consciousness, 175
  as source of design, 74
  ignoring, 308
  in robots, 188
  transfer of, 345
Learning-by-chunking, 280
Leiber, J., 338, 343, 396
Leibniz, Gottfried Wilhelm, 266, 276
Lenat, D., 74, 166, 273, 396–397
Leopard sawing, 298–299
LePore, E., 63, 397
Level of explanation, 262, 281, 360
  algorithmic, 230–233
  architectural, 280
  biological vs. psychological, 280
  cognitive, 91, 229
  computational, 230–233
  hardware, 230–233
  intentional, 112n
  knowledge, 189, 232, 253, 283, 284n
  Marr's three, 230–233, 251–253, 313–314
  personal, 77
  phenomenological, 185–186, 202–203
  semantic, 201, 203
  software, 129–130
  subpersonal, 362
Levesque, H., 93, 397
Levine, J., 177, 397
Lévis, Duc de, 379n
Lewis, D., 359
Lewontin, R., 124–125, 255, 289
Lexicon, Philosophical, 220n
Life, Game of, 105–112, 208, 256, 262
Lifton, R., 44, 397
Linguistics, 221
Lion, speaking, 306
Liquids, 82–83
LISP, 129, 222, 266
Loadstone, soul of, 154
Lobster, as self-conscious, 24
Localization fallacy, 126
Locke, John, 142–143, 145–146, 149, 186,
  397
Lockwood, M., 136, 343–344, 347, 397
Loebner, Hugh, 27–29
Loebner Prize, 27–29
Loewer, B., 63, 397
Logic, 270
  temporal, 200
Logical positivism, 226n
Logical space, 129–130, 285

Logicism, in AI, 269–270
Loui, R., 210
Lovely properties, 144–145
Lucas, J., 169, 397
Luddism, 374
Luna moth, 174–175
LUNAR, 11, 14
Lying, 290, 303, 319

Mach bands, 113
MacKay, D., 356
Macromolecules, 158
Maggots, 342
Magic, 191
  explanation of, 186–187
  phenomenological, 204
  stage, 235
Makhoul, J., 312
Mammals, infinite number of, 362
Mangan, B., 159, 397
Manifest image, 104–105, 209–210
Mann, D., 50n, 397
Map, as store of information, 329–330
Marais, E. N., 39–40, 397
Margolis, H., 347n, 397
Marijuana, 62, 64
Marijuana-sniffing dog, 71, 76
Marr, D., 213, 230–234, 251, 254–255,
  313–314, 360, 397
Martian, watching the Super Bowl, 110
Martin, M., 52
Massachusetts Institute of Technology
  (MIT), 153, 160, 215, 217–218, 228,
  267–268
Materialism, 65, 84, 155, 216, 268
  Cartesian, 132–133, 136
  eliminative, 95, 99, 119–120, 135, 327,
  361–362
Mattering, 351
  to a robot, 169
Maxwell's Equations of Thought, 269
Maynard Smith, J., 233n
McCarthy, J., 181, 183, 184n, 189n, 197–
  198, 202, 207–208, 211, 221–222, 232,
  266n, 327, 397–398
McClelland, J., 215, 221, 226, 398, 400
McCulloch, W., 356
McDermott, D., 200, 203, 398
McFarland, D., 307
McGinn, C., 351, 398
McGrath, S., xi
McMaster University, 121

McPhee, J., 369, 398
Meaning, 62, 67–68, 77, 236, 265, 290. *See also* Content; Intentionality
  discrimination of, 356–357
  endowing states with, 186
  as explanatory, 62–63
  individuation by, 185–186
  natural, 69
  real, 321
  theories of, 60, 65–67
Meaning-tracking, 76
Measure, of belief, 329
Mechanism, 63, 65–66, 72, 235, 357, 359–360
Medium
  consciousness as distinct from, 175
  as nonfungible, of consciousness, 159
Melville, Herman, 344–345
Meme, 378
Memory, 59–60, 93–94, 137, 227, 229–330
  computer, 282
  dynamic, 245
  entry into, 364
  episodic, 248
  long term, 246, 258, 278
  management, 286n
  semantic, 278
  working, 258, 278, 284
Meno's paradox, 286n
Mental clay, 211
Mentalese, 85, 111
Mentalistic
  idioms, 325, 357
  psychology, 185
  terms, 202
  vocabulary, 172
Meta-linguistic concepts, 326
Metaphier and metaphrand, 211
Metaphor, 212
Meta-tricks, 210–211
Meteorology, 228–229, 232
Meyer, J.-A., 323n
Micro-taking, 133–134
Midgley, M., 338, 343
Midnight snack problem, 187, 191–192, 196
Mill, John Stuart, 381n, 382, 398
Miller, G., 356, 398
Miller, J., 121
Miller, S. D., 49, 398
Millikan, R., 204n, 313, 363, 398

Milne, A. A., 134
Mind
  as the brain, 324
  as chaos, 268–269, 271
  Crystalline, 268–269, 271
  as Gadget, 268, 271
  as inexplicable, 268
Mind's eye, 147
Mining the past, 59, 63–65, 72, 78
Minsky, M., 40n, 197–199, 215, 240, 268, 398
MIO grunt, 301–305, 307, 316–322
Miracles, 38
Missionary and cannibals problem, 197–198
MIT. *See* Massachusetts Institute of Technology
Mitchell, M., 237, 398
Moby-Dick, 344–345
Model
  annotated, 285
  cognitive, 323
  computational, 223, 239, 246, 272, 310
  inconsistent, 212
  mental, 285, 278
Modularity, 231
  of belief fixation, 71–72
  of Jaynes' account, 125–126, 129–130
Modus ponens, 188
Money, 128
Money-pump, 326
Montaigne, Michel, 338, 343
Montefiore, A., 307n
Monte Verità, 307
Moody, T, 171–172, 176, 398
Moon rocks, 11
Moore, R., 182n
Moral attitudes, 338–339
Moral First Aid Manual, 367, 381, 384
Morality, 362, 368–384
  lack of, in state of nature, 126–127
Mother Nature, 69, 76, 255, 259, 314
Mulhauser, G., 171, 398
Multiple Drafts Model of consciousness, 131, 133, 173–174, 245, 364–365
Multiple Personality Disorder (MPD), 31–58
  neurophysiology of, 49
Muscles, artificial, 155, 167
Muskie, Edmund, 18
Mutation, 75
MYCIN, 16

Mystery, 154–155, 176, 184, 217, 268,
    338–339, 347, 350

Nagel, T., 122, 219n, 327–328, 337, 339,
    343–344, 346–348, 398
Names, 204
Narcissism, 209
Narrative, 134
Narratization, 125
Narrow content, 284, 363
NASA, 25
Naturalism, 361–362
Natural kinds, 268
Natural language parsers, 308–309
Natural ontological attitude, 99
Natural selection, 66–71, 75, 78, 125, 199,
    300
Nature vs. nurture, 163
Nautical Almanac, 382
Nazi doctors, 44
Nazis and Jews, 52
Necessity, insight into, 366
Need to know, 292
Neglect, unilateral, 168
Neisser, U., 221, 398
Nelkin, N., 95n, 98, 398
NETTalk, 238
Neural networks, 156, 163, 256
Neuroanatomy, 240, 258–259
Neuromodulators, 240
Neuron, 356
Neurophysiology, 216
Neuroscience, 95, 138n, 278, 348
  computational, 85, 241
Newell, A., 13, 189, 219n, 220–223, 232,
    253–254, 258, 272, 277–286, 356, 360,
    399
Newfie joke, 86
New look psychology, 251
New Orleans, Battle of, 136
New School for Social Research, 337, 351
Newton, Isaac, 105, 127
New York Review of Books, 31
Nietzsche, Friedrich, 399
Nilsson, N., 196, 393
Nisbett, R., 272
Nissen, M. J., 49, 399
Noble, D., 307n
Noblesse oblige, 379–380
Noise, 81, 91–92, 100, 103–104, 110–112,
    114, 116, 119
  motor, in Cog, 155, 167

Nonmonotonic reasoning, 197–200, 203
Norepinephrine, 43
Norman, D., 215, 221
Numbers, 114
  vs. numerals, 281–282

Ojemann, G., 121
Oleic acid, 315
Olfaction, 349
  in vultures, 341
O'Neill, O., 383n, 399
Ontology, 95, 98, 104–105, 107, 109, 365
Operant conditioning, 67
Operationalism, 9–10, 177, 328–329
Opinion, as distinct from belief, 89–90,
    363
Opponent process, 167–168, 342
Opportunism, in design, 163m, 225
Optimal
  design, 312–313, 360
  foraging strategy, 315
  performance, 311
  vs. suboptimal, goals, 280
Optimality, assumption of, 254–255
Oracle, 308
Orangutans, 304
"Order which is there," 111, 116
Ordinary language, 137
Original understanding, 75–76
Origin chauvinism, 156, 169
Ornstein, R., 142, 399
Orwell, George, 138
Orwellian vs. Stalinesque, 134–136, 235
Oswald, Lee Harvey, 138–139
Other minds, problem of, 292, 341
"Ought" implies "can," 367
Oversimplification, as research strategy,
    211, 279, 308–309
Oxford, 356

Pain, 126, 133, 145–146, 169, 173–174,
    279–280, 344, 347, 351–352
  in Cog, 161–162
  unconscious, 351
Panda's thumb, 269
Pandemonium model, 40n, 43–44, 227
Panglossianism, 124, 342
Parallax, 345
Parallel, 164
  architecture, 163, 165, 239
  processes, 226, 240, 245
  terraced scan, 240

Paramecia, 309, 326
Paranoia, 13–15
Parfit, D., 379n, 399
PARRY, 13–15
Parser, 15, 29, 308–309
Partee, B., 269
Pattern, 95–121
  of behavior, 70–71
  real, 360
  recognition, 229–230
Peirce, C. S., 44, 399
Pensacola (Fla.), 207n, 210
Perception, 229–230, 239, 251–252, 259,
  266, 270
Perceptrons, 227
Performance model, 313–314
Perpetual motion machine, 63
Peter Pan, 48
Phenomenal
  beliefs, 174
  consciousness, 350
  qualities, 141
Phenomenology, 186, 188, 191, 202–203,
  235–236, 240, 308
Philosophers
  and AI, 265–276, 286
  misuse of Turing test by, 5
  theories of, 278
Philosophical method, 261–263
Philosophy of mind, 275, 290
Phonology, 312
Physicalism, 184. See also Materialism
Physical stance, 63, 120n
Physical symbol system, 223n, 245. See
  also Symbol manipulation
Physics, 229
  Einsteinian, 105
  folk, or naive, 82–83, 104, 187n, 212
  of Life, 208
  Newtonian, 105
Physics-worship, 268
Piano vs. autoharp, 375–376
Pierre, what he believes, 363, 365
Pigeon color vision, 145
Pineal gland, 132–133
Pirates of Penzance, 383
Pixel, 100
Planning, 185, 189, 191, 193–195, 203, 209
Plato, 40, 258, 274–275, 284
Plover, injury-feigning or distraction dis-
  play in, 76–77
Poetics Today, 289

Point of view, of a bat, 348
Polger, T., 171–176
Pooh-sticks, 134
Pop out, 162
Popper, Karl, 185
Possibility in principle, 67, 74, 154, 157,
  159, 305
Potemkin village, 16
Poundstone, W., 105n, 107–109, 399
Pragmatics, contribution of to MPD, 57–
  58
Preconscious, 128, 130
Predicament, 213
Predicate, 204
Predicate calculus, 93, 227
Prediction, 108, 110, 116–120, 208, 382–
  383
  and computational tractability, 105
  by intentional stance, 97–98, 292, 325
Pre-established harmony, 65–67, 73, 78
Prejudice, 5
Premack, D., 89, 289, 326, 400
Pribram, K., 227n, 356
Primary and secondary qualities, 142–
  143
Prisoner's dilemma, 233n
Privileged access, 61
Probability, 247
  subjective, 194
  theory, 198
Problem-solving, 216, 222, 240–241, 243,
  280
Problem-space, 281, 284n
Proceduralism, 278
Procedural semantics, 282
Process, 203–204
  of design, 73–74
Production systems, 223n, 278–279
Productivity, 329
Program, Master, 269–271
Programming, dynamic, 315
Proof of concept, 240
Propositional attitudes, 88, 113, 363, 365
  representation of, 330
Propositions, 82–83, 86, 88, 92, 190
  as measures of belief, 114–115, 203, 329
PROSPECTOR, 16
Prosthetic vision, 159
Proteanism, 44
Proteins, in a robot, 155
Protocol analysis, 238
Proust, Marcel, 98n, 349

Psycholinguistics, 58, 221
Psychology, 69, 95, 97, 360
  academic, 83
  cognitive, 89–90, 221
  folk, 81–94, 97–98, 104, 110–111, 113,
    118–119, 152, 216, 229, 350, 361
  pholk, 152
  as uninteresting, 267
Psychology Today, 289
Psychosemantics, 60, 71
Purchase, definition of, 326
Putnam, F., 33n, 49, 400
Putnam, H., 234n, 265–276, 400
Putrescine, 341
Pylyshyn, Z., 181, 182n, 207n, 211, 220,
  285, 400

Qualia, 141–152, 172–173, 365
  absent, 141, 365
  inverted, 141
Qualification problem, 197–198
Quasi-indicator relations, 69
Quick-probe assumption, 6, 8–10, 19
Quiescence, principle of, 383
Quillian, J., 87
Quine, W. V. O., 95n, 98, 110, 114, 116–
  117, 118n, 219n, 282, 292, 356–357,
  361, 365–366, 400
Quotation, bit map as, 100

Rabbit, divided consciousness in, 345–
  346
Radical translation, indeterminacy
  of, 114, 116, 118n, 120, 292, 357,
  361
Ramachandran, V., 213, 255, 314, 400
Ramsey, W., 85–87, 90–91, 400
Random, 67, 98, 101, 111–112
  acting at, 208
  vs. pseudo-random, 100
Raphael, B., 313, 400
Raritan, 31
Rather, Dan, 137
Rational
  agent, 298, 323, 325, 331
  self-interest, 105
Rationale, free-floating, 76, 300, 315
Rationality, 265, 280, 294, 311, 360
Raw feel, 141
Realism, 88, 95–121, 131–132, 328, 361,
  363, 365
  about consciousness, 134–135

industrial strength, 98, 100, 114, 117,
  120
  intentional, Fodor's, 84–85, 87
  about MPD, 44–49
  psychological, 195
  with a capital "R," 89, 90, 98, 114
Reality, psychological, 203
Real time, 308–309, 381, 384
Reason, giving a, 294
Recognition, of patterns, 100, 102, 229–
  230
Recursion, 236
Re-entrant circuits, 278
Reference, 168–169
Reflection, 77, 347
Reflective equilibrium, 194
Registration, 325
Regress, infinite, 361–362
Reichenbach, H., 96
Reiter, R., 200, 400
Reitman, W., 241
Relevance, 197
Relevant implication, 182
Reliability, 69
Representation, 208–209, 211, 217, 222,
  239, 245, 259, 274n, 363, 366
  explicit, 269–270
  mental, 190
  procedural, 276
  transformation of, 72
Reproduction, 154
Re-representation, 77, 347
Res cogitans, 58
Research and development (R and D),
  314
Resolution theorem proving, 195
Responsibility, 360
Reverse engineering, 269
Revonsuo, A., 131n, 141n
Right stuff, 64
Rigidity assumption, 251
Ristau, C., 289, 400
Rituals, initiation, 54–55
Robinson Crusoe, 367
Robot, 66, 70, 74, 78, 129, 209–210, 252,
  255, 309, 330 358–359. *See also* autom-
  aton
  beliefs of, 327
  color vision in, 147–152
  discriminatory competence of, 339–340
  giant, 72–73
  humanoid, unlikely, 25

as merchant, or purchaser, 326
self-conscious, 25
Robotics, as a waste of time, 166
Robotics and Autonomous Systems, 307
Robot Theater, 192n
Robustness, 275
Roitblat, H., 323n
Rorty, R., 95n, 98–99, 118–120
Rosenbloom, P., 272, 279
Rosenthal, D., 144–146, 400
Routines, 192
Ruby, Jack, 138–139
Rule, 222
 formal, 217
 for thinking, 232
 of thought, 112
Rule-following, 112, 233
Rule-governed
 processes, 217
 thinking, 230
Rumelhart, D., 215, 221, 400
Russell, Bertrand, 270
Ryle, Gilbert, 191n, 219n, 356–357, 365–
 366, 401

S4OS, 47
Saccade, 160
Sagan, Carl, 379
Satanic rituals, 53
Scare-quotes, 70
Schank, R., 16–17, 23, 198–199, 212, 240,
 267, 401
Scheme / content distinction, 118
Schiffer, S., 63, 401
Schindler's List, 157–158
Scientific image, 105
Scripts, 199, 212, 240
Seals, 341–342
Searle, J., 122, 159, 184, 219n, 220–221,
 268, 328, 350n, 357, 401
Secondary and primary qualities, 142–
 143, 145
Secrets, 320–321, 337
Seek-Whence, 238
Sejnowski, T., 226, 393
Selection pressure, 112
Self, 38, 43–45, 60, 78
 fictive, 38–39, 41–42
 multiple, 133
 proper, 38–39
 substantial, 77n
Self-consciousness, 23–24

Self-creation, 58
Self-design, by Cog, 166
Self-designing systems, 112
Self-monitoring, 24, 211
Self-organizing systems, 245
Self-refutation, 171
Self-repair, 78
Self-replication, 124
Selfridge, O., 40n, 204n, 227, 401
Sellars, Wilfrid, 104, 112n, 209, 401
Semantic
 ascent and descent, 282
 engine, 63, 357
 level, 201
 properties, 222
 relations, 185–186
Semantics, 217, 228, 281
 of color words, 143
 of connectionist nodes, 91–92
 denotational, 72
 functional role, 283–284
 of natural language, 270
 vs. syntax, 62, 189
Semi-stack, 247
Sentences, 328
Sententialism, 86–87, 189–190, 328, 339–
 340
Sentience, 347, 351
Serial computer, 165
Sex, 173
Seyfarth, R., 289, 306, 316–322
Shakespeare, William, 182
SHAKEY, 196
Sharpe, R., 98n, 401
Sherlock Holmes method, 292, 298, 303,
 306, 316–317, 319
Sherrington, C. S., 133n, 364, 401
Shoham, Y., 210, 212
SHRDLU, 309
Side effects, unforeseen, 257
Silicon, 340
Simon, H., 13, 23, 221–223, 232, 234n,
 238, 310, 356, 393
Simplification, of models, 246
Simulated annealing, 226–227
Singer, P., 338, 343, 348, 379n, 383n, 401
Singer, W., 138n
Sjölander, S., 346, 401
Skinner, B. F., 313
Sloan Foundation, 215n
Sloman, A., 281, 401
Smith, A., xi

Smith, B. C., 221, 401
Smith, G., 95n, 112n, 376, 401
Smith, P., 96–97, 401
Smolensky, P., 215, 226, 401
Snake, 346, 351
Snapshots, beliefs as, 203
Snowden, C., 50n, 401
Snyder, D., 401
Soar, 241, 272, 278–281, 285, 286n
Social contract, 127
Society for Philosophy and Psychology, 267
Sociology, 138
Software, 129–130, 230
Soul, 38–39, 70, 154, 324, 340
Space
  abstract, 211
  behavioral, 211
  logical, 129–130, 285
  problem, 225, 281
Specs, clarifying the, 310–311
Spectrum inversion, 172
  in a robot, 150–152
Speech acts, 305, 321
Speech recognition, 308, 312
Speech understanding programs, 249–250. See also Hearsay II; HWIM
Speed, and intuition, 340
Sphex wasp, 191–192
Spielberg, Steven, 157
Spinoza, Baruch, 190, 270
Squid, 238
SRI, 15–16
Stabler, E., 223n, 224n, 401
Stack, 240. See also Semi-stack
Stalin, Joseph, 138
Stalinesque, 134–136
Stalnaker, R., 363
Stance. See Design, stance; Intentional, stance; Physical stance
Stanton, B., xi, 215
Stanton, H., xi, 215
State of nature, 126–127
Statistical mechanics, 226
Statistics, 227
Stein, L. A., 153, 160, 167
Stereotypes, 198–199
Stereotypic behavior, 334
Stich, S., 85–87, 90–91, 220, 401
Stories, 212–213
Strong AI, 168
Strong AL, 262

Style, 366
Subcognitive pressure, 239
Suber, P., 95n
Subjectivity, in a robot, 151
Subpersonal level, 77n
Suffering, 133, 338–339, 351–353
Supervenience, 77
Surprise, 193
Suspect properties, 144–145
Swamp-man, 156
  Dretske's version of, 74–75, 78
Syllogism, practical, 111
Symbionts, possible role in consciousness, 159
Symbol, 282–285
  active, 41n, 245–246
  grounding of, 168–169, 248
  manipulation of, 72, 217, 222, 224, 228, 245, 281, 284
  as movable, 278
  vs. nonsymbol, 92
Symbolic information, 227
Symmetry, vertical, 102, 315
Syntactically definable processes, 72
Syntactic engine, 63, 222, 357
Syntactoscope, 111
Syntax, 217
  vs. semantics, 62, 65, 328

Tabletop, 238, 244–248
Tape, rewinding the, 246
Tapeworms, consciousness of, 343
Tarski, Alfred, 270
Taylor, C., 220, 357, 401–402
Taylor, J., 377n
Taylor, P., 315, 394
Taylor, W. S., 52, 402
Technology, 367–384
Technophilia, 367–368
Teleological function, 359–360
Television, 255
Termite, 39
Thagard, P., 241, 272
Thales, 154
Thatcher, Margaret, 17
Theaetetus, 274–275
Theorem-proving, 244
Theory of mind, 289
Thermostat, 327, 329, 331, 358, 362
Thinking, essence of, 5
Thinking thing, computer as, 21

Third-person perspective or point of
  view, 339, 343, 356–357
Thomas, E. M., 338, 402
Thompson, R., 142
Thought experiment, 68, 223, 231–232,
  261, 273, 275, 290–292, 306, 357,
  365
  Cog as, 168
  as constrained by AI, 271–272
  vs. real experiment, 154
Three Cousins, 66–67, 69
Three Mile Island Effect, 383
Time
  and intelligence, 190
  pressure, 207
  real, 270, 275
  of representing, 135
Tinkerer, evolution as, 269, 271
Top-down strategy, 123–125, 204n, 224,
  249–250
  vs. bottom-up, 216, 226, 249–259
Toxin, 342
Toy
  environment, 200
  problem, 196, 238, 308
  world, 236, 240
Track, keeping, 203–204
Transduction, 131, 138
Translation, indeterminacy of, 114, 116,
  118n, 120
Transparency, of mind to itself, 43
Trial and error learning, 78
Tropism, 199
Truth, 326
Tufts University, 18, 31, 95n, 267, 337n,
  366, 376
Turing, Alan, 3–6, 10, 21–23, 166, 241,
  266
Turing machine
  interpretation of, 118n
  universal, 3, 108–109
Turing test, 3–29, 243, 266
  zimbos in, 173
Turkle, S., 122, 402
Twin Earth, 64, 284, 365
Two-bitser, 75n
Tylenol, 382

Umwelt, 320
Understanding, 59–80
Unity, of consciousness, 134
Unthinkable, in several senses, 267

Uphill analysis and downhill synthesis,
  257
Use-mention error, 127–128, 281–282
User-illusion, 346, 357
Utilitarianism, 382

Valéry, Paul, 59
Valium, effect on MPD patient, 49
Value vs. perceived value, 63
Vance, Cyrus, 16–18
van Gulick, R, 77n, 402
Vecchi, M., 226, 394
Verificationism, 135–136
Vervet monkeys, 290–306, 316–322
Virtual machine, 81, 129–130, 207, 228,
  271, 363
  in Cog, 165
Virtual muscles, 167
Virtual reality vs. real world robotics,
  166–167
Vision, 102, 230–231
  prosthetic, 159
  theories of, 255
Vitalism, 155–156
Vivisection, 338
Volition, 345
von der Malsburg, C., 138n
von Kempelen, Baron, 313
von Neumann, J., 108
von Neumann architecture, 281
von Neumann bottleneck, 241
von Neumann machine, 230
Vulture, turkey, 341–343, 349

Waltz, D., 74, 167, 402
Warhol, Andy, 137–138, 377
War of 1812, 136
Waterhouse, L., 213, 402
Weather forecasting, 382
Weizenbaum, J., 13–14, 375n, 402
Wernicke's area, 114
Weyhrauch, R., 221
Whale, sperm, 344–346
"What is it like" question, 60, 122, 327,
  337, 339, 343–349
Wheels, 200–201
  cognitive, 200
White, S., 95n, 363
Whitehead, Alfred North, 270
Whiten, A., 77, 333, 402
"Why" explanations, 63, 70, 254
Wiener, Norbert, Forum, 368n

Wimsatt, W., 104n, 402
"Winner take all," 227
Winnie the Pooh, 134
Winograd, T., 7, 220, 267, 309, 402
Witelson, S., 121
Witness, no extra, 286
Wittgenstein, Ludwig, 184n, 219n, 306, 402
Wonder tissue, 204n, 225n, 308
Woodruff, G., 289
Woods, W., 11, 312, 402
Wooldridge, D., 191–192n, 402
Workspace, 258
World knowledge, 7, 15, 74, 167, 187–189, 195, 309
World Wide Web, 29

Yonas, A., 209, 402
Young, J. Z., 356

Zabludowski, A., 118n, 402
Zadeh, L, 220
Zero, as a number, 327
Zimbo, as reflective zombie, 172–176
Zombie, 159, 171–177, 340